SUFFERINGS
OF EARLY QUAKERS

EAST ANGLIA AND
EAST MIDLANDS

1649 to 1690

Cambridgeshire, Essex, Huntingdonshire,
Leicestershire with Rutland,
Lincolnshire, Norfolk, Northamptonshire,
Nottinghamshire and Suffolk

Facsimile of part of the 1753 edition
by JOSEPH BESSE

with new Introduction and
newly compiled Index of People and Places
by Michael Gandy BA FSG

SESSIONS BOOK TRUST
York, England

Facsimile reprinted in reduced size with new Introduction
and Indexes

by William Sessions Limited
The Ebor Press, York, England

ISBN 978-1-85072-374-5

© 2007

_____

FOREWORD

IN 1753, JOSEPH BESSE published his detailed account of the sufferings of Quakers throughout England, Ireland, Scotland, Wales, New England and West Indies from 1650, when Quakers were 'first distinguished by that name', to approximately 1689, when the Act of Toleration at last gave some protection to Dissenters. The work has now become a standard source for Quaker genealogy and social history.

The two volumes of this substantial work, long out-of-print, comprise 824 and 648 pages, subdivided into regions and English counties. So for cost and other reasons our small family Book Trust (a registered charity) decided to publish a series of regional volumes beginning with Yorkshire in 1998. We continued in 2000 with the other North England counties, together with the Isle of Man; next in 2001 with America (New England and Maryland) together with West Indies (Antigua, Barbados, Jamaica and Nevis) and Bermuda. London and Middlesex followed in 2002; in 2003 Ireland, Scotland and Wales; in 2004 South-West England and in 2006 Southern England, ranging from Bedfordshire to Sussex and including Hampshire and the Isle of Wight.

Skilled indexing services have again been provided by Michael Gandy BA, Fellow of the Society of Genealogists and founding chairman of the Quaker Family History Society, who has many Quaker branches in his ancestry. Trustees wish to express their appreciation to him for these specifically compiled Indexes of People and of Places.

William K Sessions
Chairman Sessions Book Trust

INTRODUCTION

Michael Gandy

EVER SINCE IT APPEARED IN 1753, Joseph Besse's *Collection of the Sufferings of the People called Quakers* has been the first port of call for anyone interested in 17th century Quakerism at local level. Arranged county by county, and then extending to New England and Maryland, the Caribbean (especially Barbados), Ireland, Scotland and continental Europe, Joseph Besse drew together the most interesting or indicative examples of what individual Quakers had suffered for the Truth between approximately 1650 and 1690. The work is densely packed with names, dates and places; snapshots from the lives of ordinary people, our ancestors, the atmosphere built up by an unrelenting chronological catalogue of persecutions, sometimes thwarted but usually bravely borne, 'for the testimony of a good conscience'.

The work is particularly valuable because it pre-dates the establishment of the Quakers in Pennsylvania. A great many of the families of the early settlers appear in the *Sufferings* and so their home area can be identified.

The background to publication was described by Norman Penney in 'The Story of a Great Literary Venture' (1). In 1727 London Yearly Meeting had passed the following minute:

> On a proposition made to this Meeting by James Dickinson, seconded by divers countyes, this Meeting desires Friends of ye meeting for sufferings to take upon them ye care of collecting and digesting by proper persons ye sufferings and imprisonments of Friends for Tythes and on all other accounts, into proper heads from ye beginning of our being a People to this time.

Under the supervision of a committee, Joseph Besse (the final 'e' is pronounced) began the work of sorting the material already held at Gracechurch Street Meeting House in London and of bringing up to date the records of sufferings in the provinces. The work took twenty six years to complete, though there were a number of very valuable interim volumes. In 1753 1000 copies of the final work were printed of which 719 were sent straight to subscribers. The remainder were advertised at 22 shillings (£1.10p) and in 1755 100 were distributed to 43 Quarterly Meetings expressly intended for the use of such Friends as are not of ability to purchase the Work, or to be lent occasionally to People of other Persuasions, where there is Prospect of Service.

Fifty copies were sent to Philadelphia and it was also proposed to present copies to 'some great Personages...as proper and seasonable Occasion may offer'.

As the above implies Besse's *Sufferings* commanded immediate respect and was used as both an authority and a source of inspiration. It was by its nature an abstract and there is plenty more material in the sources from which it was drawn. W.C.Braithwaite says of it, 'The work is conscientiously done, and may be generally relied on' (2). Its great value is its accessibility. Once Quakers have been identified and localised in Besse, researchers know that a much longer search in the Quarter Sessions, the Books of Sufferings, the Digests of Births, Marriages and Deaths and elsewhere, is likely to be worthwhile.

In a more recent article (3) David M.Butler uses the *Sufferings* to plot the peaks and troughs of Quaker persecution in each county and attempts some analysis. He demonstrates not only that persecution came in waves according to the national political climate but that there were local variations depending on the attitude of the local magistrates and, above all, of the local vicar or the lay impropriator who was the immediate financial loser when Quakers refused to pay tithes. After the Restoration in 1660 Quakers were never seen as politically dangerous and in many cases they were respected for their moral stand even while the Letter of the Law was invoked against them. On the other hand many of those in authority were outraged by their refusal to conform and persecuted them with enthusiasm.

In a short introduction Besse himself described 'the principal Points wherein their conscientious Nonconformity rendered them obnoxious to the Penalties of the Law'. These were:

"**Their refusal to pay Tithes** which they esteemed a Jewish Ceremony abrogated by the Coming of Christ. They also considered that the Levitical Priesthood, which took Tithes, being changed, a change also of the Law which enjoined the Payment of them did necessarily follow: And that there being no Precept either of Christ or his Apostles, enjoining them to be paid under the Gospel, his Disciples are totally freed from all Obligation thereunto.

"**Their refusal to pay Rates or Assessments** for building and repairing Houses or Places appropriated to the Exercise of such a Worship as they did not approve of; the pretended Consecration of which Places they looked upon as an unwarrantable Superstition

"**Their constant Obedience to the Precept of Christ *Swear not at all*** which they would not in any case transgress. For they did not believe that any human Law or Power upon Earth could justify them in the known Breach of a positive Command such as they esteemed that of our Saviour to be in respect of Swearing. In this point they were acted by an invincible Constancy, and supported steadfast in the Faith, through Bonds, Imprisonments, Banishments, and even Death itself.

"**Their Disuse of the Custom of uncovering their Heads,** or pulling off their hats, by way of Homage to Men, which they accounted an undue and unscriptural Respect of Persons and a Misapplication of that outward Signification of Honour and Address which they appropriated to God only. This Custom had not the sanction of any written Law yet the omission of it was deemed a Contempt, and frequently punished by Fines and Imprisonment.

"**Their Christian Resolution of assembling publickly for the Worship of God** in such manner as was most agreeable to their Consciences, from which nothing could deter them; and in which they stood much exposed to the malice of their Adversaries, who always knew where to find them. In this they manifested an intrepidity, sometimes astonishing, even to those who came to their Meetings on purpose to molest them.

"**The Necessity many of them found themselves under of publishing the Doctrine of Truth** which they were persuaded of, and of reproving Vice and Immorality openly in the Streets and Markets, and sometimes even in the Places appointed for the publick national Worship. From the worst of those whom they so reproved they met with ungrateful Returns of manifold and barbarous Abuses, which were too often encouraged by Authority of the Magistrates, who ought to have restrained them.

"**Their refusing to make Use of the established Priests or Ministers,** either in Marrying, Burying, or any other Case, and conscientiously withholding the fees customarily paid on those Occasions. Hence proceeded many Prosecutions against them, especially in the Ecclesiastical Courts, where they generally issued in Excommunications, the Consequences of which often were Imprisonments on Writs *de Excommunicato capiendo*, during the pleasure of holy Church. By this means many of this People were buried alive [imprisoned], and became sacrifices to the Interest of domineering Ecclesiasticks, in causes of which the secular Power never had any Cognizance, but through their Misrepresentations.

"**Their Testimony against Wars and Fighting;** the Practice whereof they judged inconsistent with those Precepts of Christ, *Love your Enemies. Do Good to them that hate you.* Wherefore they refused either to bear Arms themselves, or to hire others in their Stead. This exposed them to Fines, and Seizures of their Goods, and sometimes even to corporal Punishments at the arbitrary Will of Military Officers.

"These Points of their religious Dissent were to them of very great Weight and Consequence; in the Observance of which they experienced an inward Peace and Tranquillity of Mind, strengthening and enabling them to persevere in the Way of their Duty; and indeed their Patience and Constancy in enduring so great a Fight of Afflictions, for the sake of their religious Testimony, was as cogent and convincing a Demonstration of the Sincerity therein, as can reasonably be expected."

About this edition

This facsimile of part of Besse's *Sufferings* is taken from the 1753 edition in *two volumes, independently numbered*. All the material in this volume appears in Volume One of Besse.

Modern indexes of surnames and places have been compiled. Original pagination has been retained and, for the most part, original spellings of names and places. However a cross-reference has been inserted so the form as used in the text should appear in the index.

As in previous volumes a number of considerations mean that the number of references stated may be more than the number of appearances of the actual word. References such as 'at the same meeting' have been indexed under the appropriate place and references to officers, such as Justices, Mayors or Priests have been indexed under the appropriate surname where this is known. Some people are referred to by their christian names when their surname has been used earlier.

The most difficult problem arises with continuous references to people as 'he' and 'she' and here common sense has been used.

Notes to Introduction:

1. Penney, N.	Journal of the Friends Historical Society Vol 23 Nos 1-2 (1926)	
2. Braithwaite, Wm.C.	*The Second Period of Quakerism* (1919; reprint 1979) p285n	
3. Butler, D.M.	'Friends' Sufferings 1650 to 1688: a comparative summary'. Journal of Friends Historical Society Vol 55 No 6 (1988)	

Recommended reading on early Quakerism in England:

Braithwaite, Wm.C. *The beginnings of Quakerism to 1660.* (1912. 2nd ed 1981)

Braithwaite, Wm.C. *The second period of Quakerism.* (1919. 2nd ed 1979)

Lloyd, A. *Quaker social history 1669-1738.* (1950)

Milligan, E.H. and Thomas, M.J. *My ancestors were Quakers: How can I find out more about them?* (1983. 2nd ed 1999). SoG

Nickalls, J.L. (ed.) *The Journal of George Fox.* (1975)

Penney, N. *The First Publishers of Truth.* (1907)

Punshon, J. *Portrait in Grey: a short history of the Quakers.* (1984)

George Fox Rides into Cambridge

That Evening I posted to Cambridge; and when I came into the Town, the Scholars hearing of me were up and were exceeding rude. I kept on my Horses Back, and rid through them in the Lords Power (and they cried he shines he glistnes) but they unhorsed Amor Stoddart before he could get to the Inn. When we were in the Inn they were so rude there in the Courts and in the Streets that the Miners, the Carters and Colliers could never be Ruder. The People of the House asked us, What we would have for Supper? as is the usual way with Inn-keepers. "Supper!" said I "were it not that the Lords Power is over them, these Rude Scholars look as though they would pluck us to pieces and make a Supper of us." They knew I was so against their Trade the Trade of Preaching, which they were there as Apprentices to learn, that they raged as bad as ever Dianas Crafts-men did against Paul.

G. Fox his Journal

Courtesy Friends House Library

See caption at foot opposite
also
see main text at foot of
page 86 following
"The Synagogue of Satan"

Courtesy Friends House Library

C H A P. VI.

CAMBRIDGESHIRE,
and ISLE *of* ELY.

A N N O 1653.

Perfecution of
of E. Wil-
liams and M.
Fifher.

T H E earlieſt Account of the Sufferings of this People in *Cambridge-*
ſhire bears Date in the ſame Month wherein *Oliver Cromwell* had
aſſumed the Title of Protector, *viz.* in *December* 1653, when *Eliza-*
beth Williams and *Mary Fiſher*, the one about fifty, and the other
about thirty Years of Age, came from the North of *England* to *Cambridge*,
and diſcourſing with ſome Scholars of *Sidney-Suſſex* College, concerning Matters
of Religion, the Scholars aſked them *How many Gods there were?* The Women anſwered, *But one God*, and told them, *they had many whom they made*
Gods of, reproving their Ignorance of the *true God and his Worſhip*. Whereupon
the Scholars began to mock and deride them: The Women, obſerving the
Froth and Levity of their Behaviour, told them *they were Antichriſts*, and that
their College was a Cage of unclean Birds, and the Synagogue of Satan. Such ſevere
Reprehenſions are uſually moſt offenſive to thoſe who moſt deſerve them:
Complaint was forthwith made to *William Pickering*, then Mayor, that two
Women were preaching: He ſent a Conſtable for them, and examined them
whence they came, and where they lay laſt Night? They anſwered, that *they were*
Strangers, and knew not the Name of the Place, but paid for what they had, and
came away. He aſked *their Names*: They replied, *their Names were written*
in the Book of Life. He demanded their Huſbands Names: They told him,
they

they had no Husband but Jesus Christ, *and he sent them.* Upon this the Mayor grew angry, called them Whores, and issued his Warrant to the Constable *to whip them at the Market-Cross till the Blood ran down their Bodies*; and ordered three of his Serjeants to see that Sentence, equally cruel and lawless, severely executed. The poor Women, kneeling down, in Christian Meekness besought the Lord *to forgive him, for that he knew not what he did*: So they were led to the Market-Cross, *calling upon God to strengthen their Faith*: The Executioner commanded them to put off their Clothes, which they refused. Then he stript them naked to the Waste, put their Arms into the Whipping-post, and executed the Mayor's Warrant far more cruelly than is usually done to the worst of Malefactors, so that their Flesh was miserably cut and torn : The Constancy and Patience which they expressed under this barbarous Usage was astonishing to the Beholders, for they endured the cruel Torture without the least Change of Countenance, or Appearance of Uneasiness, and in the midst of their Punishment sang and rejoiced, saying, *The Lord be blessed, the Lord be praised, who hath thus honoured us, and strengthened us thus to suffer for his Name's sake.* After which they kneeled down, and, like the Proto-Martyr *Stephen,* prayed God *to forgive their Persecutors, for they knew not what they had done.* As they were led back into the Town, they exhorted the People *to fear God,* not Man, telling them, *this was but the Beginning of the Sufferings of the People of God*: A Prædiction which was verified by the Sequel of what their Friends in that Place afterward underwent. Then were they thrust out of the Town, no Man daring to shew them any Countenance, or give them any Relief, for though many did secretly commiserate their Case, yet none had Courage to oppose the Current of popular Prejudice, and the misapplied Power of the Magistrate.

ANNO 1655.

William Grownes of the Isle of *Ely,* summoned to serve on a Jury there, for refusing to Swear, suffered Distress of his Goods to the Value of 3 *l.* 8 *s.*

On the Day called *Trinity-Sunday,* four Men and four Women, coming from a Meeting at *Little-Port,* were stopt by the Watch, and by order of a Magistrate sent to the Goaler, who shut them up, together with their Horses, all Night, and great Part of next Day, in a Place where they had no lodging but on dirty Pease Straw, which the Hogs had before lain on.

Clement Crabb, taken at a religious Meeting, was imprisoned eleven Weeks till the Sessions, and then discharged, without any Charge exhibited against him.

George Tingy and *William Waring,* both of *Royston,* and *Benjamin* and *Thomas Brett* of *Mildred,* for going to a Meeting on the First-day of the Week, suffered near six Months Imprisonment in *Cambridge* Castle.

Boniface Norris, aged near eighty, for riding to a Meeting about two Miles from his Dwelling, was sent to Prison, where he fell sick, and being permitted to go Home, a few Days after died. During his Imprisonment, his Wife, having publickly reproved his Persecutors for their Hypocrisy, was also committed to Prison, where she lay six Months.

For the same Cause, of openly testifying against the Corruption of the Times, several others were imprisoned, to wit, *Henry Foster* seven Weeks : *Philip Williamson* almost a Year : *Anne Blakely* half a Year : *Anne Cock* and *Anne Wilson,* three Months. These Imprisonments were by Warrants from the Magistrate, which, however illegal, carried with them the Face of Authority. But at other Times the rude People with grievous Blows, Abuses, and Insults, avenged themselves on those who reproved them : By such Abuses of the Populace, *Samuel Fulbeck, Henry Place,* and *Margaret Kellam,* suffered much.

Thomas Lightfoot, through the Malice of some high Professors at *Cambridge,* whose Hypocrisy he had testified against, was accused of Blasphemy, in saying, *The Scripture was not* THE WORD OF GOD ; an Expression, which though clearly defensible in the Sense he spake it, wherein that *Title* is *properly* and *essentially*

Marginal notes:

CAMBRIDGE-SHIRE, &c. 1653.

Cruel Whipping.

1655.

Distresses for not Swearing.

Cruel Confinement.

Imprisonments for Meeting.

Death of B. Norris in Goal, and Imprisonment of his Wife.

Illegal Imprisonments.

Rage of the People.

T. Lightfoot *accused of Blasphemy.*

essentially ascribed to *Christ* only, was made criminal in him, and he was thereupon imprisoned, and Endeavours were used to have taken away his Life, but God preserved him.

James Parnell, for publishing a *Declaration* against corrupt Ministers and corrupt Magistrates, was imprisoned in *Cambridge*, and lay there two Sessions.

In this Year several Persons, for Tithes demanded worth but 2 *l.* 2 *s.* had their Goods taken by Distress to the Value of 8 *l.* 10 *s.*

ANNO 1656.

Robert Letchworth, for Tithes under 12 *s.* in Value, suffered a Year's Imprisonment ; and *Jeremy Rose*, for a Demand of 5 *s.* for Tithes, was imprisoned six Months, though his Goods had been taken away for the same Demand to four Times that Value.

Edward Wright and *John Feast*, for not paying Tithes, were imprisoned six Months, and put in Irons as if they had been Felons.

For the same Cause were imprisoned, *Thomas Payne* about seven Months, *Christopher Lancaster* about twelve Months, *John Smith* near twenty Weeks, *John Smith* the Younger about seventeen Weeks, *Robert Kent* eleven Weeks, *Walter Crane* three Months, and *Robert Crabb*, who being taken sick in Prison, was permitted by the Goaler to go Home, where he soon after died.

Henry Clifton, riding through *Upwell*, was taken by a Constable, and carried to a neighbouring Justice, who, after some Reproach and Derision, sent him to another Justice about four Miles distant, who, without any legal Cause, sent him to Prison, where he lay in the Dungeon among condemned Men for a considerable Time.

It was at this Time adjudged penal to entertain any *Quakers*, and for that Cause only, *William Holmes* and *Thomas Jobson* were indicted at the Assizes, sent to Prison, and afterwards fined ; and the *Former* had taken from him by Distress, two Mares worth 8 *l.* and the *Latter* an Horse worth 10 *l.* Even *Christian Charity* it self was by some Magistrates reputed *criminal*, and *Richard Hubberthorn* and *Richard Weaver* were sent to Goal only for visiting *Anne Blakely* in Prison ; and the said *Richard Hubberthorn*, for not departing the Town at the Mayor's Command, was sent to the House of Correction for three Months ; as were *George Clark* and *Edward Salmon* for working on a Fast-day.

George Nash, Thomas Poole, and *John Cranford*, were imprisoned near two Months for refusing to pay 1 *s.* toward the Sexton's Wages.

ANNO 1657.

In this and the next former Year, for Demands of 25 *l.* 16 *s.* 4 *d.* for Tithes, were taken by Distress from sundry Persons, Goods worth 70 *l.* 15 *s.*

Robert Aspelon, chosen Constable, and refusing to Swear, had his Goods taken away to the Value of 70 *l.* 11 *s.*

ANNO 1658 *and* 1659.

When neither the arbitrary Proceedings of the Magistrates, nor the Insults of the People, could deter the Persons called *Quakers* from their Christian Duty of assembling together to worship God, the *younger Fry* of Scholars in *Cambridge*, animated by those who should have restrained them, manifested, by their wicked Behaviour and barbarous Abuses, that their College had been justly denominated by the first mentioned Christian Women who suffered there, *a Cage of unclean Birds*, and *the Synagogue of Satan*. 'Twas customary with them, when any of this People passed the Streets to or from their Meetings, to throw Dirt and Stones at them, to tear their Clothes, and spit in their Faces. In their publick Meetings the Scholars insulted them by breaking the Windows, throwing great Stones, and shooting Bullets in, to the Hazard of their

CAM-
BRIDGE-
SHIRE,
&c.
1658 *and*
1659.

their Lives.   When *William Allen*, who was frequently concerned to preach in those Meetings, was declaring, they would run through the Meeting-house like wild Horses, throwing down all before them, halloeing, stamping, and making a Noise, as if several Drums had been beating, to prevent his being heard : While he was speaking they threw Stones at him, broke his Head in several Places, cut his Face, and bruised his Body : He neverthelefs persisted in his known Duty undismayed.   In like manner did they abuse others of the Assembly, pulling off the Womens Headclothes, and daubing their Faces with Filth and Excrements.   Some of these Barbarities were acted in the Sight of the *Senior Fellows*, and *Proctor* of the College, who shewed no Dislike thereat : and when Alderman *Nicholson*, a sober and moderate Man, grieved at such Inhumanity, complained to the *Proctor*, desiring him to use his Authority to keep the Scholars quiet, he churlishly answered that *he could not, nor would not.*

In these two Years, for Demands of 12 *l.* 9 *s.* 11 *d.* for Tithes, were taken by Distress from sundry Persons, Goods worth 27 *l.* 4 *s.* 5 *d.*   Among which the Case of *Dorothy Motley* might have moved Compassion, who being a poor Widow with seven Children, and her Tithe demanded by the Priest but 3 *s.* 4 *d.* had taken from her a Cow worth 4 *l.* and no Overplus returned, nor Account given.

In 1659 for 6 *s.* 4 *d.* demanded for Steeple-house Rates, were taken Goods to the Value of 1 *l.* 9 *s.* 6 *d.*

ANNO 1660.

Soon after the Restoration of King *Charles the Second*, a Letter was presented to him, subscribed by *nine and twenty* Sufferers at a Meeting in *Cambridge* on the 2d of the Fifth Month 1660, which, giving a just *Idea* of the Continuance of the Persecution there, and of the Christian Plainness and Simplicity of Address then used by them to Persons in the highest Authority, is as follows, *viz.*

" *To King* CHARLES *the Second,* &c.

"   WE are not a People forward to complain without great Cause, nor
"   backward or unwilling to abide the good Pleasure of the Lord, in
"   filling up the Measure of the Afflictions of Christ in our Bodies, while
"   others are filling up the Measure of their Sins : But the Things that have
"   lately happened to us at *Cambridge*, being altogether contrary to thy Decla-
"   rations for Freedom, and Protection, to them that submit to thy Govern-
"   ment and live in Peace, and much to the Dishonour of thy royal Engage-
"   ment particularly made to us, thy Authority being pretended for the foulest
"   Misdemeanours and highest Insolences, whereby thou mayst be abused as
"   well as we, as declaring for one Thing and intending another, and much
"   Evil may proceed if such Things are suffered : Therefore we would not hide
"   it from the King, that Remedy may be had against such presumptuous Of-
"   fenders, or at least the like prevented for the Time to come, that the
"   Judgments of God, may, if possible, be diverted, that are ready to fall
"   upon this Nation, without speedy Repentance and Reformation, for the
"   Wrong done unto his Children and Servants, and thou mayst be preserved
"   in the evil Day from the Wrath of the Lamb, who is making War with
"   the Nations, and passing his dreadful Doom and Sentence upon the *Whore,*
"   the *false Prophet*, and *Throne* of the *Beast.* Be it known unto thee, O King,
"   that on the 2d Day of the fifth Month, as we were gathering together to
"   a general Meeting, at the usual Place there, being our own hired House, a
"   Tumult of Scholars, lewd Women, Townmen, and Boys, gathered also
"   about the Meeting-place like the Men of *Sodom* ; not content with the for-
"   mer Injuries, Insolences, and Indignities, acted and expressed toward the
"   Lamb's Followers about a Month before, neither ashamed nor afraid to do
"   the same Things again, though the Heads and Governors both of Town
"   " and

" and Univerfity were made acquainted with the former Riot, but rather en-
" couraged, in that their deferved Punifhment was delayed : Some of them
" prepared with Excefs of Drink, that they might forget all Humanity, and
" fhew no Mercy, fuffered none to pafs thither without fome Abufe or other,
" ftopping and thrufting us to and fro, throwing fome down, or throwing
" Dirt or Filth upon their Clothes, or in their Faces ; and alfo beating fome
" back again, and not fuffering them to go into the Meeting, mingling
" much Scoffing, Reviling, and Threatning, with the reft of their Mifufages ;
" and not ceafing there, fell upon us in our peaceable Meeting, as we were
" waiting upon the Lord in Fear, ftriking at thofe they could reach,
" flinging at others, and making an hideous Noife, with Scoffing, Laugh-
" ing, Railing, Shouting, knocking, drumming upon the Boards, and fome-
" times throwing Wildfire and Gunpowder into the Meeting, to drown
" the Sound of that which was fpoken to us in the Name of the Lord, and
" continually exercifing themfelves in one Act of Mifchief or other, to make
" a Difturbance, and weary us out of the Place ; and when they faw they
" could not do it by all thofe Means, they brake and battered down the
" Doors and Walls next the Street with Bolt-hammers and other Engines, and
" though we minded them of the King's Declaration, wherein he promifed
" Liberty to tender Confciences, at his firft coming into *England*, and fhewéd
" them the Unlawfulnefs of their Doings, affaulting, breaking in upon us,
" and beating us in our own hired Houfe ; they called us Rebels, and pre-
" tended the King's Order for what they did, and ran violently upon us, and
" ufed us as if our Lives were all at their Mercies, haling, thrufting us out,
" and ftriking both Men and Women (though not lifting up an Hand againft
" them) without any Pity or Refpect to Age or other Condition, with Clubs,
" great Splinters, and Pieces of the Doors and other Timber : And though
" they that entred the Houfe beat us with fo much Cruelty, yet would not
" their Outguard let us pafs, till they alfo had fatisfied their bloody Minds
" in beating us again, fo that very many of us were forely hurt and bruifed.
" Twenty two had their Blood fhed ; one fo lamed that he was left behind
" unable to walk abroad, and a Woman almoft killed by their cruel Ufage ;
" and befides this, fome of us loft our Hats, and many of us had our Clothes
" rent and much befpattered and daubed : And yet our Perfecutors were not
" fatisfied with all this : When they had driven us from the Houfe, and
" cleared the Streets of us, they returned and quite battered down the reft of
" the Walls and Bays on each Side of the Meeting-houfe, next two Entries,
" and laid it all open to the Streets, then fought and hunted up and down the
" Meeting-houfe again for us, and them they lighted on did very much abufe,
" and affaulted an *Alderman*'s Houfe where fome of us lodged, and beat the
" Man of the Houfe at his own Door, and departed not fo long as it was
" light. *And we whofe Names are hereunto fubfcribed were Sufferers, and are*
" *Witneffes that thefe Things are true before written.*

John Moone	Jeremy Herne	Jofiah Cole
William Pepper	Stephen Crifp	John Oftler
John Ainfloe	Gregory Tingy	William Warbies
John Parker	Daniel Wallis	Stephen Hart
John Webb	Benjamin Lunt	Thomas Harris
Daniel Ward	William Turner	Thomas Payne
George Clark	Giles Fifher	James Allen
John Forfter	William Witham	John Pollard
Henry Marfhall	Philip Williamfon	Thomas Roufe
John Adams	Jeremy Wood.	

Befide the Subfcribers, many others partook of the like Abufes, to which their
publick Meetings continually expofed them, for being confcious of their own
Innocence, they difdained thofe mean Arts and Subterfuges, under which Men
of

of evil Defigns are wont to palliate their Treachery. Of thefe were *Venner* and his Accomplices, called the *Fifth Monarchy Men,* who in the Winter this Year made an Infurrection in the City of *London,* thereby incenfing the Government, and raifing a Storm of Perfecution, wherein the peaceable *Quakers* greatly fuffered, for in the Month called *January* this Year, *one Hundred* and *twenty fix* of this People were committed to Prifon for refufing to take the *Oath of Allegiance,* of which Refufal, their confcientious Obedience to the Precept of Chrift, *Swear not at all,* was their only Motive. Of this Number were committed,

Imprifonment of 126 for refufing to Swear.

To the Caftle in *Cambridge,* being the County Goal	59 Perfons
To the *Talbooth* Prifon there	8
To *Wifbich* Goal	8
To *Ely* Goal	51
In all	126

The Ufage they met with in *Cambridge* Goal is defcribed in the following Letter, from one of the Prifoners there to a Friend in *London,* viz.

" *Dear Friend,*

" MY dear Love to thee and all faithful Friends and Brethren, in Bonds
" and out of Bonds : God Almighty keep you all faithful to the End :
" This is to let thee know how it is, and hath been with us, in *Cambridge-*
" *fhire* and Town. They have been very cruel and violent towards all Friends,
" fparing none, neither Widows nor fatherlefs Children, but haled all before
" them called Juftices, and they fent all to Prifon : Many Widows about
" fixty, fome feventy Years old, and they left fome of the Houfes without
" Inhabitant, and fome little Children in the Streets, without any to look after
" them for feveral Days : Such was the Cruelty that I was moved to write
" a few Lines to them, a Copy whereof I have fent thee. They brought
" in one Day about fixteen Women, a great Part of them Widows, and moft
" of them all very poor in the Outward, having but little but as they did earn
" it by Day-labour, and they put them into the *Shire Hall,* where they were
" kept all Night without any thing to lie upon, and thefe Women were kept
" about four Days, and then the Goalor came and thruft them out, not having
" any Order, and took from them what Bedding they had gotten in, and doth
" keep it for Fees. We are already about thirty one Men in the County Goal,
" and nine Men in the Town Goal, and fixteen Women.——Upon the Se-
" cond-day laft, the Men called Juftices, fent the Clerk of the Peace to let
" us know, that it was the King's Pleafure to free us of the Oath, and if we
" would enter into a Bond to live peaceably, and not to have any Meeting
" or Conventicle for one Year's Time, we might have our Liberty : To
" which we anfwered by one Confent, *We could not for Confcience-fake, being*
" *the Lord's free Men.* And that Day I was moved to write a few Lines to
" them called Juftices, and fent it to them where they fat in *Cambridge,* a Copy
" of it I have fent alfo. Friends here are finely kept, and well content to lie
" upon Straw. Farewell.

A Letter de-fcribing the Ufage of the Prifoners.

"   Thy dear Friend and Brother in the Bonds of the Gofpel,

Cambridge *County Goal,* the 31ft of
    the *Eleventh Month* 1660.   " JOHN AINSLOE."

The Letters above-mentioned which *John Ainfloe* fent to the Juftices, were as follows, *viz.*

CAM-
BRIDGE-
SHIRE.
&c.
1660.

1*st* Letter
from J. Ain-
sloe *to the*
Juſtices.

The *Firſt* LETTTER.

" *Friends!*

" HAVE you forgotten there is a God, or do you think he hath forgot-
" ten his People, or do you think to change his Decree, or turn his
" Arm backward, that you thus act concerning his People, who ſeek not the
" Harm of any, but the Good of all, neither can they be charged with
" Wrong they have done to any, neither is Guilt found with them that Man
" can charge upon them, but only concerning our God, becauſe we cannot
" deny our God, and ſwear contrary to his Command ; therefore are we per-
" ſecuted and impriſoned, and Widows Houſes left deſolate, and the Fatherleſs
" left in the Streets ; the like hath not been heard of in Ages paſt, nor did
" this Nation ever meet with the like. O conſider, the Lord ſees and hath
" Reſpect to the Widow and Fatherleſs, though you have none : *Friends*, this
" is your Day, you ſhould do well to uſe it well, left God ſhorten it, and
" when you cry, God will not anſwer, and when you need Pity, you find
" none : Conſider that the Breath of all Men is in the Power of the Lord,
" and he can take it from them when it pleaſes him, and he will ſhorten the
" Days of the Wicked, and bring Deliverance for his People. Therefore
" conſider, and take Warning, and leave off perſecuting the innocent People
" of God, left God caſt out you as he hath done them before you, who
" were found guilty in that Thing, though not in ſo great a Meaſure. *Friends*,
" conſider that the Cry of the Poor and Fatherleſs, and the Deſolation of the
" Widow, enters into the Ears of the God of Heaven whom we ſerve,
" and he will plead our Cauſe one Day, until which Time we wait with
" Patience. Only it was upon my Spirit to lay theſe Things before you in
" Love, that you might repent before your Meaſure be filled up, and then
" no Place of Repentance will be found.

" *From a Lover of Peace and Righteouſneſs, and the Welfare of all Men,*

 25th of the Eleventh   " JOHN AINSLOE."
 Month 1660.

The *Second* LETTER.

" *Friends!*

" WE are bound with a ſtronger Bond than Man can bind, and this is the
" Bond of Peace and Unity, with which Bond we are bound to God to
" love him, and honour him above all, and our Neighbour as our ſelves, which
" is to us of greater Price and Value, than any Tie Men can lay upon us, and
" other Bonds cannot we enter into for Conſcience-ſake, but they who are
" out of this Bond in the Strife and ſtriving Nature one with another, of
" them Bond may be required for their good Behaviour ; but the Lord hath
" redeemed us out of Strife, and we are come to witneſs him who hath taken
" away the Occaſion of War, and Plots, and evil Contrivances againſt any
" Man ; and we wiſh and deſire from our Hearts the Welfare of all Men,
" and their Proſperity in that which is good, and if any wiſh otherwiſe, or be
" found acting otherwiſe, they are not of us : Bond may be required of them.
" This being conſidered by you in the Fear of the Lord, you will ſee no
" Reaſon why Bond ſhould be required of us. This is written in Behalf of
" my ſelf and many Brethren now Priſoners of the Lord, for witneſſing forth
" a good Conſcience towards God and towards Man, in *Cambridge* Town and
" County Goals.

 28th of the Eleventh   " JOHN AINSLOE."
 Month 1660.

Thus in an innocent Plainneſs, and with Chriſtian Courage, did this Sufferer
repreſent to the Magiſtrates, the Caſe of himſelf, and of his Friends in Priſon,
and in ſo doing cleared his own Conſcience, and left them the leſs excuſable in
                                                                    their

their Proceedings. The Bonds which were required of this People, would have restrained them from their religious Meetings, and therefore were by them refused.

And in another Letter, some Time after, the said *John Ainsloe* says,

"SOME of us are kept in and not suffered to go out to ease our selves, but must do it where they lie, and others of us shut up in Dungeons and Holes, where they keep their Felons, and Witches, and Murderers, and so thronged, that they have but Room to stir one by another, and the Places do smell so nasty, that it were enough to poison any Creature, but that the Lord is our Preserver ——— There is about twelve of us, poor labouring Men, that have nothing to live on but their own Labour, and they have been kept from it these eight Weeks, and had nothing but as others of us relieve them. Many of the Prisoners are sickly with Colds.

CAMBRIDGESHIRE. &c. 1660.

Reason for refusing Bonds.
Extract of another Letter from J. Ainsloe.

" JOHN AINSLOE."

This hard and close Confinement was prejudicial to the Health of many of them, and occasioned the Death of *Joseph Holmes*, who together with his Father and Brother, were imprisoned.

Death of J. Holmes in Prison.

In this Year *Edward Peashy* for a Demand of 6 s. for Tithes, had his Goods taken by Distress to the Value of 5 l.

Distresses, &c.

George Thorowgood, for opening his Shop on the Day called *Christmass-day*, was committed to Prison.

ANNO 1661.

1661.

The same *George Thorowgood*, for a Fine imposed on him for opening his Shop on an Holiday, so called, had his Goods taken away to the Value of 15 s.

Distress for opening Shop.

Mary Prior of *Over*, an aged and religious Widow, appearing at Sessions on a Summons for absenting herself from the publick Worship, was committed to Prison, where she fell sick and died, and was buried in *Cambridge* Castle Yard on the 5th of the Tenth Month this Year.

Death of M. Prior.

Stephen Blow and the Widow *Peachy*, for 7 s. of them demanded for Tithes, had their Goods taken away to the Value of 10 l. 13 s.

In the same Year *James Tims*, and *Francis Gerrard*, were imprisoned in *Cambridge* Castle, on an Attachment out of the Exchequer, for not paying Tithes.

ANNO 1662.

1662.

Eleanor Harwood, *Anne Barbary*, *Thomas Thorowgood*, *Mercy Padley*, and *Blanch Sutton*, were imprisoned on an Indictment for Absence from the National Worship : They were kept five Days and five Nights without any Bed to lie on, though one of them had a young Child sucking at her Breast. For the same Cause *Robert Letchworth* was imprisoned, and afterwards detained on a Writ *de Excommunicato capiendo* : And *Samuel Cater*, *Thomas Hawkes*, and *Samuel Fuller*, were by Order of Sessions committed to Prison, and continued there ten Weeks.

Imprisonments for Absence from the National Worship.

In the Second Month this Year, *Joseph Stevens* and *Edith Stevens*, both of *Over*, were committed to Prison for Tithes, and in the next Month *Thomas Goodwin* and *John Smith*, of *Hardwick*. *Samuel Fulbigg*, for a Demand of 7 s. for Tithe, had his Goods taken to the Value of 2 l. 10 s.

Robert Letchworth, for refusing to Swear, had taken from him two Cows worth 7 l.

ANNO 1663.

*1663.

Causeless Imprisonment.*

In this Year *Jeremy Rose* was arrested and imprisoned, for he knew not what, unless the Name *Quaker* had intitled him to such Usage.

James

James Tims, *Robert Skeile*, *Richard Read*, and *John Adams*, for refufing to bear Arms in the County Militia, had their Goods taken away to the Value of 19 l. 13 s. 4 d.

Jeremy Rofe, for 2 d. demanded for Tithe of Grafs worth but 18 d. fuffered Diftrefs of his Goods to the Value of 2 l. 10 s.

In the fame Year *Walter Crane* of *Horfed*, had been detained in Prifon fixteen Months on a Writ *de Excommunicato capiendo* for Tithes. And by like Writs for the fame Caufe were *Robert Steel* and *John Ruf* confined in *Wifbech* Goal.

On the 16th of the Second Month this Year, *Thomas Richardfon*, *Francis Bugg*, and *John Ives*, taken by Conftables at a Meeting, were committed to *Ely* Goal, and at the Affizes about five Months after, had the Oath of Allegiance tendred them, and for refufing it were remanded to Prifon, where *Thomas Richardfon*, above fixty Years of Age, through Want of Firing and other Neceffaries, and lodging on Straw in Winter Time, was taken fick, and died on the 13th of the Eighth Month 1665, after two Years and an Half Confinement. The other two continued there fix Months after his Death.

Henry Fofter of *Sutton*, was taken from his own Houfe by rude Soldiers, who with Sword and Piftol fo terrified his Wife, big with Child, that fhe fell in Travel before her Time, and both Mother and Child died : He was fent to *Wifbech* Goal till the next Affizes, and then, together with *William Conftance*, and *John Tye*, who were taken from a Meeting at *Chatteris*, was remanded to Prifon, where they continued many Months.

In the Month called *November* this Year, *John Ainfloe*, *Robert Falkner*, and *John Hollowell*, after a Meeting at *Wellingham*, were taken by the Sheriff and fent to Prifon till the next Affizes, four Months after, when a Bill of Indictment was found againft them, *for refufing to hear Common-prayer, and being at an unlawful Meeting :* Upon which they were recommitted till another Affize.

Robert Skeile and *John Rofe* were imprifoned on a Writ de *Excommunicato capiendo*, for abfenting from the National Worfhip.

William Wilkinfon, fummoned to the Seffions, and appearing with his Hat on, was fent to Prifon.

In this Year were taken from feveral in this County for refufing to pay towards Rates for Repairing the parochial Worfhip-houfes, Goods worth 2 l. 13 s. 8 d.

A N N O   1664.

In this Year were taken on Account of Tithes from *Stephen Blow*, for a Demand of 13 s. Goods worth 2 l. 6 s. and from *Stephen Wilfon* and *Richard Bond*, for about 40 s. demanded, Goods worth 12 l. 10 s.

Benjamin Cranwell was this Year committed to *Cambridge* Caftle for Tithes, where was alfo *James Blakely* the Elder, who lay there feveral Years.

George Thorowgood and *John Clark*, taken at a Meeting, were imprifoned, the Former ten Days, and the Latter two Months.

William Fifon and *Jonas Scrooks*, for being at a Meeting, were fent to Goal by *William Holder* a Prieft, and Juftice of the Peace.

George Thorowgood, *William Williams*, and *John Lowder*, for refufing to Swear, were imprifoned by Order of Seffions fifteen Months : This *William Williams* was a very poor Man with many fmall Children : His Wife, hoping to get fome Relief, applied to *William Fifher*, one of the County Juftices, at *Wifbech*, reprefenting the hard Condition of her numerous Family ; to which he, more like a *Canibal* than a *Chriftian*, replied, *If fhe wanted Food, fhe might take her Children, fry them for Stakes, and eat them.* The faid Juftice died not long after in much Trouble and Horror of Mind.

Richard Steaton, *Reuben Stevens*, and *William Pepper*, were imprifoned on Writs de *Excommunicato capiendo*, though wholly ignorant of any Procefs in the Ecclefiaftical Court againft them.

Clement Crabb the Elder, and *William Hart*, were imprisoned at *Wisbech* eighteen Months, for Absence from the National Worship ; as were *Edward Peachy, Daniel Peachy, Walter Peachy*, and *Stephen Blow*, fourteen Weeks, also *Edward Wright* and *John Webb* suffered Imprisonment some Time for the same Cause.

Several others had extravagant Seizures made on them for Nonconformity to the publick Worship, viz.

*Imprisonments
for Absence
from the pub-
lick Worship.
Extravagant
Seizures.*

	l.	s.	d.
John Dring of *Money*, sixty three Beasts worth	183	0	0
Ezekiel Palmer, seven Cows worth	22	0	0
Dorothy Motley, an industrious Widow, having six Children, six Kine worth	20	0	0
John Phipps of *Meexel*, eight Beasts worth	32	0	0
Richard Clarkson of *Chatteris*, fourteen Kine worth	30	0	0
	287	0	0

Some of the Cattle thus seized, were sold for half, and others for a quarter of their Value, few People caring to purchase them, the Innocence of the Sufferers affecting the Consciences of their Neighbours, who commiserating their Case, generally refused such Pennyworths.

ANNO 1665.

Joseph Nunn of *Littleport, John Dring, Thomas Paine, Anne Crabb*, and *Elizabeth Aspelon*, for not paying Tithes, had Goods and Cattle taken from them to the Value of 18 *l.* And *William Boughton* for a *Mortuary*, suffered by Distress 2 *l.* 10 *s.*

Richard Bedmell, and *William Wadingham*, of *Doddington, Robert Smith, William Wilkinson*, and *Thomas Dorman* of *Littleport*, and *Henry Wadely*, for Demands on them of 14 *l.* 4 *s.* 2 *d.* for Tithes, had Cattle and other Goods taken from them to the Value of 92 *l.* 13 *s.* 8 *d.* When the Priest of *Littleport* made Seizure of *Dorman's* Goods, he was reproved for taking Tithe for Calves, where none was due, and put in Mind of the Apostle *Paul's* Example, who *coveted no Man's Goods*, &c. to which he answered, *I matter not what* Christ *said, nor what Paul said ; I will have a Calf.* An Expression denoting, that he was more concerned for the *Profits* than the *Duty* of his Office.

ANNO 1666.

John Wayman and *Thomas Wayman*, both of *Over*, for a Demand of 5 *s.* for Tithe, were imprisoned in *Cambridge* Castle at the Suit of *Dudley Pope* Impropriator.

At *Ely* Assizes in the Month called *April* this Year, several who had been long in Prison at *Wisbech* for refusing the Oath of Allegiance, were set at Liberty.

ANNO 1667.

Robert Rayment, William Witham, Thomas Paine, and *Elizabeth Aspelon*, were imprisoned for Absence from the National Worship.

William Wilkinson, fined 60 *l.* for Meeting, died a Prisoner after two Years Confinement.

ANNO 1668.

Francis Emerson was imprisoned in *Cambridge* Castle for Tithes at the Suit of *John Philips* and *Joseph Kettle* : *Edward Peachy* and *John Blow* were also imprisoned there on an Attachment for Tithes.

C A M-
BRIDGE-
SHIRE,
&c.
1669.

*Diftreffes and
Imprifon-
ments.*

ANNO 1669.

Richard Cope, for refufing to bear Arms, fuffered Diftrefs of his Goods to the Value of 30 *s.*

In the fame Year, *John Adams, Thomas Gray, William Wells, William Crofs, Edward Fuller, William Nix,* and *Philip Williamfon,* were fent to Prifon for not paying Tithes, and continued there feveral Years.

1670.

*Great Spoil by
the Conven-
ticle Act.*

At Ely.

ANNO 1670.

By an Act of Parliament made this Year againft Conventicles, whereby Informers were encouraged with Part of the Fines, great Spoil of Goods was made in this County and Ifland; *viz.*

At *Ely* were taken from *Francis Bugg*, for being at feveral Meetings, Goods worth 42 *l.* 18 *s.* 4 *d.* And from feveral other Inhabitants there, to the Value of 47 *l.* 4 *s.* 2 *d.*

Among thefe was *George Thorowgood,* a poor Man, who having all his Houfhold Goods, Bed and Bedclothes taken from him, was forced to lodge on Straw ; after which, when fick, his Profecutors took away his Sheets and Shirt. Several, who, being fhut out of their Meeting-place, met in the Street were forely beaten, and *Stephen Clarkfon* knockt down by a Blow, which he complained of till his Death about five Months after.

At *Chatteris* and *Sutton* in the Ifle of *Ely,* were taken from about twenty Perfons, Goods to the Value of 61 *l.* 6 *s.* 8 *d.*

Richard Cope and *Robert Stanton,* Conftables, refufing to ferve one of the Warrants for thefe Diftreffes, were fined 5 *l.* each; and for *Non-payment,* Cope had taken from him four Cows worth 9 *l.* and *Stanton* four Cows worth 11 *l.*

At *Linton* were taken from feveral Perfons, Goods worth 59 *l.* 3 *s.* 9 *d.*

At *Cambridge,* for Meetings held there, Goods worth 54 *l.* 4 *s.* 6 *d.* One *William Brafier,* at whofe Houfe fome of thofe Meetings were, had all his Goods taken away, even his working Tools, and Bedding, fo that he was conftrained to lie on the Boards. *Edward Cooke* had the Bedding for himfelf and Family taken away, with his Children's Cradle, fo that the poor Babes contracted Sicknefs by lodging on Straw, and one of them died. Alfo *Nicholas Froft,* for permitting a filent Meeting in his Houfe, fuffered the Lofs of all his Goods.

At *Littleport* in the Ifle of *Ely,* were taken from feveral Perfons, Goods to the Value of 54 *l.* 18 *s.* 8 *d.* Among which is the Cafe of *Samuel Cater,* who was fined 25 *l.* for Preaching in *Norfolk,* from whence the Magiftrates there fent a Warrant to the Juftices of *Ely,* where he dwelt, and his Goods and Timber were taken by Diftrefs before he came Home.

From *John Adams* of *Hadenham,* then a Prifoner, for Meetings at his Houfe, were taken Goods worth 49 *l.* 8 *s.* 4 *d.* And from *Edward Fuller* to the Value of 35 *l.* 2 *s.* 4 *d.* One *Woodward,* a Member of the Church of *England,* refufing to affift in carrying thofe Goods, was forced to pay 5 *l.* Fine ; and wanting but 2 *d.* of that Sum, the Juftice would not abate it. This *Woodward,* afterward on his Death-bed, expreffed much Satisfaction in fo fuffering.

At *Over,* feveral, who met there, had their Cattle and Goods diftrained to the Value of 156 *l.* 6 *s.* 6 *d.* *John Ainfloe,* fined 20 *l.* for Preaching there, had nine Cows taken worth 30 *l.* which when the Parifh Officers refufed to fell below their Value, Juftice *Hatton,* who impofed the Fine, fold to his own Clerk and the Informer for 12 *l.* Some other of the Cattle were bought by *Sackvil Wade* Lord of the Manour of *Over,* who gave this Reafon for buying them, *viz.* " That he, feeing rafcally Fellows purchafe thofe Goods at low Rates, " had bought them with Intention to let the Owners have them again at the " fame Price :" But he was ignorant that the Owners would not buy their own Goods again, though never fo cheap. The Purchafers were generally
Men

CAM-
BRIDGE-
SHIRE,
&c.
1670.

Severity of a
Juſtice.

Men of little Reputation, ſuch as inferior Conſtables, and *Informers*, one of whom, *Edward Wells*, a Cobler of *Cambridge*, by buying ſuch Bargains became a Grazier.

For Meetings at *Royſton*, were taken Goods worth 47 *l.* 12 *s.* One of the Juſtices who granted Warrants for theſe Diſtreſſes was *James Wilmot*, a keen Man for ſuch Service, who bid the Officers leave the Sufferers neither Diſh nor Spoon, nor Seat to ſit on. By ſuch Direction they thought themſelves warranted in Stripping *William Witham* of the Coat from his Back, and telling him, that next Time they would ſend him home naked: Alſo in taking from the Wife of *Philip Williamſon*, then impriſoned for his Religion, the Firing provided for herſelf and Children; and from *Edward Mayes* and his Wife, both very aged, their Bed and Bedclothes; and from the Widow *Aſhwell*, above eighty Years of Age, the Bed ſhe lay on.

At *Oakington*, *Great Abington*, *Balſham*, *Fulliborne*, and *Hogington*, they made Diſtreſs of Cattle and Goods to the Value of 126 *l.* 2 *s.* 8 *d.* In which Diſtreſs they ſhewed no Compaſſion, taking from *Suſanna Gunn*, a poor induſtrious Woman, even the *Bread-Corn* ſhe had gleaned.

At *Swanzey* they took from *Nicholas Walker* and *John Norris*, Goods worth 22 *l.*

In this Year *Joſeph Townſend* having a Booth at *Sturbridge* Fair with Goods to ſell, went to viſit his Mother in *Cambridge*; an Informer ſeeing him go in, ſuſpected a Meeting there, and perſuaded three *Doctors* of the Univerſity, Juſtices of the Peace, to come thither from their Place of publick Worſhip; who coming, found only three Perſons beſide the Family: Vext at the Diſappointment, they charged a Conſtable with *Joſeph Townſend*, and in the Evening tendred him *the Oath of Allegiance*, and for refuſing it committed him to Goal. When there, upon Information of his being at a Meeting in the Forenoon of the ſame Day, they fined him, and ordered Goods to be taken out of his Booth to the Value of 10 *l.* They kept him cloſe Priſoner there during the Fair, to his very great Detriment, though ſeveral of his *Chapmen* offered 1000 *l.* Bail for his Liberty; and his Wife, who came from *Northamptonſhire* to take Care of his Goods, offered herſelf to lie in Priſon in his ſtead.

Edward Smith of *Linton*, and *John Bing* of *Over*, were impriſoned for refuſing to Swear.

For a Meeting at *Cambridge* on the 27th of the Ninth Month this Year, the whole of the Fines were laid on *Elizabeth Underwood* of *Cheſterton*, from whom, ſhe then dwelling with her Son, they took all the Goods they could find of hers.

Violent, about this Time, were the Proceedings of *Edward Patrick* a Juſtice of the Peace, who with one *Rickman* an Apparitor, came to the Meeting at *Littleport*, took the Names of thoſe who were met, turned them out by Violence, took in their own Horſes, made a Fire, and ſat down drinking and carouſing. When they went away they ordered the Doors to be lockt up. Then charging ſeveral Perſons to attend them, they went to the Burying Ground purchaſed by the ſaid People, and made Uſe of by them for twelve Years paſt; where the Juſtice with his own Hands pulled down the Pales, while his drunken Attendants brake them in Pieces, digged up the Poſts, and levelled the Fence with the Ground.

At another Meeting the ſame Perſons pulled down *Samuel Cater* preaching, and ſtruck him twice: And while he was Praying, pulled him off his Knees by the Noſe. They knocked down *Stephen Clarkſon*, ſo that he complained of the Blow till he died about five Months after.

On the 29th of the ſame Month they repeated their Inſults, beating and abuſing many, and throwing ſome of their Hats into the Dirt. They alſo took away the Forms of the Meeting-houſe.

In this Year *Edward Redmel* and *William Wadingham*, both of *Doddington*, were impriſoned in *Wiſbech* Goal for Tithes.

In this Year alſo *Henry Tims*, *George Read*, and *John Pigg*, ſuffered eight Months Impriſonment for refuſing to bear Arms in the County *Militia*.

ANNO

*Violence of
Juſtice Pa-
trick.*

ANNO 1671.

Ezra Purcas was committed to Priſon for refuſing to pay 3 s. demanded of
him for *Smoke-penny, Garden-penny,* and *Eaſter-Offerings.*

In the Month called *April* this Year, the aforementioned Juſtice *Patrick* in
much Fury entered a Meeting at *Littleport,* violently beating both Old and
Young, till he broke his Staff, and then taking another out of a Warden's
Hand repeated his Blows, and throwing ſeveral Women down in the Street,
ſaid, *If he killed them he could anſwer it.* Then he ſent two young Men to
Bridewell, where they were cruelly whipt, and detained till Seſſions.

1672.

*Releaſe of
Priſoners.*

ANNO 1672.

In this Year many of this People under Confinement, for refuſing to take
the Oath of Allegiance, were diſcharged by the King's Letters patent, of whom
were releaſed out of *Cambridge* Caſtle, *Edward Smith, John Bing, William
Witham, Edward Sutton, Robert Matthews, Giles Pemberton, Philip Williamſon,
Thomas Rivers, Francis Holcroft,* and *Jacob Rogers.*

In the ſame Year died, Priſoners for Tithes, *Reuben Stevens* and *Bennet Cranſ-
well,* both of *Over,* and *Thomas Gray* of *Hadenham.*

1673.

*Diſtreſſes for
Meeting.*

ANNO 1673.

George Taylor of *Cheſterton, John Smith* of *Over, John Ainſloe,* and *John Norris,* for being at a Meeting held in the Houſe of the ſaid *John Norris* at *Wellingham,* ſuffered Diſtreſs of their Goods and Cattle to the Value of 37 *l.* 16 s.
Alſo for a Meeting at *Mildenhall,* were taken from *Francis Bugg* and *John
Burgeſs,* Goods worth 32 *l.* 10 s.

1674.

*Grievous Op-
preſſion of a
poor Man.*

ANNO 1674.

For Meetings held at *Cambridge,* Seizures were made on divers Perſons to
the Amount of 11 *l.* Of theſe was *William Brazier,* a poor Shoemaker, who,
after Diſtreſs of his Houſhold Goods, was ſpoiled of his working Tools, his
wearing Apparel, and his Wood for firing: And when reduced to lodge on
Straw, they took from under him the Sheets which covered that Straw:
Nevertheleſs his Zeal and Conſtancy continued immoveable.

John Elgar of *Papworth,* for a Meeting at *Eltiſley,* had Cattle taken from
him worth 6 *l.* 10 s.

*Death of 4
Perſons in
Priſon.*

In this Year *John Adams* of *Hadenham,* died a Priſoner for Tithes; as did
alſo *John Feaſt* of *Sutton, John Beadles* of *Chatteris,* and *Peter Hill* of the ſame.

1675.

*Diſtreſſes for
Tithes,*

*and for
Meetings.*

ANNO 1675.

John Prime of *Wilbrum,* at the Suit of *Thomas Witham* a Prieſt, had his
Houſhold Goods, and other Things taken by Diſtreſs to the Value of 74 *l.*
for a Demand of three Years Tithe for a Farm of but 22 *l. per Annum* Rent.

In this Year ſeveral Perſons, who had met together at the Houſe of *Matthew
Beeſley* of *Oakington,* ſuffered by Diſtreſs made on their Goods and Chattels to
the Value of 61 *l.* 17 s. 6 d. And *Henry Boſtock* for being at a Meeting at
Wellingham, had Malt taken from him worth 6 *l.* 10 s.

*Hard Caſe of
G. Friend
and his Fa-
mily.*

George Friend, informed againſt by *Edward Swanton* a Prieſt, for being at a
Meeting at *Lakenheath,* had all his Goods taken from him, and himſelf with
his Wife and four or five ſmall Children, were obliged to lodge on Straw in the
Cold of Winter. The Goods taken were carried to the informing Prieſt's
Houſe.

ANNO

Anno 1676.

Gabriel Walker of *Swaffham-Bulbeck*, was committed to *Cambridge* Caſtle on a Writ *de Excommunicato capiendo*, at the Suit of *Malin Sawerby* Prieſt, for *Eaſter-Offerings* and Tithes of half a Rood of Saffron-Ground. He was confined in a cloſe Dungeon, where, for want of Air in Summer, and Fire in Winter, his Life was endangered. He was continued in this hard Impriſonment near four Years after.

Cruel Confinement of G. Walker.

James Houghton of *Downham*, was impriſoned in the Iſle of *Ely*, on a Writ *de Excommunicato capiendo*, where he lay above four Years, for refuſing to pay 16 d. toward the Repairs of the Pariſh Worſhip-houſe. Alſo *Henry Harlow, Nicholas Froſt, Thomas Edmundſon,* and *Henry James,* for like Demands of 3 s. 6 d. each, were detained Priſoners at *Cambridge* above ſix Years.

Tedious Impriſonments.

In this Year was levied by *Exchequer* Proceſs, for Abſence from the National Worſhip, whereby two Thirds of their Eſtates were forfeited to the King on old Statutes made againſt *Popiſh* Recuſants,

	l.	*s.*	*d.*
From *John Prime* of *Wilbrun*, Goods worth	88	0	2
Richard Webb of *Weſtwickham*, to the Value of	26	10	0
	38	10	3

Diſtreſs by Exchequer Proceſs.

Anno 1677.

1677.

By like Proceſſes for the ſame Cauſe, were taken from the ſaid *Richard Webb*, and *John Prime, Henry Boſtock* of *Quy; John Harvey* of *Linton*, Grocer, and *Edward Smith* of the ſame, Goods to the Value of 65 l. 17 6 d. And from *John Smith* and *George Naſh*, both of *Over*, Goods worth 97 l. 11 s. 7 d. The ſelfiſh View of ſome Officers, in executing ſuch Proceſſes, is ſhewn by the Anſwer which *Iſaac Smith*, an under Sheriff, gave when he was told that it would be of leſs Detriment to the Sufferers to take *live Cattle* than *Houſhold Goods*, his Reply was, that *he had more Need of Houſhold Stuff, being ſhortly to go and keep Houſe himſelf.* This was proved to a Committee of Parliament.

More Diſtreſſes by Proceſs out of the Exchequer.

Anno 1678.

1678.

Thomas Amey of *Great Abington*, impriſoned in *Cambridge* Caſtle, on a Writ *de Excommunicato Capiendo*, at the Suit of *John Boulton*, Vicar, for a Claim of Oblations and Tithe of Wild Pigeons, was remaining under that Confinement a Year and an Half after.

Long Impriſonment for trivial Claims.

Anno 1679.

1679.

At *Chatteris* in the Iſle of *Ely*, exorbitant Seizures of Cattle were made for ſmall Tithes, at the Suit of *William Strong* Vicar, *viz.*

	Demanded				Cattle taken		
	l.	*s.*	*d.*		*l.*	*s.*	*d.*
For	4	0	0	of *Francis Cooper*, to the Value of	40	0	0
	0	10	0	of *Ellis Basford*	7	10	0
	1	1	0	of *Edward Claxon*	22	0	0
	5	11	0			69	10	0

Exceſſive Seizures.

The ſame Vicar took from *John Worth*, for a Claim of Tithes, Cattle worth 13 l. 10 s. and for the ſame Tithes detained him alſo in Priſon twenty Months.

CAM-
BRIDGE-
SHIRE,
&c.
1679.

Seizures by
Exchequer
Proce/s.

In this and the next preceding Year were taken by *Exchequer* Proceſs for Abſence from the National Worſhip, from

	l.	*s.*	*d.*
Richard Pettit of *Stow cum Quy*, Wheelwright, ten Cows worth	22	0	0
Henry Boſtock of *Quy*, a Cow and an Horſe worth	5	10	0
John Prime of *Wilbrum*, fourteen Cows worth	32	15	6
Robert Salmon of *Shudicamps*, and his Widow, to the Value of	7	6	8
John Smith of *Over*, a Mare and a Gelding worth	16	0	0
Richard Webb of *Weſt-Wickham*, ſeven Horſes, and other Things, worth	52	0	0
Edward Smith of *Linton*, and *Jacob Baker* of *Weſt-Wooton*, Goods worth	5	15	6
	141	7	8

1680.

ANNO 1680.

Joſeph Endon of *Boſley*, for 30 s. demanded for Tithes, had two Cows taken from him worth 7 *l.*

1682.

Diſtreſſes, &c.

ANNO 1682.

Stephen Blows, for a Meeting in his Houſe at *Soham* in the Iſle of *Ely*, had taken from him eight Cows worth 26 *l.* 15 s. and ſeveral others alſo had Goods taken away for the ſame Meeting worth 10 *l.* 10 s.

Taken by *Exchequer* Proceſs, for Abſence from the National Worſhip, from *Nicholas Sparks* of *Linton*, Goods worth 10 *l.* 12 s.

For the ſame Cauſe were committed to *Cambridge* Caſtle, *Nicholas Walker*, *John Holmes*, *George Hanſcomb*, and *Robert Hanſcomb*, all of *Swanzey*; alſo *Robert Adams*, and *William Page* of *Over*.

1683.

Impriſonments
and Diſtreſſes
for ſeveral
Cauſes.

ANNO 1683.

Edmund Roſe of *Chatteris*, was impriſoned for Tithes at the Suit of *William Strong* Vicar.

Nine Perſons, convicted for a Meeting at *Littleport*, ſuffered Diſtreſs of Goods to the Value of 11 *l.* 16 s. 6 d. And ſixteen others, for refuſing the Oath of Allegiance, tendred them at the Quarter Seſſions, were committed to Priſon; two of whom, *Samuel Fullbegg*, and *John Toppin*, ſoon fell ſick and died Priſoners.

For Abſence from the National Worſhip, were taken from *Nicholas Spark* of *Linton*, Goods worth 6 *l.* 4 s. and from *John Webb* of *Balſham*, to the Value of 9 *l.* 14 s.

And for the ſame Cauſe were committed to Priſon, *Vincent Wayman* of *Cottenham*, *Edward Peachy*, *Thomas Blows*, and *Stephen Blows*, all of *Soham*; alſo *Gabriel Walker* of *Swaffham-Bulbeck*.

1684.

ANNO 1684.

Taken for Tithes from *Jeremiah Roſe* of *Chatteris*, for 20 s. demanded, two Cows worth 6 *l.* and from *Philip Eldin* of *Marſh*, for 7 *l.* Demand, a Mare, Colt, and ſixty Sheep, worth 35 *l.*

W. Page died
a Priſoner.

William Braſier of *Cambridge*, was committed to Priſon on a Writ *de Excommunicato capiendo*. And in this Year *William Page* died a Priſoner.

1685.

3 Perſons im-
priſoned.

ANNO 1685.

John Langran of *Taſt*, and *Thomas Hanſcomb* and *Richard Maſters* of *Swanzey*, were committed to Priſon for Abſence from the National Worſhip.

ANNO

ANNO 1686.

John Prime was imprisoned for Tithes in *Cambridge* Castle. In this Year King *James the Second* issued a Proclamation for releasing out of Prison such as were detained either on Writs *de Excommunicato capiendo*, or by *Exchequer* Process, or otherwise at the King's Suit : By which Means were discharged fourteen or fifteen of the Persons beforementioned, together with *Samuel Cater*, *Robert Letchworth*, *Robert Read*, *William Crofs*, and *Robert Skeele*.

J. Prime.
K. James's
Proclamation.

ANNO 1690.

1690.

Henry Slater of *Elme* in the Isle of *Ely*, prosecuted for 10 s. Tithe at the Suit of *Charles Dimock* Priest, had taken from him a Cow and Mare worth 4 l. 5 s.

In the same Year *Henry Wadelow*, *John Goom*, and *Clement Pain*, had their Corn taken for Tithes to the Value of 6 l. 14 s.

Distrefses for Tithes.

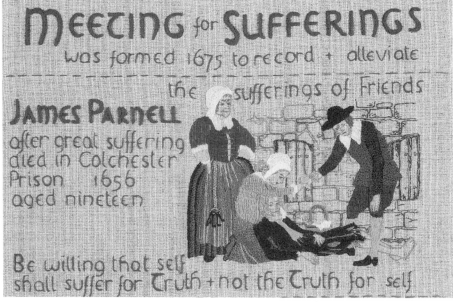

Courtesy Quaker Tapestry, Kendal   See "James Parnel" text opposite

C H A P. XIV.

E S S E X.

Anno 1655.

Sufferings of
J. Parnel.

THE firft Sufferings in this County which occur to our Notice, were thofe of *James Parnel,* who, when fixteen Years of Age, was convinced of the *Truth* by the Miniftry of *George Fox,* then Prifoner in the Dungeon at *Carlifle.* He gave early Proofs of his Patience and Conftancy by fuffering Imprifonment in *Cambridgefhire,* of which we have already made mention in our Account of that County, pag. 86 foregoing. Being about eighteen Years of Age, he came into *Effex,* preaching the Doctrine of the Gofpel with fuch Efficacy, that many were convinced, and among others *Stephen Crifp,* afterward an eminent Teacher of the fame Doctrine. *Parnel,* as he was coming out of *Nicholas* Steeple-houfe in *Colchefter,* where he had been exhorting the People to Repentance, was met by a blind Zealot who ftruck him a violent Blow with a great Staff, faying, *There, take that for Chrift's Sake:* To whom the innocent Sufferer meekly anfwered, *Friend, I do receive it for Jefus Chrift's Sake.* From thence he went to *Coggefhall,* where the *Independent* Profeffors had appointed a Faft, on purpofe to pray againft the fpreading of Error, by which they meant the *Quakers* Doctrine. The Prieft, who officiated on that Occafion, uttered many Invectives againft that People, fuch as Prejudice and Prepoffeffion had furnifhed him with. *James Parnel* ftood ftill till the Prieft had done, and was coming down from his Pulpit, when, thinking it his Duty to undeceive the People, he faid to the Prieft, *I am ready to prove that the* Quakers *are not on a Sandy Foundation, and that thou art a falfe Prophet and Deceiver.* After fome Words had paffed, a Perfon ftanding by accufed *Parnel,* faying, *that he owned no Church:* He replied, *That's falfe.* Then being afked, *What Church he owned?* He anfwered, *The Church in God.* Whereupon the Prieft faid, *That was Nonfenfe.* But *Parnel* taking a Bible out of his Pocket, fhewed, that it was a *Scripture Expreffion,* and charged the Prieft with *Blafphemy* in calling it *Nonfenfe.* On his coming out of the Steeple-houfe he was apprehended, and, after Examination, committed to *Colchefter* Caftle, by a Warrant figned by four Juftices, containing the following Charge, *viz.*

" THAT the faid *James Parnel*, with many other Perfons of his
" gathering together, did in a riotous Manner enter into the Parifh
" Church at *Great-Coggefhall*, and there being a great Number of Chriftians
" met in the faid Church, to hold and keep a Day of publick Humiliation
" and feeking of God, and being in order thereunto then exercifed in the
" Divine Worfhip and Service of Almighty God, he the faid *James* did
" then and there ftand up, and told the Minifter *he blafphemed and fpake*
" *falfly*, and ufed many other reproachful Words againft the faid Minifter,
" and afterward he departed the faid Church, and went into the common
" Highway in the faid Town of *Great-Coggefhall*, with a great Number of
" Perfons his Followers, who kept there unlawfully together, and fome of
" them gave out menacing and threatning Speeches, tending to the Breach of
" the Peace, and againft the Law ; and alfo the faid *James* cannot give us a
" very good Account of himfelf, where he was laft fettled, or of his Life
" and Converfation, but doth farther appear to us to be an idle and diforderly
" Perfon."

To this *Mittimus J. Parnel* afterward publifhed an Anfwer, in a Book called
The Fruits of a Faft, printed by *Giles Calvert*, *Anno* 1655, wherein he fhews
the Errors and Inconfiftencies of the Charge againft him, juftifying the Peace-
ablenefs of his own Demeanour at that Time ; and alfo gives a folid and
Chriftian Account of the Work of God upon his Soul, and the Neceffity
laid upon him to teftify againft the Formalities and *Will-Worfhip* of *Man's* In-
vention.

Being in Prifon he was clofely confined, and at the Time of the next Affizes, held a few Weeks after at *Chelmsford*, he was faftned to a Chain with
Felons and Murderers, and fo led above twenty Miles through the Country,
remaining chained both Night and Day.

Brought among Felons to the Affizes.

At his Trial he was brought to the Bar hand-cuff'd, but the People ex-
claiming againft that Cruelty, at his next Appearance the Manacles were taken
off. The Judge feemed refolved againft him, faying, *that the Lord Protector
had charged him to punifh fuch Perfons as fhould contemn either Magiftrates or
Minifters :* And in his Charge to the Jury, he directed them to bring him in
Guilty, which they readily did : He was fined 40 *l.* and fent again to Prifon till
Payment. And the Goaler was ordered not to let any *giddy-headed People*,
by which was meant *his Friends*, come at him.

The Judge prejudiced againft him.

The *Goaler* obferved his Orders, to which the Cruelty of his own Difpofition
alfo inclined him, for he would fuffer none to come to him but fuch as abufed
him ; and the Goaler's Wife, equally cruel, not only ordered her Servant to
beat him, but ftruck him with her own Hands, fwearing *fhe would have his
Blood*. When his Friends fent him Victuals, fhe ordered the other Prifoners to
take it ; and when a Bed was fent him, fhe refufed to let him have it, but
conftrained him to lodge on the hard damp Stones. After this he was put into
an Hole in the Caftle-Wall, not fo wide as fome Bakers Ovens, which Hole
being a great Heighth from the Ground, and a Ladder, ufed to go up by, being feveral Feet too fhort, he was obliged to climb up and down by a Rope
to fetch his Victuals or other Neceffaries : For when his Friends would have
given him a Cord and a Bafket to draw up his Food in, the cruel Keeper
would not fuffer it. By lying long in that damp Hole, his Limbs were be-
numbed ; and as he was going up the Ladder with his Food in one Hand,
attempting to lay hold on the Rope with the other, he miffed his Aim, and
fell down on the Stones, by which he was fo wounded in his Head, and bruifed
in his Body, that he was taken up for dead. Then they put him into an Hole
underneath the other, there being two Stories of fuch narrow vaulted Holes in
the Wall : Here, when the Door was fhut, was fcarce any Air, there being
no Window or Place befide to let it in. Thus bruifed with the Fall, and fhut
up where he could hardly breath, there was little Hope left of his Life.
Whereupon

His clofe and cruel Confine-ment.

E S S E X.
1655.

Whereupon two of his Friends, *William Talcot* and *Edward Grant*, wealthy Tradefmen of that Town, offered to be bound in fufficient Bonds, and *Thomas Shortland*, another of his Friends; offered to lie in Prifon in his Stead, fo that he might have Liberty to go to *William Talcot*'s Houfe till he might recover of his Bruifes, but this was denied. Nor would the Goaler fuffer him to walk fometimes in the Yard, as other Prifoners did. It happened once, that the Door of his Hole being open, he went forth into a narrow Yard between two high Walls, at which the Keeper in a Rage lockt up the Door and fhut him out in the Yard all Night, in the cold Time of Winter. His Conftitution being much impaired by cruel Ufage and hard Imprifonment, after ten or

His Death, and Charaɛter.

eleven Months he fell fick and died. Two of his Friends, *Thomas Shortland* and *Anne Langley*, were prefent at his Departure. When Death approached, he faid, *Here I die innocently :* And a little after, *Now I muft go.* He had often faid, that *One Hour's Sleep would cure him of all.* The laft Words he was heard to fpeak were, *Now I go*, and then ftretching himfelf out, flept about an Hour, and breathed his laft. He died a Youth, about nineteen Years of Age, but approved himfelf a ftrong Man in Chrift, and having an Eye to the Eternal Recompence of Reward fet before him, perfevered faithful to his End through manifold Sufferings, with a remarkable Innocence, Patience, and Magnanimity. His Perfecutors, inftead of repenting of their Cruelty, the apparent Caufe of his Death, raifed a flanderous Report of his haftning his own End by willfully abftaining from Food : But that Report was proved falfe by the Teftimony of credible Witneffes, who were frequently with him during his Sicknefs ; and to whom that groundlefs Calumny was a clear Indication of the *deep-rooted Malice* of thofe who invented it.

Their Teftimony to the Light of Chrift gave great Offence.

ANNIS 1656, 1657, 1658, and 1659. Many in this County were zealoufly concerned to publifh the Doɛtrine of the *Light* of *Chrift*, and the Neceffity of Obedience thereunto, for which Caufe they frequently went to the publick Places of Worfhip, waiting for the moft part till the Prieft had ended his Sermon, and then declaring to the People their own Experience of the Work of Truth, reproving Sin in all, and exhorting to Repentance and Amendment of Life ; they alfo publickly teftified againft Superftition and Will-Worfhip, and fpared not to caution Men to beware of being feduced by falfe Teachers, who regarded more their own Intereft and Promotion, than the Purity of their Doɛtrine. This plain and Chriftian Teftimony, however effeɛtual to the Converfion of many, gave great Offence to thofe who hated Reformation, and particularly incenfed the Priefts, who having no fmall Influence on the Magiftrates, excited them to fupprefs the Meffengers of fuch Tidings, whom they

Many Imprifoned.

mifreprefented as Difturbers of the publick Peace and Worfhip, under which Pretence they procured the Imprifonment of *William Monk* of *Sandon* two Years and four Months ; *John Claydon* of *Hadftock* fixteen Months ; *Anne Langley* at one Time ten Weeks, and at another Time fifteen Weeks ; *George Rofe* about five Months ; *William Allen* of *Samford* about a Year ; *Stephen Huberfty* of *Burnham* five Weeks ; *John Davidge* in the Houfe of Correɛtion a Month ; during which Time none of his Friends were fuffered to vifit him ; *Martha Simonds* four Months, and two of her Friends, who came to fee her, three Days. Befide thefe were imprifoned for the fame Caufe, *John Sewel* of *Geftlingthorp*, *John Child* of *Felfted*, *Samuel Skillingham*, *Mary Cooke*, *Jonathan Bundock* of *Weft-Bergholt*, *Thomas Shortland*, *Stephen Crifp*, *Edmund Crofs*, *Anne Stammage*, *John Eve*, and *Anne Child*. Alfo *Matthew Hodfon*, *Joane Defborow*, *Edward Grant*, and *John Hall*. *Anne Humphry* was imprifoned in Bridewell, where *John Tomlin*, *Margaret Gray*, and *George Ede*, were not only clofe

Some whipt. Others fet in the Stocks.

confined, but alfo cruelly whipt. At *Saffron-Walden*, *William Robinfon* was imprifoned, and *George Whitehead* fet in the Stocks. Others there were whofe Chriftian Advices and Exhortations met with Returns of illegal and barbarous Abufes from the Populace, the worft of whom, animated by the Priefts, and

Many Infults and Abufes.

unreftrained by the Magiftrates, treated them moft inhumanly : Many and grievous were the Infults, Stonings, Beatings, Bruifes, Scoffings, and Revilings, patiently

patiently endured by *John Child, Anne Child, John Chandler, Henry Fell, Robert Debnam, Mary Bourne, Zachary Child,* and others. At *Halstead, John Isaac,* having a Concern to warn the People, and unwilling to give Offence, committed the same to Writing, which he left at the Steeple-house; for this he was sent to Prison, and afterward fined twenty Marks.

Their religious Constancy in Meeting.

The religious Zeal of this People, in frequenting their Assemblies for Worship, obliged them to travel to the Places where they were held, which being sometimes at a confiderable Diftance, their going to or coming from them on the Firft-day of the Week, was called a *Breach* of the *Sabbath,* and punifhed by Fines, Diftrefs of Goods, or Imprifonment. For this Caufe *Samuel Skillingham* and *Zachary Child* going to a Meeting at *Weathersfield,* were ftopt by Wardens in the Street, and forely beaten and abufed by a Juftice's Clerk: And for the fame Caufe *Elizabeth Court* was fent to the Houfe of Correction, where fhe was whipt, and fuffered much cruel Ufage, being kept without Candle or Fire in the cold Winter, when fhe was fick of an Ague. *John Child,* for riding to a Meeting, had his Horfe taken away, and kept from him three Weeks, and then return'd Home without Bridle, Saddle, Pillow, or Cloth, all which they detained for a pretended Forfeiture. *Edmund Crofs, John Pike, Jeffery Bullock, Richard Waite,* and *William Halley,* were taken out of a Meeting at *Horfley,* and fet in the Stocks fix Hours, for coming thither on the *Sabbath-day.* For the fame Caufe *Edward Morrell* and *Anne Child,* by the Direction of the Prieft of *Stebbing,* were taken from a Meeting there, and kept under Guard in an Alehoufe all Night. And under the like Pretence *Richard Potter* and *William Suffall* were committed to Prifon. The Wife of one *John Chopping* being feen going homeward, on that Day, her Hufband was fined, and had his Goods diftrained. *Zachary Child* and *Anne Child* returning from *Colchefter,* where fhe had been to vifit her Hufband in Prifon, were kept by an officious Conftable at *Braintree,* detained all Night in an Inn-yard in cold Weather, and next Day were fined 10 s. each. Some were imprifoned on an Accufation of working on the Firft-day of the Week, a Pretence with which the extream Superftition of thofe Times furnifh'd thofe who were addicted to it, and gave them an Opportunity of perfecuting Men more religious and righteous than themfelves, and better qualified to difcern the Nature of the true *Chriftian-Sabbath,* and of that *perpetual Reft* from the *Bondage* of *Sin,* which the true Believers in Chrift are entred into: Hence proceeded the Imprifonment of *Thomas Chitham, Thomas Shortland,* and *John Tomlyn:* And under the fame Pretence *Thomas Lee* of *Steeple* was fined 20 s.

Punifhed as Sabbath-breaking.

Nature of the Chriftian-Sabbath.

Richard Norton of *Coggefhall,* for Fines of 6 l. for refufing to Swear, had his Goods taken away by Diftrefs: And *Griffith Perry,* for the fame Caufe being fined 20 s. fuffered the Lofs of two Cows valued at 11 l.

Diftrefs.

In thefe Years we have divers Inftances of exorbitant Seizures for Tithes, *viz.*

l.	s.	d.		l.	s.	d.	
For 50	0	0	Demand, were taken from *John Pollard* of *Steeple,* Corn, &c. to the Value of	322	0	0	*Exorbitant Seizures for Tithes.*
6	0	0	*Mofes Davie* of *Felfted*	28	0	0	
5	0	0	*John Crofier*	23	0	0	
0	10	0	*Robert Adams* of *Feering*	5	10	0	
2	10	0	*Griffith Perry* of *Linfel*	20	0	0	
2	14	0	*John Adams* of *Hadftock*	27	0	0	
0	10	0	*Samuel Warner* of *Boxted*	5	10	0	
17	9	0	*John Choppin*	25	15	0	
20	0	0	*Robert Nichols* of *Colne*	50	0	0	
10	0	0	*Jofiah Smith* of *Little-Samford*	45	0	0	
1	19	0	*John Cakebread* of *Great-Samford*	6	10	0	
For 116	12	0	Demanded, Taken to the Value of	558	5	0	

ESSEX.
1656 *to*
1659.

*Imprifonments
and Diftreffes
for Tithes.*

The above-named *John Pollard* was alfo imprifoned in *Colchefter* Caftle four-teen Months, in the Upper Bench five Months, and in the Fleet fome Years after.

Sarah Cadney of *Much-Braxfted* had taken from her, for Tithes, by Diftrefs, two Cows worth 11 *l.*

Among thofe who were Prifoners for Tithes in *Colchefter* Caftle, were *John Crofter* and *Mofes Davie*, who continued there twenty one Weeks ; *John Adams* fix Months ; *Robert Abbott* of *Colne*, and *Thomas Mumford* of *Saling*, two Years and four Months ; *Henry Smith* of *Saling* three Months ; the Widow *Balls* and her Son *William Balls* twenty Months ; though the Son was not at that Time the Occupier of any Land : *Edward Morel* of *Thaxted* nine Weeks ; *James Potter* of *Marks-Tey* was committed in *November* 1658, and continued feveral Years ; *Thomas Ellam* and *John Evans*, both of *Much-Eafton* ; alfo *John Emfon* and *William Crow*, both of *Barfield*, committed in the Year 1659, remained there fome Years : *William Enniver* of *Broxted* was imprifoned for Tithes twenty two Weeks.

In thefe Years *Robert Ludgater*, *Thomas Creek*, *Richard Horton*, *Richard Ames*, *Samuel Norton*, *William Boggs*, the Widow *Balls*, and *Richard Lack*, fe-verally fuffered the Seizure of their Goods, for refufing to pay the ufual Affeffments toward the Repairs of the Parifh Worfhip-houfes.

For not bear-ing Arms.

John Furly of *Colchefter*, for refufing to fend an Horfe and Man, when fummoned to ferve in the County Militia, fuffered by Diftrefs to the Value of 3 *l.* 5 *s.* Alfo *Arthur Condon*, for a Demand of 4 *s.* toward the Charge of the Trained-Bands, had a Coat taken from him worth 20 *s.*

For Marrying.

Francis Marriage of *Stebbing*, was imprifoned in *Colchefter* Caftle for being Married in another Manner than according to the Form of the Directory.

A remarkable Occurrence.

We fhall next make mention of a remarkable Incident which occurred at *Halfted*, where one *William Simfon*, under a religious Concern, paffed through the Streets, with his Body naked, as a Sign to the People, when an ill-minded Man named *John Folks*, gave him feveral cruel Strokes with a Whip. *William* bearing it patiently, faid to the Standers by, *Mark the End of that Man* : It fo happened that a fhort Time after, *Folks*, walking into his Yard feemingly in good Health, fell down dead immediately.

A Meeting at Harwich.

ANNO 1660. On the 16th of the Month called *May* was a Meeting at *Harwich*, appointed fome Days before, it being on the Firft-day of the Week, to which about forty Perfons were coming over the River in Boats, (a thing ufual on that Day for People coming to the National Worfhip) but the Mayor would not fuffer them to come on Shore ; and when *Robert Graffingham*, an Inhabitant of that Town, and Shipwright to the Admiralty, fent his own Boat with two Servants to fetch over fome of his Friends, the Officers forbad it, and by the Mayor's Order put the faid Servants in the Stocks, and kept them there feveral Hours : However, fuch Friends as were in the Town met, and the Houfe was foon filled with fober and peaceable People, to whom *George Fox* the * Younger was preaching, when a great Company of rude Sea-men and others came, who being prevented by the Prefs of People from coming near to abufe the Preacher, curfed and fwore moft outragioufly, fome of them threatning to pull down the Houfe, others crying out, *The King is now com-ing, who will hang or banifh you all. George Fox* hearing their abominable Oaths and Imprecations, was much grieved in Spirit thereat, and in a pious Zeal againft their Wickednefs, uttered thefe Words, *Wo, Wo, unto the Teachers and Rulers of this Nation, who fuffer fuch Ungodlinefs as this, and do not feek to fupprefs it.* Some of the People forthwith reported, or perhaps mifreported, this to the Magiftrates, who prefently fent the High Conftable and others to fetch *George Fox* by force out of the Meeting-houfe into the Street, where the Mayor

was,

---

* So called by his Friends, to diftinguifh him from the other *George Fox* who had been longer a *Minifter* among them.

ESSEX.
1660.

Prosecution of
G. Fox jun.
and R. Graf-
fingham.

was, who haftily commanded him to Prifon: *George* defired to know what Law he had tranfgreffed, for that it was unjuft to imprifon him without legal Caufe. The Mayor anfwered, *You fhall know that afterward,* and fo he was hurried away to Prifon unexamined. *Robert Graffingham* in brotherly Love accompanied him to the Goal, and when the Rabble, as they paffed the Street, abufed him, faid to the Conftables, *You ought to fee the Peace kept, and not fuffer the Prifoner to be abufed.* After he had been fome Time in Prifon, a *Mittimus* was fent figned by the Mayor and two others, wherein they charged him with *caufing a Tumult, and difturbing the Peace of the Borough:* Thus imputing to the innocent Man the Guilt of that Difturbance which was raifed by thofe who abufed him. As juftly might *Lot* and the Angels have been charged with caufing a Tumult in *Sodom,* when the Wicked furrounded *Lot's* Houfe. Nor was it the Aim of the Magiftrates of *Harwich* to punifh diforderly Perfons, for while *George Fox* was there in Prifon, it was frequent with Drunkards both Day and Night to pafs by, and coming to the Grate of the Prifon would curfe him bitterly, ftammering out Oaths through Drunkennefs, and then crying out, *God fave King* Charles, *he will hang all the* Quakers *and* Anabaptifts: Thefe Perfons went unreproved: But if any fober Men came to difcourfe with him, the Mayor had ordered *they fhould not be fuffered;* and the Goaler's Servant would throw Water upon, or otherwife abufe them. The Mayor and other Magiftrates bufied themfelves fo much about this *innocent Man,* that they fent up fuch an Information to the Parliament, as produced the following Order of the Houfe of Commons, viz.

Order of the Houfe of Commons.

" *Monday, May* 21ft. 1660.

" THE Houfe being informed that two *Quakers,* that is to fay, *George*
" *Fox* and *Robert Graffingham,* have lately made a Difturbance at *Har-*
" *wich,* and that the faid *George Fox,* who pretends to be a Preacher, did
" lately in his Preaching there, fpeak Words much reflecting on the Government and Miniftry, to the near caufing of a Mutiny, and is now committed
" by the Mayor and Magiftrates there.

" *Ordered,* that the faid *George Fox* and *Robert Graffingham* be forthwith
" brought up in Cuftody, and that the Sheriff of the County of *Effex* do receive them, and give his Affiftance for the conveying them up accordingly,
" and delivering them into the Charge of the Serjeant at Arms attending this
" Houfe.

" *Ordered,* that the Thanks of this Houfe be given to the Mayor and Magiftrates of *Harwich* for their Care in this Bufinefs.

" WILLIAM JESSOP,

" *Clerk of the* Common's Houfe *in Parliament.*"

The Complaint againft *Graffingham* feemed to arife from the Prejudice of the Mayor, who had before faid to him in the Hearing of feveral People, *If I could get you out of Town, I could eafily deal with the reft of the* Quakers.

The foregoing Order was brought to *Harwich* by the Sheriff of *Effex,* feveral armed Men attending him; upon which *George Fox* was taken out of the * Hole where he had lain ten Nights, and delivered up to them to conduct to *London.* On the Road thither they met *Robert Graffingham* going homeward, with an Order from the Commiffioners of the Navy to refit one of the King's Frigates then in *Harwich* Port; notwithftanding which, the Sheriff took him back to *London,* and delivered them both into the Cuftody of the Serjeant at Arms, who committed them the fame Night to *Lambeth-Houfe,* with an Order, *that few of their Friends fhould come at them, and if any did, that Perfons fhould*

G. Fox *and* J. Graffing-
ham *delivered to the Cuftody of the Serjeant at Arms.*

---

* A Place not four Yards in *Length,* and lefs in *Breadth.*

ESSEX.   *ſhould be preſent to hear what they ſaid, and that all Letters to or from them*
1660.   *ſhould be read before Delivery* ; which was ſtrictly obſerved for ſome Time. They
were cloſe confined to their Chamber above ſix Weeks, from whence they ſent
the following Letter, *viz.*

Their Letter
to the Speaker.

" *To the* Speaker *of the Houſe of* Commons :

" *Friend,*

" WE deſire thee to communicate this encloſed to the Houſe of *Commons*,
" it being a few innocent, juſt, and reaſonable Words to them, though
" not in the eloquent Language of Man's Wiſdom, yet it is in the Truth
" which is honourable. We are Friends to Righteouſneſs and Truth, and to
" all that are found therein.

" *Robert Graſſingham.*
" *George Fox."*

Encloſed was their Caſe, directed

" *For the Houſe of* Commons *aſſembled in Parliament at*
" Weſtminſter, *viz.*

Their Caſe
incloſed.

" *Friends,*

" BY your Order touching us, dated the 21ſt of the Third Month called
" *May*, we underſtand you have been falſly informed concerning us, by
" ſome who have falſly accuſed us. Therefore this is our juſt and reaſonable
" Requeſt, that we, together with our Accuſers, may Face to Face be brought
" before you, and if any Thing can be juſtly proved againſt us, worthy of
" Death or Bonds, we ſhall not refuſe either. But if there can be nothing
" juſtly proved againſt us, then ought our Accuſers to be aſhamed, and we to
" be acquitted.
" Now we do believe it to be unjuſt and unreaſonable, that a Man ſhould
" be haled out of a peaceable Meeting, as one of us was at *Harwich* in *Eſſex*,
" and ſent to Priſon without being examined, or a *Mittimus*, (only for declar-
" ing againſt the Curſing and Wickedneſs of the rude People, and againſt ſuch
" as ſuffer ſuch Ungodlineſs, and do not ſeek to ſuppreſs it) and there be
" kept ten Nights, and from thence to be tranſported unto this Place, and that
" we ſhould be here confined to our Chamber, as we have been for about
" three Weeks laſt paſt, ſeeing nothing is proved againſt us, nor we yet brought
" to an Examination, neither did your Order expreſs any ſuch Confinement.
" So theſe Things are laid before you in Plainneſs, that Juſtice may be herein
" done by you.
" By us who are Sufferers for Righteouſneſs-ſake, and we have and
" ſhall have Peace in our Suffering, and in writing our ſelves
" thus, except we were convinced by the Law of God, or
" any juſt Law of our Nation to the contrary.

Lambeth-Houſe *the* 15th *of the*
Fourth Month called June 1660.

" *G. Fox* the Younger.
" *R. Graſſingham."*

Their Caſe
printed.

The Speaker not anſwering their Requeſt, they publiſhed their ſaid Caſe in Print,
and got it delivered to the Members of Parliament ; but no Notice was taken
of it, becauſe it was not drawn in the uſual Form, and inſcribed, *To the*
Right Honourable, &c. a Title which the Priſoners conſcientiouſly ſcrupled to
uſe. After they had been fourteen Weeks in Cuſtody without any Examination,
upon a Motion made by a Member of the Houſe, the following Order was
iſſued,

" *Thurſday,*

" *Thursday*, the 20th of *August* 1660.

" **O**RDERED, that *George Fox* and *Robert Graffingham*, who, by Virtue
" of a former Order of this House, were taken into Cuftody by the
" Serjeant at Arms attending this Houfe, for fome Difturbances at *Harwich*,
" be forthwith releafed and fet at Liberty, upon Bail firft given to render
" themfelves, when they fhall be in that Behalf required."

Order for their Releafe.

" **WILLIAM JESSOP**,

" *Clerk of the* Common's Houfe *in Parliament.*"

Neverthelefs they were ftill detained for the Serjeant's Fees, who demanded
50 *l.* befide 10 *s.* a Week for their Chamber Rent, though they were put in the
higheft Room of a lofty Tower, not fit to lodge in, till they had the Windows
repaired at their own Charge. They not complying with thefe unreafonable
Demands, the Day before the Parliament rofe, (notwithftanding an *Act* of Obli-
vion and Indemnity which had paffed that Seffions, and their own Order aforefaid) they made another Order, *viz.* " That it fhould be referred to the
" King's Privy Council to confider of them, and to give fuch Order touch-
" ing them, as to their Liberty, or to continue under Reftraint, as they fhould
" find confiftent with the publick Peace, and in the mean Time to re-
" main in the Serjeant's Cuftody." By this Order they were detained a confiderable Time longer ; all this unneceffary Buftle having been made about two
plain, honeft, and harmlefs Men, to their very great Lofs and Hardfhip, for
no other Offence, than that *one* of them had exhorted the People to Truth and
Righteoufnefs, and exclaimed againft the Abominations of the Times, and the
other had countenanced him in fo doing.

Detained for Fees.

Another Order of the Houfe.

In *December* this Year, *John Furly* of *Colchefter* had the Oath of Allegiance
tendred him by *John Shaw* Recorder, and refufing it was fent to Prifon, but
after five Days difcharged till the Seffions, where the fame being again tendred
him and refufed, he was remanded to Prifon, and kept there ten Weeks.

Oath tendred to J. Furly.

On the 13th of the Month called *January*, *John Harvey*, *George Court*,
John Webb, *Samuel Peachy*, *Samuel Read*, *John Claydon*, *John Day*, *Jacob
Baker*, *Walter Crane*, *John Simon*, *John Churchman*, *Robert Churchman*, *George
Churchman*, *Thomas Amy*, *Edmund Clark*, *Thomas Day*, *John Stinton*, *John Ellis*,
and *Michael Pettitt*, were taken out of a Meeting at *Hadftock*, and carried to
Saffron Walden, and thence to a Juftice of the Peace at *Dunmow*, who tendred
them the Oath, and on their refufing to Swear, fent them to the Seffions at
Chelmsford, where the Oath was again tendred them, and for refufing to take
it they were fent to *Colchefter* Caftle, where they remained a confiderable Time.

19 Committed to Prifon.

On the 20th of the fame Month, *John Inghill*, *Jofeph Burnifh*, *Edward
Grant* jun. *Nicholas Prigg*, *Edwin Harrifon*, *Richard Quick*, *Thomas Bayles*, *John
Crumplin*, *George Wetherly*, *John Partridge*, *John Havens*, *Zachary Welch*, *John
Defbrow*, *Thomas Moffe*, *Michael Thorn*, *John Crouch*, *Thomas Shortland*, *Na-
thanael Plumfted*, *John Bifhop*, *William Quick*, *Zachary Catchpool*, and *Thomas
Burgis*, were taken out of a Meeting at *Colchefter*, and by the Recorder and
other Juftices committed to Prifon for refufing to take the Oaths of Allegiance
and Supremacy, and detained there nine Weeks.

22 More fent to Prifon.

On the fame Day *William Williams*, *Peter Peachy*, and *Thomas Brewer*, taken
out of a Meeting at *Eaft-ham*, were fent to *Colchefter* Caftle for refufing the
Oaths. Alfo *Jofeph Smith*, *William Bridge*, *John Harding*, *George French*, *John
Knowles*, *Griffith Perry*, *Thomas Ellis*, *Thomas Sewell*, *William Sewell*, *William
Adcock*, *John Turner*, and *Jofiah Clark*, were taken out of a Meeting at *Thax-
ted* by the Mayor's Order, and had to the Seffions, whence for refufing the
Oath they were fent to Prifon, where they lay above three Months.

Sundry others imprifoned.

On the 27th, *Edwin Morrell*, *John Potter*, *Thomas Eve*, *John Clark*, *Richard
Sewell*, and *Thomas Eltham*, being at a Meeting in the fame Town, were fum-

More Impri-fonments.

ESSEX.
1660.

An Occurrence worthy of Notice.

Others committed for refusing the Oaths.

Case of A. Smith.

Imprisonment of S. Crisp and others.

Divers taken at a Meeting in Baddow.

Tithes.

Suffering of R. Levitt and others.

moned to appear before the Mayor next Day, who tendred them the Oath, and for refusing it sent them to Prison, where they lay eleven Weeks. On the same Day *John Salmon, William Hudson, Thomas Lea, John Raven,* and *John Davidge,* taken in a Meeting at *Steeple,* were carried from Place to Place, and at length to some Justices at *Colchester,* who tendred them the Oaths, and sent them to Prison : At the Time when they were apprehended, some of those who took them charged *Thomas Lea* with being a Preacher, and called for a Bible to hear whether he could read : He opening the Book, without Design, at 2 *Chron.* xx. 11, 12. read to them the Text, viz. *Behold, how they reward us, to come to cast us out of thy Possession, which thou hast given us to inherit ? O our God, wilt thou not judge them ? for we have no Might against this great Company that cometh against us, neither know we what to do, but our Eyes are upon thee.* A Text very suitable to the Occasion, and it was remarkable, that it occurred so seasonably without looking for ; but whether that happened *casually* or *providentially,* we presume not to determine.

In the same Month *Griffith Perry,* and his Son of the same Name, were taken out of a Meeting at the House of *Edwin Morrell,* and committed to Prison by an Order of Sessions for refusing the Oaths : Also *Daniel Deacon* of *Colchester,* taken from a Meeting there, was for the same Cause sent to Goal, and continued there above ten Weeks. At *Harwich* about the same Time, *William Palmer, John Vandewall* and *Edward Boyce,* were taken from their own Houses, and, for refusing to take the Oaths, were by the Mayor and another Justice sent to Prison. At *Tolsbury, John Rolfe* speaking to the People by way of Exhortation, in the Grave-Yard, was carried before a Justice of the Peace, who tendred him the Oaths, and for refusing them, sent him to *Colchester* Castle.

About this Time *Andrew Smith,* for refusing to pay Tithes, was imprisoned in *Colchester* Castle seven Months, and after that in the Fleet above four Months, and had his Goods taken away to the Value of 26*l.* There were also Prisoners for Tithes in the same Castle, *Francis Marriage, John Chopping, Thomas Ames, Thomas Chapman,* and *William Fretton.*

ANNO 1661. *Stephen Crisp* was apprehended at a Meeting at *Harwich,* and by a Justice of the Peace there, who had ordered his *Mittimus* to be written before his Examination, committed to Prison. On the next Day was committed for having been at the same Meeting, *William Marloe, Edward Boyce,* and *Mary Vandewall,* who after three Weeks were brought to the Sessions, where a Bill of Indictment was preferred against them, but the Grand Jury refusing to find it, the Oath of Allegiance was tendred them, and they were sent back to Prison. During their Confinement, several who came to visit them, were by the Justice's Order detained there, viz. *Joseph Burrough, John Hawes, William Ellis, Jonathan Goddard, Thomas Garnford,* and *William Skinner.*

In the same Year *Robert Conyers, William Fretton, Robert Davidge, Robert Godfrey, Thomas Leage,* and *John Davidge,* were taken at a Meeting at the House of *Thomas Fretton* in or near *Great-Baddow,* and by the Justices sent to *Colchester* Castle, with a *Mittimus* expressing, that *they were met together and exercised in Preaching, and other spiritual Duties.*

In this Year also *Thomas Fretton* was again imprisoned at *Colchester* for not paying Tithes. And the Widow *Balls* of *Horsley,* for 9*s.* 10*d.* demanded for Tithes, suffered the Loss of five Cows worth 20*l.*

ANNO 1662. *Robert Levitt* of *Stebbing,* having had Judgment passed against him for Tithes on the Statute of treble Damages, was committed to Prison, and while there was sued in the County Court, and had his Corn taken away to the Value of 50*l.* notwithstanding which he remained a Prisoner about three Years. In this Year also *John Adams* of *Hadstock, George Bacon, Griffith Perry, John Cakebread* of *Old-Samford, John Crosier* and *Samuel Skillingham,* both of *Felsted, Thomas Fraling, Thomas Brand,* and *Edmund Raven,* were imprisoned for Contempts upon Prosecutions in the *Exchequer* for Tithes. In the same Year *George Barnard* of *Finchingfield,* for two Years Tithe

Tithe of a Farm of 50 *l. per Annum*, had Goods taken from him which were fold for 40 *l*. Alfo *Jofiah Smith* of *Little-Samford*, the Rent of whofe Farm was 78 *l. per Annum*, had taken from him Barley, Wheat, and Cows, to the Value of 66 *l*. 15 *s*. 6 *d*.

ANNO 1663. Exceffive were the Seizures made in this Year for Tithes: *George Barnard* had Goods taken from him worth 30 *l*. *Jofiah Smith* Barley, Wheat, and Oats, fold for 42 *l*. 10 *s*. *Robert Levitt* to the Value of 20 *l*. And *Thomas Cole* of *Lexden*, for an original Demand of 20 *s*. fuftained the Lofs of eleven Cows and a Bull worth 50 *l*. In the fame Year *John Raven* was fent to Prifon for refufing to anfwer upon Oath to a Bill exhibited againft him for Tithes. *Exceffive Seizures.* *Imprifonment of J. Raven.*

In this Year was a grievous Perfecution of this People for their religious Meetings at *Colchefter*, where *William Moore*, then Mayor, exerted the utmoft of his Authority to opprefs them. *Grievous Perfecution at Colchefter.*

On the 25th of *October* he came and forcibly broke up the Meeting, fending *Stephen Crifp* and *John Pike* to Prifon. On the 28th of the fame he came again, and having difperfed the Meeting, he committed *Thomas Brown* and *Thomas Gainford*. And on the 1ft of *November* he fent Prifoners alfo to the *Moothall, Thomas Bayles* and *George Wetherly*. This Method proving ineffectual, a Party of the County Troops were employed to go to the Meeting, where they beat fome, and carried others to Prifon, having firft broke the Forms, Seats, and Windows of the Meeting-houfe. After this, being kept out of their Meeting-houfe, they affembled in the Street, fometimes in the Cold and Rain, not daring to decline their Duty for thofe Inconveniencies: Thus they continued conftantly meeting twice a Week, on the Firft and Fourth-days of the Week, at their appointed Hour, till the 6th of *December*, when a Troop of Horfe, who came to Town the Day before, armed with Swords, Piftols, and Carbines, rode in furioufly among them, crying out, *What a Devil do you here?* Some with their drawn Swords, and others with their Carbines, laying on without Mercy, both on Old and Young, Men and Women, beat and bruifed many exceedingly, chafing them to and fro in the Streets, after which they broke into feveral Houfes to the Terror of the People. There were alfo taken by the Troopers and committed to Prifon, *John Havens, Henry Havens, Benjamin Hall, William Quick, John Shaft*, and *Thomas Brunton*. And about the fame Time, *William Havens, Thomas Cole, Robert Dednam*, and *Nathanael Gibfon*, were committed to Goal by the Mayor. *Many bruifed.*

On the 13th of *December* the Troopers came again, having added to their former Weapons great Clubs, one of which was above four Inches round: With thefe they knockt down many in the Streets, where fome lay as dead, and many were fo difabled and bruifed, that they could not get off their Clothes, nor feed themfelves for feveral Days after. Remarkable was the Patience and Meeknefs of one of the Sufferers at this Time, who, when a Trooper was beating him with his Sword, and the Blade fell out of the Hilt, took it up, and gave it him again, faying, *I will give it thee up again: I defire the Lord may not lay this Day's Work to thy Charge.* After they had difperfed the Meeting, four of the Troopers met a poor fickly Man about a Quarter of a Mile from the Meeting-place, and riding up to him, afked him *whether he was a Quaker?* He not denying it, they beat him fo, that the Spectators thought he would have died on the Place, and he had probably been killed, but that he was taken into an Houfe; howbeit he was difabled from getting his Bread, or providing for his Family a long Time after. *Many knockt down in the Streets.* *A poor fickly Man almoft kill'd.*

On the 16th, the Fourth of the Week, fome of the Troopers came early to the Meeting, and grievoufly abufed thofe few that were met, purfuing them on foot into the Houfes and Yards.

On the 27th of *December* thirty eight Troopers came riding among the Friends, who were met in the Street, moft defperately, and fo cruelly beat them with Clubs and Carbines as moved Compaffion and Tears in the Standers by. As the Soldiers forced fome away by Violence, they drove them upon others *Barbarous Beatings.*

others of their Comrades, whom they had placed as Centinels in the Paſſages, who with Clubs beat them afreſh, till the Fleſh of ſome of them was become like a Jelly, their Blood for the preſent ſtagnated, and their Limbs deprived of Uſe, which barbarous Treatment was attended with dreadful Oaths, and horrid Imprecations, to the Grief of the Souls of thoſe whoſe Bodies had been thus inhumanly uſed.

Furious At-
tack of the
Soldiers.

On the 3d of the Month called *January*, about ſixty of the Friends being met at the uſual Place, the Soldiers, ſome on Foot, and ſome on Horſeback, fell furiouſly upon them, as if they would have ſlain them all, with Clubs and Carbines knocking down ſeveral, and amongſt others an old Man, whom they beat ſo unmercifully, that ſome of their Abettors perſuaded them to deſiſt, for they had ſo beaten him that he was unable to go Home without Help. Another, aged ſixty five, was followed a great Way by one on Horſe-back, and three on foot, who beat and abuſed him ſo, that it was very much queſtioned whether one of his Arms would ever recover its Uſe. *Solomon Fro-*

An Inſtance of
conjugal Af-
fection.
Death of
E. Grant.

mantle a Merchant, was ſo grievouſly abuſed and beaten, that he loſt much Blood, and yet the barbarous Troopers did not deſiſt : His Wife, fearing left he ſhould be killed, fell down upon him to cover and protect him from their Blows, many of which ſhe received on her own Body. *Edward Grant*, Father of *Fromantle*'s Wife, about ſeventy Years of Age, was knockt down, and ſur-vived the fatal Stroke but a few Days. Among theſe Sufferers was alſo *Giles*

G. Barnadiſ-
ton.

Barnadiſton, a Man of Note, brought up in Learning at one of the Univerſities, and who had been formerly a Colonel. He, convinced of the Truth as held by this People, willingly bore his Part of this Storm of Perſecution, in the hotteſt of which he conſtantly attended religious Meetings, and undauntedly hazarded his Life for his Teſtimony.

Iron Spikes in
the Soldiers
Clubs.

On the 6th of the ſame Month the Soldiers had put into their Clubs Iron Spikes, ſharpened with a File, with which they hurt many, particularly an ancient Woman of good Repute, whom they wounded in twelve ſeveral Places, ſome of the Soldiers being ſo cruelly wanton, that they made Sport of running thoſe Iron Spikes into Peoples Bodies, ſcoffing and jeering them when they ſtarted or flinched at the Pain.

The Troopers
wearied.

After this the Troopers, finding the Conſtancy of the Sufferers invincible, ge-nerally began to relent, and abate of their former Violence, ſo that they inclined to commiſerate thoſe whom they could not conquer, and grew aſhamed of fighting againſt thoſe whom no Abuſes could provoke to reſiſt them : So that there was a Calm or Repoſe for two or three Weeks, till the Mayor and Re-corder, diſpleaſed at their Backwardneſs, puſht them on again to act againſt their Wills ; ſo that on the 24th of the Month called *January*, about twenty of them on Horſeback went to the Meeting-place with Trumpets ſounding, and puſht the Friends away, but with leſs Violence than formerly.

Paſſages
guarded.

On the 27th of the ſame Month they endeavoured to prevent their Meeting, by guarding the Paſſages thither, ſtopping and forcing back ſuch as they ſaw coming.

On the 31ſt the Soldiers took Poſſeſſion of the Ground before the uſual Time of Meeting, and ſo kept them from aſſembling that Day.

Fined for
Meeting.

On the 7th of the Month called *February*, the Soldiers came as uſual, and carried about ſixteen of the Perſons aſſembled to their Head-Quarters at the *White-Hart*, whither the Mayor and Recorder came after Sermon, and fined them 12 *d.* each for being abſent that Day from *Divine Service*, as they call'd it, making a meer Jeſt and Sport of their own Proceedings, telling one, *they would have her Scarf*, another, *her Petticoat*, &c.

Fines repeat-
ed.

On the 14th of the ſame Month the Troopers came early, and took the Friends as they came, one or two at a Time, whom the Mayor ſent to Priſon for being at an unlawful Aſſembly, although there was none that Day, there being not five of them together, except the Troopers, which the Mayor recollecting, fined them 12 *d.* each for not hearing *Divine Service*, and ordered them to be kept in Priſon till they paid it : But in that alſo he acted extrajudicially,

which

which the more knowing Magiſtrates perceiving, procured the Diſcharge of the Priſoners after eight or ten Days.

On the 21ſt they took the Friends, five or ſix at a Time, as they came to the Meeting, and the Mayor ſent ſome to Priſon, and threatned others.

On the 28th the Friends met together in one of their Grave-Yards, whence the Soldiers drove them out without much Hurt. But the gentle Behaviour of the Soldiers at this Time was owing to their own Humanity, and not to any Reſtraint put upon them by either the Mayor or other of the Magiſtrates.

ANNO 1664. At *Colcheſter* the Violence of Perſecution, though much abated, was not yet wholly ceaſed, for on the 10th of the Month called *April,* the Soldiers came to the Meeting-place with Trumpets ſounding, and took away about twenty Perſons to the *White-Hart,* of whom four were ſent to Priſon. *Perſecution at Colcheſter abated.*

At the Quarter Seſſions on the 22d of the ſame Month, thirteen of thoſe who had been in Priſon were indiĉted for being at an unlawful Aſſembly, and recommitted. One other, who had been taken in the Street by himſelf, was acquitted, after he had been wrongfully impriſoned twenty three Weeks. But notwithſtanding his Innocence, the Goaler yet detained him for an unreaſonable Demand of Fees.

On the 1ſt of the Month called *May,* the Soldiers took eight Men, and carried them to the *White-Hart,* where they were ſeparately examined before the Mayor, and upon the Soldiers Evidence committed to Priſon, with a ſtriĉt Charge to the Goaler not to give any of them Liberty, on Pain of loſing his Place.

Leaving *Colcheſter* let us turn to *Halſted,* where were about two Hundred Soldiers commanded by Captain *Turner,* who on the 13th of the Month called *March* 1664, ſet a Guard in the Way to the Meeting-place, and ſtopped all they ſuppoſed to be *Quakers,* and carried them to the Market-houſe, where they kept them about an Hour: Being diſmiſſed they went direĉtly to the Meeting-houſe, and there ſat together in Silence: About an Hour after Captain *Turner,* with other Officers and Soldiers, came down, and ſet a Guard of Muſquetiers at the Door; then the Captain went in and demanded twice, *Where is your Preacher?* No Anſwer being given, he ſaid no more but, *Ye Rogues, get ye out,* and inſtantly fell to ſtriking violently on Old and Young, Men and Women, without Diſtinĉtion: In like manner did the reſt of the Officers, and as they drove them out, the Guard of Muſquetiers ſtruck them again with their Muſquets, ſo that moſt of them were ſorely bruiſed, and the Blood of ſeveral ran down. After that the Soldiers brake in pieces the Walls and Windows of the Houſe, carried away the Doors, pulled down the Chimneys, and the main Dorman of the Houſe, ſo that the Floor of the Chamber fell in. Then they gave away, carried off, and ſold what they pleaſed. The Damage done to the Houſe was computed to be more than 25*l.* The Names of ſome who were preſent, and ſuffered by theſe Abuſes, were *Thomas Iſaac, Edmund Pryor, James Allen, Richard Bunting, Daniel Pryor, William Bunting, Richard Norden, Edmund Manly, William Bappon,* and *William Swan.* *Perſecution at Halſted.*

In the ſame Year *Edward Morrell, Joſeph Smith, John Clark, William Bridge, Margaret Clark, Thomas Archer, John Wood,* and *Robert Beard,* were impriſoned by Writs *de Excommunicato capiendo,* obtained after Proceſs againſt them in the *Eccleſiaſtical Courts* for being abſent from the eſtabliſhed Worſhip. *Impriſonments by Writs de Excom. Cap.*

In this Year alſo *John Woodward, Mary Cotton, John Empſon, John Cakebread,,* and *Thomas Chiſwell,* were ſeverally committed to Priſon for refuſing to pay Tithes. There was alſo taken by Diſtreſs *and for Tithes.*

From		*l.*	*s.*	*d.*			*l.*	*s.*	*d.*	
	John Chopping for	11	10	0	Demand, Corn worth		27	2	0	
	William Fritton	1	19	0	A Cow worth		5	0	0	*Diſtreſſes for*
	Thomas Fritton	4	0	0	Six Cows worth		36	0	0	*Tithes.*
For Demands of		17	9	0	were taken to the Value of		68	2	0	

ESSEX.
1664.

Profecution of
J. Smith.

Fines and
Imprifonment
for Meeting.

Tithes.

Exchequer
Procefs.

Severe
Seizure.

Imprifon-
ments.

Trained Bands.

Execution for
Tithes.

Grievous Spoil
of T. Cole's
Goods.

Treble
Damages.

From *Thomas Cole* of *Lexden*, nine Cows worth 30 *l.* were taken by Diftrefs for Tithes: From *Robert Levitt*, three Cows and Corn worth 16 *l.* And from *Jofiah Smith*, Corn to the Value of 36 *l.* 6 *s.* 10 *d.* The fame *Jofiah Smith*, for not fending a Man to ferve in the *Militia*, was by the Deputy Lieutenants of the County fined 5 *l.* for which they took from him an Horfe worth 6 *l.* In this Year alfo *Thurfton Read* was imprifoned in the *Moothall*, by *William Moore* Mayor of *Colchefter*, for teaching School without Licenfe, and continued there till he died.

ANNO 1665. The aforefaid *Jofiah Smith* was again fined 5 *l.* for not ferving among the *Militia*, and had an Horfe taken from him worth 12 *l.* which Horfe the Officer who made the Diftrefs kept for his own riding. Befides this, the Deputy Lieutenants, *Altham* and *Lumley*, with one Major *Turner*, and about ten armed Horfemen, entred the faid *Jofiah's* Houfe in his Abfence, under Pretence of fearching for Arms, and carried away a Fowling-piece worth 30 *s.* On his coming Home he was taken by three of the Horfemen, left behind for that Purpofe, and detained Prifoner by Major *Turner*, who for fome Time would not let him have a Bed to lie on. This Ufage, as they told him, was for being a Friend to the *Quakers.*

On the 2d of the Month called *Auguft* this Year, *Thomas Salthoufe*, *Thomas Yoakley*, *William Williams*, *Edmund Bolt*, and *Samuel Hicks*, were fined 5 *l.* for being at a Meeting in *Eaft-Ham*, and for Non-payment were committed to the Houfe of Correction at *Barking* for two Months.

ANNO 1666. On the 24th of the Month called *April*, *Jonathan Bundock* was committed to Prifon, at the Suit of *William Collingwood*, for Tithes.

ANNO 1667. On the 1ft of the Month called *April* this Year, *William Woolfey* was committed to Prifon on an *Exchequer* Procefs for Tithes. And in the next Month *Mary Barker*, *William Boggas*, and *Richard Emerton*, were fent to Goal for the fame Caufe; as was alfo *Stephen Holman* on the 14th of the Month called *July.*

Grievous was the Diftrefs made this Year on *Thomas Cole* of *Lexden*, who for two Year's Tithe valued at 40 *s.* had taken from him at the Suit of *John Smith* Prieft of *Mary's* Parifh in *Colchefter*, eleven Seam and three Bufhels of Wheat, eighteen Seam of Barley, and 25 Seam of Oats, in all worth 54 *l.*

In the fame Year *Samuel Thornton*, *John Swinton*, *John Furly*, *Edward Melfop*, *James Parke*, *George Taylor*, *Daniel Vandewall*, *John Goodwin*, and others, were committed to Prifon by Order of *Thomas Garrard* Mayor of *Harwich*, for affembling together at a religious Meeting in that Town.

John Furly the younger, and *George Wetherly*, both of *Colchefter*, were fined for refufing to furnifh Soldiers for the Trained-Bands: The former of them fuffered Diftrefs of Goods to the Value of 18 *l.* and the latter of 2 *l.* 0 *s.* 6 *d.*

Some Time before this *Jofiah Smith* of *Little-Samford*, having been fued for Tithes on the Statute for treble Damages, had taken from him by an Execution eighteen Cows, three Horfes, a Waggon, fourteen Seams of Barley, nine Seams of Wheat, twenty one Seams of Malt, and other Things to the Value of 140 *l.* So that within the Space of about five Years the Diftreffes made upon his Goods for Tithes, amounted to 400 *l.* being more than the whole Rent of his Farm for that Time, which was but 78 *l. per Annum.*

ANNO 1668. *Thomas Cole*, profecuted at the Suit of *John Nettles* Prieft of *Lexden*, for two Years Tithe valued at 10 *l.* had taken from him by an Execution, two Horfes, one Mare, ten Cows and Bullocks, forty four Sheep, twenty Lambs, and five Seam of Wheat, in all to the Value of 64 *l.* At the Time of this Seizure the Prieft ftood by, encouraging the Bayliff againft the Sufferer, by calling out *Difable him, difable him:* By which he difcovered his own perfecuting Difpofition, and the Bent of his Inclination to ruin his Neighbour.

ANNO 1669. *Thomas Fritton* was profecuted at the Suit of *Robert Sturrel* Prieft of *Much Stambridge*, on the Statute for treble Damages, and had taken from

from him for Tithe of 16 *l.* Value, fixteen Cows and a Bull worth 56 *l.* which **ESSEX.** the Officer fold for 40 *l.* and threatned to come again for more. 1669.

Robert Levett was profecuted for Tithe in the County Court, at the Suit of *John Sorrel* jun. an Impropriator; and had taken from him in this and the next *Tithes.* fucceeding Year, Goods worth 23 *l.*

ANNO 1670. On the 5th of the Month called *June*, *Henry Wroth* Juftice, *Diftreffes for* being informed of a Meeting at *Waltham-Abbey*, went thither with fome Atten- *a Meeting at* dants. He caufed the Names of feveral prefent to be taken, and granted his *Waltham-* *Abbey*, Warrant, by which were taken the fame Day from *Thomas Bennett*, Cloth worth 70 *l.* which the Officers laid up in the Veftry-Room of the Steeple-houfe. And at the fame Time they alfo took Goods from *Edward Tomfon*, *Jofias Levett*, *Mary Bennet* Widow, and *Richard Pridan*.

For Meetings at *Harwich* were taken

		l.	*s.*	*d.*	
From	*Daniel Vandewall* Goods worth	2	3	6	*and for Meet-*
	John Vandewall		0	0	*ings at Har-*
*	*William Brambam*		19	6	*wich.*
	Mary Vandewall, Edward Boyfe, Hefter Matthews, and *William Mark* }	2	6	7	
	William Marlow	5	13	0	
	Hannah Mace	2	1	4	
	George Taylor	1	0	0	
		48	3	11	

For Meetings at the Houfe of *John Churchman* in *Wendon*, were taken

		l.	*s.*	*d.*	
From the faid	*John Churchman* at feveral Times, Goods worth	13	6	6	*and at Wen-*
	Matthew Day of Newport	23	5	0	*don, &c.*
	Anthony Pennifton	8	12	0	
		45	3	6	

For Meetings at *Chifwell* were taken

		l.	*s.*	*d.*
From	*Samuel Reader* Goods worth	4	6	7
	William Winter, James Pettitt, William Pinner, and *Thomas Cornwell* }	3	5	6
		7	12	1

For Meetings at or near *Thaxted* were taken

		l.	*s.*	*d.*
From	*Jofeph Smith,* at four feveral Times, Goods worth	50	17	9
	Edwin Morrell at feveral Times	51	10	0
	Thomas Nottay Timber worth	21	5	0
	William Bridge, Sufan Hayward, Rebecca Saward, Thomas Ellis, and *Rebecca Fann,* Goods worth }	9	8	10
	Thomas Jarvis, William Ofborn, and *Thomas Johnfon*	6	16	0
	John Claydon of *Hadftock*	26	7	10
	Bridget Bingham, Mary Woodward, and *Thomas Miller,*	2	1	6
		168	6	11

For

---

* *William Brambam* had not a Bed left him, nor was he worth fo much more as was thus taken away.

ESSEX.
1670.

For Meetings at *Coggeſhall*,

	l.	s.	d.
Samuel *Cater*, for Preaching, was fined	20	0	0
Taken alſo from *Robert Ludgater* ſen. *Robert Ludgater* jun. Widow *Guyon*, and *Robert Clark*, Goods worth	7	4	0
Widow *Mootham*, *John Guyon*, *William Sewel*, and *John Garrett*	4	8	0
John Clark, *Nathanael Sparrow*, and *Robert Adams*	8	2	0
Robert Evans, *John Gage*, and *Cornelius Curtis*	3	10	0
Edward Mines and *Richard Pemberton*	1	19	0
	45	3	0

Sentence of Premunire paſt upon R. Richardſon.

At the Quarter Seſſions at *Chelmsford*, on the 1ſt of the Month called *July*, *Richard Richardſon* and *Chriſtopher Taylor*, having been bound to appear there for teaching School without Licenſe, appeared accordingly : But the Juſtices not finding ſufficient Cauſe to proceed againſt them on the Matter they were charged with, tendred to *Richard Richardſon* the Oath of Allegiance, and committed him to Priſon for refuſing to take it : At the next Aſſizes he had Sentence of *Premunire* paſt upon him, and was continued in Priſon about two Years and a Quarter, where he ſuffered much through Extremity of Cold and cruel Uſage, being often ſhut up among the Felons.

Officers of Coggeſhall fined.

Poor Man's Clothes taken away.

Meeting-houſes ſhut up.

Releaſe of Priſoners.

About this Time *Hunwick* and *Maxie*, two Informers, eager of their Prey, and finding the Officers at *Coggeſhall* not ſo forward to diſtrain Mens Goods as they were to inform againſt them, made their Complaint to the Juſtices, and cauſed a Churchwarden, two Conſtables, and four Overſeers, to be fined 5 *l.* each for NegleČt of what was called their Duty. Theſe Informers were ſo rapacious, that meeting *Robert Clark* a poor Man, after a Meeting in the Street, they ſtript his Coat from off his Back, and carried it off. The like they did alſo to *Nathanael Gage*. The Meetings in that Town were for a conſiderable Time held in the Street, the Officers having excluded them from the Uſe of their Meeting-houſe by nailing up the Doors.

ANNO 1672. In this Year were diſcharged out of the Common Goal for this County, *Richard Richardſon*, *Edwin Morrell*, *Joſeph Smith*, *John Clark*, *Margaret Clark*, *William Bridge*, *Thomas Archer*, and *Nathanael Plumſted*, by Virtue of a general Amneſty then granted to this People by King *Charles the Second* under the Great-Seal of *England*.

What happened to ſome noted Informers.

We think proper here to inſert ſome Remarks which were made by obſerving Perſons concerning ſome noted Informers, and others who had ſignalized themſelves by their eager Proſecutions and ill Uſage of this People, *viz.*

John Cullington a Fiſherman of *Harwich*, and a noted Informer againſt Meetings there, was found drowned, whether by Accident, or through Deſpair is uncertain, but the latter not improbable, for he had expreſs'd himſelf to be under a grievous Trouble and Concern of Mind for what he had done. His dead Body was caſt on ſhore at a common Landing-place near the Sea-ſide.

Randal Poole a Taylor of the ſame Town, a Man who had been in good Credit, took up the Buſineſs of an Informer, to follow which he negleČted the Care of his lawful Vocation. After which he habituated himſelf alſo to Gaming and Drinking, ſtriving by that Means to ſtifle the Checks of Conſcience, which nevertheleſs grew ſo ſtrong that he was conſtrained to acknowledge, *that he was ſo troubled in Mind, that he was afraid he ſhould be diſtraČted.* This Trouble produced Repentance, ſo that he afterward deſiſted, and lived quietly.

John Hunwicks, an Informer of *Braintree*, had been a Shopkeeper of good Reputation there, but ſeeking to enrich himſelf by the Spoil of his Neighbours, he proceeded with much Uneaſineſs. At length, when on his Death-bed, he ſent for *Solomon Skinner*, and others whom he had proſecuted, intreating them to forgive him, and to pray to God for him, telling them he was fo troubled in Confcience, that he could not die in Peace.

A certain Soldier, who had been an Informer, when taken fick, declared, *that he was never quiet in his Mind fince he had meddled with the* Quakers, *and that he would never do it again.*

The Goaler's Wife, who had been inftrumental in many Injuries, Affronts, and Abufes to *Richard Richardfon*, and others of this People in Prifon at *Chelmf-ford*, in her laft Sicknefs was under much Remorfe of Confcience when fhe reflected on her Cruelty toward them, often crying out, O *yon Men!* O *yon Men.* And under much Trouble on their Account fhe died. So remarkable was the Patience and Meeknefs with which thofe Sufferers, for the Caufe of Religion, endured the Abufes, Revilings, and Contradictions of Sinners, that it fenfibly affected the Confciences of their Oppofers, by the convincing Evidence it carried with it of their Innocence and Integrity. *Death of the Goaler's Wife.*

Meeknefs of the Sufferers.

ANNO 1673. *James Potter* of *Marks-Tay*, for a Demand of 6*l.* for Tithes, had taken from him at the Suit of *Peter Otger* an Impropriator, five Cows and three other Kine, valued at 22*l.* 10*s.* and the Bayliff judging that infufficient, came again and took another Cow worth 3*l.* 10*s.* *Diftrefs for Tithes.*

ANNO 1674. *John Shackerly*, *Thomas Tyler*, *Edward Tomfon*, *Chriftopher Taylor*, and *Thomas Bennet*, were indicted at the Seffions for Abfence from the National Worfhip, by the Procurement of *Edward Claydon* an Informer : And for the fame Caufe *Jofias Levett* and *Richard Pridden* were indicted at the Affizes. *Indictments at Seffions and Affizes.*

ANNO 1675. Taken for Meetings at *Saffron-Walden*,

		l.	*s*	*d.*	
From	*Anthony Pennyftone*, Goods worth	8	5	8	*Diftreffes for Meetings.*
	Samuel Reader and *William Pinnerfon*	13	12	0	
	Thomas Cornall, *James Pettitt*, and *John Pettitt*	7	15	0	
At PEDMARSH,					
From	*Katharine Stow*, for a Meeting at her Houfe	26	12	0	
At SOUTHMINSTER,					
From	*Henry Hafleham*, for a Meeting at his Houfe	28	5	4	
	John Reynolds, *Edmund Sewel*, and *John Woodward*	16	15	0	
	William Freeton of *Mundon*, an Horfe worth	10	0	0	
At ROYDEN,					
From	*John Page* and *Henry Feaft*, three Cows worth	14	0	0	
		125	5	0	

ANNO 1677. Taken for a Meeting at *Dedham*,

From	*Samuel Groom*, at whofe Houfe it was held, Goods worth	13	3	6
	Job Spurgeon, *Robert Mixer*, and *Splendine Rand*	2	11	0
	Abraham Vangover and *Samuel Warner*	1	1	0
		16	15	6

ANNO 1678. *Thomas March* was profecuted in the *Exchequer* by *William Secker* a Prieft at *Leigh*, for eight Years Tithe of a Farm of 26*l.* *per Annum.* The Prieft obtained a Decree for 53*l.* 13*s.* 4*d.* being double the Value of the Tithes, and 15*l.* 10*s.* 10*d.* Cofts of Suit, for which his Goods were taken away to the Value of 100*l.* He alfo fuffered about two Years Imprifonment at the Suit of the fame Prieft. *Exchequer Procefs.*

On the 9th of the Month called *April* this Year, the following Perfons were Prifoners in *Chelmsford* Goal for Tithes, viz.

Edmund Raven of *Creffing*, at the Suit of *Richard Cooke*.
John Marfhall of *Finchfield*, at the Suit of *Samuel Bifhop* Prieft.
Michael Pettitt of *Wimbifh*, at the Suit of *Edward Haward* Prieft.
Edward George of *Thaxted*, at the Suit of *Robert Raynard* Prieft.
William Ofbefton, *John Harding*, and *John Barnard* of *Alfaftone*. *Lift of Prifoners at Chelmsford.*

Ifrael

ESSE X.
1678.

Ifrael Roberts of *Belfham,* at the Suit of *Robert Poole* Prieft, for three Years Tithe of a fmall Farm of but 11 *l. per Annum* ; though during his Imprifonment the Prieft Yearly took Corn off his Ground for Tithes.

Jofiah Smith of *Horfley,* at the Suit of Prieft *Tillyers.*

Thomas Cragg of *Belfham-Pauls,* at the Suit of *John Thomas* Prieft.

William Palmer of *Geftlinthorp,* at the Suit of *John Godwin* Prieft.

John Battell of *Rabnefs,* at the Suit of *Ifaac Read* Prieft.

At the fame Time alfo were Prifoners there, *Katharine Stow* the Elder, and *Katharine Stow* the Younger, at the Suit of *William Treffel* Prieft of *Pedmarfh,* for a Claim of 2 *d.* each for *Eafter-Offerings,* for which they had then fuffered two Years and two Months Imprifonment, and were ftill continued.

Imprifonments on Procefs Ecclefiaftical,

Abraham Bell, and *Mary* his Sifter, were profecuted in the Ecclefiaftical Court for 9 *s.* 4 *d.* each, demanded for their Rate by the Churchwardens of *Felfted,* and upon a *Significavit* of Contumacy were committed to *Chelmsford* Goal, where they were clofely confined.

and for Abfence from the publick Worfhip.

About the fame Time alfo were imprifoned for Abfence from the National Worfhip, *Thomas Bennet* and *Thomas Tyler* of *Waltham-Abbey,* who had lain there eight Months : *James Potter* of *Marks-Tay, John Raven* of *Feering,* and *Mary Cockerton* of *Kelvedon.* The faid *Thomas Bennet* had alfo Two-thirds of his Eftate feized by a Procefs in the *Exchequer,* on the Statute made againft *Popifh* Recufants.

In this Year alfo *Thomas Ifaac* and *James Allen* of *Halfted,* were imprifoned at *Chelmsford,* at the Suit of *John Sewel,* for refufing to pay the ufual Affeffment toward the Repairing the Steeple-houfe there.

Imprifonments by a Writ de Excom. Cap.

ANNO 1679. On the 2d of the Month called *April, Zachariah Child, Abraham Bell,* and *Mary Bell* Widow, were imprifoned by a Writ *de Excommunicato capiendo,* at the Suit of *William Surrey,* then Churchwarden of *Felfted,* for refufing to pay his Rate.

Diftreffes.

ANNO 1680. In this Year *Samuel Parmentor* of *Otten-Belfham,* and *Robert Poole* of *Paul's-Belfham,* fuffered Diftrefs of their Goods for abfenting themfelves from the publick Worfhip.

Imprifonments for Tithes.

ANNO 1681. About the Month called *January* this Year, *William Reynolds* of *Great-Chefterford,* was imprifoned in the County Goal for refufing to pay fmall Tithes, at the Suit of the Prieft of *Strettell.*

Fines for Meeting.

ANNO 1682. In the Beginning of the Month called *June* this Year, was a Meeting at *Flamfted-End,* for which Fines were impofed, and Diftrefs of Goods made on *Thomas Taylor, Thomas Abraham, John Shackerly, Samuel Stanbridge, John Bufh,* and *Thomas Bennet,* to the Amount of 9 *l.* 6 *s.* 3 *d.*

On the 4th of *December* in the fame Year, at *Saffron-Walden,* the Friends being kept out of their Meeting-houfe, held their Affembly in the Street,

Oath tendred,

whither the Magiftrates came, and tendred the Oath of Allegiance to *Robert Freak* and *Richard Mansfield* of *Afhden,* and *Thomas Trigg* of *Littlebury,* and for

Refufers fent to Prifon.

refufing to take it fent them to Prifon. On the 18th of the fame Month, being fhut out and affembled as before, the Magiftrates went and tendred the Oath to *Anthony Pennyftone, Humphry Smith, Thomas Simons, Henry Starr, John Scotcher, John Allen, Samuel Taylor,* and *Thomas Waite,* and committed them alfo to Prifon for refufing to take it : And at a Seffions about nine Months after they were fined 20 *l.* 16 *s.* 8 *d.* and Diftreffes made on the Goods of divers of them ; but *Samuel Taylor* and *John Allen* not having whereon to make Diftrefs, were recommitted to Prifon for three Months longer.

Severe Diftrefs.

In the Month called *January* this Year, *James Matthews* of *Weft-Ham,* for a Meeting in an Houfe adjoining to his Dwelling, and for his Wife's Preaching there, fuffered Diftrefs of Goods to the Value of 104 *l.* 13 *s.* 3 *d.*

Diftrefs for Meeting at Plaiftow,

For a Meeting at *Plaiftow,* and for *William Falkner's* Preaching there, Goods were taken by Diftrefs from *George Brown* and *Robert Bailey* to the Value of 12 *l.* 15 *s.* 9 *d.*

and for Abfence from the National Worfhip.

In this Year alfo, *Roger Elcock* of *Much-Baddow,* and *Jofeph Parmentor* and *Thomas Cragg,* both of *Paul's-Belfham,* fuffered Diftrefs of their Goods for being abfent from the National Worfhip.

ANNO

ANNO 1683. *William Shepherd* of *Wickham*, for a Demand of eight Years Tithe, valued at 10 s. *per Annum*, was prosecuted in the County Court, at the Suit of Dr. *Browning*, and suffered Distress of his Houshold Goods to the Value of 5 l. 5 s.

John Slaughter of *Upminster*, for a Demand of 39 s. for Tithe, had a Cow and other Things taken away worth 11 l.

Richard Reeve of *Colchester*, and *Josiah Smith*, were still continued Prisoners for Tithes. And on the 3d of the Month called *March* this Year, *Thomas Wiseman* was committed to Prison by an Attachment out of the *Exchequer*, at the Suit of *Samuel Croxal*, Priest of *Tolsunt-Knights*, for Tithes.

On the 22d of the Month called *July* this Year, *John Matthews* of *Harwich*, *Job Spurgeon* of *Dedham*, *Stephen Moore* and *Stephen Arnold* of *Lawford*, taken at a Meeting, were committed to *Chelmsford* Goal by Warrant from Justice *Smith*: They were after a few Weeks bailed out till Sessions: But on their Appearance there on the 3d of *October*, they were required to give Sureties for their good Behaviour, which refusing to do, they were recommitted to Prison, where three of them lay upon Straw about fifteen Weeks in the Midst of a Winter remarkable for Extremity of Cold, but the fourth, *Job Spurgeon*, being so weak that he was unable to lie down, sat up in a Chair the most Part of that Time.

About this Time several Distresses were made for Absence from the National Worship, by which were taken

	l.	*s.*	*d.*
From *Samuel Parmentor*, *Israel Roberts*, *Robert Poole*, and *Thomas Miller*, Goods worth	3	10	0
Robert Elcock, *Joseph Parmentor*, *Thomas Cragg*, and *Thomas Mullar*, to the Value of	4	10	0
	8	0	0

Richard Pitman, *John Larking*, *Thomas Tyler*, *John Shackerly*, and *Thomas Bennett*, were convicted before Justice *Fox* of *Cheshunt* in *Hartfordshire*, for being at a Meeting at *Flamsted-End*, and by his Certificate of that Conviction, directed to Justice *Wroth* of *Layton* in *Essex*, a Warrant was issued to the Constables of *Waltham-Abbey*, by which Distresses were made on the Goods of the Persons convicted to the Amount of 8 l. 17 s.

By Virtue of a Warrant granted by *John Tendering* Justice, upon Information of their being at religious Meetings, Distresses were made by the Officers of *Hatfield-Peverill*, by which were taken

	l.	*s.*	*d.*
From *Philip Woolridge*, *Hugh Nichols*, *Martha Nichols* Widow, *Katharine Blundall*, and *John Spencer*, Goods worth	4	14	0
John Smith, *Thomas Walford*, *John Lea*, and *Richard Cast*	4	13	0
Paul Gatewood, *John Webb*, *Elizabeth True*, and *Edward Eatney*	2	0	6
	11	7	6

The Constables, who made these Distresses, reported, that the convicting Justice had directed them to take for 5 s. as many Goods as were worth 5 l. A Direction favouring more of *furious Zeal* than an equal Distribution of Justice.

John Rand of *Little-Baddow*, *Phineas Barnard* of *Mountnessing*, *Thomas Sewel*, *Joseph Lark*, *John Silvester*, *John Marshall*, *John Cakebread* of *Samford*, *John Wastell*, *John Butcher*, *Francis Eve*, *William Sutton*, *James Warner*, and *Edward Eatney*, were summoned to appear before the Justices at the Petty-Sessions, on the 2d of *December* 1683, for no other apparent Cause than their religious Dissent

ESSEX.
1683.

Released at the Affizes.

Indictments for 20l. *per Month.*

Attachment for Tithes.

Sundry Imprisonments.

Imprisonment by a Writ de Excom. Cap. Trained-Bands.

Illegal Act of Colonel Turner.

Imprisonment of M. Cockerton.

Tithe of Corn.

sent from the Religion established by Law : When there, they were required to find Sureties for their good Behaviour, which they, having given no just Occasion of Offence, refused to do, and were therefore committed to *Chelmsford* Goal, and detained there three Months, till the Affizes, when they were set at Liberty by Judge *Jones*, on Bond given for their Apearance at the Affizes following : At which Affizes *John Child* of *Felsted*, *John Bunting* of *Halsted*, *John Cakebread* of *Samford*, and *William Swann*, and several others were indicted on the Statute of 20l. per Month, for Absence from the National Worship : *Michael Pettitt* was also prosecuted for the same Cause.

ANNO 1684. On the 9th of the Month called *May*, *John Norden* and *Nathanael Sparrow* were committed to Prison by an Attachment issued out of the Court of Chancery on a Prosecution there for Tithes, at the Suit of *John Heath* a Distiller of *London*, Executor to *Thomas Cooke* late Priest of *Stisted*.

In the same Month, upon an Information of meeting together for religious Worship, *John Dunbar*, *Simon Joslin*, *John Griffin*, and *John Plumb*, were committed to Prison by Justice *Ballett* of *Hatfield Broad-Oak*, and continued there till the next Affizes, when they were recommitted by the Judge. The same Justice *Ballett* caused *Richard Burles* of *Feering* to be taken up, as he was passing the Street, and committed him to Prison.

In this Year *Thomas Houchin* of *Feering*, was committed to Prison by a Writ de *Excommunicato capiendo* : And *Thomas Turner* of *Coggeshall*, for refusing to pay toward the Charges of the Trained-Bands, had Goods taken from him to the Value of 10s.

We conclude our Account of this Year with an illegal and arbitrary Proceeding of Colonel *Turner*, and others at *Thaxted*, who lock'd and naild up the Door of the Meeting-house there, which the next Day they opened again, taking away the Forms, Benches, and Stand, all which, together with the Window-Shutters of an Apartment, they carried to a Green not far from the Town and burnt them.

ANNO 1685. *Mary Cockerton* a Widow, was a Prisoner in *Chelmsford* Goal, having been committed thither on a Prosecution for Tithes.

ANNO 1690. In this Year *John Mascall* of *Finchingfield*, and *John Cakebread*, had Corn taken from them for Tithe, to the Value of 4l. 3s. 6d.

C H A P. XIX.

HUNTINGTONSHIRE.

ANNO 1655.

THE earlieſt Sufferers in this County were *John Cranwell* and *Thomas Purcas*, who, for their conſcientious Refuſal to pay Tithes, were committed to Priſon : And while there, the former for a Demand of 12 *l.* for Tithes, ſuffered Diſtreſs of his Goods to the Value of 21 *l.* and the latter for a Claim of 1 *l.* 7 *s.* ſuſtained a Loſs of 4 *l.* Beſides which, the Prieſts who proſecuted them, or their Agents, took out of their Fields in Harveſt, what Quantities of Corn they pleaſed. In like Manner the Claimers of Tithes entred into the Grounds of *Ephany Taylor* Widow, *Thomas Golding*, and *William Nixon*, and took, under Pretence of Tithes, what they thought fit, without rendring any Account of their Doings.

Imprisonments and Distresses for Tithes.

ANNO 1657. On the 19th of the Month called *January* this Year, *Simon Sanford* was proſecuted in the *Exchequer* for Tithes under 5 *s.* Value, and committed to *Huntington* Goal, where he lay ſeventeen Months, till diſcharged by Order of a Committee of Parliament. In this and the preceding Year, ſeveral Perſons for Demands of 2 *l.* 10 *s.* 6 *d.* for Steeple-houſe Rates, ſuffered by Diſtreſs of their Goods to the Value of 9 *l.* 9 *s.*

Imprisonments.

Distresses.

ANNO 1658. *John Apthorp* was impriſoned at *Huntington* for Tithe, and thence removed to the *Fleet* in *London*, where having ſome Liberty to walk abroad, a malicious Informer repreſented him as a dangerous Perſon, and cauſed him to be taken by a Party of Soldiers and committed to *Newgate*. As ſoon as he was diſcharged thence, he returned again to the *Fleet*, where he continued Priſoner about a Year. *Thomas Parnell* alſo ſuffered many Months Impriſonment for Tithes under 20 *s.* in Value, for which he had been proſecuted in the *Exchequer*.

Persecution of J. Apthorp and T. Parnell.

ANNO 1659. *Daniel Maddy* was by ſome Juſtices of the Peace committed to Priſon for refuſing to Swear, but at the next Aſſizes was releaſed by Judge *Hales*. About the ſame Time *Richard Jobſon* and *Thomas Jobſon* were taken out of their Beds, and kept under Guard at the *Crown* Inn at *Huntington* twenty four Hours : After which, though they refuſed to Swear, they were diſmiſt, but their Houſes, as alſo that of *Robert Raby*, were ſearched for

Variety of Prosecutions.

HUNT-
INGTON-
SHIRE.
1659.

Arms, on a groundlefs Sufpicion of their Difaffection to the Government. In this Year alfo *Leonard Ellington* was committed to *Huntington* Goal, for coming in with his Hat on into the Court of the Mannour of *Warbois*, of which he was a cuftomary Tenant. About this Time alfo, *Richard Pierpoint* and *Richard Chatteris*, of *Erith*, for appearing before a Juftice of the Peace with their Hats on, were fent to Prifon : At the next Seffions they were fined 10 s. each, and for Non-payment continued in Prifon feventeen Weeks. *Thomas Swan* was alfo committed to Prifon on the 26th of *September* this Year for Tithes, and continued there above two Years In this Year for Demands of 1 l. 15 s. for Tithes, were taken from feveral Perfons in this County, Goods to the Value of 3 l.

*Many Impri-
fonments for
not Swearing.*

ANNO 1660. On the 12th of the Month called *January* this Year, *Robert Ingram* and *John Parnel* were taken by a Party of Horfe from their own Houfes, and carried before the Commiffioners at *Huntington*, who fent them to the Common Goal there for refufing the Oath of Allegiance. Next Day fome of their Friends vifited them in Prifon ; of which, Notice being given, a Party of Horfe furrounded the Goal, crying out, *A Meeting, a Meeting*, and thofe who came to vifit the Prifoners were imprifoned with them : But the Day following were difcharged by the Magiftrates, faying, *We fhall foon have them again*, for they had heard of a Meeting appointed at *Southo* on the Morrow. Accordingly fome armed Men on Horfeback were fent thither, who apprehended *John Crook, Benjamin Thornly, Thomas Bunby, Richard Jobfon, John Deare, Anthony Chandler, Daniel Maddy, Thomas Marfhall, Giles Fifher, William Bing, Henry Maddy,* and *Richard How*, who being carried before the Juftices, and refufing to take the Oaths, were fent Prifoners to *Huntington*, where they found others of their Friends imprifoned for the fame Caufe, two of

*Deaths of
S. Sanford
and F. Lamftead.*

whom, *Simon Sanford* and *Francis Lamftead*, died Prifoners fhortly after, the Former on the 18th of the Month called *February* this Year, and the Latter on the 7th of the next Month : In which Month alfo, *William Marlow, Samuel Nottingham,* and *Robert Gray*, were fent to Prifon for the like Teftimony againft Swearing. At the Affizes in the fame Month, called *March*, moft of the aforefaid Prifoners, for refufing the Oath, were fet at Liberty by Judge

*Three detained
as dangerous
Perfons.*

Hales ; but * *John Crook, Benjamin Thornly*, and *Robert Ingram*, were ordered to continue till another Affize, they being caufelefsly reprefented as Ringleaders and more dangerous than the reft : *John Parnel*, though difcharged as to the Oath, was by an Action laid againft him for fmall Tithes, detained above five Years longer in Prifon, at the Suit of *John Heath*, Prieft of *Hemingford-Abbot*.

*Sufferings for
Tithes.*

ANNO 1661. *Thomas Golding*, of *Colne*, was committed to *Huntington* Goal for Tithes, at the Suit of Dr. *Gunning*, (afterward Bifhop of *Ely*) and continued Prifoner more than three Years. He had alfo taken from him a Mare worth 40 s. for pretended Dues for Tithes of Wool and Lambs. About the fame Time *Ellen Ingram*, a poor Widow of *Colne*, had an Horfe taken away worth 40 s. for a Demand of 3 s. 4 d. for Tithe of one Rood of Corn.

*Imprifonments
for Meetings.*

John Ainfloe, Philip Taylor, Thomas Jobfon, and *Thomas Rivers*, as they were going to a Meeting, were apprehended at *Godmanchefter*, and by an officious Juftice fent to Prifon : As were alfo in the Month of *October* this Year, *John Samms, Richard Jobfon, William Sterling, Robert Smith*, and *Robert Raby*, who had been taken in a Meeting at the faid *Raby*'s Houfe in *Huntington*. In this

*Abufes for
Opening Shop.*

Year alfo *Robert Raby, Richard Jobfon*, and *Katharine Lanford*, fuffered many Abufes for having opened their Shops on the 30th of the Month called *January*. *Richard Jobfon* was alfo profecuted in the Ecclefiaftical Court for Marriage-Fees, by a Prieft who had not been concerned in Marrying him, he having taken his Wife in a publick Affembly before many Witneffes, without employing any Perfon of that Function.

ANNO

---

* *John Crook*, who had been a Juftice of the Peace in *Bedfordfhire*, was convinced by the Preaching of *George Fox* in 1654, and foon after was left out of the Commiffion.

ANNO 1663. *John Parnel*, for refusing to pay Tithes, had seven Loads of Hay taken from him worth 7 *l.*

In this Year *Anne White*, and *William White* her Son, were taken from their own House at *Eltin* by Constables, who conveyed them to a Justice of the Peace, and by him they were sent to *Huntington* Goal for refusing to take the Oath of Allegiance.

ANNO 1664.   On the 28th of the Month called *August*, of twenty Persons who were taken out of a Meeting at *John Cranwell*'s of *Erith*, eighteen were committed to Prison.   In this Year also *Thomas Purcas* of *Bluntsham*, and *William Sterling* of *Godmanchester*, for Absence from the National Worship, suffered Distress of Goods to the Vaule of 1 *l.* 3 *s.* 8 *d.*

In this or the preceding Year, *Robert Falkner* and *Thomas Bell* were met on the Highway by *Nicholas Johnson* a Justice of the Peace, who forced them to his House, and thence sent them to Prison till next Sessions, when appearing before the Justices with their Hats on, they were sent back to Prison, where they lay till the Assizes, at which Judge *Twisden* seemed inclinable to discharge them, but said, *he could not, because they were not legally before him.*   At an ensuing Sessions they were released by a private Order from the Justices, after twenty Weeks Imprisonment without any legal Cause.   And in this Year *John Peacock* was excommunicated for not paying pretended Dues to the Priest.

ANNO 1667.   *John Parnel*, at the Suit of *Griffith Lloyd* an Impropriator, was imprisoned in *Huntington* Goal, and thence removed to *London.*   On Trial a Verdict was given against him for 9 *l.* 12 *s.* Tithe upon the Statute for treble Damages, for which his Goods were taken by Distress to the Value of 30 *l.*

ANNO 1668.   In this Year *Roger Chamberlain*, of *Offord-Cluny*, suffered Distress of his Goods to the Value of 4 *l.* for refusing to pay Tithe.

ANNO 1669.   The said *Roger Chamberlain* had taken from him for Tithe, Corn to the Value of 20 *l.*

In this Year *Leonard Barringer*, *William Lamb*, *Thomas Cooke*, *Christopher Lindsey*, and *Robert Ingram*, were taken from a Meeting at *Somersham*, and sent to Prison, where they lay five Weeks.   On the 10th of the Month called *August*, *John Crook*, *Thomas Parnel*, and *John Peacock*, taken at a Meeting in the House of *Leonard Ellington* at *Warbois*, were committed to Prison till the Assizes, where an Indictment was preferred against them on the Statute of 35 *Eliz.* but Judge *Hales* declaring the Indictment to be invalid, they were set at Liberty.   In the same Year *Samuel Nottingham*, *Richard Snazdale*, *Edward Lambert*, *Richard Proud*, *Richard Taylor*, *Thomas Lorimer*, *William Moll*, *Henry Avelyn*, and *William Mitchel*, were taken from a Meeting at the said *Samuel Nottingham*'s House in *Ramsey*, and being carried before *Henry Williams* Justice, he tendred them the Oath of Allegiance, and for refusing it sent them to Prison till next Sessions, when they were ordered to appear at the following Assizes, where they were indicted, and fined 5 *l.* each, for which Fines *Edward Lambert* and *Richard Taylor* suffered Distress of their Goods ; and *Thomas Lorimer*, *William Moll*, and *Henry Avelin*, were continued Prisoners three Months longer.

ANNO 1670.   *John Parnel* was again cast into Prison for Tithes, at the Suit of *Griffith Lloyd* Impropriator.   He had also taken from him Corn, for Tithes, to the Value of 46 *l.*

On the 15th of the Month called *July*, the following Persons, taken at a Meeting in the House of *Thomas Abbott* of *Ives*, suffered Distresses of their Goods by Warrants from the Justices, viz.

	l.	*s.*	*d.*
Tobias Hardmeat, *William Martin*, *David Tisdale*, *Robert Raby*, *John Apthorp*, *Robert Ingram*, *Richard Jobson*, and *Samuel Nottingham*, to the Value of	17	15	4
John Parnel, *Daniel Abbott*, *William Gray*, *Reuben Eldred*, Widow *Abbott*, *William Field*, and *Thomas Parnel*.	9	13	0
	27	8	4

Margin notes:

HUNT-INGTON-SHIRE. 1663.

Imprisonments for refusing to Swear.

18 Sent to Prison.

Distresses.

Imprisonments.

Excommunication.

Prosecution for Tithes.

Distress.

Tithes.

Imprisonments.

Tithes.

Distresses for Meeting.

In

HUNT-
INGTON-
SHIRE.
1670.

In the next Month *William Starling* of *Godmanchefter*, for a Meeting at his Houſe, had his Goods taken away worth 24 *l.* 12 *s.* 6 *d.* And for the ſame Meeting were taken from *Thomas Lifter*, an Horſe and a Cow worth 8 *l.* which Horſe, valued at 6 *l.* was ſold to Juſtice *Williams*, one of thoſe who iſſued the Warrant, for 45 *s.* And the Cow, worth 40 *s.* was ſold to his Clerk for 16 *s.* 6 *d.* From *John Vintner*, for the ſame Meeting, they took a Cart and Wheels worth 3 *l.* 10 *s.*

Horfes feized.   For another Meeting at *William Starling*'s, the Informers went to the Inns, and ſeized ſeveral of the Friends Horſes before Conviction.

For other Meetings in this County were taken

	l.	*s.*	*d.*
Diftreffes for Meetings. From *Robert Lifter*, *John Lifter*, *Tobias Hardmeat*, *John Parnel*, *Robert Stow*, and *John Whitehead*, Goods worth	25	10	8
Tobias Hardmeat at another Time, a Cow and an Horſe worth	6	0	0
which were ſold to the Brother of Juſtice *Heron* for 45*s.*			
From *Tobias Hardmeat* at a third Time, Goods worth	7	0	0
which were ſold by Inch of Candle for 2 *l.* 5 *s.*			
From *Chriftopher Maidftone*, for himſelf and his Wife, though ſhe was not at the Meeting, Goods worth	12	0	0
Thomas Parnel, for a Meeting at his Houſe in *King-Rippon*, were taken Goods to the Value of	19	0	0
which were ſold to Juſtice *Johnfon*'s Servant, for his Maſter, for 9 *l.* 7 *s.*			
From *Robert Falkner*, for a Meeting at his Houſe in *Somerfham*, Goods worth	29	10	0
Rofe Pont Widow, *Richard Snazdale*, *Thomas Golding*, *Jafper Robins*, *John Offly*, *Samuel Nottingham*, and *John Blake*, Goods to the Value	19	12	0
Richard Jobfon, for a Meeting at his Houſe	8	10	0
John Cranwell of *Erith*, for a Meeting at his Houſe	25	0	0
Thomas Peel, *Robert Raby*, *Jafper Lifter*, *John Cranwell*, *William Triftram*, *Richard Laxton*, and *William Field*, Goods to the Value of	19	19	0
	172	1	8

Many of the ſame Perſons being preſent at the Meetings in ſeveral Places, had repeated Informations againſt them, and were often diſtrained on, ſo that beſide the Seizures already mentioned, there were alſo taken this Year

	l.	*s.*	*d.*
From *David Tifdale*, *Thomas Purcas*, *Thomas Cooke*, *William Wright*, *Tobias Hardmeat*, *Daniel Abbott*, *Francis Rogers*, *Elizabeth Gray*, *William Star-ling*, *Jafper Robins*, and *Rofe Pont*, Goods worth	44	11	8
Richard Taylor, *Thomas Burgis*, *Richard Snazdale*, *Stephen Clarkfon*, *Leonard Ellington*, * *Blanch Peacock*, *Reuben Eldred*, *Henry Gilings*, *John Lifter*, and *Simon Jackfon*, to the Value of	33	5	2
	77	16	10

Taken

* Wife of *John Peacock* who was then in Priſon.

Taken alfo for a Meeting at *Blythorne*,

l.   s.   d.

From *Nicholas Tomfon, John Arthur, Thomas Robins,*
John Leighton, William Fowler, William Bing, } 32 6 6
and *Leonard Baker,* Goods worth

For a Meeting at *William Starling*'s in *Godmanchefter*, were Goods taken

l.   s.   d.

From the faid *William Starling, Samuel Nottingham,*
Richard Snazdale, Rofe Pont, and *Wil-* } 26 0 0
liam *Wright,* to the Value of

Many of thefe Diftreffes were very rigorous and fevere : When *Jafper Lifter* **Warrants rigoroufly exe-**
had all the Goods in his Houfe taken away, he being very poor, and lame, **cuted.**
going on Crutches, and having three fmall Children, defired of Juftice *He-*
ron that a Blanket might be returned him to cover his Children, but that
Favour was denied him.   Alfo when *William Fowler* and *Leonard Baker* had
all their Goods feized, except a few old Forms and Stools of little Value, the
Juftices ordered the Officers to take all worth carrying away, and to burn the
reft.   And when *John Tomfon*, a very poor Man, was returned by the Officers
as infolvent, the Juftices ordered, that *if he had two Coats, they fhould take one*
of them.   Alfo when *Robert Stow*, of *Ellington*, had his Houfhold Goods all
taken from him, the Officers faid *they muft diftrain his Bees.*   Thefe Inftances
fhew how unmercifully the Warrants on thefe Occafions were executed, and
how void the Breafts of Perfecutors were of common Charity and Compaffion.

ANNO 1671.   In this Year feveral of this County fuffered Imprifonment **Imprifonments**
for not paying Tithes, *viz.   Thomas Afhton,* who continued in Prifon eighteen **for Tithes.**
Months : *William Newberry* nine Months : *Jafper Lifter* and *Robert Lifter*
thirty four Weeks, for a Demand of 2 s. 6 d. each : *Tobias Hardmeat* thirty
Weeks : *Reuben Eldred* twenty Weeks : And *William Starling* feventeen Weeks.
And in this Year *Roger Chamberlain* had taken from him for Tithes, Corn
worth 4 l. 5 s.

ANNO 1672.   *Richard Johnfon* and *Robert Raby*, being elected Aldermen **Fines for**
of *Huntington*, for refufing to take the Oath required on their Admittance into **not Swearing.**
that Office, were fined twenty Marks each, and committed to Prifon, where
they continued fifteen Weeks, and were afterward fued to an Outlawry.

John Tomfon and *John Peacock* were excommunicated for Abfence from the **Excommuni-**
National Worfhip : And for the fame Caufe *Samuel Nottingham, William Ham-* **cations.**
mond and *Edward Lambert*, fuffered Diftrefs of Goods to the Value of 16 s. 6 d.

In this Year *John Peacock, Robert Ingram, Francis Penn, Robert Whitehead,* **Releafe of**
Elizabeth Throftle, and *John King*, were difcharged from their Imprifonment in **J. Peacock**
the Common Goal at *Huntington* by the King's Letters Patent, generally ex- **and others.**
tended to the People called *Quakers* then under Confinement.

ANNO 1674.   Taken by Diftrefs for religious Meetings,

l.   s.   d.

From *Tobias Hardmeat, William Gray, Roger Chamber-* }
lain, *and Robert Alfop*, Goods to the Value of } 2 6 8 **Diftreffes.**

For Fines impofed for Abfence from the National Worfhip, Goods were
taken by Diftrefs,

l.   s.   d.

From *Thomas Cook, Edward Chriftenthwaite, William*
Bavin, Thomas Bundy, William Gill, William }
Hawkins, John Seaborn, James Fern, and *John* } 3 14 0
Purcas, to the Value of

Before thefe Diftreffes were made, feveral of them had fuffered thirteen Days
Imprifonment for refufing to pay thefe Fines.   For the like Caufe *William*
Wright,

HUNT-
INGTON-
SHIRE.
1675.

*Fines and
Diſtreſſes.*

*A Burial
deemed a
Conventicle.*

Wright, Edward Abbott, Robert Alſop, and *John Stevenſon,* were alſo impriſoned.

ANNO 1675. On the 28th of the Month called *March, John Parnel, John Peacock, Richard Taylor, Thomas Peele, Richard Jennings, John Fills, William Gills, William Hawkins, Thomas Cooke, Edward Chriſtenthwaite, John Barringer,* and *Leonard Barringer,* were fined for being at a Meeting at *Erith,* and ſeveral of them ſuffered Diſtreſs of Goods to the Value of 2 *l.* 14 *s.*

On the 14th of the Month called *June,* ſeveral Perſons, who attended the Interment of *Robert Falkner* in the Burying-ground at *Somerſham,* were fined on the Evidence of two Informers who ſwore it to be a Conventicle : The Amount of the Sums taken by Diſtreſs on that Occaſion was 87 *l.* 7 *s.*

On the 19th of *October,* for a Meeting at the Houſe of *Thomas Blundy* of *Bluntſham,* were taken

Diſtreſſes.

	l.	*s.*	*d.*
From *Tobias Hardmeat, Richard Taylor, Thomas Poole, John Barringer, Thomas Seaborn, William Bavin, John Nunn,* and *Benjamin Thornly,* Goods worth	31	14	0

And for a Meeting held in the Barn of *Amy Peacock* of *Erith,* were taken

	l.	*s.*	*d.*
From *Amy Peacock, Laurence Dunk, Richard Baſſe, Sarah Green, Benjamin Thornly,* and *Samuel Nottingham,* Goods worth	12	0	0
And for being at ſeveral other Meetings, *Edward Chriſtenthwaite, Richard Triplo, Thomas Peele, Thomas Burgeſs, Richard Taylor,* and *Leonard Barringer,* ſuffered Diſtreſs of Goods to the Value of	27	2	0
	39	2	0

*Fines for
Meeting.*

ANNO 1676. On the 23d of the Month called *April,* for a Meeting at *Amy Peacock's* in *Erith,* where *George Whitehead* preached, *Tobias Hardmeat* and *Thomas Parnel* were fined 10 *l.* each : And *Richard Baſſe, Benjamin Thornly, Edward Chriſtenthwaite* and *William Bavin,* had Goods taken from them worth 2 *l.* 8 *s. William Pryor,* a young Man of *Somerſham* was fined 5 *s.* The Officers came when he was in Bed, and took away all his Clothes except one Stocking. He, being poor, was obliged to borrow Clothes to wear, till by his Induſtry he could repair the Loſs.

*Impriſonments
on Writs de
Excom. Cap.*

On the 7th of the Month called *February, George Clapham* was committed to Priſon by a Writ *de Excommunicato capiendo,* having been proſecuted by Dr. *Pocklington* in the Eccleſiaſtical Court for not going to his Pariſh-Church, and for not receiving the Sacrament. For the ſame Cauſes alſo, *William Poole, James Paris, Richard Chamberlain, Benjamin Bennett,* and *Nathanael Cawthorne,* were ſeverally impriſoned on Writs *de Excommunicato capiendo,* at the Promotion of *Duellin Salmon,* a Regiſter of the Commiſſary Court of the Biſhop of *Lincoln.*

*Impriſonments
for 16 d.*

ANNO 1678. *John Purcas* was impriſoned by a Writ *de Excommunicato capiendo,* at the Suit of *William Drury,* for a Claim of Tithes of but 16 *d.* Value.

Long Impriſonments.

On the 6th of the Month called *March* this Year, *Thomas Aſhton* and *William Newberry,* were remaining Priſoners in *Huntington* Goal, where the Former of them had been three Years and ten Months, and the Latter three Years and five Months, both of them for Tithes, at the Suit of *William Sweepſon* Impropriator.

In this Year alſo, the following Diſtreſſes were made by Warrants iſſued out of the *Exchequer,* for Seizure of two Thirds of the Yearly Value of their Eſtates, viz.

From

	l.	*s.*	*d.*	HUNT- INGTON- SHIRE. 1678.
From *Samuel Nottingham*, Cattle worth	36	5	0	
John Ellis, Kine and Bedding worth	8	10	0	
Richard Taylor, Corn worth	30	0	0	
Thomas Golding, a Gelding worth	3	10	0	*Diftreffes for*
And three Cows from one of his Tenants, worth	6	13	4	*two Thirds of*
Richard Proud, Goods worth	3	19	2	*Eftates.*

	88	17	6

ANNO 1679. Taken by *Exchequer* Procefs for Abfence from the National Worfhip,

	l.	*s.*	*d.*	
From *Nathaniel Nurfe*, *John Offly*, *Samuel Nottingham*, *Richard Proud*, and *Thomas Golding*, Goods worth }	48	2	0	*Diftreffes.*

ANNO 1680. *James Fenn*, chofen Conftable, and refufing to take the ufual Oath to qualify him for that Office, was committed to Prifon. *Imprifonment for refufing to Swear.*
At the Affizes at *Huntington* on the 12th of the Month called *Auguft* this Year, eleven Perfons were profecuted as *Popifh* Recufants, and the Grand Jury found Bills of Indi&ment againft them, *viz.* *William Starling*, *Jafper Robins*, *William Wright*, *Robert Lifter*, *John Lifter*, *Thomas Lifter*, *Thomas Robins*, *Richard Laxon*, *William Martin*, *John Apthorp*, and *William Nokes*. *Indi&ments,*
The Accounts of Corn taken out of the Field for Tithe from Perfons of this Perfuafion in this County, from the Year 1673 to the Year 1680 inclufive, amounted to 436*l.* 14*s.* 8*d.* *Tithe of Corn.*
ANNO 1681. In this Year on Proceffes out of the *Exchequer*, and on Prefentments at the Affizes and Seffions, Goods were taken by Diftrefs to the Value of 58*l.* 10*s.* 10*d.* And for Fines upon the Conventicle A&, to the Value of 5*l.* 1*s.* *Variety of Fines levied.*
ANNO 1682. For Abfence from the National Worfhip feveral Perfons had their Goods taken by Diftrefs to the Amount of 28*l.* 14*s.* 6*d.* *Diftreffes.*
ANNO 1683. *Reuben Eldred*, a Miller in *Fen-Stanton*, had been profecuted in the Ecclefiaftical Court for Tithes of a Windmill, at the Suit of *Robert Blennel* Prieft of that Parifh. During the Profecution *Eldred* died, leaving *Tobias Hardmeat* his Executor. A few Weeks after his Death, the Parfon cited *Tobias* for the fame Tithes, which he, refufing to pay, was about two Years after, on a Certificate of Contumacy, committed by two Juftices to Prifon without Bail or Mainprize, till he fhould comply with the Ecclefiaftical Injun&ion. His Commitment was in *December* 1683, a Winter remarkable for Extremity of Cold. The fame Prieft alfo profecuted *Elizabeth Gray* in the Ecclefiaftical Court for Tithes : She was a poor Widow of about eighty Years of Age, and fo infirm that fhe could fcarce go out of her Houfe : Yet the Profecutor was fo hard-hearted, as to apply to the Juftices to fend her to Prifon, the Ecclefiaftical Court having certified her to be contumacious. But the Juftices refufed in regard of her Age, faying, *What do you bring this Woman to us for ? fhe is fitter for her Grave than to be brought hither.* So they would not fend her to Prifon. Thus the Compaffion of the Juftices fruftrated the cruel Intent of the Parfon. But he, difappointed of his Defign againft the ancient Woman, cited her Son *William Gray* into the Court for the fame Claim of Tithes, and procured a Certificate of Contumacy againft him ; but upon Examination before the Juftices, he appearing to be only as a Servant to his Mother, they difcharged him, though the Prieft's Advocates, *viz.* *Salmon* a Regifter, and *Newman* a Pro&or of the Ecclefiaftical Court, ftrenuoufly urged the Juftices to fend him to Prifon. Thus both Mother and Son were preferved by the Moderation of the Civil Magiftrate, from being facrificed to the arbitrary Proceedings of Ecclefiaftical Power. *Tithes of a Windmill.* *Cafe of a poor ancient Widow, profecuted by an hard-hearted Prieft.*

In

HUNT-
INGTON-
SHIRE.
1683.

Death of
N. Caw-
thorne.

Imprifon-
ments.

In the Month called *June* this Year, *Nathanael Cawthorne* was committed to the Fleet Prifon in *London*, at the Suit of *Robert Purchafe* Tithe-farmer of the Parifh of *Witton*. In which Prifon he died on the 31ft of *December*. During his Sicknefs, fome of his Friends, confidering the extream Rigour of the Seafon, applied to the Profecutor to grant the poor Man a little Liberty, but could not prevail with him. Thus he laid down his Life in Confirmation of the Teftimony he bore againft the Antichriftian Yoke and Oppreffion of Tithes.

ANNO 1684. About the 2d of *December*, *Richard Jobfon* and *Elijah Lovel* of *Huntington*, were accufed before the Mayor and other Juftices of the Peace, for being at three feveral Meetings in the faid *Richard Jobfon*'s Houfe: Upon their refufing to find Sureties they were fent to Prifon. At another Meeting in the fame Place, *William Starling*, *John Stevenfon*, *William Triftram*, *John Lifter*, *Jafper Robins*, *Caleb Walker*, and *Thomas Robins*, were likewife taken and committed to Goal. They were confined in an open Chamber, the Windows unglazed, and no Chimney in it, in a cold Winter Seafon, where they remained Prifoners about four Months. For the fame Caufe alfo, *Jofeph Fowler*, *Thomas Afhton*, and *Abigail Looke*, were fent to Prifon. Several of the Perfons fo committed, were afterward indicted and fined as *Guilty of a Riot* ; though nothing could be more peaceable than their religious Affemblies.

Excommunica-
tion.

ANNO 1685. In this Year were remaining Prifoners on Writs de Excommunicato capiendo, in the County Goal at *Huntington*, *William Poole*, *James Paris*, *Benjamin Bennett*, *Roger Chamberlain*, *John Purcas*, *David Teafdale*, and *Daniel Abbott*, which two laft had lain there about two Years, having been profecuted in the Ecclefiaftical Court for a fmall Sum demanded toward repairing the Steeple-houfe at *Ives*.

Diftreffes.

Richard Snazdale, for abfenting himfelf from his Parifh-Church, fuffered Diftrefs of eleven Oxen worth 72 *l.* though they were fold but for 15 *l.* For the fame Caufe were taken from *John Barnes*, *Gabriel Hampfhire*, *Richard Taylor*, *Thomas Smith*, *Tobias Hardmeat*, *Samuel Nottingham*, and *Richard Proud*, Goods worth 45 *l.* 17 *s.* 6 *d.*

Prifoners re-
leafed.

At the Affizes this Year, *George Clapham*, *James Paris*, *William Poole*, *Roger Chamberlain*, and *Benjamin Bennett*, were difcharged from their Imprifonment by Virtue of King *James the Second*'s Proclamation for a free and general Pardon.

Tithes in kind.

ANNO 1690. The Accounts of Tithes taken in kind, viz. in Corn and other tithable Matters in this County, from the faid People, between the Years 1680 and 1690, amounted to 1006 *l.* 5 *s.* 4 *d.*

C H A P.

*Reputed birthplace of
George Fox (1624-1690/1)
at Fenny Drayton, Leicestershire
– from* The Friend *of 1892.
Courtesy of Friends House
Library.*

C H A P. XXIII.

LEICESTERSHIRE,
and R U T L A N D.

A N N O 1652.

*Sufferings of
E. Muggle-
ston,*

O N E of the firſt Sufferers in this County was *Edward Mugglefton,* an ancient Man of *Swanington,* who was twice obliged to appear at *London,* ninety Miles from his Dwelling, before a Committee of Parliament appointed to enquire into the State of ſuch Preachers as had been plundered during the Civil Wars : While he was attending on them, at that Diſtance, a Seizure was made of his Goods at Home to the Value of 8 *l.* 10 *s.* for a Claim of 2 *l.* 15 *s.* 6 *d.* for Tithes.

and C. Lewis. In the ſame Year *Chriſtopher Lewis,* of *Harby,* was cited before a Juſtice by the Prieſt of that Pariſh (who had before taken out of his Fields what Corn he pleaſed) for 18 *s.* 2 *d.* pretended to be yet due for Tithe : The Juſtice granted a Warrant, by which the Officers took from him a Cow worth 3 *l.* 10 *s.*

*Several Impri-
ſonments.*

ANNO 1653. *Richard Farmer,* of *Twycrofs,* after the Pariſh Prieſt had ended his Sermon there, attempted to read a Paper of Chriſtian Exhortation to the People ; for which Office of Love he was committed to Priſon, and lay there till the next Aſſizes, where ſeveral of the principal Inhabitants certifying that he had not diſturbed them in their Worſhip, he was ſet at Liberty, without any Notice taken of the Injuſtice done him. In the ſame Year *William Simpſon,* for propoſing a Queſtion to the Prieſt of *Brampton,* after his Sermon, was ſent to the Houſe of Correction at *Leiceſter,* and detained there five Weeks. About the ſame Time *Grace Swan* and *Anne Juxon,* after the publick Worſhip was ended at *Leiceſter,* where the ſaid *Anne* would have read a Paper of Chriſtian Advice to the People, were both confined in the Town-hall ſome Hours, and then *Anne* was ſent to *Leiceſter* Goal, where ſhe lay about five Weeks in a very cold Winter.

ANNO 1654. In the Month of *September*, *William Dewſberry* was imprifoned at *Leiceſter*, but releaſed again the next Day. On the 24th of *December*, *John Whitehead* was alſo put into Prifon there, but difcharged two Days after. On the 25th of the fame, *John Carr* was committed to the Dungeon there, but fet at Liberty again at the next Seffions. The Imprifonment of theſe Men was merely arbitrary, no Breach of any Law being charged againſt them ; but their preaching to the People was very difpleafing to the eſtabliſhed Teachers of thoſe Times, who monopolized that Office, purely for the Sake of the Profits annexed to it by Law. About this Time alſo, *John Boyer* and *Thomas Cave*, having fpread ſome religious Books at *Leiceſter*, were imprifoned by the Mayor's Order : At the next Seffions they were difcharged : But though it appeared that the Mayor had taken away from them and others of their Friends about 500 Sheets of printed Books, they could not obtain the Reſtitution of them, nor any Recompence for that illegal Seizure of their Property.

ANNO 1656. *Edward Mugglefton*, after a Profecution in the * *Exchequer* for Tithes, was committed to Prifon at *Leiceſter*. While he lay there his Son was profecuted for the fame Tithe, though known to be but a Servant to his Father.

ANNO 1658. *Zachary Gilby*, of *Thiſtleton*, was imprifoned in *Oakham* Goal by an Attachment out of the *Exchequer* : He was confined there about ſixteen Weeks amongſt Felons in a cold naſty Place. *John Riddiſh* was alſo imprifoned there, on an Attachment, about the fame Time, for Tithe of ten Groats Value, he being a poor labouring Man, and having a Wife and five ſmall Children : The Woman in her Diſtrefs applied to the Prieſt his Profecutor to intercede for his Liberty, and took one of her little Children with her, judging that might be a Means to move his Compaffion : But the Prieſt, void of Pity, thruſt them out of Doors, and churliſhly told her, *She might get her Huſband out again how ſhe could.*

ANNO 1659. For refufing to pay the ufual Rates made for the Repairing of the Steeple-houfes, *Edward Mugglefton*, for a Demand of 6 s. 8 d. had Goods taken from him worth 1 l. 3 s. And *Thomas Orton* and his Son, for a Claim of 1 l. 0 s. 4 d. ſuffered Diſtrefs of Goods to the Value of 2 l. 13 s. 4 d.

Matthew Rudkin, becauſe his Confcience reſtrained him from taking an Oath, was fined, and had his Goods taken away to the Value of 1 l. 3 s. 6 d.

ANNO 1660. The Sufferings of this People in the prefent Year are well expreſſed in

" A Copy of a Letter written from *Leiceſter* Goal, dated the 20th of the Twelfth Month 1660.

" *Friends,*

" IT lieth upon us to give an Account of our Sufferings, we being in Num-
" ber twenty five, which are imprifoned becauſe we cannot Swear, we
" expecting that more will be brought to Prifon. We be under the Oppreffion
" of a cruel Goaler, who refufeth to let us have neceſſary Provifion brought to us,
" and one who is a Friend, which we have employed for that Purpoſe, when
" ſhe hath made Provifion ready for us, and brought it to the Door,
" the Goaler hath feveral Times turned it back with cruel threatning Words,
" ſaying, *He would break her Neck if he took her coming in at the Door.* And
" many of us, being very poor Men in the Outward, fcarce able to provide
" for our Families, when at Liberty, and ſome of us being fifteen or ſixteen
" Miles from our outward Beings, and ſo unable to buy ourſelves Provifions
" at the Goaler's exceffive Rates. Some of us have been imprifoned five
" Weeks : One, his Wife being near the Time of her Delivery of Child, his
Friends

---

* The Prieſt, who profecuted *Edward Mugglefton*, among other extravagant Charges, fwore that *Edward* ſtruck him, and that he durſt not go to gather his Dues for fear of him. In which he expoſed his Malice, and was believed by no Body.

" Friends defiring but a fhort Time for him to go and fpeak to his Wife, his Bro-
" ther offering to ftay in his Room the Time, was denied : Another was brought
" to Prifon from his Wife, fhe being delivered of a Child but two Days be-
" fore. And fome of our Friends, being brought to Prifon, had their Coats
" taken off their Backs by the Soldiers, and not reftored again : Another
" Friend's Wife being very weak, and not likely to continue long, fhe defiring
" much to fee her Hufband, who defired upon Security, fo much Liberty of
" the Goaler to go and fee her, but he denied it ; It lying much upon the
" Friend to go and fee his Wife in that Condition, he acquainted one of the
" Commiffioners with it, who fent his Warrant to the Goaler to fet the Friend
" at Liberty, and that fhould be his Difcharge, but the Goaler kept the
" Warrant and refufed to let him go, except he would pay him a Mark Fees.
" We are forced to hire Rooms at exceffive Rates, by reafon that we cannot
" have a free Prifon to hold us, fo as that we might lie down, there being
" fo many Debtors and Felons in it. Three of the Friends who are im-
" prifoned are *Northamptonfhire* Men : One, whofe Name is *William Vincent,*
" who had been imprifoned at *Northampton* near fourteen Months, it being
" but two Weeks after he was put out, but he was brought to Prifon here,
" he being a Man in much bodily Weaknefs, with many running Sores upon
" him, and by outward Appearance is not likely to continue long, his Wife
" alfo being in the Town, and bringing him fome warm Food, which fhe
" had provided for him, was turned back, and not fuffered to bring it him.
" Likewife the Goaler denies to let him have a Candle at his own Charge,
" whereby he might drefs his Sores, it being a dark Place, where he is lockt
" up by Daylight ; likewife not fuffering a few Boards, which were their own,
" to hold the Straw up, but did take them from them.

" Subfcribed by

Edward Mugglefton	*Robert Bakewell*	*Robert Day*
John Evatt	*William Perkins*	*Richard Farmer*
John Elliott	*Peter Hincks*	*Roger Sturgis*
Richard Read	*Samuel Ward*	*Thomas Falkner*
George Power	*Robert Cliffe*	*William Gregory*
Thomas Orton	*John Swann*	*William Horton*
William Smith	*William Vincent*	*William Tomfon.*
Thomas Marfhall	*William Line*	
Robert Pimm	*George Almon*	

ANNO 1661. *Richard Poole* was taken at a religious Meeting, and fent
to Prifon, where he lay feveral Months. On the 23d of *September* this Year,
Thomas Taylor, going towards *Swanington*, was met by a Company of Soldiers,
who paffing fimply by them, without pulling off his Hat, fome of them cried
out, *A Fanatick*, and rode after him, brought him back, kept him Prifoner
that Night, and next Day hurried him to and fro, till at length two Country
Juftices committed him to *Leicefter* Goal for refufing the Oath of Allegiance :
For which Caufe alfo *William Dracutt, Daniel Smith, Robert Day, Robert Cliffe,
John Doubleday, Nicholas Juxon, Humphry Woolrich, George Brown, Thomas
Palmer, Thomas Goodman,* and *James Smith*, were this Year committed to Pri-
fon. On the 4th of *November, Edward Mugglefton* the Elder, after two or

three Weeks Sicknefs, died a Prifoner, having been under clofe Confinement
about five Years. He laid down his Life in *fweet Peace with the Lord*, to the
Teftimony of whofe Truth he had been faithful and obedient.

On the 30th of *December*, *Roger Sturgis* and *Alice* his Wife, with four other
Friends, went to vifit *William Fellows*, then fick in Bed, and as they fat by
him, a Conftable, with Soldiers and others armed with Swords and Staves,
came in, dragged them out of the Houfe, kept them Prifoners all Night at

an Alehoufe, and next Day carried them feven Miles to a Juftice's Houfe, who, hearing the Cafe, that they were only vifiting the Sick, fet them at Liberty, except one Woman, whom he ordered the Officers to carry to the High Conftable : Three of her Friends went with her, and the High Conftable, whofe Name was *James Oliver*, fent them all to *Leicefter* Goal by a *Mittimus*, fo apparently illegal, and out of Form, that the Goaler refufed to receive them. Thus after much ill Ufage, and hurrying to and fro feveral Days, they were fet at Liberty. *Illegal Imprifonments.*

About this Time *John Boyer*, of *Leicefter*, for no other Caufe that he knew of, but that he did not pull off his Hat to the Earl of *Gray*, was beaten by one of his Servants with a great Cudgel about the Head, till he was very bloody, and then ftruck down among the Willows into the Water, and there left for dead. After fome Time, recovering a little, he got Home with much Difficulty, but from that Time quite loft his Eyefight, and fhortly died of the Bruifes he had received. *Cruel Beating of J. Boyer.* *His Death.*

ANNO 1662. In this Year *John Swann*, *William Smith* the Elder, *William Smith* the Younger, and *William Perkins*, were imprifoned in the County Goal at *Leicefter* for Tithes. In the fame Year *John Edinborough* and *Robert Day*, for 14 *d.* demanded for Steeple-houfe-Rates, had Goods taken from them worth 12 *s.* *Edward Marriott*, for the fame Caufe, alfo fuffered Diftrefs of his Goods. *Tithes and Steeple-houfe Rates.*

William Bramfton was imprifoned five Weeks for refufing to Swear, and for the fame Caufe was fined 5 *l.* *Imprifonment for not Swearing.*

In the Month called *Auguft*, at *Leicefter* Affizes, *Richard Church*, *George Barford*, *William Caunt*, *Richard Read*, and others, were fent to Prifon for refufing to Swear.

On the 2d of *September*, the Lord *Behmen*, alias *Swords*, having received Information of an intended Meeting at *Swanington*, came thither with armed Men, before the Meeting was begun ; and caufed nine Perfons there to be apprehended and fecured that Night, and next Day fent them to Goal by the following *Mittimus*, viz. *For Meeting.*

" *To the Keeper of his Majefty's Goal for the County of* Leicefter.

" **W**HEREAS upon Complaint made, that feveral *Quakers* and dif-
" affected Perfons were to meet at *Swanington*, at an unfeafonable
" Time, to the Difturbance of his Majefty's good Subjects, and contrary to
" an Act in that Cafe provided : Thefe are therefore to command you in
" his Majefty's Name to receive into your faid Goal, and there fafe to keep
" the Bodies of the Perfons underwritten, until fuch Time as they be thence
" delivered by due Courfe of Law. Hereof fail not at your utmoft Peril.
" Given under my Hand and Seal the 3d of *September* 1662. *Mittimus of 9 Perfons to Leicefter Goal.*

" **T. Swords.**

" *George Fox*   *Sufanna Frith*   *Edward Mugglefton*
" *William Smith*   *Joane Brockefby*   *Thomas Fowkes*
" *Margaret Bayly*   *Henry Walker*   *Joane Roe.*"

Upon this *Mittimus* they were kept in Prifon about a Month till the Seffions, when no fufficient Caufe appearing to juftify their Confinement, they were fet at Liberty.

At the fame Time alfo *Leonard Fell*, *Samuel Hooton*, and *William Sly*, were Prifoners in the fame Goal : Many others were taken out of their religious Meetings and committed to Prifon, viz. *Thomas Allen*, *John Allen*, *William Timfon*, *John Carter*, *John Warren*, *John Trefter*, *William Line*, *William Green*, *Samuel Wilfon*, *Obadiah Wilkins*, *Nicholas Pawley*, *Thomas Palmer*, *Joane Wilkins*, *Anne Line*, *Mary Wood*, *Anne Cane*, *Anne Smith*, and *Sarah Lea* : Some of thefe *Other Prifoners.*

LEICES-
TER-
SHIRE,
&c.
1662.

Imprifonment and Diftreffes.

were detained in Prifon feven Weeks, and others three Months. Several others, for their Conftancy in affembling together, were fined, and for Non-payment, both fuffered Imprifonment and Diftrefs of Goods, of which Number were,

	Fines.				Sums levied.		
	l.	*s.*	*d.*		*l.*	*s.*	*d.*
Samuel Hooton, who for	5	0	0	fuffered Diftrefs of Goods worth	11	0	0
William Marfhall,	3	6	8		6	0	0
Richard Leake,	3	6	8		6	10	0
Matthew Rudkin,	2	0	0		8	0	0
Nicholas Juxon,	3	6	8		4	0	0
Edward Mugglefton,	2	0	0		5	0	0
For	19	0	0	Taken	40	10	0

Imprifon-
ments.

Unhealthy
Confinement.

For refufing
to Swear.

Imprifonments
for feveral
Caufes.

Cruel Ufage.

John Shilcock, for Meeting, had a Cow taken from him worth 4*l.*

ANNO 1663. *Richard Jarvis*, a poor labouring Man, fuffered twelve Weeks Imprifonment for Tithes of fmall Value. And *Robert Day* of *Clawfon*, who had been in Prifon a confiderable Time, was this Year difcharged.

Elizabeth Doubleday, taken at a Meeting at *Silby*, was fent to Prifon at *Leicefter*, where fhe was confined among Felons in a very unhealthy Manner, feventeen Women being fhut up in one Room but four Yards long, and two Yards broad.

Thomas Saunderfon was fined for refufing to Swear, and had his Goods taken away to the Value of 1*l.* 10*s.* Alfo *Richard Church*, after five Weeks Imfonment for a Fine of five Marks for refufing to take an Oath, had two Cows taken from him worth 5*l.* 10*s.*

ANNO 1664. In this Year *Nathanael Newton*, *Henry Sidons*, *William Medcalf*, *Francis Allen*, *John Palmer*, *William Bodycoat*, and *William Sibly*, having been taken at a Meeting, were committed to Prifon. *John Evans*, of *Wigfton*, was alfo imprifoned for refufing to pay Tithes : He was cruelly ufed, being fometimes clofe fhut up in a filthy ftinking Dungeon, and at other Times in a Room over a Common *Jakes* or Houfe of Office. He continued in Prifon about eighteen Months.

ANNO 1666. Taken this Year by Diftrefs for Tithes,

Diftreffes for
Tithes.

			Demand.			Sums taken		
			l.	*s.*	*d.*	*l.*	*s.*	*d.*
From	Thomas Fellows,	for	1	12	0	Goods worth	12	0	0
	Roger Sturgis,		0	12	0		5	0	0
	Richard Church,		1	6	0		3	0	0
	For		3	10	0	Taken	20	0	0

Extent.

Other Suffer-
ings.

Exceffive
Spoil.

Long Imprifon-
ment for
Tithes.

The faid *Thomas Fellows* and *Roger Sturgis*, had alfo an Extent taken out to feize their Land, and were committed to Prifon, *Robert* being an infirm old Man, and almoft blind.

Francis Child, of *Harborough*, for being prefent at religious Meetings, was fined 20*l.* and fent to Prifon for Non-payment.

William Sly, *William Hooton*, *William Wells*, *Thomas Herrick*, *John Evans*, *Francis Brawton*, and *Samuel Pawley*, being taken at a Meeting and carried before a Juftice of the Peace, he tendred them the Oaths, and committed them to Prifon.

ANNO 1667. From *Edward Hallum*, of the Vale of *Bevoir*, the Claimers of Tithe took one Fifth of his Barley, and one Sixth of his Beans : From *John Doubleday* they took whole Fields of his Corn : And from *John Evans* twice as much as the Tithe came to.

William Smith, of *Croxton*, being fubpœna'd into the *Exchequer* for Tithes of 6*s.* Value, appeared there in Perfon, but not anfwering in Form by an Attorney, nor upon Oath, the Procefs went on, and at his Return Home he was taken from his Wife and feven Children, and committed to Prifon, where he lay above fix Years, to the exceeding great Oppreffion of himfelf and Family, he being poor. *Robert Day* was alfo imprifoned on an *Exchequer* Procefs for Tithes. *William Willows* and *Thomas Walker*, of *Rodly*, the Former for a Demand of 20*s.* and the Latter for 4*d.* for Tithes, were fubpœna'd into the *Exchequer*, where they perfonally appeared, but not anfwering upon Oath, were fent to Prifon for Contempt, as if they had not appeared. *Richard Gibfon* was alfo committed to Prifon, and detained there feveral Years, at the Suit of *Matthew Honeywood*, Dean of *Lincoln*.

On the 22d of the Month called *March*, a religious Meeting was held at *Syfon*, to which an Officer with Soldiers, and many rude People, came, and without any Warrant dragged the Affembly out of their Meeting-place. They took *William Horton* and fet him in the Stocks : After which they drew him, with his Head on the Ground, over a Stone Bridge, and then threw him into a Wheelbarrow, to the bruifing of his Body : Two Shepherds, whom they charged to affift them, refufed, faying, *They knew not but the Man might die by the Abufes given him, and that they might come into Trouble as acceffary to his Death.* After this they tied him on Horfeback, fome crying, *Throw him into the Mill-pond*, and others, *Stick a Knife in him.* As they were carrying him to Juftice *Babington's*, they were informed that he was not at Home, wherefore they brought their Prifoner tied on the Horfe to *Syfon* again, to an Alehoufe, where they laid him on the Floor, and made their Sport of him. At length they took him before Juftice *Patchin*, a Magiftrate of Clemency and Moderation, who ordered him, and the reft of his Friends informed againft, to appear at the next Monthly Meeting of the Juftices ; they accordingly appeared at the Time and Place appointed, but the Juftices were not there, only their Clerks, fo that no Procefs was made againft them. Neverthelefs Juftice *Babington* afterward fent for feveral of them, and fined fome of them 30 *s.* and others 40 *s.* for refufing to Swear.

ANNO 1668. On the 19th of the Month called *April, Matthew Whatoff, Thomas Burbridge, Richard Frank, William Pollard, John Whatoff,* and *William Fawkes*, taken at a Meeting, were fined five Marks each. In this Year alfo, *Patrick Levingfton*, a *Scotchman*, taken out of a Meeting at *Syfon*, was committed to the County Bridewell at *Leicefter* for fix Months. *John Wilford, Thomas Hanfon, Conftance Blanchly,* and *Anne Ford*, were taken at a Meeting in *Harby*, and committed to Prifon. *John Wilford* was again imprifoned fourteen Days for a Meeting at his Houfe : This was done by the Procurement of the Prieft of *Nether-Broughton*, who was heard to fay, that *Wilford* would foon be imprifoned the third *Time*, and then banifhed. And to a Perfon who afked him, *What muft become of the poor Man's Wife and Children ?* the hard-hearted Prieft replied, *Let them all perifh together.*

Michael Woodcock, of *Gilmourn*, was taken from his Wife and Children, and imprifoned upwards of three Years, though while he was in Prifon the Tithe-mongers took away his Corn off the Land in what Quantities they pleafed, from fome Fields half the Crop, and from others the Whole.

ANNO 1670. On the 25th of the Month called *January*, a Meeting was held for Church-Affairs, and to relieve the Neceffities of the Poor, at the Houfe of *John Penford* of *Kirby-Mucklow*. Thither came the Informers, and found them confulting together about Works of Charity. *John Penford* defired them to look into the Books of Account, then lying open, that fo they might not mifreprefent the Caufe of their Meeting. The Informers went and got a Warrant to bring *John Penford, William Wells, John Carr,* and *Richard Woodland*, before the Juftices at *Market-Bofworth.* They appeared accordingly, and were charged with being at a feditious Conventicle ; they defired that the Informers might give in their Depofitions in their Hearing, but the Juftices would not grant it ; for indeed they were fo partially difpofed, that one of them, the Lord *Beaumont*, told *John Penford*, whom he knew to have a confiderable Eftate, that *he would bring him to Poverty.* They fined *John Penford* 20*l.* for

LEICES-
TER-
SHIRE,
&c.
1670.

*Arbitrary
Proceedings.*

for his Houfe, and 10 *l.* for a Preacher though no Preacher was there ; they alfo fined feveral others 3 *l.* 6 *s.* 8 *d.* each, fo that the whole amounted to 50 *l.* *Penford* and *Woodland* appealed to the Quarter Seffions, and retained Council to plead their Caufe there : But fo arbitrary were the Juftices, that they refufed to try the Appeal, unlefs the Appellants would firft take the Oaths of Allegiance and Supremacy, which they refufing to do, the Court awarded treble Damages againft the Plaintiffs, as if they had been caft upon Trial, though it was apparent, that they had both Law and Equity on their Side.

*A moving
Cafe of* J.
Wilford, *a
poor Man.*

In this Year many were fined for their religious Meetings by the Conventicle Act, and had their Goods taken away by Diftrefs to the Amount of 107 *l.* 19 *s.* 4 *d.* Among thefe was *John Wilford,* who was fined 20 *l.* for Preaching. When the Officers came to feize what he had, for he was very poor, they heard his Children crying, *Father, will they take the Loaf ?* This moved them to Compaffion, infomuch that they trembled and wept, and departed for that Time : But fhortly after returned and took away his Cow, the only One he had, by which the poor Children were deprived of Milk, though not of Bread : In fhort, all the Goods he had being infufficient to fatisfy the Fine, the Officers made Return of the Warrant, declaring upon Oath, *that they had not left him worth any Thing.*

*Diftreffes for
Meetings.*

ANNIS 1671 and 1672. In thefe Years the Sufferings of this People, for their religious Affemblies, were general : And the Goods and Chattels which were taken from them by Diftrefs, in this County, for their Conftancy in this particular Point, amounted to 333 *l.* 13 *s.* 8 *d.*

*Releafe of
Prifoners.*
J. Penford
*imprifoned by
a Writ de
Excom. Cap.*

*Many impri-
fonments.*

In the Year 1672, *Laurence Farmer* and *William Chriftian,* then Prifoners in *Leicefter* Goal, were fet at Liberty by the King's Letters Patent. In the fame Year *John Penford,* of *Kirby,* for refufing to pay toward the Repairs of the Steeple-houfe, was excommunicated, and by a Writ *de Excommunicato capiendo* committed to Prifon, where he continued two Years.

ANNO 1674. On the 9th of the Month called *April,* Samuel *Wilfon* was fent to Prifon on a Writ *de Excommunicato capiendo,* at the Suit of *Jofiah Bond,* Vicar of *Mary's* Parifh in *Leicefter,* for 40 *s.* demanded for nine Years Tithe, though he occupied nothing titheable, but the Vicar pretended a cuftomary Claim upon the Houfe he dwelt in. In the latter Part of the fame Month, *Sarah Litherland,* a Widow, having fix fmall Children, was committed to Prifon on a Profecution in the Bifhop's Court, for 7 *s.* claimed for Tithes, at the Suit of *Robert Hill,* Vicar of *Whitwich.* In this Year alfo, *Thomas Dafh,* of *Hinckly,* Labourer, for refufing to pay fmall Tithes, was imprifoned on a Writ *de Excommunicato capiendo,* at the Suit of *George Naylor* Prieft. Likewife *Thomas Follows,* of *Whetftone,* Hufbandman, was committed to Prifon by the following *Mittimus,* viz.

" Leicefterfhire *fs.*

" *To the Keeper of his Majefty's Goal at* Leicefter *in the faid County.*

T. Follows's
Mittimus.

" WE fend you herewithal the Body of *Thomas Follows,* of *Whetftone*
" in the faid County, Hufbandman, for refufing to become bound
" with fufficient Sureties before us in Recognizance, to the Ufe of our Sove-
" reign Lord the King, to give due Obedience to the Procefs of the Judge
" of his Majefty's Ecclefiaftical Court of the Arch-Deaconry of *Leicefter,* in a
" Caufe of Subftraction of Tithes there commenced againft him by Mr. *Thomas*
" *Robinfon,* Clerk of *Enderby* and *Whetftone* aforefaid, requiring you to keep
" him in your faid Goal, without Bail or Mainprize, until he fhall become
" bound with fufficient Sureties to give due Obedience to the faid Procefs,
" according to the Statute in that Cafe made in the 27th Year of King *Henry*
" *the Eighth,* Cap. 20. And hereof you are not to fail. Given under our
" Hands and Seals the 27th of *February* 1674.

" THO. BEAUMONT.
" THO. STAVELY."

By like Warrants, granted by the Juftices upon *Significavits* out of the LEICES-
Eccléfiaftical Court, *John Marriott* and *William Parker* were imprifoned at the TER-
Suit of *John Ray* of *Long-Clawfon*, the Former of them for a Demand of 6 s. SHIRE,
and the Latter of 3 s. for one Year's Tithe. In this Year alfo, *Thomas Poole*, 1675.
of *Eventon*, was fent to Prifon for Tithes. Significavits.

ANNO 1675. In this Year a Book was publifhed, and prefented to the
King and Parliament, intitled, *The continued Cry of the Opprefled for Juftice*,
from which we have taken the following Certificate, *viz.*

"FOR a Meeting at *Long-Claxton* or *Clawfon*, four Perfons were fent to Cruel Perfe-
" Prifon, and fo much Goods at divers Times taken from fome of the cution at
" faid Meeting, that they had not a Cow left to give the young Children ton.
" Milk : Their very Bedclothes, working Tools, and wearing Clothes, efcaped
" not the Violence or Avarice of the Perfecutors ; the total Sum amounted
" to above 236 l. Nor did this fatisfy our Perfecutors, for they cruelly drag-
" ged fome Women in the Streets by the Necks, till they were near ftifled,
" tearing the Clothes off their Heads and Backs. One Woman that gave
" fuck was fo beaten and bruifed on her Breaft, that it feftered and broke,
" with which fhe hath endured many Weeks Mifery and Torture : Another
" Woman of feventy five Years of Age was violently thrown down upon the
" Ground by one *W. Guy* Conftable ; the Men were forely beaten, drawn and
" dragged out of the Meeting, fome by the Heels, fome by the Hair of the
" Head, and fome fo bruifed, that they were not able to follow their Day-
" Labour. Others they whipt in the Face till the Blood ran down. There
" was one they furioufly trod upon, till the Blood gufhed out of his
" Mouth and Nofe. To complete the Matter, the Informers took away from
" one of the Prifoners his Purfe and Money, as if he had not been a quiet
" Neighbour, but a Prifoner of War : Nor was this accidental, but Defign :
" No fhort Fit of Cruelty upon an extraordinary Provocation, for at this
" bitter Rate have they treated them for feveral Months.

Witneffes,	" EDWARD HALLUM
	" WILLIAM MARRIOTT
	" JOHN WILFORD
	" WILLIAM SMITH
	" RICHARD PARKER."

Hence the Reader may form a juft *Idea* of the violent Manner in which
the Informers ufually proceeded in breaking up and difperfing thofe Meetings,
the Particulars of which Abufes it would be fcarce poffible to enumerate.

ANNO 1676. In this Year *George Power*, of *Swanington*, was committed Imprifonments
to Prifon for fmall Tithes, at the Suit of *John Brintnal* Prieft : Alfo *William* for Tithes.
Timings, of *Sileby*, Shepherd, was fubpœna'd into the *Exchequer*, and afterward
imprifoned, at the Suit of *Richard Saunders* Impropriator.

ANNO 1679. In this Year, *John Smith*, a notorious Informer, who had Practices of
long followed that fcandalous Employment in *Nottinghamfhire*, to the Ruin of J. Smith an
many honeft Families there, removed into this County. His firft Attempt Informer.
was on the 22d of the Month called *June*, at a Meeting in the Houfe of
Edward Erbery of *Broughton*, where he found about fixteen Perfons fitting in
Silence : He uttered feveral provoking Expreffions on purpofe to induce one
or other of them to fay fomething, that he might have a Pretence to Swear
there was a Speaker ; but this ftale Policy of his failed him, for they all
continued filent. Upon this he, with his Companion, a Fellow who had been
in Goal for Felony, took the Names of fuch Perfons as the Conftable, who
was with them, knew ; and carried the Reft before Juftice *Cole*, who fined E. Erbery's
Edward Erbery for his Houfe 20 l. The Informer with Officers, having got Houfe broke
the Juftice's Warrant, broke open *Edward*'s Houfe, and took away his Houfe- open.

LEICES-
TER-
SHIRE,
&c.
1679.

*Apprehenfion
of* T. Pitftow
and others.

*Fine for not
aiding the
Officers.*

hold Goods, above the Value of the Fine, not leaving his Wife, an ancient ſickly Woman, ſo much as a Bed to lie on. The ſaid *Edward Erbery* was then in Priſon ; for he, with *Thomas Pitſtow* of *Southwark*, and *John Swan* of *Little-Pealting*, had been taken ſome Time before after a Meeting at *Brough-ton*, where *William Cotton*, Prieſt of that Place, apprehended *Thomas Pitſtow* under Pretence of his being a *Jeſuit*, and carried him before his Brother *Cotton*, a Juſtice of the Peace, who tendred the Oath of Allegiance to all three of them, and upon their Refuſal to take it ſent them to Priſon, where they lay near two Years after. It happened while the Informer and Officers were ſeizing *Edward*'s Goods, one *James Packer*, of *Dunton*, riding that Way, was by them charged to aſſiſt them, which he refuſed to do, wherefore upon their Complaint to the Juſtices he was fined 5 *l.*

On the 29th of the ſame Month, for a Meeting held at the Widow *Townſ-end*'s, in *Broughton*, upon the Information of the ſaid *John Smith*, by Warrant from Juſtice *Cole*, were taken

*Diſtreſſes for
Meeting.*

	l.	*s.*	*d.*
From the ſaid *Widow*, Houſehold Goods, and her Daughter's wearing Apparel, to the Value of }	23	0	0
William Brooks, Goods worth	00	19	0
Richard Bailey, ſeven Heifers worth	12	0	0
Sarah Hilton, Goods worth	4	0	0
	39	19	0

Nicholas Pawley, of *Whetſtone*, by the ſaid *Smith*'s Information, was fined 10 *l.* 5 *s.* for being at a Meeting on the 6th of the Month called *July.* Next Morning the ſaid Informer, with a Conſtable, took from him a Cow which they ſold for 20 *s.* they alſo employed Men to threſh out all the Corn and Peaſe the poor Man had, which they ſold for 10 *l.*

William Allen, of *Whetſtone*, was alſo fined 10 *l.* 5 *s.* through *Smith*'s Information, which a Kinſman, not of his Perſuaſion, paid.

Thomas Shenton, of *Coſby*, was fined for himſelf and his Wife 5 *l.* 10 *s.* for being at *Broughton* Meeting, and, by Warrant from the aforeſaid Juſtice *Cole*, the Officers took two Cows, and five Ewes and Lambs, which the Conſtable could not preſently ſell, wherefore the Juſtice fined him 5 *l.* for Neglect of his Office, which he was obliged to pay ; and then the Juſtice granted his Warrant to other Officers, who broke open *Shenton*'s Doors, and took all the Goods in his Houſe, and upon his Grounds : But ſome of his Neighbours, to prevent his Ruin, laid down the Money, and took Part of the Goods for their Satisfaction.

*Lord Beau-
mont's oppreſ-
ſive Order.*

John Evatt, a very poor Man, for a Meeting at his Houſe, was fined 10 *l.* 5 *s.* for which the Officers ſeized his Goods of little Worth : But the Lord *Beau-mont*, one of the Juſtices, commanded the Officers to ſell them if it were but for the thirtieth Part of their Value ; whereupon they ſold all they had taken for 7 *s.* *William Howett* was fined 5 *s.* for being at the ſame Meeting, and 10 *l.* for the Poverty of *Evatt*, for which his Goods were diſtrained, and ſome of them ſold : But the Informer complaining againſt the Pariſh Officers,

*Pariſh Officers
fined.*

viz. *John Bradſhaw* Churchwarden, *Henry Pim* Overſeer, *John Gettly* Third-burrow, and *Michael Pim* Conſtable, the Juſtice fined them 5 *l.* each for Neglect of their Office : But they afterward proving the *Informer*'s Complaint to be falſe, after much Trouble and Coſt, had their Fines remitted.

*Diſtreſſes for
Meetings.*

William Marſhall, of *Wimſwould*, for two Meetings at his Houſe, was fined 20 *l.* and had a Cow taken from him worth 2 *l.* 13 *s.* 4 *d.* which was ſold to *Smith* the Informer for 1 *l.* 6 *s.* 8 *d.* At the ſame Meeting, *John Fox* had Goods taken from him to the Value of 23 *l.* 15 *s.* his Houſe being broke open to come at them. Moſt of thoſe Goods were bought by *Smith* the Informer for 7 *l.* Wherefore, under a Pretence of a Deficiency, they returned and took away more to the Value of 30 *s.* From *Elizabeth Shepherd* they took an Hog worth

worth 10 *s*. Some of the Officers being unwilling to make thefe Diftreffes, the Informers got Warrants againſt them, directed to the High Conftables, who made Diftrefs of the Officers Goods, fo that they were forced to pay above 20 *l*. to have their Goods again : After which the Informer, *Smith*, caufed them to be fent to Goal, and to be bound over to the next Seffions to execute their Warrants : By fuch Means this impudent Informer, fupported by the Authority of the Juſtices, kept the Parifh-Officers in Fear of him, againſt whofe Oath it was difficult to defend themfelves.

ANNO 1680. On the 28th of the Month called *March, Smith* the Informer came to the Houſe of *John Evans*, of *Wigſton*, when the Meeting was difperfing, and feveral of the People gone, and no Preaching had been there : Neverthelefs Juſtice *Cole* fined *John Evans* 20 *l*. for which the Officers diftrained his Cows, and fold three of them. On the 4th of the next Month the faid *John Evans* was fined by the fame Juſtice 30 *s*. for being at a Meeting at *Knighton*. And for a Meeting at his own Houfe on the 11th of the fame Month, Juſtice *Beaumont* fined him 5 *l*. For thefe Fines the Officers made feveral Diftreffes, taking at one Time five Beafts and two Swine, and they were fold at *Leiceſter* ; at another Time they took twenty five Sheep out of his Field, and fold them ; and at a third Time they carried away two of his beft Horfes and fome Hay out of his Yard. Befide all which, for a Meeting at *Knighton* on the 13th of the Month called *June*, for Fines for himfelf and Family, and the Poverty of others, they took away two Cows worth 3 *l*.

Taken alfo for Meetings,

	l.	*s.*	*d.*
From *Francis Broughton* and *Samuel Pawley*, Goods worth	1	8	0
Richard Chamberlain, feven Beafts worth	12	0	0
John Vittal, five Beafts and a three Years old Colt worth	14	0	0
Samuel Wilfon, of *Leiceſter*, a Mare, two Cows, and an Heifer, worth	11	0	0
John Penford, of *Branſton-Gate*, three Cows worth	14	0	0
Godfrey Smith, of *Burton*, feven Beafts worth	20	0	0
Elizabeth Wale, *John Evans*, *Margaret Townfend*, *Richard Bayly*, and *William Brooks*, Goods worth	8	10	0
John Ward the Younger, of *Knighton*, a Copper and his working Tools to the Value of	20	0	0
Anne Wells Widow, four Mares, three Heifers, eight Cows, a Calf, feven Swine, feven Quarters of Malt, and fix Strike of Wheat, valued at	49	10	0
Richard Read, of *Syleby*, Bedding, Looms, and other Goods, worth	10	0	0
	160	8	0

From *Thomas Poole*, a poor Man, they took his Bed and other Goods worth about 7 *l*. In making which Diftrefs they took even the Cradles his Children lay in , they alfo took a Child out of the Bed and laid it on the Floor, and made the Bed a Part of their Spoil.

In this Year *John Penford* was again fined 20 *l*. for a Meeting held at his Houfe in *Kirby-Mucklow*, for fupplying the Neceffities of the Poor, and other Works of Charity. *John Dixon*, Prieft of the Parifh, hearing of the Meeting, informed *Wenlock Stanley*, of *Branſton*, thereof by Letter, who fent three of his Servants to be at the Meeting ; and though they heard neither Praying nor Preaching there, yet the Lord *Beaumont* and Juſtice *Roberts* fined *John Penford* not only for the Houfe, but alfo 10 *l*. for a Preacher, though no Preacher was there. He appealed again to the Quarter Seffions, but the Juſtices there refufed to hear his lawful Plea, and gave treble Damages againſt him.

There

LEICES-
TER-
SHIRE,
&c
1680.

Clofe Pri-
foners a long
Time.

Diftrefs and
Imprifonment.

Proceedings of
J. Smith *the*
Informer.

Barbarous
Actions at
Broughton
Meeting.

Invincible
Conftancy in
Meeting.

Oaths tendred.

There lay at this Time clofely imprifoned in *Leicefter* Goal, *Samuel Harper* of *Harborough, Daniel Fox* of *Thruffington, John Wilsford* of *Fenny-Stanton* in *Huntingtonfhire, Samuel Brown* of *Leicefter* Apothecary, *John Elliott* of *Nor-kilworth* Hufbandman, and *John Johnfon* of the fame Place Shepherd: The five laft mentioned had been Prifoners about four Years in *November* 1680, on Writs *de Excommunicato capiendo,* having been profecuted in the Ecclefiaftical Courts for not going to the publick Worfhip. For which Caufe alfo *Michael Woodcock, Elizabeth Hill, William Bromfton, John Stevenfon, Henry Brown, John Brooks,* and *William Webfter,* fuffered Imprifonment.

Richard Chamberlain, for frequenting religious Affemblies, had three Cows taken from him worth 10 *l.* And *Richard Bayley* fuffered about three Years and an Half Imprifonment for refufing to Swear.

ANNO 1681. On the 15th of the Month called *May,* the Informer *John Smith,* and his Servant, came to *Thorp* in the Parifh of *Broughton,* where a Meeting had been, but was over, and the Friends gone homeward before he came: He rode after them, and by Violence forced fome of them back again to an Alehoufe, and took their Names. Then he went to Juftice *Cole,* and informed of a Meeting which he had not feen; whereupon the Juftice fined *Thomas Follows* 10 *l.* 5 *s.* *William Brooks* 6 *l.* 10 *s.* and *Edward Erbery* 3 *l.* for which Diftreffes were forthwith made, by which they took from *W. Brooks* upwards of 15 *l.* They had a little before taken all *Edward Erbery's* Goods, but he having bought fome few Neceffaries fince that Seizure, they took them away to the Value of 3 *l.* 10 *s.*

In *November,* Endeavours were ufed by perfonal Cruelties, and barba-rous Treatment, to diffolve the Meeting at *Broughton.* The principal Agents therein were *William Cotton* Prieft of that Parifh, *William Read* Churchwarden, *Robert Bent* Overfeer, and *Richard Moore* Conftable: Thefe Parifh-Officers firft declared, *That they had a Warrant empowering them to break up the Meeting after what Manner they pleafed.* The Method they chofe, was to animate certain rude young Fellows to infult and abufe the Perfons affembled: Thefe Young-fters being afkt for their Warrant, anfwered *that they were fet on by the Parifh.* They rufht into the Meeting, laid violent Hands on the Perfons affembled, pluckt them out of the Meeting, and dragg'd them to and fro in the Dirt, the Officers ftanding by and reproaching the Sufferers, telling them, *they might have ftaid at Home.* On the 4th of *December,* thefe young Ruffians came early to the Meeting, pull'd down the Fire and threw it about the Houfe: Then they dragged out *Elizabeth Hill* through the Dirt, till fhe was almoft dead. Some of the Neighbours afking, *Whether they meant to kill the Woman?* They anfwered, *What care we, Mr.* Cotton *bid us.* When fhe feemed near expiring, one of them faid, *Let us fee if her Teeth be fet:* Another putting his Finger into her Mouth, and perceiving her to breathe, faid, *Let us at her again; the Devil is in her, and we will fqueeze him out.* Then one of them went to the Con-ftable, and returned, faying, *The Conftable bid them proceed, and if any took her Part, to ferve them in like Manner.* At length, leaving her for dead, they affaulted the Reft, flinging Dirt upon them, and tearing their Clothes: They fell violently upon *John Brooks,* dragg'd him backwards over an high Door-Cell, and tore his Clothes: They alfo dragg'd out *William Brooks* and others, throwing them one upon another, fo that the Spectators thought they would have murdered them. But all thefe horrid Abufes could not deter this People from the Performance of their Chriftian Duty. On the 11th of the fame Month they came again at their ufual Hour, but found the Door of the Meeting-houfe lockt, and the Gate nail'd up: Wherefore they met in the Yard, whither the Officers came, and took the Men into Cuftody, and furioufly dragg'd away the Women. Next Day *John Brooks* and *William Webfter* were carried before Juftice *Cotton,* the Prieft's Brother, and another Magiftrate, who tendred them the Oaths, and fent them to Prifon. By this Time moft of the Men be-longing to the Meeting being fhut up in Goal, the Women yet continued ftedfaft, and

CHAP. 23. *of the* People *called* QUAKERS. 341

LEICES-
TER-
SHIRE,
&c.
1680.

and being deprived of their Meeting-houſe, provided another to aſſemble in, being in the ſame Pariſh.

On the 18th of the ſame Month the Women met, *viz.* *Elizabeth Hilton,* *Jane Hilton, Anne Griffith, Alice Griffith, Elizabeth Hill,* and others, whoſe Sufferings at that Time are related by themſelves in the following Words, *viz.*

" Friends being come to the other Meeting-houſe, where they were per-
" mitted to go, and quickly theſe rude Youths came in again, and fell to
" drawing us and throwing us on Heaps on the Floor, then dragged out ſome
" by the Head and Heels, and went and fetch Dirt and rubbed on our
" Faces ; and the Prieſt's Man, whoſe Name is *Thomas Ambroſe,* came into
" the Houſe, and ſaid to the Youths, *Daub them ſoundly, for it is no Matter*
" *if they were all put into the Mill-Dam.* So the Youths going on with their
" cruel pulling and haling, while the Prieſt's Man was there, pulling of us
" by the Heads, as if they would have ſtrangled us, and by our Arms, as if
" they would have pulled our Joints aſunder. And thus they continued, (as
" Friends ſuppoſed) about half an Hour : And the Prieſt's Man ſaid, *His Maſter*
" *was one of the beſt Men in* England, *for if every one would ſerve them ſo, this*
" *Hereſy would be rooted out.* So when we were off from the Meeting-
" Ground, and in the Street coming homeward, one of the Youths fell to
" gathering up Dirt, and threw in the Face of *Elizabeth Hilton,* and took an
" Handful of Dirt, and following of her, caught her by the Hood, and
" holding her behind the Head with one Hand, crammed the Dirt in her
" Mouth with the other. So *Elizabeth* being near ſpent, and leaning on a
" Gate, he caught her by the Head and daubed her ſo, that her Life being
" in Danger, two Friends (as ſoon as they could get to her) came and led
" her towards an Houſe ; but before ſhe could get to the Houſe, the Youths
" came on again, and threw *Elizabeth Hilton* and *Elizabeth Hill* down in the
" Street, and ſaid, *That before they ſhould go into the Houſe they would ſpend*
" *their Blood.* And with much ſtriving *Elizabeth Hilton* got near the Door to
" go to an Houſe, but one of the Youths caught her by the Hood, and
" held her by the Hood till ſhe was near ſtrangled, and when his Hands
" were looſed, *Elizabeth Hilton* had a ſore Fall over the Door-Cell to her great
" Hurt; So the Neighbours came in, and they being affrighted, and Friends
" much ſpent by their barbarous Cruelties, the Conſtable was ſent for, but
" he came not ; but one of the Youths came in, and ſeeing how it was, ſaid,
" *I think ſhe is dying indeed, but if ſhe do, ſhe is fitter for the Devil.* Never-
" theleſs all neceſſary Means for her Recovery were uſed, yet ſhe lay at
" *Broughton* where ſhe had the Hurt, near three Weeks, before ſhe got Home,
" being near two Miles from the Place of her outward Abode, and then
" they brought her Home, though weak. There was but one young Man, a
" Friend, at this laſt Meeting, they having (before theſe Cruelties were acted)
" been by a wicked Informer, *John Smith,* very much ruinated by ſpoiling of
" their Goods, and ſince, (by the Inſtigation of this vile and wicked Prieſt
" *Cotton)* ſent moſt of our Men Friends to Priſon, and have now ſtruck at
" the Lives of thoſe that are left, by his wicked Agents.

" Before theſe Tranſactions were thus acted, *Thomas Ambroſe,* the Prieſt's
" Man, ſaid, *That nothing would drive them away, but either Fire or Water,*
" *and if the Houſe was his he would burn it on their Heads :* And ſaid to the
" Officers, *that* Elizabeth Hilton *would be put into the Well :* And they
" aſked, *Who ſhould do it ?* And he ſaid, *He would.*"

As the *Sufferings* inflicted on theſe innocent and religious Women were re-
markably cruel and unjuſt, ſo their Chriſtian Patience under ſuch barbarous
Uſage was the more conſpicuous, by which they were ſupported and enabled to
abide ſtedfaſt through ſo great a Torrent of Oppoſition.

ANNO 1682. On the 10th of the Month called *May,* for a Meeting at
the Houſe of *John Adams* in *Great-Bowden,* were taken,

				l.	*s.*	*d.*

*Sufferings for
Meeting.*

From   the faid *John Adams*, two Cows, two Heifers,
and fome Houfhold Goods, to the Value of } 22 11 0

Hannab Fifh, twenty nine Lambs, Hogs, a Waggon, two Calves, a Sow and Pigs, worth } 16 2 0

Francis Broughton, a poor Weaver, his Loom,
and Houfhold Goods, worth } 4 16 6

William Smith, Houfhold Goods to the Value of   10 10 8

————————
54 0 2

In the fame Year, for Meetings at *Leicefter*, were taken,
From   *Samuel Wilfon*, Goods worth above   10 0 0
Elizabeth Wall, almoft all fhe had, valued at   5 0 0
Samuel Brown, Goods worth   4 0 0
Richard Smith, his own and his Wife's Apparel,
their Childrens Bedding, and other Things,
to the Value of } 3 2 0

Thomas Poole, Goods worth   1 10 0
Thomas Hall, Money and Goods to the Value of   3 4 8
Sarah Davis, Goods worth   0 17 0

————————
27 13 8

*For being at
a Funeral.*

For being prefent at the Burial of the Wife of one
Edward Eafterton, the faid *Edward* himfelf was fined
5 *l.* 5 *s.* and had his Goods taken away to the Value of } 6 10 0

Thomas Pitftow, for preaching there, was convicted by
the Oaths of two Informers, who neither faw nor heard
him, and had his Doors broke open, and his Goods taken
away to the Value of } 9 0 0

Richard Crowley, for being at the fame Burial, had
Timber taken from him worth } 14 10 0

Thomas Marfhall, for being at the fame Funeral,   10 5 0
John Webfter, three Cows valued at   6 10 0

————————
46 15 0

*Falfe Infor-
mation.*

Richard Read, on a falfe Information of his being at the faid Burial, was
fined 10 *s.* though he was at that Time fick in Bed. Several alfo of the Neighbours, not *Quakers*, were fined for being at the fame Funeral, and paid their
Fines.

*Meeting at
the Houfe of
J. Fox.*

ANNO 1683. On the 15th of the Month called *July* was a Meeting at
the Houfe of *John Fox*, of *Wimfwould*, to which *Smith* the Informer came with
a Conftable and Headborough. The Informer coming in lockt the Door, and
took out the Key. Then they took down the Names of thofe that were met.
On the 23d, *Smith* brought a Warrant figned by *Richard Lifter*, of *Thorp-
Arnold*, a Juftice of the Peace, directed to the Conftable, Headborough,
Churchwardens, and Overfeers of *Wimfwould*, of the Execution of which they
gave the following Certificate :

*Certificate of
executing a
Warrant.*

" WHEREAS we the Officers of *Wimfwould* in the County of
" *Leicefter*, with *John Smith* of *Hoton* in the fame County, whofe
" Names are under-written, by Virtue of a Warrant to us directed from Juf-
" tice *Lifter* of *Thorp-Arnold* in the faid County, to levy 21 *l.* on the Goods
" and Chattels of *John Fox* of *Wimfwould* in the County aforefaid, we the faid
" Officers, with *John Smith* abovefaid, upon the 23d Day of *July* 1683, by
" Virtue of the faid Warrant did enter into the faid Houfe of *John Fox*, and
" other

" other Ground, and did make Seizure of all the Goods and Chattels of the
" faid *John Fox*, and did make Sale of the fame to *Jofeph Fox*, of *Wimfwould*
" aforefaid, for 21 *l*.   Which Sum of 21 *l*. we do acknowledge the receiving
" of, and do acquit him of the fame.   Witnefs our Hands,

" THOMAS WARNER, *Conftable.*
" THOMAS CONSTABLE, *Overfeer."*

The Juftice and the Informer in this Cafe, having received two Thirds of the *Divifion of* Money, would not truft the Overfeer with the Poor's Part, but ordered it to *the Poors* be paid to the Conftable, with a Charge for him to diftribute it among fuch *Part.* Poor as were of the National Church only, and that no Diffenters fhould partake of it : A Caution as to the *Quakers* unneceffary, for the pooreft of them would not have accepted any Part of the Gain of fuch Oppreffion.

On the 26th of the Month called *January*, *William Purdy*, of *Daulby*, for *Fines for* being at two Meetings, was fined 11 *l*.   10 *s*. by the faid Juftice *Lifter* upon *Meetings.* *Smith*'s Information, and had taken from him Goods to the Value of 50 *l*. but fold to a Neighbour upon Payment of the Fine for 11 *l*. 10 *s*. Alfo *Valentine Gregory* of *Statborn*, for being at a Meeting, had Goods taken from him worth 9 *l*. 18 *s*.

About the fame Time the faid *John Smith* came to a Meeting at *Claxton*, *More Profe-* and having charged the Conftables to keep the Doors, he took the Names of *cutions for* the Friends affembled, and about two Weeks after, by Warrants from Juftice *Meeting.* *Lifter*, made a Seizure of the Goods of *William Hawley*, *Thomas Doubleday*, *John Webfter*, *John Merriott* jun. *Richard Jarvis*, and *Henry Brown*, to the Value of 15 *l*. which the Officers paid into the Hands of Juftice *Lifter*.   At another Meeting at *Claxton*, about a Fortnight after the Former, *Smith* came again and took Names, and procured a Warrant, by which Diftreffes were made on the Goods of *Edward Merriott*, *William Doubleday*, *John Webfter*, and *William Parker*, to the Value of 4 *l*.

The Informers, *Smith*, and another whofe Name was *Warner*, were exceed- *Informations* ing bold, and would fometimes make Informations upon mere Conjectures, *on Conjecture.* which being given in upon Oath, were efteemed by the Juftices a fufficient Ground for Conviction.   A remarkable Inftance of this Kind happened in the Cafe of *Jofeph Holt* and *Auguftin Allen*, both of *Rutlandfhire*, who, on the 13th of the Month called *February* 1683, being feen by the Informers in a Yard near the Houfe of *William Chapman* in *Somerby*, where a Meeting was fometimes held, they at all Adventures made Information to Juftice *Lifter* of the faid Perfons being at a Meeting.   The Juftice, as forward to convict as *Forward Con-* the others to inform, accepted their Evidence, and laid a Fine of 6 *l*. on *victions of* *Jofeph Holt*, and 5 *l*. 10 *s*. on *Auguftin Allen*, and becaufe they dwelt in another *fome Juftices.* County, the Juftice fent a Certificate of their Conviction to Sir *Edward Noel* of *Whitwell* in that County ; and the faid *Auguftin Allen* had four Cows taken by Diftrefs worth 9 *l*. which his Wife, not of his Perfuafion, redeemed by paying his Fine ; though indeed the Perfons had not been at the Meeting for which they were convicted.

About the fame Time, *Smith* meeting *John Richards* on the Highway, fuppofed him to be coming from a Meeting ; and went to Juftice *Lifter* and pofitively fwore what he only imagined.   The Juftice prefently granted his Warrant againft *Richards* as lawfully convicted before him of being that Day at a Conventicle at *William Chapman*'s Houfe ; which, though true, *Smith*, who fwore it, did not know.   Upon this Conviction *Richards* had four Cows taken from him worth 14 *l*.

ANNO 1684.   On the 22d of the Month called *June*, *John Fox* was again *Repeated Dif-* fined 20 *l*. 10 *s*. for fuffering a Meeting at his Houfe, upon *Smith*'s Informa- *treffes on J.* tion, who on the 24th at four in the Morning, while the faid *John Fox* was *Fox.* in Bed, came with Officers and fearched the Yard and Outhoufes, but finding little

*Fines for a
silent Meet-
ing.*

*A Meeting-
house plun-
der'd.*

*Other Dis-
tresses.*

*Wicked Beha-
viour of
Smith the In-
former.*

*More Spoil on
the Goods of
J. Fox.*

*Goods sold to
the Informer
much under
Value.*

*Information
against T.
Penford and
others for
Meeting.*

little there, urged the Officers to break open the House, which they were unwilling to do, but to pacify the Informer promised to pay the Fine. On the
last Day of the same Month the Officers came again and entred the House,
and carried away in two Carts, Goods to the Value of 20 *l.* but sold them for
10 *l.* *Edward Belton, William White, Elizabeth Shepherd,* and *Mary Marshall,*
were convicted, and fined for being at the same Meeting.

On the 8th of the Month called *July,* the Mayor of *Leicester,* and two
other Justices, came to the Meeting there, which was held in Silence: They
caused the Persons assembled to be taken out of the Place, and fined *Mary
Wood* 20 *l.* for the House, *Elizabeth Wall* 10 *s.* *Richard Smith* for his Wife 10 *s.*
and *Thomas Aslin* for his Wife 5 *s.*

On the 28th of *September, Smith* came to a Quarterly Meeting, and took
Names, and made Information, upon which *Mary Wood, Elizabeth Wall,* and
John Penford, were fined; and in consequence of these and the former Fines,
the Officers shortly after took all the Forms and a Bedstead out of the Meeting-
house; and from the said *Mary Wood* her Bedding, Bedsted, and other Things,
leaving her nothing to lie on, nor scarce to sit on. From *Elizabeth Wall,
Richard Smith, Thomas Aslin, John Penford,* and *Richard Crowly,* they took
Goods and Apparel worth 11 *l.* 1 *s.* And from *Samuel Brown,* for himself and
his Wife being at Meetings, Goods to the Value of upwards of 15 *l.* *Thomas
Marshall* was also fined 4 *l.* for being at the same Meetings.

On the 16th of *November,* Information was again made of a Meeting at
John Fox's House, and Justice *Lister* again fined him 20 *l.* And on the 2d
of *December,* the Informers, *Smith* and *Warner,* came to *Fox*'s House. *Smith*
tarried there till *Warner* fetcht the Officers: *John Fox* desiring to see the Warrant, *Smith* let him read it, which he did, till he came to a Clause mentioning
more than five Persons beside the Family, which *Fox* said was not true.
Then *Smith* snatcht the Warrant out of his Hand, kicking him, and calling
him *Son of a Whore:* Such rugged Behaviour was usual with that Kind of Men.
Warner soon returned with the Officers, and a Cart and Horse, and *Thomas
Stubbs,* a Carpenter, whom they employed to take down the Bedsteds, while
the Informers and Officers loaded away the other Goods. So they left very
little of any Value, except the Bed which his Wife lay sick on. They took
away even their Meat and Drink, and the Casks their Beer was in. They also
took the Matting that was nail'd to the Floor, and a Bench that was fastned
to the House: They pickt up a Copper which was fastned in a Furnace, and
carried it away. They also took away a Cow and Hay out of his Yard. The
Value of the Goods taken at this Time was about 14 *l.* 3 *s.*

On the 29th of the same Month, *Smith* and *Warner* having heard that the
poor Man had in the mean Time got some Bedding again, and other Necef-
saries into his House for his Family, some of whom, for want of Beds, had been
obliged to lodge elsewhere; they came again with Officers, and *Smith,* to
shew his Authority, threatned the Officers, *that if they left any Thing in the
House worth a Penny, he would make it cost them 5 l. a Man;* upon which they
swept away all they could find. They continued ransacking the House till
about eight in the Evening, when, the Weather being very cold, the said *John
Fox* and his whole Family, *viz.* his Wife, four small Children, the eldest not four
Years old, and two Maid-Servants, were constrained to lodge at other Houses,
having neither Bed nor Bedclothes left, by which they and the Children contracted much Cold. The Goods taken at that Time were valued at 8 *l.* 11 *s.* 3 *d.*
but sold to *Warner* the Informer for 2 *l.* 2 *s.* 6 *d.*

Mary Marshall, a poor ancient Woman, for being at a Meeting in the said
John Fox's House, had fourteen Pounds of Linen Yarn and her Bedclothes taken
from her, to the Value of 1 *l.* 12 *s.*

On the 23d of *December, Smith* and *Warner* gave Information to *Thomas
Ludlam,* Mayor of *Leicester,* against *Thomas Penford,* whom the Mayor fined
10 *l.* for the Poverty of the Owner of the Meeting-house, and 10 *s.* for his
own being there, for which the Officers seized seven Quarters of Wheat worth
about

about 17 *l*. 10 *s*. *Samuel Watſon* for himſelf and Wife being at the ſame Meeting, had taken from him Wheat worth 9 *l*. And *John Evans*, for a Meeting at his Houſe in *Wigſton*, was fined 20 *l*. and had an hundred and thirty Sheep taken from him valued at 30 *l*.

For a Meeting at the Houſe of *Dorothy Evatt*, were taken

	l.	*s.*	*d.*
From the ſaid *Dorothy*, Goods worth	0	18	0
Thomas Glover, Goods worth	5	0	0
Richard Newcomb, of *Caſtle-Dunningſon*, all his Goods, not a Bed, Diſh, nor Spoon, left, but he, his Wife, and Children, were obliged to lodge at a Neighbour's Houſe	30	0	0
Iſaac Giſburne, of *Kegworth*, Goods worth	6	0	0
	41	18	0

*More Fines
for Meeting.*

The ſaid *Iſaac* was fined 15 *l*. upon a falſe Information, for Preaching, but not having Goods enough to ſatisfy that Fine, the Officers gave the Informers Money out of their Pockets.

William Launder, of *Long-Hoton*, had Goods taken away, and among other Things his Loom, wherewith he, being a Weaver, wrought for the Support of himſelf, and his aged Mother, to the Value of 5 *l*. *George Beriſford*, of *Lockington*, had working Tools and other Goods taken from him to the Value of 10 *s*. 6 *d*. *William Hewett* alſo had his Goods ſold for a Fine of 3 *l*. 10 *s*. but they proving too little, the Officers agreed with the Informers as well as they could. *Edward Hallum*, of *Hoſe*, had Goods taken from him to the Value of 20 *l*. 10 *s*.

*Working Tools
diſtrained.*

ANNO 1685. In this Year our Accounts make mention of thirty three Perſons remaining Priſoners at *Leiceſter*, viz.

*33 Priſoners
at Leiceſter.*

1. On Writs *de Excommunicato capiendo*, thirteen, namely.

Thomas Daſh, who had been Priſoner above eleven Years ; *Richard Bayley*, about ſix Years ; *William Bramſton* and *John Stevenſon*, about three Years ; *John Johnſon*, *John Elliott*, and *Daniel Fox*, about eight Years. *Elizabeth Hill*, about five Years. Alſo *Benjamin Smart*, *Richard Chamberlain*, *John Vital*, *William Smith*, and *Michael Woodcock*.

*Long Impriſon-
ments.*

2. For Abſence from the National Worſhip, two, namely, *Richard Sharp* and *John Webſter*.

3. For refuſing to Swear, eighteen, namely,

Thomas Pitſtow, *Edward Erbery*, and *John Swann*, who had continued Priſoners about ſix Years. Alſo *Thomas Corby*, *Margaret Burton*, *Jane Ireland*, *Anne Clark*, *Hannah Smith*, *William Smith*, *Francis Child*, *Samuel Heyrick*, *William Sibley*, *Judah Carter*, *Thomas Mackerneſs*, *Mary Ward*, *Mary Webb*, *Thomas Underwood*, and *John Warren* ; who had been ſent to Priſon by an Order of Seſſions.

ANNO 1686. The before-mentioned Priſoners were generally ſet at Liberty upon the Proclamation iſſued by King *James the Second* for a free Pardon. Their religious Aſſemblies were held with leſs Interruption, and Informations againſt them diſcouraged. *Smith*, the old Informer, was curbed in his Attempts by the King's Direction, as appears by the following Letter, directed

*Diſcharge of
Priſoners.*

" *To the Right Honourable the Earl of* Huntington, *one of his*
   " *Majeſty's moſt Honourable Privy Council, Chief Recorder*
   " *of* Leiceſter, Cuſtos Rotulorum *of the County of* Leiceſter.

" M Y L O R D, *Whitehall, Dec.* 7. 1686.

" T H E King being informed that *John Smith*, a common Informer,
   " doth very vexatiouſly proſecute the *Quakers* in the County of *Lei-*
   " *ceſter*, and in the Town and County of *Nottingham*, and his Majeſty being

*Duke of New-
caſtle's Let-
ter.*

" pleafed to extend his Favour to thofe of that Perfuafion, his Majefty would
" have your Grace direct the Juftices of Peace to give no Sort of Countenance
" to the faid *John Smith*, and his Profecution againft the *Quakers*. MY LORD,
" I am for his Grace the Duke of *Newcaftle*, one of his Majefty's moft Honour-
" able Privy Council, *&c.*

" *Your Grace's moft faithful humble Servant,*

" SUNDERLAND, P."

Upon this Difcouragement which the Juftices were directed to give the Informers, and fuch as made a Trade of Preying on confcientious Subjects, the
Perfecution in this County abated : Wherefore we take our Leave of *Leicefterfhire*, and proceed to *Lincolnfhire*.

C H A P. XXIV.

L I N C O L N S H I R E.

A N N O 1654.

*Firft Sufferer
E. Hooton.*

THE firft Sufferer among this People in this County was *Elizabeth
Hooton*, who for bearing her Teftimony to the Truth in the Place of
publick Worfhip at *Beckingham* was imprifoned five Months.

*Sufferings for
feveral Caufes.*

ANNO 1655. The faid *Elizabeth Hooton* was again imprifoned twelve
Weeks for exhorting the People to Repentance : Which *William Teff* alfo attempting to do in the Steeple-houfe at *Raifon*, was dragged out thence by the
Head and Feet. In this Year alfo, *Edmund Woolfey*, being chofen Conftable,
and refufing to take the ufual Oath to qualify for that Office, was fined 5 *l.*
And in the fame Year, *John Pidd*, of *Beckingham*, for refufing to pay Tithe,
fuffered ten Weeks Imprifonment.

*Imprifonment
of T. Brom-
ley for not
Swearing.

His Death in
Prifon.*

ANNO 1657. *Thomas Bromley*, fummoned to ferve on a Jury, and refufing to Swear, was fined 4 *s.* and fuffered Diftrefs of his Goods to the Value
of 8 *s.* He was afterward imprifoned in *Lincoln* Caftle, at the Suit of the
Prieft of *Fillingham*, where, after four Months, he died, being old and infirm,
and fometimes wanting Neceffaries. The Woman, who kept the Goal, pitying
his Age and Poverty, gave him Leave now and then to go into the Town to
earn fomewhat toward his Support ; but for her Lenity, *Ralph Hollingworth*, his
Profecutor, petitioned the Judge to have her fined. He laid down his Head
in Peace, as a faithful Witnefs againft the Antichriftian Oppreffion of Tithes.
John Harvey, of *Spalding*, fined 10 *s.* for refufing to Swear, had his Goods
taken away to the Value of 21 *s.*

*Perfecution of
W. Willows
and T. Ed-
wards for not
Swearing.

Cloth taken
away.*

William Willows and *Thomas Edwards*, becaufe they could not take an Oath,
were refufed their Freedom of *Bofton* Corporation, to which they had a Right,
and *William Willows* was fo exceffively fined by the Mayor for opening his
Shop, that he was obliged to remove his Habitation.

William Wallace, a *Scotchman*, ftanding to fell Cloth in *Bofton* Market, had
fome of his Goods taken away by the Mayor's Order, under Pretence that he
had no Right to fell any there, but in Reality for being a *Quaker*, fince that
Privilege was not denied to other *Foreigners*.

*For not taking
off his Hat.*

George Reeve, of *Spalding*, being fummoned to the Quarter Seffions, appeared
there with his Hat on, for which he was fent to the Houfe of Correction as
a Difturber of the Peace.

Edmund

Edmund Woolfey, riding through *Boston* to a Meeting, was fined for travelling on the *Sabbath*, and had his Mare taken from him by the Mayor's Order. He was shortly after committed to *Lincoln* Goal, at the Suit of *Francis Ball*, an Impropriator, or Farmer of Tithes : After about a Year's Imprisonment he died : A faithful and conscientious Man, and acknowledged to be so even by his Prosecutor, who said, *He believed* Edmund *would have paid him his Tithe, had he thought them his Right.*

ANNO 1658. *Arnold Trueblood* was committed to *Lincoln* Goal for Tithes, and after many Weeks Confinement died there.

In the same Year *John Pidd*, of *Beckingham*, was again imprisoned six Months : Also *John Seele*, of *Liverton*, a poor Labourer, was committed to Prison for a small Demand for Tithes : And *Robert Anglesaw*, for a Claim of 4*l.* was imprisoned till an Acquaintance of his paid the Prosecutor 9*l.* 16*s.* Also *Richard Pidd* and *Joseph Stokes* were detained several Weeks in *Lincoln* Castle for Tithes, till discharged by Order of a Committee of Parliament.

Hezekiah Croft, of *Egle*, for a Demand of 6*l.* 13*s.* 4*d.* for Tithes, was imprisoned seventeen Weeks, and after his Release thence, had his Cattle taken away to the Value of 40*l.* Also *John Wressel, James Hutchenson*, and *John Johnson*, were kept in Prison till some of their Relations, for Demands of 1*l.* 15*s.* 10*d.* for Tithes, paid their Prosecutors 6*l.* 10*s.*

Edward Edwards, of *Ancots* on the Isle of *Axholme*, was prosecuted for Tithes to an Execution, when, to prevent the Seizure of his Bed and Goods, his Mother paid the Prosecutor 20*l.*

John Whitehead, Robert Fowler, and *George Reeve*, for uttering some Christian Exhortation to the People assembled in their Place of Worship at *Boston*, were clapt up in Prison, and the said *George Reeve* had Irons put upon him as if he were a Felon, and was kept in that Manner in a cold Place in Winter. *William Teff*, for reproving some People in the Street at *Market-Raison* for their Swearing and Prophaneness, was barbarously used, and both he and his Wife were beaten and stoned out of the Town. Also *Edmund Woolfey*, for publickly testifying against their Use of vain Sports and Gaming, was by the rude People at *Heapham* sorely beaten and abused, and had much of his Blood spilt.

ANNO 1659. *Robert Whitman*, of *Dunnington*, and *Vincent Frotheringham*, and his Son, were imprisoned for Tithes in the Castle at *Lincoln*. *Richard Parnell*, of *Epworth*, for 3*d.* ½*d.* demanded by the Priest for Smoke-penny, had taken from him about *Midsummer* this Year, Goods worth 13*s.* Several others in this and the two preceding Years, for Demands of 1*l.* 17*s.* 2*d.* for Steeple-house Rates, had Goods taken from them to the Value of 7*l.* 0*s.* 4*d.*

ANNO 1660. In the Month called *April, William Teff, Edward Willey*, and *John Capes*, were committed to Prison for Tithes. And *Thomas Hampsted*, of *Wightstone*, for a Demand of 1*l.* 19*s.* for Tithes, had his Goods taken away to the Value of 10*l.* *Robert Parker*, for a Claim of 2*l.* 15*s.* Goods worth 10*l.* 3*s.* 4*d.* and *James Watson*, for 7*l.* Goods to the Value of 21*l.* In the same Year *Alexander Cheesman, Robert Peckover, Thomas Graves, William Berrier*, and *George Reeve*, for Demands of 4*l.* 13*s.* 6*d.* for Tithes, had Goods taken from them to the Amount of 9*l.* 3*s.* Also *William Phillips*, for the same Cause suffered Distress of Goods to the Value of 5*l.* 5*s.* And *Richard Robinson* had three Sheep and two Lambs taken away for a Claim of 11*s.* for Tithes.

On the 8th of the Month called *May, John Smith* and *Robert Harrison*, both of *Sixhill*, being cited to appear before the Justices for not paying toward the Repairs of the Steeple-house, and appearing with their Hats on, the Cause for which they were summoned was let drop, and the Justices sent them to Goal for a pretended Contempt of Authority in standing covered before them.

ANNO 1661. *Thomas Richardson* was committed to the County Goal on an Attachment out of the *Exchequer* for Tithes.

On

LINCOLN-SHIRE. 1657.

Death of E. Woolfey *in Prison. His Character.*

Death of A. Trueblood.

Other Imprisonments for Tithes.

Prosecutions for Tithes.

G. Reeve *iron'd.*

Cruel Usage.

Prosecutions for several Causes.

Imprisonment and Distresses for Tithes,

and for Steeple-house Rates.

Pretended Contempt.

Imprisonment of T. Richardson.

On the 13th of *November* this Year, *John Whitehead*, taken at the Houſe of *Humphry God* at *Binbrough*, was by the Juſtices ſent Priſoner to *Lincoln* Caſtle, where he lay three Months.

*Imprisonment
of J. White-
head.*
ANNO 1662. *John Whitehead* was again committed to Priſon by the following *Mittimus*, viz.

*Second Impri-
sonment of
J. White-
head.*
" *To the Keeper of his Majeſty's Goal at the Caſtle of* Lincoln,
" *or to his Deputy or Deputies there.*

" Lincoln-Lindſey.

His Mittimus.
" **F**ORASMUCH as *John Whitehead*, of *Owſwick* in the County of *York*,
" was, upon Complaint brought before us this Day, by Warrant, for uphold-
" ing private Meetings, contrary to an Act of Parliament made and provided;
" and being tendred the Oath of Allegiance by us, being two of his Majeſty's
" Juſtices of the Peace for the ſaid Parts and County, according to the Sta-
" tute in that Caſe made and provided, did refuſe to take the ſaid Oath.
" Theſe are therefore in the King's Majeſty's Name to charge and command
" you, immediately upon Receipt hereof, to receive him the ſaid *John White-
" head* into your ſaid Goal, and him there ſafely keep without Bail or Main-
" prize until the next general Goal-Delivery, to be holden at the ſaid Caſtle
" of *Lincoln*, for the ſaid County : And hereof you are not to fail, as you
" will anſwer the Contrary at your Perils. Given under our Hands and Seals
" this 9th Day of *July*, in the fourteenth Year of his Majeſty's Reign, *Annoq*;
" *Dom.* 1662.

" **MARTIN LISTER,**
" **JOHN BOSWELL.**"

*Commitments
of many for
not Swearing.*
About the ſame Time *William Morris*, *William Bancroft*, and *John Cleaſby*, were committed to the ſame Priſon for refuſing to Swear. At the Aſſizes on the 19th of the Month called *July*, they were ordered to remain in Priſon till the next Quarter Seſſions ; but the Juſtices releaſed *William Bancroft* ſooner, in Compaſſion to his old Age and Infirmities ; *William Morris* was alſo diſcharged at a petty Seſſions intervening. At the Quarter Seſſions on the 7th of *October*, *John Whitehead* and *John Cleaſby* were indicted for refuſing the Oath of Allegiance, fined 5 *l.* each, and recommitted till Payment. On the 14th of *December*, *Vincent Barrow*, *John Thetting*, *Thomas Torkſey*, *Robert Kelſey*, *Peter Moody*, *Thomas Barrow*, *Charles Tate*, *John Clark*, *William Clark*, *Richard Parnell*, *John Spicer*, and *Thomas Halifax*, were taken at a Meeting, and for refuſing to Swear, committed to Priſon. At a general Seſſions on the 15th of the next Month they were fined 30 *s.* each, and ſet at Liberty.

*Many other
Imprisonments.*
On the 5th of *October*, *Samuel Davy*, *Henry Wilſon*, *Gregory Sherwin*, *William Carnall*, *John Thompſon*, *Stephen Willoughby*, *George Reeve*, *John May*, *Suſan Thomas* , *Margaret Smith*, *Rebecca Preſton*, and *Ellen Wilſon*, were committed to *Spalding* Priſon, but after five Days were all ſet at Liberty, except *Samuel Davy*, to whom the Juſtices tendred the Oath of Allegiance, and upon his Refuſal to take it ſent him to *Lincoln* Caſtle, where he continued Priſoner about twenty two Weeks. On the 12th of the ſame Month, *Thomas Summers*, *Chriſtopher Clark*, *John Scotney*, *Edward Fiſher*, *John Sandby*, and *Thomas Mathers*, were apprehended at a religious Meeting, and committed to *Spalding* Priſon, where they continued about a Quarter of a Year.

At a Seſſions held at *Caſtor* on the 14th of the Month called *January*, *Thomas Markham*, *Robert Rockhill*, *William Williamſon*, *John Rockhill*, and *Thomas Benſon*, were fined 20 *s.* each, having been taken at a Meeting, and detained in the Cuſtody of the Conſtable till that Seſſions. About the 5th of the next Month, *James Taylor*, *Thomas Norton*, and *Robert Walker*, three poor

Men,

Men, were committed to *Lincoln* Caftle for Tithes. And at the Affizes on the
19th of the Month called *March*, *John Cleafby*, after eight Months Imprifonment, for refuſing to Swear, was ſet at Liberty.

ANNO 1663. At a Quarter Seffions on the 28th of the Month called
April, *John Whitehead*, after more than nine Months Imprifonment for refuſing
to take an Oath, was difcharged by the Juftices, upon the Interceffion of
Captain *Fofter*, a compaffionate Man, and one who bore fome Authority under
the Earl of *Lindſey*. During his Imprifonment, *John Titman*, *Edward Tifdale*,
and *George Billers*, were committed to the fame Goal, and lay there three
Months, for abfenting themſelves from the publick Worſhip.

*Difcharge of
J. White-
head.*

On the 22d of *December*, *Charles Howett*, of *Grantham*, Baker, after a
Profecution in the Ecclefiaftical Court for not coming to his Parifh Church,
and not hearing Divine Service there, was Excommunicated, and by a Writ
de Excommunicato capiendo committed to *Lincoln* Caftle.

*Imprifonment
on a Writ* de
Excom. Cap.

ANNO 1664. *Robert Boguly*, of *Croyland*, profecuted for Abfence from
the publick Worſhip, was committed to Prifon by a Writ *de Excommunicato
capiendo* on the 30th of the Month called *May*. And by a like Writ, for the
fame Cauſe, *William Hayworthingham*, of *Somercotes*, was alfo fent to Goal on
the 25th of the Month called *Auguſt* in the fame Year ; and about the fame
Time *William Brown*, of *Croyland*, and *William Parnell*, of *Epworth*.

*Imprifonments
on Writs* de
Excom. Cap.

ANNO 1665. On the 28th of the Month called *March*, *Roger Williams*,
of *Lincoln*, Sadler, and on the 10th of *September*, *William Berrier*, *Robert
Scott*, *John Afhton*, and *William Powton* ; and on the 27th of *December*,
William Anthony, of *Wefton*, Hufbandman, were committed to Prifon on Writs
de Excommunicato capiendo, in Confequence of Profecutions in the Spiritual
Courts for Non-Attendance at the publick Worſhip.

ANNO 1666. In the Month called *July*, *Robert Richardfon* was imprifoned in *Lincoln* Goal by the Sheriff's Warrant, upon an Attachment out of
the *Exchequer* on a Profecution there for Tithes.

*On Attach-
ment.*

ANNO 1667. In *September*, *William Clark* and *Robert Freeman*, and in
the Month called *January*, *William Garland*, of *Gainſborough*, having been
profecuted in the *Exchequer* for Tithes, were committed to Prifon by Attachments out of that Court.

*Exchequer
Profecutions.*

In this Year, for refuſing to take an Oath when tendred them at a Court-Leet,

	l.	*s.*	*d.*	
Thomas Parnell ſuffered Diftrefs of Goods worth	8	0	0	*Diftreffes for
not Swearing.*
William Maffey of *Sutton*, to the Value of	2	3	0	
John Morley of *Adlin-Fleet*, to the Value of	1	3	0	
	11	6	0	

Alfo *Chriftopher Wilfon*, of *Adlin-Fleet*, had fix Bufhels of Barley taken from
him for the fame Cauſe.

ANNO 1668. *Vincent Frotheringham*, of *Hykeham*, was committed to
Prifon in the Month called *January*, on an Attachment out of the *Exchequer*
for Tithes. And about this Time *Joseph Pope*, of *Irby*, after he had ſuffered
Diftrefs of Corn, Wool, Sheep, Hogs, Hay, and other Things, to the Value
of 18*l.* 12*s.* 10*d.* for Tithes claimed by *John Harnefs*, Prieft of that Parifh,
was by the Prieft's Influence on the Bayliff of the Town, and his Application
to the Steward of the Lady *Hollis*, and their Mifreprefentations to her, turned
out of his Farm.

*Profecutions
for Tithes.*

ANNO 1669. On the 19th of the Month called *Auguft*, *George Craggs*,
Prieft of *Anderby*, with three Servants, came to *William Cliff*, of that Town,
as he was lading his Corn, and demanded Tithes, which, becaufe *William* refufed to give him, the Prieft ordered his Servants to ftrike the faid *William*
and *Katharine* his Wife, ſaying, *They are excommunicated Perfons, and if you
knock them on the Head, there is no Law againft you : I will be your Warrant :
The Way is clear.* This Prieft called himself a *Proteftant*, but was eager to

*Unufual Bar-
barity of the
Prieft of* An-
derby *in abu-
fing a Man and
his Wife.*

LINCOLN-
SHIRE.
1669.

*throwing her
down, so that
she miscarried.*

*After which
he imprisoned
the Man.*

*Death of
that Priest,
and Remarks,
thereon.*

Exchequer
Prosecutions.

*Distresses for
Meetings.*

put in Practice the worst Part of *Popery :* His Servants not anfwering his Purpofe, he himfelf ftruck the faid *Katharine* with a Fork, and her Hufband defiring him to forbear and not abufe his Wife, who was then with Child, the
Prieft enraged took up another Fork, and pufht her violently on the Body
feveral Times, and threw her down ; he alfo faid to his Servants in his Fury,
Fetch my Sword, I will be revenged of them. In fhort, the poor Woman was
forely affrighted, much hurt and bruifed, fo that fhe foon after mifcarried of
two Children, one of which had plain Marks of the Blows received, and fhe
her felf was in great Danger of her Life. Within a few Days after this Barbarity to the Woman and her unborn Babes, the Prieft alfo caft her Hufband
into Prifon by a Writ *de Excommunicato capiendo,* by that Means burying the
Man alive, whom he could not excite his Servants to kill. It happened
within a few Weeks after that the Prieft himfelf alfo died : Upon whofe Death,
obferving People made fuch Reflections as naturally did rife from the recent
Notice they had taken of the Man's *Imprifonment,* the *Injury* done to his Wife,
and the *Death* of her two Children, as aforefaid.

In this Year alfo, *Samuel Trouting, Robert Smith, John Potter,* and *Robert
Atkinfon,* were imprifoned by Attachments on Profecutions in the Court of
Exchequer for Tithes.

ANNO 1670. On the 5th of the Month called *June, Thomas Richardfon,*
of *Mumby-Chapel,* for a Meeting at his Houfe, fuffered Diftrefs of Goods to
the Value of 29 *l.* 6 *s.* 8 *d.* Alfo *William Pidd, John Betts, George Waters,
John Waters, Thomas Atkin,* and *Thomas Swafh,* for being at the fame Meeting, had Goods taken from them worth 3 *l.* 18 *s.* 10 *d.* In the fame Year the
faid *John Waters,* for a Meeting held at his Houfe, had Goods taken from
him worth 29 *l.* And from *Thomas Richardfon* and *William Cliff,* for being at
that Meeting, Goods were taken worth 18 *s.*

For Meetings at *Gedney* in *Holland,* Goods were taken

	l.	*s.*	*d.*
From *Robert Binks,* for a Meeting at his Houfe, to the Value of	20	0	0
Nathanael Gregg, for a Meeting at his Houfe	15	0	0
Richard Kitton, for his * Wife	1	4	0
Nathanael Gregg, Thomas Johnfon, Thomas Sowter, Richard Wilfon, George Reeve, and *Henry Wilfon*	5	11	1
Edward Tifdell, for a Meeting at his Houfe	13	10	0
Alice Prefton, James Fiddill, and *Stephen Willoughby*	2	14	0
George Sherwin and *William Clark*	1	18	0
Ralph Anthony, of *Wefton,* for a Meeting at his Houfe	12	0	0
John Scotney, for being at that Meeting	2	9	0
John Titimus, of *Moulton,* for a Meeting at his Houfe	5	14	0
Samuel Waters, Thomas Mathers, and *John Speck*	2	7	0
	82	7	1

*Sudden Death
of a persecu-
ting Priest,
and of an In-
former.*

A bufy Informer at this Time, named *John Hunleby,* was warned by one
Lancelot Marfhall of the Judgments of God upon Perfecutors, and put in Mind
of the fudden Death of one *William Carter,* Prieft of *Honington,* a Promoter
of Perfecution there, and very active in caufing Diftreffes to be made, who, as
he was coming from the High Conftable's Houfe, was ftruck with Sicknefs,
and foon after found dead in his Bed, unknown to the People where he lodged.
Hunleby took this Friendly Monition amifs, and was very angry, and threatned the Friends at the Meeting where it was given, warning them to appear
before the Juftice next Morning. But fo it happened that *Hunleby* was fuddenly

---

* The Informers fwore fhe was at a Meeting when fhe was ten Miles diftant.

denly ſtruck with a mortal Diſeaſe that Night, ſo that he died a lingering
Death; and his own Siſter reported, *that ſhe never ſaw any Perſon die ſo ſtrangely.*

	l.	*s.*	*d.*
Taken from * *Thomas Everett*, of *Honington*, for Meetings at his Houſe, Goods worth	40	0	0
John Peachel, of *Carleton*, to the Value of	14	18	0
Charles Howett, Henry Howett, Chriſtopher Smith, John Killingley, and *John Richardſon*	2	11	4
Joſeph and *Benjamin Roper*, Goods worth	1	0	0
† *Thomas Summers* and *John Wilkinſon*	3	11	0
	62	0	4

	l.	*s.*	*d.*
Taken from *Richard Pidd*, of *Beckingham*, for Meetings at his Houſe, Goods worth	17	3	6
Richard Burdett, William Burdett, and *Mary Parker*	2	12	4
John Green, George Lucas, and *John Trueblood*	2	17	0
	22	12	10

For Meetings in the Iſle of *Axholme*, and at *Gainſborough*, and Places adjacent, were taken

	l.	*s.*	*d.*
From *John Urry*, Goods to the Value of	18	0	0
Chriſtopher Edwards	33	10	0
John Pilſworth and *Richard Parnel*	1	16	9
William Edlington, Alice Tate, and *John Clark*	9	1	0
Robert Everett, Peter Naylor, and *Thomas Taylor*	4	16	4
Adam Foſter, George Boulder, and *Thomas Tee*	6	8	0
Thomas Peele and *Henry Simpſon*	14	10	0
Henry Garland	37	3	0
	125	5	1

Taken alſo for other Meetings,

	l.	*s.*	*d.*
From *John Walcott*, of *Helperingham*, Goods worth	2	0	0
John Pidd, Henry Carlton, Mary Sharp, John Mower, and *Margery Carnell*	2	10	0
	4	10	0

There had been taken, ſome Time before, for abſenting themſelves from the National Worſhip,

	l.	*s.*	*d.*
From *Henry Wilſon*, of *Gedney*, for himſelf and Wife	2	13	4
Robert Aſhton, Richard Pitman, and *Thomas Birks*	3	18	0
	6	11	4

ANNO 1671.   On the 25th of the Month called *July*, for a Meeting at the Houſe of *John Willoughby*, of *Wigtoft*, on a pretended Information of a
Preacher's

---

* Several Perſons, who had purchaſed ſome of *Thomas Everett*'s Goods, were ſo troubled in Mind that they could not reſt till they had reſtored them to the Owner.
† The ſaid *Thomas Summers*, for telling the Perſons who made the Diſtreſs, that they did not act according to Law when they took Goods, which he told them were not his, was proſecuted at the Quarter Seſſions, and committed to Priſon.

*Diftreffes on
flender Infor-
mation.*

Preacher's being there, of which the only Evidence was, that one of the Informers heard a Man fay, *Lord* ; Goods were taken by Diftrefs

	l.	*s.*	*d.*
From *William Dixon* and *William Barrows,* to the Value of	13	10	0
Robert Whiteman, John Fotherby, and *William Sawyer*	5	7	6
Judith Birks, John Willoughby, and *Richard Patman*	10	18	0
Mary Mitchell, William Bladefmith, and *William Birks*	8	13	0
Taken alfo from *Robert Grimball,* Goods worth	10	0	0

	48	8	6

*Imprifonments
for Tithes.*

ANNO 1672. In *September, Robert Reader,* of *Garthorp,* was committed to Prifon for Tithes, at the Suit of *Robert Barnard* Impropriator : In the Month called *January, William Bladefmith,* of *Swinefhead,* was alfo imprifoned for Tithes at the Suit of *John Newton :* And in the fame Year *Henry Wilfon,* of *Gedney,* was committed on a Common-Pleas Writ, at the Suit of *Peregrine Moore* Prieft : Alfo *John Potter* and *William Garland* were fhut up in *Lincoln* Caftle by an *Exchequer* Procefs for Tithes, at the Suit of *John Coop* a Prieft.

*Diftreffes for
not Swearing.*

Thomas Scott and *Robert Afhton,* of *Crowle,* for refufing to take an Oath, when fummoned on a Jury, were fined, the Former 40*s.* and the Latter 5*l.* and had taken from them, the Former an Horfe worth 6*l.* and the Latter Goods to the Value of 7*l.* 10*s.*

*Releafe of
Prifoners.*

In this Year King *Charles the Second* iffued his Letters Patent for difcharging out of Prifon the *Quakers* then confined at the King's Suit, by which *Ralph Harbottle, John Williamfon, Charles Howett, Richard Parnel, William Hagworthingham, Roger Williams, William Cliff, William Phillips,* and *John Bayley,* were releafed from their Imprifonment in *Lincoln* Caftle.

*Sundry Profe-
cutions.*

ANNO 1673. In the Month called *May, Chriftopher Edwards, Thomas Halifax* and *John Robinfon,* all of *Epworth,* and *Richard Parnel,* of *Haxfey,* for refufing to pay *Eafter-Offerings,* were fent to Prifon at the Suit of *James Gardiner* a Prieft. *Thomas Parnel* had taken from him, for Tithes, an Horfe, a Colt, four Cows, and two Steers worth 20*l.* at the Profecution of *William Dorner,* Prieft of *Willingham.* Alfo *Robert Grimboll,* for the fame Caufe, had four Steers taken away worth 10*l.*

Thomas Scott was this Year again fummoned on a Jury, and for refufing to Swear, again fined 5*l.* for which Goods were taken from him to the Value of 10*l.* *Thomas Pickance* and *Thomas Humphry* had alfo their Goods taken by Diftrefs for refufing to Swear ; and *Thomas Waddington,* becaufe he would not take the Oath of a Churchwarden, was excommunicated.

*Imprifonments
for Tithes.*

ANNO 1674. On the 15th of the Month called *May, Robert Reader* was imprifoned for Tithes, at the Suit of *Robert Barnard.* In the fame Month *William Edlington,* of *Crofland* in the Ifle of *Haxfey,* and in the Month called *July* following, *Robert Berrier,* of *Crowle,* were committed to *Lincoln* Caftle, by Writs *de Excommunicato capiendo,* at the Suit of *Edward Coggin* and *Thomas Poynter* Impropriators.

*Imprifonments
for trivial
Claims for
Tithes.*

On the 17th of the Month called *June, Chriftopher Edwards, John Robinfon,* and *Thomas Halifax,* after above a Year's Confinement at *Lincoln,* were carried up to *London,* and there committed to the *Fleet* Prifon, at the Suit of *James Gardiner* Prieft of *Epworth,* whofe Demand on all three of them did not amount to more than four Shillings. On the 3d of the Month called *Auguft, Thomas Wrefsle* was fent to Prifon by an Attachment out of the *Exchequer,* and in *September, James Dixon,* of *Crowle,* was brought Prifoner to *Lincoln* Caftle by a Writ *de Excommunicato capiendo,* at the Suit of *Solomon Afhburn* Prieft ; as was alfo *Thomas Everett* by the fame Writ. On the 8th of *October, John Clark,* of *Garthorp, Matthew Ganmore,* and *Joane Marfhall,* of *Ludington,* Widow, were imprifoned for not paying *Eafter-Offerings,* at the Suit of *Thomas Pinder* Prieft. Taken alfo about this Time from *Edward Cheefman,* for Tithes, Goods worth 16*l.* 19*s.* 8*d.* at the Suit of *Robert Barnard*

*Eafter-Of-
ferings and
Tithes,* &c.

Barnard Impropriator : And from *Thomas Everett*, by *John Towne* Impropriator of *Sudbrook*, Goods to the Value of 10 *l.*

Taken alfo this Year, for refufing to pay Steeple-houfe Rates, from *William Molls*, *Samuel Trotting*, and *Herbert Ingram*, for 12 *s.* demanded, Goods worth 1 *l.* 9 *s.* And from *Chriftopher Bavin* Goods worth 2 *s.* 8 *d.*

Taken likewife for Abfence from the National Worfhip,

		l.	*s.*	*d.*	
From	*Richard Burdett*, *James Roper*, and *John Killingley*, Goods worth	5	19	6	*Diftreffes for Abfence from the National Worfhip.*
	John Richardfon, *William Maffey*, and *Daniel Brittain*	8	0	0	
		13	19	6	

George Waters, for attending religious Meetings, fuffered Diftrefs of Goods to the Value of 23 *l.* And *Thomas Richardfon* and *William Pidd* to the Value of 1 *l.* 4 *s.*

ANNO 1675. For a Meeting at the Houfe of *Alice Bunbee*, of *Potter-Hanworth*, Widow, were taken by Diftrefs,

	l.	*s.*	*d.*	
From the faid Widow *Bunbee*, Cattle worth	20	0	0	*Diftreffes for Meeting.*
Peter Bunbee and *Nicholas Johnfon*, to the Value of	8	0	0	
	28	0	0	

Abraham Morris, of *Lincoln*, Mercer, for being at the fame Meeting, was fined 10 *l.* for a Preacher, and 5 *l.* for himfelf, for which they took Stuff out of his Shop which coft him 19 *l.* 7 *s.* 8 *d.* He appealed to the Quarter Seffions, but got no Relief.

In this Year *Thomas Everett*, for not paying Tithes, had four Draught-Bullocks taken from him worth 20 *l.* And *John Baldock*, of *Wainfleet*, for refufing to pay toward the Repairing of the Steeple-houfe, was committed to Prifon on a Writ *de Excommunicato capiendo*. *For Tithes and Eafter-Offerings.*

ANNO 1676. On the 26th of the Month called *March*, *Katharine Cliff* was committed to Prifon for Tithe, at the Suit of *John Owberry*, Prieft of *Anderby*. On the 8th of the Month called *June*, *Thomas Brown* was fent to Prifon for Tithes, at the Suit of *John Hackley*, Prieft of *Partney*; and on the 5th of the Month called July, *James Watkins* and *John Watkins*, of *Wadington*, were imprifoned at *Lincoln* on a Writ of Rebellion for not paying Tithes, at the Suit of *John Barnard* their Parifh Prieft. *Imprifonments for Tithes.*

In this and the preceding Year, feveral Perfons in this County had Corn taken out of their Fields to the Value of 17 *l.* 7 *s.* 6 *d.*

ANNO 1677. About this Time *William Brown* and *Robert Man*, both of *Belton*, were committed to *Lincoln* Caftle, at the Suit of the Churchwardens, fo called, on a Writ de *Excommunicato capiendo*. *Thomas Everett* had his Hay taken by one *Wharton*, Prieft of *Carlton*, to the Value of 3 *l.* and from feveral others was Corn taken to the Amount of 13 *l.* 0 *s.* 8 *d.*

ANNO 1678. On the 10th of the Month called *Auguft*, *Alice Bellows*, of *Lincoln*, was committed to the Caftle there, at the Suit of *John Thomas*, Prieft of *Wapload*. And on the 22d of *November*, *Thomas Robinfon*, of *Brant-Brough-ton*, and *Samuel Hall*, were fent to the fame Prifon at the Suit of *John Chapple* Prieft. The faid *Thomas Robinfon* had alfo his Cattle taken by Execution to the Value of 15 *l.* 15 *s.* In this and the preceding Year, Corn was taken from *Thomas Everett* to the Value of 17 *l.* 10 *s.* And in this Year feveral other Perfons had alfo their Corn taken away to the Amount of 17 *l.* 3 *s.* 1 *d.* Taken alfo for Demands of 1 *l.* 15 *s.* 5 *d.* ½ *d.* for Steeple-houfe Rates, from feveral Perfons, Sheep, Hogs, and other Things, worth 8 *l.* Alfo *Thomas Parnel*, for refufing to pay the Parifh Clerk's Wages, had an Horfe taken from him worth 2 *l.* 19 *s.* *Imprifonments, Execution and Diftreffes for Tithes and other Caufes.*

LINCOLN-SHIRE.
1678.

From *Thomas Robinson*, of *Brant-Broughton*, for being at a Meeting at *Beckingham* on the 24th of the First Month 1677-8, were taken four fat Bullocks worth 34*l.* 10*s.* by Warrant from *Christopher Nevil*, of *Harmston*, a Justice of the Peace. And by another Warrant from the same Justice, for a Fine of 40*l.* for another Meeting at the same Place, on the 31st of the First Month 1678, he had taken from him eighteen of his best young Sheep, one Pair of Steers, four Draught-Bullocks, and four fat Bullocks, worth 44*l.* 11*s.* The four fat Bullocks were sold by *Thomas Kelsey* the Constable to *John Cupp* a Butcher, who hearing on what Account they were taken, declined his Bargain. Then all the ten Steers and Bullocks were drove to *Grantham* Market, but no Body would buy them; thence they were driven to *Sleeford*, where one *Parker* bought the four fat Bullocks for 27*l.* but when he understood that they had been taken by the Act, he also threw up his Bargain. Then they drove the Beasts to *Lincoln*, but could find no Chapman, for the People looking on them as the Spoil of Conscience, would not buy them. At length the Constable drove them all to Sir *Christopher Nevil* the Justice, by whose Warrant they had been taken, but he, after keeping them fourteen Days, and finding no Purchaser, and being unwilling to take them himself, restored them to the right Owner, on Consideration that the same or others of like Value would probably be upon the Land at any Time: For he, though willing to execute the Law according to his Office, was of a more generous Disposition than to seek Advantage to himself by the Loss of his Neighbours. The eighteen Sheep worth about 14*l.* were sold privately out of the Market to a poor Man of *Grantham* for 10*l.* 7*s.* The chief Promoter of this Prosecution was *John Chapple*, Priest of *Brant-Broughton*, who perceiving the Constable not forward in making Distresses, and breaking up Meetings, sent him a menacing Letter, *viz.*

" *Brant-Broughton, April* 9th, 1678.

Priests Letter to a Constable.

" THOMAS KELSEY,

" I CANNOT but wonder that any King's Officer should be so back-
" ward in executing the King's Laws, as I find you to be: Methinks you
" should have gone to Sir *Christopher Nevil*, had you had no other Inducement
" thereto save only Civility to Sir *Francis Fane*, who desired you so to do:
" You cannot now, as you did then, pretend the Want of an Horse. I have
" sent my Man on purpose to join with you in giving Information to the
" Justices concerning the late Conventicle held at *Broughton*, and if you refuse
" to act, I have ordered my Man to make his Complaint to the Bench. If
" your Landlord, Mr. *Pierpoint*, be informed how you and others have be-
" haved your selves in this Business, I know that he will not thank you for
" your Remisness; for whatever his Tenants at *Broughton* may be, sure I am,
" he is a Person more zealous for the Church. No more at present, from

" *Your Friend,*

" JOHN CHAPPLE."

Priests excite Justices to prosecute.

By such Means as this the Parish Officers were sometimes prompted to act against their own Inclinations, the Priests exciting the Justices to punish by Fines and Imprisonment for Neglect of Duty such of them whose Christian Moderation made them unwilling to prosecute their conscientious Neighbours.

Tithes.

ANNO 1679. In this Year sundry Persons had Corn taken out of their Grounds for Tithe to the Value of 169*l.* 13*s.* 5*d.*

On the 13th of the Month called *August*, *William Brown*, of the Isle of *Haxsey*, was carried Prisoner to the Castle at *Lincoln*, at the Suit of *Robert Barnard* Tithe-farmer. On the 16th of *September*, *Thomas Cutforth*, of *Epworth*, was committed to the same Prison, at the Suit of *Richard Horrin*, Priest of *Haxsey*. On the 19th of *November*, *William Smith*, of *Fishtoft*, was also sent to the same Goal, at the Suit of *Joseph Tridell* Tithe-farmer, and on the 27th of of the Month called *January*, *Robert Killingley* was committed thither at the Suit of *Michael Mitchel*, Prieſt of *Pinchbeck*.

Taken this Year, for not paying Steeple-houſe Rates, from *Euſtace More-croft*, and others at *Sepſey*, Goods worth 4 *l.* 16 *s.* 2 *d.*

At the Aſſizes at *Lincoln*, in the Month called *April* this Year, *Thomas Swaſh* was convicted on the Statute of 20 *l.* per Month for one Month's Abſence from the National Worſhip. And *Thomas Billing* was proſecuted on the ſame Statute, and committed to *Lincoln* Caſtle.

ANNO 1680. In the Month called *May*, *John Hopkins*, of *Weſton*, and *Jonah Titimus*, of *Marton*, for not paying the Repairs of the Steeple-houſe there, were impriſoned by Writs *de Excommunicato capiendo*. And on the 18th of the next Month, *Robert Aſhton*, *Robert Berrier*, *James Dixon*, and *Francis Brown*, all of the Pariſh of *Crowle* in the Iſle of *Haxſey*, were committed to *Lincoln* Caſtle for refuſing to pay ſeveral Sums demanded of them for Wages of the Pariſh-Clerk, and were continued Priſoners there till the next Aſſizes. In this Year alſo *John Ayſtrope* was Priſoner in this County on a Writ *de Excommunicato capiendo*.

ANNO 1681. Taken, for Tithe of Corn and Pulſe, out of their Fields from ſeveral Perſons in this County, to the Value of 88 *l.* 4 *s.*

ANNO 1682. In *November* was a Meeting at a Place called St. *Martin*'s belonging to the Town of *Stamford*; to which came an Informer, named *Hankins*, of *Market-Deeping*, and another Perſon whom he had hired to aſſiſt him. Theſe brought with them ſome Pariſh-Officers, and without producing any Warrant carried thoſe that were met before a Juſtice, and made Oath, that *William Collington*, of *Stamford*, preached in that Meeting, when indeed he had not, but the Meeting was held throughout in Silence : However the Juſtice certified the Mayor of *Stamford* according to the Information ſworn before him, whereupon the Goods of the ſaid *William Collington* were ſeized to the Value of 20 *l.*

John Whitehead was committed to Priſon at *Lincoln* on the 22d of the third Month 1682, for preaching at an Aſſembly at the Houſe of *Thomas Sowtor*'s in *Sutton* : At the Aſſizes on the 31ſt of the Fifth Month then next following, the Oath of Allegiance was tendred him by the Judge, and he recommitted till the next Aſſizes, which was on the 5th of the Month called *March* 1682-3, at which he was indicted, and committed to Priſon again under Sentence of Premunire.

Taken this Year from ſundry Perſons, for Tithe of Corn and other Things, out of the Fields, to the Value of 76 *l.* 12 *s.*

ANNO 1683. In this Year the Amount of Corn, Pulſe, &c. taken out of the Field from ſeveral Perſons in this County, was 42 *l.* 17 *s.* 4 *d.*

Taken from *William Hobman*, of *Phiſerton*, for 7 *s.* 4 *d.* demanded for repairing the Steeple-houſe there, Goods worth 2 *l.* 1 *s.* 6 *d.*

Jane Redſmith, a poor Widow, for a Meeting at her Houſe in *Stamford*, had all her Goods taken from her to the Value of — 10 *l.* 0 *s.* 0 *d.*

	l.	*s.*	*d.*
Taken alſo from *William Collington* and *Elizabeth Moll*, for being at the ſame Meeting, Goods worth	0	15	0
Taken by Diſtreſs, for a Meeting at the Houſe of *Francis Brown*, of *Crowle*, a Mare, two Cows with Calves, ten Quarters of Malt, and other Corn, to the Value of	16	15	2
	27	10	2

Taken alſo for Abſence from the National Worſhip, from *William Brown*, *Jane Davis*, *Edward Cheeſman*, and *John Pilſworth*, Goods worth 2 *l.* 0 *s.* 6 *d.* And from *Joſeph Medly*, *William Aſhby*, *William Yates*, and *John Eldridge*, to the Value of 1 *l.* 13 *s.* 6 *d.*

Thomas Heads, of *Thurlby*, had his Goods ſeized ſeveral Times for frequenting religious Meetings : At length for a Meeting at his Houſe on the 24th of the

LINCOLN-
SHIRE.
1683.
the Month called *June*, the Officers took all the Houſhold Goods he had left, worth about 30 *s.* and ſo exceedingly rigid were they in the Seizure, that they pulled the Bedclothes away from under his Wife then lying in with Child. They came ſeveral Times after to ſearch for more Goods, but finding none, went their Way diſſatisfied, muttering to themſelves the old Proverb, *Where nothing is to be had, the King muſt loſe his Right.* Taken alſo for Meetings at ſeveral Times, from *Joſeph Lee*, of *Boven*, Goods worth 1 *l.* 18 *s.* 6 *d.* From *John Milner*, of *South-Witham*, a Cow, Sheep, and other Things, to the Value of 7 *l.* 10 *s.* And from *William Rant*, of *Swineſhead*, ſeven Beaſts worth 14 *l.*

For Tithes.   ANNO 1684. Taken this Year, for Tithe, out of the Fields from ſeveral Perſons, Corn, Pulſe, &c. to the Value of 51 *l.* 0 *s.* 6 *d.*

On the 19th of the Month called *April*, *Samuel Everett*, *William Brown*, *Robert Killingley*, *Thomas Wreſsle*, and *Thomas Robinſon*, were Priſoners in *Lincoln* Caſtle for not paying Tithes ; alſo *John Baldock*, *James Dixon*, *Edward Cheeſman*, *John Ayſtrope*, *Robert Everett*, and *William Turner*, impriſoned on Writs *de Excommunicato capiendo*, for refuſing to pay Tithes and Steeple-houſe Rates : And *Thomas Atkins*, *Polyxena Hicks*, *Thomas Stubs*, *Edward Hairby*, *Richard Page*, and *Daniel Page*, who having been taken at their religious Meetings, were ſent to Priſon by an Order of Seſſions. *John Toobit* was at the ſame Time a Priſoner on the Statute of 20 *l.* per Month for 100 *l.* for five Months Abſence from the National Worſhip.

For Sunday
*ſhillings, ſo
called.*   In this Year alſo, for Weekly Fines of 1 *s.* called *Sunday* Shillings, impoſed for Abſence from the *Pariſh-Church*, were taken from *Thomas Heads*, *John Milner*, *John Simſon*, *Robert Parkinſon*, and *Elizabeth Sugden*, Goods and Apparel worth 4 *l.* 9 *s.* 6 *d.* This *Elizabeth Sugden* was a poor Servant, from whom they took her beſt Clothes worth 16 *s.*

*Eccleſiaſtical
Proceſs.*   On the 15th of the Month called *June*, *Richard Darking*, *Thomas Clifton*, and *Richard Grantham*, all of *Gedney*, were cited into the Eccleſiaſtical Court, at the Suit of *Auguſtin Finch*, Prieſt of *Gedney*, and they not appearing, the Court certified Sir *John Oldfield* and *Walter Johnſon* Juſtices, of their Contempt, who thereupon committed them to the Houſe of Correction at *Spalding*.

*At a Meeting
for Care of
the Poor.*   On the 3d of the Month called *July* was a Meeting for Church-Affairs, ſuch as providing for the Poor, and the like good Offices, at the Houſe of *Joane Wray*, of *Fulbeck*, Widow : Intelligence was given of this Meeting to Juſtice *Thorold*, of *Grantham*, by a rambling Woman, who uſed to ſtroll about the Country begging, and blowing an Horn. Upon this *Beldam*'s Information the ſaid Juſtice *Thorold* and *Chriſtopher Beriſford*, of *Lednam*, another Juſtice,
J. White-
head *fined
for Preaching.*   came to the Meeting and found *John Whitehead* exhorting his Friends to Charity and Liberality, ſuitable to the Occaſion of their Meeting. The Juſtices took the Names of moſt that were preſent, and fined them, for which Fines Juſtice *Thorold* granted Warrants of Diſtreſs, by which the Officers took

		l.	*s.*	*d.*
*Diſtreſſes for
the ſame
Meeting.*	From *Joane Wray*, ten Beaſts and thirty eight Sheep worth	41	0	0
	Thomas Robinſon, of *Brant-Broughton*, two Steers	9	0	0
	John Richardſon, of *Hough*, Corn worth	5	5	0
	John Whaley, of *Normington*, a Pair of Oxen	7	0	0
	Henry Pickworth, of *Sleeford*, Goods worth	6	0	0
	Thomas Everett, of *Haverbolm*, Pewter	0	8	0
	Thomas Everett, *Anne Frotheringham*, *Joſeph Frotheringham*, *William Bunby*, and *William Hobman* }	2	15	2
	John Killingley, *John Green*, and *William Gabitas*	1	5	0
		72	13	2

The Beaſts and Sheep taken from *Joane Wray* were driven from Market to Market, but no Body would buy them : At length one *Edward Wright* redeemed them by paying the Fine of 20 *l.* without her Knowledge.

John

John Frotheringham was committed to Prifon by a Seffions Procefs againft him, for Abfence from the National Worfhip.

On the 19th of the Month called *April* this Year, *John Whitehead* was imprifoned under Sentence of *Premunire* for refufing to take the Oath of Allegiance, and *Thomas Hooton* was for the fame Caufe fent to Prifon by an Order of Seffions.

J. Whitehead premunired.

Thomas Heads, for refufing to Swear that his Mother was buried in Woolen, though he offered to have affirmed the fame, was fined, and had taken from him a Cow, and other Things, to the Value of 3 *l.* 10 *s.*

For refufing to Swear.

On the 19th of the Month called *July*, *Mary Waterman*, of Stegnefs, Widow, was taken Prifoner by an Attachment for Tithes, at the Suit of *Thomas Tomfon* Prieft, and on the 17th of *October* following was removed to *Lincoln* Caftle.

Attachment.

On the 4th of the Month called *January*, *John Ingram*, of Cubet in *Holland*, was taken by a Writ, de *Excommunicato capiendo*, and committed to *Lincoln* Caftle for refufing to pay 9 *d.* toward the Repairs of the Steeple-houfe at *Wefton* : And *Thomas Orflin* was alfo committed at the fame Time for 4 *d.* demanded for the fame Ufe. Likewife *William Turner*, who was then in Prifon, had four Beafts taken from him by the Wardens of *Anderly*, valued at 7 *l.*

Imprifonment on a Writ de Excom. Cap.

ANNO 1685. About the 12th of the Month called *April*, *Thomas Toinby* and *Jofeph Frotheringham*, with *William Hobman*, were taken at a religious Meeting, and fent to Prifon by the Mayor and Recorder of *Waddington*. Alfo *Richard Stanly*, *Robert Stanly*, *James Watkins*, and *Thomas Archer*, for being at the fame Meeting, had their Names given in to the Mayor, who fent Soldiers for them, and committed them to Prifon. At the Seffions not long after they were indicted for a Riot, fined and fent back to Prifon. But *William Hobman* and *Thomas Toinby* were fet at Liberty upon fome of their Relations paying their Fines.

Profecutions for Meeting.

On the 20th of *September*, Henry *Clipfon*, a Juftice's Clerk, came to the Meeting-houfe at *Tanby-Woodfide*, when the Meeting was ended, fome of the Affembly being on the Road homeward, and others with their Horfes in their Hands ready to depart ; *Clipfon* finding no Body in the Houfe was in a Rage, calling them *Rogues* and *Whores*, and defperately fwore that there had been a Conventicle, and that he would make Oath of it before his Mafter, and accordingly did fo : His Mafter, *John Bond*, a Juftice, lately put into Commiffion, took his Clerk's Oath of what he had not feen, and thereupon convicted feveral Perfons, and granted Warrants for Diftrefs, which he charged the Officers to return in three or four Days at fartheft : By thofe Warrants were taken,

Random Information of a Juftice's Clerk.

	l.	*s.*	*d.*	
From *Thomas Brown*, of *Partney*, thirty one Sheep worth	17	0	0	*Diftreffes.*
John Burton, an Ewe worth	0	15	0	
George Baflington, of *Spilfby*, Wool worth	3	1	4	
Thomas Stubbs, Houfhold Goods, &c. worth	6	0	0	
Abraham Screm, two Horfes, a Swine, and Pewter	6	5	0	
Robert Brown, for 5s. Fine, an Horfe worth	5	0	0	
	38	1	4	

Upon the Information of the aforefaid *Clipfon*, and one *Jofeph Harrifon* his Affociate, of another Meeting at the fame Place, whither they came curfing and fwearing, the faid Juftice granted another Warrant on the 18th of *October*, by which were taken,

Curfing and Swearing Informers.

	l.	*s.*	*d.*	
From *Thomas Stubbs*, a Cow, an Hog, Glaziers Tools, and other Things, to the Value of	19	3	8	*Diftreffes.*
William Stanley, a Mare worth	8	0	0	
Thomas Brown, a Mare worth	5	0	0	
	32	3	8	

LINCOLN-
SHIRE.
1685.

	l.	*s.*	*d.*
Brought over	32	3	8
From *Ibraham Screm*, Goods worth	10	0	0
Robert Brown, a Bed, Bedding, Tables, Pewter, and other Goods, worth ⎬	5	10	0
	47	13	8

Seizure of working Tools.

A Neighbour of *Thomas Stubbs*, feeing him deprived of his working Tools, to prevent his total Ruin, after the Officer had fold many of his Goods, purchafed the Remainder for 2 *l.* 10 *s.* and returned to *Stubbs* his working Tools, bidding him *make Ufe of them.* For fuch was the Inhumanity of his Profecutors, that they would have bereft him of the Means of getting his Bread.

The Fences of a Burying-ground demolifhed.

About this Time alfo, the *Parifh-Officers,* of *Tanby,* came to the Burying-ground adjoining to the Meeting-houfe there, and, by an Order from the faid Juftice *Bond,* fold the Pales and Pofts, which fenced in the Ground, to one *Ambrofe Etherington,* who, with his Servant and a Carpenter, carried them away, to the Lofs of 12 *l.* which they coft: So they left the Burying-ground open and expofed to the Beafts, or to the Rudenefs of Perfons more inhuman, ufually attending on fuch mifchievous Occafions. They alfo took from a poor Woman, who dwelt in the Meeting-houfe, and was maintained by Charity, all the Goods fhe had, worth about 15 *s.* So that upon the Oaths of thofe two wicked Informers, *Clipfon* and *Harrifon,* fwearing there were Meetings where they faw none, and that there was Preaching where they did not hear any, Juftice *Bond* caufed to be taken away as many Cattle and Goods as were computed to be worth 110 *l.* 14 *s.*

Diftreffes on random Evidence.

Imprifon-ments.

In this Year alfo, *Benjamin Coggan,* of *Epworth,* was committed to *Lincoln* Caftle, being arrefted by a *Quitam* Writ, at the King's Suit, for 200 *l.* for ten Months Abfence from the Parifh-Church. Alfo *Thomas Richardfon, John Richardfon, Edward Willey, Ralph Bucknell,* and *John Leeman,* were imprifoned by Order of Seffions, for Abfence from the publick Worfhip, but at a fubfequent Seffions that Order was annulled. In this Year *Edward Cheefman* died a Prifoner, having been long confined by a Writ *de Excommunicato capiendo.*

Tithes.

ANNO 1686. In this and the next preceding Year, were taken, for Tithes, out of the Fields from feveral Perfons, Corn, Pulfe, *&c.* to the Value of 120 *l.* 19 *s.*

At a Quarter Seffions at *Spalding,* on the 14th of the Month called *January, Stephen Willoughby, John Winkley, John Ingram, Thomas Orflin, Thomas Summers, Robert Killingley,* and *Ifaac Langftaff,* were committed to Prifon upon Prefentments, for *Abfence* from their *Parifh-Church.*

ANNO 1687. Taken in this Year, for Tithes of Corn, Hay, *&c.* out of the Fields of feveral Perfons, to the Value of 55 *l.* 4 *s.*

Commitment of T. Brown.

On the 26th of the Month called *April* this Year, *Thomas Brown,* of *Hartney,* was committed to *Lincoln* Caftle by the following Warrant, *viz.*

" *To the Conftables of* Hartney, *&c.*

" Lincoln-Lindfey.

His Warrant.

" WE *Samuel Fuller* Dr. of Divinity, and *Nicholas Smith* Efq; two of his
" Majefty's Juftices of the Peace for the faid Parts and County,
" whereof one is of the *Quorum,* having received Information from the Wor-
" fhipful *William Fofter* Dr. of Laws, and Vicar-general, and Official Principal
" of the Right Reverend Father in God *Thomas,* by divine Permiffion Lord
" Bifhop of *Lincoln,* a competent Judge in that Behalf lawfully conftituted,
" by a certain Inftrument or Writing under the Seal of his Office, That *Tho-*
" *mas Brown,* of *Hartney* aforefaid, in the faid Parts and County, Miller, hath
" been duly fummoned to appear before him the faid *William Fofter,* or his
lawful

" lawful Surrogate, in the Confiftory Court of the bleffed Virgin *Mary*, of
" *Lincoln*, upon a certain Day to the faid *Thomas Brown* affigned, and long
" fince paft, to anfwer *Francis Garthfide* Clerk, Rector of the Rectory and
" Parifh-Church of *Hartney* aforefaid, in a certain Caufe of Subftraction of
" Tithes and Offerings, and other Duties of Holy-Church, which Summons
" he out of Contumacy and Obftinacy hath not obeyed; but in fuch his
" Difobedience and Contumacy doth hitherto perfift, in manifeft Contempt
" of his Majefty's Ecclefiaftical Laws : And Requeft being made to us to affift
" and aid the Vicar-general, and Official Principal, and his Surrogate, to order
" and reform the faid *Thomas Brown* in the Caufe before rehearfed, according
" to the Power and Authority to us given by Virtue of an Act of Parliament
" in that Behalf; We his Majefty's Juftices, whereof one is of the *Quorum* as
" aforefaid, do hereby charge and command you, and every of you, to attach,
" or caufe to be attached the faid *Thomas Brown*, againft whom fuch Infor-
" mation hath been given and Requeft made : And that you convey the faid
" *Thomas Brown* to his Majefty's Goal at the Caftle of *Lincoln*, there to remain
" without Bail or Mainprize, until he the faid *Thomas Brown* fhall have found
" fufficient Sureties to be bound before fome of the King's moft honourable
" Privy-Council, or fome Juftice of the Peace for the faid Parts and County,
" to the Ufe of our Sovereign Lord the King, to give due Obedience to the
" Procefs, Proceedings, and Sentences of the faid Ecclefiaftical Court, wherein
" the faid Suit or Matter for the Premifes doth depend and is. And the
" Goaler of his Majefty's faid Goal at the Caftle of *Lincoln* is hereby required
" to receive the faid *Thomas Brown* into his faid Prifon, and him there fafely
" to keep accordingly. Given under our Hands and Seals at *Lincoln* the firft
" Day of *April*, in the third Year of the Reign of our Sovereign Lord *James*
" *the Second*, King over *England*, &c. 1687.

" SAMUEL FULLER,
" NICHOLAS SMITH."

Thus was *Thomas Brown* become a Prifoner without any Profpect of being
difcharged, the original Caufe of his Profecution in the Ecclefiaftical Court
being for Tithes, with the Payment of which he could not in Confcience
comply. About the fame Time *William Bladefmith* and *William Birks* were
committed to the fame Prifon by Attachments out of the *Exchequer* for Tithes, *Attachments.*
at the Suit of *John Flefk*, Bayliff to Sir *John Newton* : And in the fame Year
Samuel Everett was alfo imprifoned there for the fame Caufe, at the Suit of
John Towne, of *Sudbrook*, Impropriator.

We mentioned before, in the Year 1684, the Imprifonment of *Mary Waterman*, and her Removal afterward to *Lincoln* Caftle : We fhall next infert a
Paper written this Year, being as follows, *viz.*

" *A* TRUE RELATION *of the Sufferings and Death of* Mary Water-
" man, *of* Stegnefs *in the County of* Lincoln, *Widow, who died
" in Prifon at* Lincoln *the 19th Day of the Second Month called
" April* 1687, *for her Teftimony againft Tithes.*

" AFTER fome vexatious Proceedings in the County Court, by *Thomas* *A Narrative*
" *Tomfon*, Prieft of *Stegnefs*, againft the faid *Mary Waterman*, and *Peter* *of the Death*
" *Waterman* her eldeft Son, who was joined Executor to her Hufband's laft *of M. Water-*
" Will, becaufe for Confcience-fake they could not give him Tithes : The *man, and the*
" faid Prieft caufed to be taken away from them Goods to the Value of *Caufe of it.*
" about 20 *l.* by a *Diftringas*, but this Proceeding being contrary to Law, they
" got thofe Goods again with much Charge : After which, *Peter* her eldeft Son
" died,

" died, whilft the abovefaid Prieft profecuted the faid *Peter* and *Mary Water-*
" *man* in the *Exchequer* for the fame Caufe, and after his Death, the faid *Mary,*
" by an Attachment, was taken Prifoner, at the faid Prieft's Suit, the 19th
" Day of the Fifth Month 1684, by *John Chambers* and *William Richardfon*
" Bailiffs, and by them kept Prifoner at *Orby* and at *Alford* till the 17th
" Day of the eighth Month in the fame Year, and then brought to *Lincoln*
" Caftle by the fame Warrant, by the Procurement of the faid Prieft, where
" fhe was detained till the Goaler was encouraged to give her fome Liberty
" by the King's Proclamation. But the Prieft by his Attorney threatning the
" Sheriff and Goaler, fhe was remanded to Prifon again, and then by a fe-
" cond Attachment, bearing Date the 19th Day of the Fifth Month 1686,
" which was delivered to the Goaler by *John Chambers* Bailiff, fhe being in
" Cuftody upon the Former, which it feems they found was weakned by
" Contempts being pardoned, and from that Time fhe was kept more clofe
" by the Procurement of the faid Prieft : So being in a fmoaky Room fhe
" grew weaker and weaker, till fhe died the 19th of the Second Month 1687,
" often in her Sicknefs thanking God, who ftrengthened her to give up her
" Life for her Teftimony againft Tithes.

" And that the aforefaid Prieft might totally ruin her and her Family, he
" alfo profecuted *Robert Waterman*, her fecond Son, who was with her as a
" Servant, and managed her Bufinefs, and by an Attachment out of the *Ex-*
" *chequer* upon the 16th of the Sixth Month 1686, the faid *Robert* was arrefted,
" and brought Prifoner to his Mother in *Lincoln* Caftle the 17th of the fame
" Month, though he was not joint Executor with her, and therefore not
" concerned to pay the Prieft Tithes. But through the Mercy of the Sheriff
" and the Goaler he had fome Liberty to go Home and order his Bufinefs."

The hard Ufage and Death of the faid *Mary Waterman* induced *John White-*
head, fome Time her Fellow-prifoner, to write to her Profecutor, the Prieft of
Stegnefs, as follows, viz.

" *Friend* THOMAS TOMSON,

" I THOUGHT good hereby to let thee know that *Mary Waterman*,
" that defolate Widow, whom thou haft been long purfuing with one
" vexatious Suit after another, died the 19th Day of this Month, being kept
" clofe at thy Suit. Therefore fearch and fee, whether in thy Skirts will not
" be found her Blood, when the Lord fhall make Inquifition, and give that
" heavy Doom mentioned in *Mat.* xxv. 41. to the End of the Chapter, on
" thofe that have not vifited his Servants in Prifon. O! where wilt thou ap-
" pear in that Day, who didft keep that innocent Woman in Prifon for Tithes,
" or to which of the Saints wilt thou turn, to find an Example for thy horrid
" Actions. None of the Priefts under the Law, except thofe two wicked
" Sons of *Eli, Hophni* and *Phineas,* which both fell in one Day, did ever
" force their Maintenance. And among the Minifters of the Gofpel, which
" Chrift fent forth, and faid, *Freely you have received, freely give,* Tithes nor
" forced Maintenance was not fo much as mentioned to be received for feveral
" Ages. Therefore be afhamed of thy Wickednefs and Hardnefs of Heart,
" and repent whilft the Lord gives thee Time and Space, that this thine Ini-
" quity may be blotted out, which is the Defire of

" *Thy Soul's Friend,*

Written the 26th Day of
the Second Month 1687.   " JOHN WHITEHEAD.

" *P. S.* And let thy Repentance be manifeft
" by difcharging her Son *Robert,* who hath
" been wrongfully detained by thee, though
" not joined *Executor* with his Mother."

Our Records do not mention how long the faid *Robert Waterman* continued in Prifon after his Mother's Deceafe.

In this Year were taken, for not paying Steeple-houfe Rates, from *Thomas Brown, Thomas Richardfon,* and *John Richardfon* his Son, Goods to the Value of 4 *l.* 18 *s.*

ANNO 1688. Taken this Year out of the Fields for Tithes of Grain, Hay, and other Things, from fundry Perfons, to the Value of 89 *l.* 2 *s.* 11 *d.*

ANNO 1689. On the 16th of the Month called *July, John Milner,* of *South-Witham,* as he was fetching Home his Hay, was met by *Francis Whiting,* Prieft of that Place, who, not having got fo much for his Tithe as he intended, did beat the faid *John Milner* with a Stick very cruelly : On the 31ft of the fame Month, as he was binding his Hay, the Prieft came to him again, and beat him unmercifully : He did alfo beat the faid *John Milner* at feveral other Times with much Cruelty, fo that he was difabled to go about his Bufinefs, and obliged to lie by it a Quarter of a Year together, by which he fuftained great Lofs and Damage : After all thefe Abufes, which the innocent Man bore with Patience, and avenged not himfelf, but committed his Caufe to him who judges righteoufly, the Prieft cited him into the Ecclefiaftical Court, where he appeared feveral Times, and as often complained to them of the Abufes he had fuffered, but to no Purpofe.

We find that in this Year the Corn taken from feveral Perfons in this County for Tithes, amounted to 100 *l.* 5 *s.* 8 *d.*

ANNO 1690. In the Month called *May, John Clark* was committed to *Lincoln* Caftle by a Common-Pleas Writ for Tithes of *Hemp, Flax, Pigs, Hens, Apples,* &c. at the Suit of *Thomas Pinder,* Merchant in *London,* Son and Executor to a Prieft of the fame Name.

In this Year alfo, the Tithe of Grain, taken from this People in this County, amounted to the Sum of 103 *l.* 13 *s.* 4 *d.*

Having thus defcribed the Sufferings in this County within the Years propofed ; we proceed to the City of *London* and County of *Middlefex.*

C H A P. XXVI.

N O R F O L K.

ANNO 1654.

Imprifonment of R. Hubberthorn.

THE firft fuffering Cafe which occurs to our Notice in this County, was that of *Richard Hubberthorn*, who for his Chriftian Concern to exhort the People affembled in the Steeple-houfe at *Wymondham*, after the Prieft had ended his Sermon, was committed to *Bridewell*, and from thence the next Day fent to *Norwich* Caftle, and kept there till Seffions. On his Appearance there, the Caufe of his Commitment was dropt, and the Juftices took Occafion from his prefent Appearing before them with his Hat on, to charge him with a Contempt of Authority, and under that Pretence recommitted him to Prifon, where he lay a long Time after.

In the Winter of the fame Year, *James Lancafter*, for warning the People in the Streets of *Norwich*, was committed to Prifon by the following *Mittimus*,

" *Norwich* ſs.

Mittimus of J. Lancafter to Norwich Goal.

" THESE are to require you to take into your Cuftody *James Lancafter*
" herewith fent, who lately came to this City from *North-Seal* in the
" Ifland of *Walney* in *Lancafhire*, and can fhew no lawful Caufe for his Coming
" hither, but only to declare the Truth, as he calls it, and did in the publick
" Market-place in this City gather together a great Company of rude and idle
" People, to the Difturbance of the Peace of this City, and him fafely keep
" untill he fhall be delivered thence according to Law : And hereof fail not.
" The 9th of *December* 1654.

To Mr. Edward Shent, *Keeper of the Common Goal in the faid City.*

" THOMAS TOFTE, *Mayor*."

With him was alfo committed *Chriftopher Atkinfon*, by a *Mittimus* of the fame Date and Direction as follows, *viz.*

" *Norwich* ſs.

*Mittimus of
C. Atkinſon.*

" THESE are to require you to take into your Cuſtody the Body of
" Chriſtopher *Atkinſon* herewith ſent, who lately came into this City from
" *Kendal* in *Weſtmorland*, and can give no Account of his Livelihood, nor
" ſhew any lawful Cauſe of his Coming hither, but only to declare the Truth,
" as he calls it.

" THOMAS TOFTE, *Mayor.*"

*G. White-
head ſent to
Priſon.*

About the ſame Time *George Whitehead*, for uttering a Chriſtian Exhortation
to the People in *Peter*'s Steeple-houſe in *Norwich*, after the Prieſt had done,
was ſent to the ſame Priſon, where not complying with the Goaler's extravagant Demands for Lodging, they * lay in their Clothes on the Floor : At the
next Seſſions for that City, *James Lancaſter* and *George Whitehead* were diſcharged by the Court, but ſtill detained by the Goaler, under Pretence of Fees,
ſeveral Weeks longer, till the Goaler died ; and his Widow, of a more merciful Diſpoſition, ſet them at Liberty. Thus they, by their Patience and Meek-
neſs, gave approved Tokens of their Innocence : While *Atkinſon*, being of a
more rough Temper, for uttering ſome bitter Expreſſions againſt his Oppoſers,
was detained longer in Priſon by Actions laid againſt him by a Prieſt and an
Attorney, and he giving way to Heat and Anger, fell from the Tenderneſs of
his firſt Convincement, and miniſtred Occaſion to the Adverſaries to ſpeak
reproachfully.

*Remarks on
the different
Tempers of the
Sufferers.*

Not long after this, *Thomas Simonds*, for aſking a Prieſt, after his Sermon,
a ſerious Queſtion reſpecting his *Doctrine*, was committed to *Norwich* Caſtle :
And *George Whitehead*, going to viſit him and another of his Friends under
Confinement, was by Order of the Mayor detained there about three Weeks,
without any Cauſe, but the arbitrary Will and Pleaſure of that Magiſtrate.
About the ſame Time *Dorothy Waugh*, for teſtifying againſt Sin in the Market-
place at *Norwich*, was kept Priſoner in the City Goal near a Quarter of a Year.

*Commitment
of many to
Priſon.*

ANNO 1655. *Thomas Bond*, being at an *Independent* Meeting in *Great-
Yarmouth*, after their Preacher had done, found a Neceſſity upon him of ſpeaking to the Aſſembly, which he began to do, when one of their *Elders*, or *Dea-
cons*, interrupted him, by thruſting him down over an high Seat, to the endangering of his Life, and after that dragged him into the Yard, when
attempting again to ſpeak to the People, he was taken and ſent to Priſon,
where he lay among Felons, and the Goaler would ſeldom admit any of his
Friends either to viſit or relieve him.

*Impriſonment
and other
Abuſes of
T. Bond.*

Richard Clayton and *Elizabeth Court*, being under the like Concern, and endeavouring to diſcharge their Duty, by exhorting the People in the Steeple-
houſe at *Wymondham*, after the Prieſt had concluded his Service, were, for their
Good-will, ill requited with Impriſonment. Alſo *Edward Warne*, for attempting the ſame good Office to a Congregation met at *Waſtfield*, was committed
to *Norwich* Caſtle, and at the next Seſſions fined 5*l*. Likewiſe *Alice Day*, for
the ſame Cauſe, ſuffered a long Impriſonment at *Norwich*.

*Diverſe other
Impriſon-
ments.*

ANNO 1656. *Robert Jacob*, of *Wymondham*, was choſen Conſtable when
he was ſo old and infirm, that in Reaſon and Juſtice he ſhould have been ex-
cuſed from that Office, nevertheleſs he was ſummoned before the Juſtices, and
becauſe he would not Swear to execute an Office he was not fit for, was committed to Priſon. The ſame Perſon ſhortly after was again committed to Priſon
for refuſing to pay Tithes, and died in Priſon for ſuch his conſcientious Refuſal,
when he was eighty Years of Age. In this Year alſo *John Goddard*, of *Rock-
land*, being ſummoned to ſerve on a Jury at the *Quarter Seſſions*, appeared there,
but refuſing to be ſworn, was fined 5*l*. and for not paying it was ſent to Priſon.

*Death of
R. Jacob in
Priſon, being
80 Years of
Age.*

*Impriſonment
of Others.*

William

---

* This was no ſmall Hardſhip, eſpecially to *George Whitehead*, then a Youth of about
eighteen Years of Age, and tenderly educated.

NORFOLK.
1656.

A charitable Inflance.

Other Impri-Jonments.

William King, on the fame Occafion, alfo refufing to Swear, was fined 40 s. *Thomas Dormer*, of *Taflingham*, refufing to take an Oath when required at Seffions, was by the Juftices fined 5 s. One of the Bench, who knew the Man's Converfation and Integrity, declared his Diflike of what they had done, and to prevent his Neighbour's Imprifonment paid the Fine in Court.

John Clifton and *Henry Lone*, were taken out of a religious Meeting, and committed to Prifon without any Breach of Law affigned. About the fame Time *John Allen*, of *Lammis*, for having a Meeting at his Houfe, was committed to Prifon, and when at Seffions that Caufe of his Commitment appeared infufficient, the Juftices, from his appearing before them with his Hat on, took Occafion againft him, and required Sureties for his good Behaviour, which he refufing to comply with, was continued in Prifon.

Diftreffes.

In this Year alfo feveral Perfons, for frivolous Demands of Tithes, amounting but to 12 s. had their Goods taken away to the Value of 4 l.

Diftreffes and Imprifonment for Tithes.

ANNO 1657. In this Year, for Tithes demanded of feveral Perfons amounting to 19 l. 9 s. 5 d. Goods were taken by Diftrefs to the Value of 51 l. 16 s. 6 d. *William Barber* was profecuted in the *Exchequer* for Tithes, and in *September* committed to *Norwich* Caftle, where he continued a long Time. *Henry Ward*, of *Helgay*, had Goods taken from him for Tithes, to the Value of 13 l. And *Chriftopher Good*, of *Markham*, to the Value of 5 l.

ANNO 1658. Taken from feveral Perfons in this County, for 18 l. 19 s. claimed for Tithes, Goods to the Value of 42 l. 13 s. 6 d.

ANNO 1659. *Abraham Howes*, *John Goddard*, and *Henry Goddard*, were imprifoned in *Norwich* Caftle, on an *Exchequer* Procefs, though the Prieft, their Profecutor, had entred the Lands of the two Latter, and taken what Corn he pleafed ; and for a Claim of 5 l. for Tithes, had taken from the firft of them two Cows worth 11 l.

ANNO 1660. The barbarous and inhuman Treatment which this People ufually met with at their religious Meetings in *Norwich*, is expreffed in the following Letter fent to the *Mayor* and *Aldermen* of that City, bearing Date,

     " *The 2d of the Fourth Month called* June 1660.

     " *Friends*,

A Letter relating the barbarous Ufage of the People at Norwich.

" UPON the Firft-day of the Week, we being met in our ufual Meeting-
" place, together with other Friends, to worfhip the Lord in Spirit and
" Truth, and to wait for Refrefhment to our Souls from his Prefence, there
" came into our Meeting-place one *Chriftopher Bennet*, Apprentice to *Zachary*
" *Mahew* in *Auftin*'s Parifh, *John Sadler* in *Paul*'s Parifh, and *John Salmon*, Ser-
" vant to the Brewhoufe without *Pickthorp-Gate* ; thefe Perfons being chief Setters
" on of others, came amongft us, and with much Cruelty fmiting, punching,
" and pulling fome of us by the Arms to hale us out of the Meeting, with fuch
" Violence as if they would have torn our Limbs from off our Bodies, and with
" Rigour pufhing us from one to another, dragging about, and affronting us
" with many unbecoming Actions, and with cruel Mockings ; and by thefe
" Perfons we have long fuffered much Cruelty, and by others whom they
" animate and encourage, whofe Names are unknown to us, who neither
" fearing the Law nor the Magiftrates, have broke open the Gate of *Jofeph*
" *Whitlock*, and have broke a new Bar and two Locks from off it, one after
" another, and have broken a Lock of an inner Gate, and the Firft-day of
" this Week broke open one of his Doors, and threw another off the Hinges,
" their ufual Cuftom being to difturb our Meetings, with throwing of Stones,
" breaking the Windows, which is to the Value of forty Foot of Glafs, thump-
" ing us on the Back and Breaft without Mercy, dragging fome moft inhumanly
" by the Hair of the Head, and fpitting in our Faces, abufing both Men and Wo-
" men, with other violent and unfeemly Actions unfit to be mentioned, alfo with
" throwing of Fire, and drawing Blood feveral Times, and feveral of them
" getting upon the Table, have violently thrown themfelves down upon the
" Heads of Men and Women, and have taken the Mire out of the Streets,
         " and

" and have thrown it at the Friends, fome of them holding the Maid of the
" Houfe, whilft others daubed her Face with Gore and Dung, fo as the Skin
" of her Face could hardly be feen. We doubt not but fome of you, to whofe
" Ear the Cry of thefe Cruelties are come, are grieved that fuch Wickednefs
" fhould be committed, and the Evil-doers not terrified, nor the Peaceable and
" Harmlefs protected in this City, but that the Authority and Magiftracy
" thereof fhould be flighted as it is, and difregarded by a Company of wicked
" lewd Fellows of the bafer Sort, fuch as affaulted the Houfe of *Jafon*, for fo
" they behave themfelves as fuch, whofe prefumptuous lawlefs Minds (if they
" fhould have an Opportunity) would not ftick to act the like Cruelty even upon
" your felves ; therefore we thought meet to give in thefe Perfons Names
" as fome of the chief Difturbers, and are ready upon their Examination to
" give Teftimony concerning their Carriages, that they may be dealt with as
" you in Juftice fhall fee fit for fuch Offenders, we have fuffered much long
" by them and others they encourage, who have fundry Times drew the Blood,
" and rent the Garments of feveral, fmote and much abufed us, who, if we
" were Offenders, we know are not to fuffer by them, but by you who are
" over the People to do them Juftice, before whom it hath been offered
" them by feveral of our Friends to appear, if they had any Evil to lay to
" their Charge. Many more Abufes we have fuffered which we could mention,
" but that they be too tedious, thefe being fufficient to let you underftand the
" Cruelty and Wickednefs by which thefe People were acted, that fo they
" may be reftrained, the Parliament having fhewed their Moderation in re-
" ftraining thofe in fome Meafure, which are thus rude in *London*.

" *Signed by*   JOHN FULLER,   EDWARD MONK,
"   JOHN BACKHOUSE,   ISAAC MARRIOTT,
"   TOBIAS ROE,   THOMAS BUDDERY,
"   ROBERT GREEN,   EDWARD MASON,
"   WILLIAM MASSAM,   SAMUEL DUNCOMB."

The foregoing Letter was prefented and read to the Magiftrates as directed, *The Bearer fent to Prifon.* but they were fo far from regarding the juft Complaints therein contained, that they fent the Bearer of it to Prifon, though under another Pretence, *viz.* his having put up fome Papers, giving Notice of a Meeting appointed, and in- viting the People to it : Under this Colour they required Sureties for his good Behaviour, and for refufing to be fo bound, committed him to Goal.

On the 15th of the Month called *January* this Year, the Conftables of *Several impri-foned for re-fufing to Swear.* *Emneth*, without producing any Warrant, took *Thomas Laycock* and *Richard Saunders* out of their Beds by Night, and next Day carried them before a Juftice, who tendred them the Oath of Allegiance, and for refufing to take it fent them to Prifon at *Lyn*, where they were kept ten Days till Seffions, and then removed to *Norwich* Caftle, whither one *Robert Turner* accompanied them, in order to bring back their Horfes ; but he going to vifit his Friends confined in the Caftle, the Mayor fent an Officer for him, and becaufe he would not take the Oaths, fent him to the City Goal. On the fame Day St. *John Buck* was taken out of his own Houfe by a Conftable and Watchmen, and carried before the Mayor of *Norwich*, who, though there appeared no reafonable Caufe to fufpect his being difaffected to the Government, yet becaufe he would not Swear, committed him to Prifon.

On the 17th, at the Quarter Seffions, *Thomas Bayly* and *John Rack* were *Many Impri-fonments, and other Abufes.* fined 40 s. each for refufing to Swear, and for not paying that Fine were fent to Prifon. On the 20th, a Juftice of the Peace, with armed Attendants, came to a Meeting at *Erpingham*, and took from thence *John Allen*, *John Soame*, and *Henry Miller*, whom he committed to Prifon. At the fame Time he ordered the Women to be dragged out of the Meeting by Force, with this Threat, *You were warned once before* ; *this is the fecond Time, and if you meet the third* *Threats of a Juftice to the Women.* *Time, we are for killing and flaying.* On the fame Day *John Watfon*,

NORFOLK.
1660.

Bartholomew Flegg, and *William Sherwood,* taken out of a Meeting at *Wyndham,* were fent to Goal for refuſing the Oath ; as were alſo *Michael Shipp* and *Edward Vineyard,* whom they took out of the Meeting. And on the ſame Day the High-Conſtable, with Horſemen and Footmen armed with Halberts, Piſtols, Swords, Pitchforks, Clubs, and Hedgeſtakes, came to the Meeting at *Pulham,* and in Time of Prayer rudely dragged out *John Laurence, Joſeph Laurence, William Barber, George Whitehead,* and others, whom they carried next Day before a Juſtice, who ſent them to Priſon. And on that Day alſo, *Henry Kettle* jun. *Anne Kettle, Elizabeth Winter, Mary Goddard, John Cockeril, Edward Rack, Suſan Taylor, Robert Elding, Margaret Elding, Elizabeth Day, Joſeph Whitlock, Edmund Garnham,* and *Andrew Bucknam,* moſt of whom were taken, by a Captain and ten armed Men with Swords drawn, out of their Meeting at *Kilverſtone,* were committed to *Thetford* Goal.

Sundry impriſoned for refuſing to Swear.

On the ſame Day, the Mayor and Recorder of *Norwich* tendred the Oath of Allegiance to *Edward Monk, Thomas Buddery, John Fuller, William Maſſam, Edward Maſon, John Ruſt, David Read, William May, Samuel Duncomb,* and *Robert Turner,* and for refuſing to take it committed them to Priſon, though ſeveral of them were poor Men, whoſe Wives and Children ſuffered at Home for Want of Neceſſaries, which they uſed to be ſupplied with by their Labour.

On the 25th, *Henry Ward,* of *Helgay,* was taken out of his Bed early in the Morning, and *Peter Gill* from his Labour, and both of them, for refuſing to Swear, ſent to Priſon. And on the 26th, *John Wymer,* of *Machum,* going homeward from *Yarmouth* Market, was taken by the Watch, kept Priſoner that Night, and next Day had the Oath of Allegiance tendred him by two Juſtices, who alſo tendred the ſame to his Wife who came to viſit him, and ſent them together to *Norwich* Caſtle. And on the ſame Day *William Farmer,* for the ſame Cauſe, was ſent to the ſame Priſon, having been taken from his own Houſe at *Crippleſham.*

On the 27th, *John Hewett, William King, Thomas King, Robert King, John Parding, Henry Peed, Thomas Barrett, John Watſon,* and *Matthew Bacon,* being met at the Houſe of *James King* in *North-Walſham,* the High-Conſtable, attended by Perſons armed with Swords, Halberts, and other Weapons, ruſhed violently in, dragged them out, and carried them before Juſtice *Rant,* who refuſed to act againſt them ; ſo they were kept that Night in an Alehouſe, and next Morning carried before two other Juſtices, who committed them to the Caſtle at *Norwich.*

Others for not paying Tithes.

In this Year alſo, *Matthew King* of *North-Walſham, William Tilney* of *Aylſham, Henry Halls* the Elder, of *Aſhbee, Benjamin Lines* of *Coulton,* and *Robert Tillet* of *Harlyn,* were committed to Priſon in *Norwich* Caſtle for refuſing to pay Tithes.

Indictments.

ANNO 1661. At a Seſſions at *King's-Lyn,* in *October,* Bills of Indictment were preferred againſt *Bartholomew Hewlet, Chriſtopher Goad,* and *Edward Caſe,* for not repairing to their reſpective Pariſh-Churches to hear divine Service, and for not finding Sureties to appear to anſwer thoſe Indictments, they were committed to Priſon. And in the ſame Year, *Anthony Oakley* of *Ellingham, Thomas Tubbin* of *Claxton,* and *John Wynne* of *Markham,* for refuſing to pay Tithes, were impriſoned in the Caſtle at *Norwich.* And *Robert Tillet* of *Harlyn,* for the ſame Cauſe, ſuffered Diſtreſs of two Cows worth 6 *l.* 10*s.*

Imprifonments and Diſtreſſes for Tithes.

Unhealthy Confinement of many at Yarmouth.

ANNO 1662. *William Hadkins, William Thirton, John Haſtings, William Mead, Iſaac Mills, Robert Camplin, George Bragg, Thomas Lawes, William Bennett, William Ward, Henry Downing, Joane Heard, Sarah Meade, Joane Caſtell, Margaret Haylett, Magdalen Fuller, Anne Stubbs,* and *Elizabeth Clements,* were taken out of a Meeting at *Yarmouth,* and ſent to Priſon, where they were kept in a Dungeon without convenient Food, Lodging, or other Neceſſaries, nor had they any Place of Eaſement, except a Tub ſtanding in the Room, the Smell of which was very offenſive, nor were they permitted to empty it, till by ſpecial Application to the Bayliffs of the Town, that Favour was granted them : After which they were removed into an upper Room, and on the 17th of of *September*, at the Seffions, the Women were fet at Liberty, and not long after the Recorder difcharged the Men alfo, there having been no regular Procefs againft them. The Bayliffs difpleafed at their Releafe, prefently committed them again by a new *Mittimus*, of which when they defired a Copy, it was denied them.

On the 9th of *November*, *Jofeph Whitlock*, *Edward Monk*, and *David Read*, were taken at a Meeting in *Jofeph Whitlock*'s Houfe by an Officer with Soldiers, and a fhort Time after, *Robert Green*, *Tobias Roe*, *William May*, and *Samuel Duncomb*, coming thither with the fame Intent of Meeting, were alfo apprehended, and prefently after them, *Ifaac Merritt*, *Thomas Buddery*, *Daniel Day*, *John Dey*, and *Edward Mafon* ; they were all carried before the Deputy-Lieutenants, who committed them to *Norwich* Caftle, where three of them were lockt down all Night, in a very frofty Seafon, in the loweft and worft Dungeon in the Prifon : After fourteen Days Confinement they were brought to Trial at the Seffions, but it not appearing to the Jury that they were a Number fufficient to make their Affembly unlawful when the Soldiers took the firft of them, they were acquitted.

In the fame Year, *Abraham Hewes* of *Hockham*, and *William King* of *Suffield*, fuffered Imprifonment for their Teftimony againft paying Tithes.

ANNO 1663. On the 7th of the Month called *February*, *Edward Shooter*, *Robert Turner*, *John Yaxley*, *Thomas Waller*, *Jofeph Whitworth*, *John Haflewood*, *Jofeph Townfend*, *Anthony Prefton*, and *Benjamin Townfend*, were taken out of a Meeting at *Lyn* by Soldiers, who after they had expofed them for fome Hours to the Derifion of the Rabble, carried them before the Mayor, who, for their refufing to take the Oath of Allegiance, fent them to Prifon, where they were kept a long Time, lodging on the bare Boards without any Fire, and when Straw was brought them to lie on, it was taken away and given to the Felons. Of thefe Perfons, fo ufed, the firft named *fix* were Inhabitants of that Town, and the other *three*, Traders who came to the *Mart*, one of whom had a Family at *Lincoln*, another dwelt beyond *Northampton*, and the third, *Benjamin Townfend*, was a Man of large Dealings, who fuffered much in his Trade by this Confinement, having fix *Pack-horfes* ftanding at great Charges at an Inn, and much Goods, fome of which were greatly damaged. Under this cruel Confinement they continued above five Months, and then

ANNO 1664. At a Seffions held on the 27th of the Month called *July*, the Oath was again tendred them in open Court, and upon their Refufal to take it, an Indictment was drawn up againft them, but their Trial put off, and they were again committed to Prifon, where leaving them to ftruggle with the Hardfhips of their Captivity, we proceed to relate the very hard Cafe of eight others of their Brethren, Sufferers at *Yarmouth*, as written and figned by themfelves, *viz.*

" WE whofe Names are underwritten, coming to *Great-Yarmouth* in *Nor-*
" *folk*, about our lawful Occafions, (and one being put into that Har-
" bour by contrary Wind, when he was returning to his Habitation in *Holland*)
" we were upon the Firft-day of the Week met together in a peaceable Manner,
" and not in the leaft to the Terror of the People, or to the Difturbance of
" the Peace of the Town or Kingdom ; and having enjoyed our Meeting
" peaceably, and being in a Readinefs to depart, at the very Inftant of Time
" came in a Lieutenant with a Conftable, together with diverfe Soldiers
" and others that accompanied them, and they took the Names of moft of the
" Men and Women that were prefent, but as for us that were Strangers, they
" carried us to the Main-Guard, where they kept us that Night, and the next
" Day we were carried before the Bayliffs of the Town, to whom we gave a good
" Account of the Occafion of our Coming to Town, and of our Determina-
" tion of departing out of the Town fo foon as our Bufinefs was difpatched,
" and that the Wind ferved (for five of us belonged to one Veffel that was
" come

NORFOLK.
1664.

" come to the Town to take in Red-Herrings for the *Straits*) but whatſoever
" we ſaid in our Defence, it ſeemed to be little regarded by them.

" And when they had examined us a little they produced their grand Snare,
" *to wit*, the Oath of Allegiance, which for Conſcience-ſake we could not
" take, nor any other Oath whatſoever, whereupon they committed us to the
" Common Goal, with a ſtrict Order (as we were told ſeveral Times) that
" none of our Friends ſhould be permitted to come at us, nor that no Manner
" of Proviſion ſhould be brought in unto us, and the Goaler being ready to
" obſerve their Order, we were kept near upon eight Weeks ſo cloſe, that in
" all that Time the Door was not once opened by the Goaler's Order (that
" we know of) to let in any Proviſion to us, and we being ſhut up in an high
" Chamber, were therefore ſo much the more ſtraitned. And when the Bayliffs
" were ſpoken to concerning the Goaler's ſevere Dealing with us, they or one
" of them replied, that *They would carry him out in what he did, and that we*
" *ſhould not have any Thing but what we had of the Goaler.* Howbeit, after-
" ward we had ſo much Privilege as to have our Victuals handed in at the
" Door. We have now remained here above twenty three Weeks, and have
" not yet been brought to any farther Trial. And we could ſay much of their
" Cruelty towards us ſince we have been committed, but the Lord hath given
" us Patience to bear the ſame for his Truth's Sake, in which we remain
" innocent Sufferers.

Yarmouth, *the* 14th *of the*
Seventh Month 1664.

" ROBERT RAINE,   EDWARD ANDREWS,
" JAMES CROW,   STEPHEN NICHOLS,
" JOHN RENT   EDWARD COXERE,
" WILLIAM CATON,   JOHN HOBSON."

Leaving them in Priſon, where the farther Time of their Continuance is
uncertain, we return to thoſe nine Perſons, already mentioned in this and the
preceding Year to be continued Priſoners at *Lyn*, where,

Sentence of
Præmunire
paſſed on 8
Perſons at
Lyn.

ANNO 1665. They were brought to Trial at the Seſſions, held on the 2d
of the Month called *April*, upon an Indictment for refuſing the Oath of Allegiance, when after a ſhort Examination their Anſwers were recorded *pro Confeſſo*,
and the dreadful Sentence of *Præmunire* was pronounced againſt them, under
which they, cheerfully ſuffering for their Chriſtian Teſtimony, returned to
Priſon, where the cruel Goaler debarred them of the uſual Liberty of Priſoners, for he cloſed up the Windows of their Room with Boards, ſo depriving
them of Light to work by, and in a great Meaſure, of Air, inſomuch that

Death of
E. Shooter.

one of them, *Edward Shooter*, through the Hardſhip of that cloſe Confinement, died there. This Goaler, *Ralph Emerton*, was a Perſon of a rugged,
moroſe, and miſchievous Diſpoſition, of which the following Inſtance is recorded, *viz.* As *Anthony Preſton*, one of the Priſoners, was ſtanding behind the
heavy thick Door of the Goal, the Goaler came and threw the Door with
Violence againſt him, intending to have cruſhed him between that and a Stone
Wall, againſt which he ſtood ; but was providentially prevented by his ſudden
perceiving it, and breaking with his Hands the Force of a Blow which might
have deſtroyed him. To thoſe who ſaw the malicious Purpoſe of the Goaler
therein, it was very obſervable, and made a deep Impreſſion on their Minds,

Sudden Death
of a Goaler.

when, but a few Hours after, they ſaw the Contriver of ſo much Harm to an
innocent Man, ſuddenly taken ill, and dead in his Chair.

16 *Impriſoned*
at Norwich.

About this Time *Thomas Buddery*, *Edward Maſon*, *William May*, *William*
Waymer, *John Defrance*, *Samuel Duncomb*, *Edward Monk*, *Peter Hewett*, *Tobias*
Roe, *Robert Green*, *William Bennet*, *David Read*, *Edmund Sewel*, *William Fal-*
lowfield, *Peter Gill*, and *John Ruſt*, were impriſoned at *Norwich*, having been
taken at their religious Meetings in that City, and ſent to Goal for refuſing
to Swear.

4 *Sentenced*
to Tranſporta-
tion.

At the Quarter Seſſions, held at *Norwich* Caſtle on the 20th of the
Month called *February* 1665, *Henry Kettle* jun. and *Robert Eden*, both of
Thetford,

Thetford, *Richard Cockerill* of *Snares-hill*, and *Edmund Rack* of *Kilverston*, convicted of the third Offence in meeting together, were sentenced to be carried from thence to *Yarmouth*, and from that Port to be transported to *Barbadoes* for seven Years.

ANNO 1666. *Henry Walker* of *Ashbee*, imprisoned on an Execution for Tithes, died this Year a Prisoner for his Testimony : And in the same Year, *Thomas Watson*, a poor Man of *Fakenham*, was fined 60*l.* for three Months Absence from the National Worship on the Statute of Queen *Elizabeth*, and though utterly unable to pay that Fine, was taken from his Wife and three Children, and committed to *Norwich* Castle : As was *John Heath*, of *Sparl*, fined in the like Sum for the same Cause. And for the same Cause of absenting themselves from the National Worship, *John Booty*, a blind Man of *Stratton-Myles*, and *Elizabeth* his Wife, suffered Imprisonment in *Norwich* Castle ; as did also *Samuel King* of *Barfer*.

ANNO 1667. *Joseph Harrison*, *Edmund Peckover*, *William Hempstoll*, *Samuel Tubby*, and *Alice Williamson*, having been prosecuted on Indictments for neglecting the publick Worship in their respective Parish-Churches, so called, were committed to Prison. And in this Year *Hilary James*, of *Snetherton*, was prosecuted in the *Exchequer* for Tithes, and by an Attachment out of that Court, committed to *Norwich* Castle. And to the same Prison were also committed about the same Time, *James Fulcher* of *Lammis*, *Peter Gill*, and *Nicholas Phillips*, upon Prosecutions for Tithes.

ANNO 1668. *Thomas Berrier* and *Robert Berrier*, both of *Upwell*, and *Simon Gee*, having been prosecuted in the Ecclesiastical Court for Tithes, were by Writs de *Excommunicato capiendo*, dated the 18th of *July* this Year, committed to Prison ; as was about the same Time, *Francis Gardener*, for the like conscientious Refusal to pay Tithes. And in the same Year, *William Monk* and his Wife, both very aged, were sent to Prison for their Nonconformity to the Manner of Worship by Law established.

ANNO 1670. On the 29th of the Month called *April*, *John Hubbard* the Elder, of *Stoke*, had his Goods taken by Distress, for his own and his Wife's Absence from the publick Way of Worship, to the Value of 80*l.*

After the coming out of the Conventicle-Act in this Year, great Spoil was made in this County, several base Fellows taking up the Trade of Informing, and the Justices readily complying with their avaricious Purpose by granting their Warrants for Distress, by which were taken as follows, *viz.*

		l.	*s.*	*d.*
From	*Robert Allen*, of *Buxton*, Goods worth	13	13	8
	Henry Appleyard, of *Saxlingham*	0	15	0
	Matthew Bacon, of *North-Walsham*, and *Andrew Robsam*, of *Banningham*	0	18	0
	William Barber, of *Gessing*	40	0	0
	William Bishop, of *Wymondham*	0	11	0
	John Brown, of *Fritten*, and *Elizabeth Bidwell*, of *Yaxham*	7	8	0
*	*John Booty*, of *Stratton-Myles*	21	0	0
	Thomas Dormer, of *Saxlingham*	1	10	0
	Lewis Geedy, of *Hempenhall*	51	0	0
	Robert Goodwin, of *Saxlingham*	7	10	0
	Joseph Harrison, of *Fakenham*	31	1	6
	John Halls, of *Shotisham*	8	0	0
	Elizabeth Halls, of *Saxlingham*	27	0	0
	John Wade, of *Twyford*	32	13	6
	Robert Southgate, of *Twyford*	29	2	0

Carr. over 272 2 8

---

* *John Booty* had been blind about twenty Years.

	l.	*s.*	*d.*
Brought over	272	2	8
From *Hugh Shelterham,* of *Twyford*	4	5	6
Richard Pulling, of *Saxlingham*	1	12	4
William Wafey, of *Bardfwell, John Goodwin,* of *Tafeborough, Thomas Tyrrell,* of *Hardwick,* and *Mary Johnfon*	12	11	0
* *Luke Lindoe,* of *Scarning*	28	1	6
Edward Pearfe and *Thomas True,* of *Eaft-Dereham*	23	0	3
William Stonnuck, of *Cranworth*	3	1	0
Robert Laft and *Samuel Pike,* of *Ellingham*	155	0	0
Peter Gill and *John Soams,* of *Aylfham*	47	13	0
William Scarning and *John Hewett,* of *Banningham*	16	2	0
William King, of *North-Walfham*	26	1	6
Robert Peartree, of *Edgefield*	15	0	0
William Hempftoll and *Edmund Peckover,* of *Fakenham*	3	5	0
Henry Miller, of *Wickmore*	40	0	0
Jeremy Lucas, Grace Palmer, and *Anne Palmer*	2	13	6
Edward King, of *Wymondham*	2	10	0
Frances Pulham, of *Runhall,* and *William Free-man,* of *Attleburgh*	1	12	0
† *John Allen,* of *Lammis,* and *John Reeve,* of *Aylfham*	2	6	6
John Laurence, of *Wramplingham*	40	0	0
Elizabeth Roufe, of *Aylfham, Abraham Houfe,* of *Rufhford,* and *Robert King,* of *Swafield*	14	7	2
Edmund Rack, of *Kilverfton*	26	0	0
William Garnham, Mary Townfend, and *Robert Spurgin,* of *Thetford*	2	5	0
Henry Kettle, of *Rufhford*	10	17	0
Henry Goddard, of *Hockham*	9	4	0
Thomas Money and *Francis Gardener,* both of *Tivetfhall*	3	0	0
	762	10	11

Bufy In-formers.

About this Time *William Barber,* of *Geffing,* was committed to Prifon on a *Significavit* of Excommunication procured by the Prieft of that Parifh, who alfo acted the Part of an Informer againft him for being at the Meeting, for which he was fined as is before mentioned. Of thofe who were active in molefting religious Meetings, about *Thetford,* was one Captain *Cropley,* who without Warrant from the Civil Magiftrate, would attempt to difperfe the Affemblies by Force of Arms : And when they afked for his Commiffion fo to do, he fhewed them his Rapier : And one of them not going at his Command, he beat him on

Captain Crop-ley's Cruelty.

---

* *Luke Lindoe* had all his Beds taken away, with other Goods, fo that himfelf, is Wife and Children, were conftrained to lodge on Straw in the cold Winter Seafon.
† The faid *John Allen* was alfo fent to Goal by the following *Mittimus,* viz.

" *Norfolk* fs.

" I herewith fend you the Body of *John Allen,* of *Lammis,* who refufeth to take the Oath
" of Allegiance, and hath feveral Meetings, and unlawful Affemblies at his Houfe, under
" Pretence of divine Worfhip, contrary to his Majefty's late Proclamation. Thefe are
" therefore to will and require you in his Majefty's Name, him fafely to keep as your Pri-
" foner, to anfwer this his Contempt at the next Affizes and General-Goal-Delivery, holden
" for this County at the Caftle of *Norwich* : And hereof fail not, Given under my Hand
" and Seal this 9th Day of *June* 1671.

To the Keeper of the King's Goal
at the Caftle of Norwich, *or to*
his Deputy in his Abfence.

on the Head with his Stick, and kickt him on the Back, to the endangering of
his Life, so that he was sick for a considerable Time after.

On the 10th of the Month called *July* this Year, two drunken Informers,
Wright and *Spendlove*, (one of whom in his Cups had said, *We will eat of the
Fat, and drink of the Sweet, and the Rogues* [the *Quakers*] *shall pay for all.*)
came to the Meeting at *Norwich*, and having procured a Warrant, caused
*William Waymer, Thomas Buddery, Anthony Alexander, John Rust, Edward
Monk, Anne Whitlock, Thomas Plumsted, Isaac Gofs,* and *Robert Miles,* to go
with them before the Mayor. As they passed the Street, the People asked,
Who were the Informers ? Some of the Friends answered, *These are the In-
formers,* pointing to them. Upon which the People expressed some Dislike of
their Practice. Hence those Informers took Occasion, and complained to
Augustin Briggs, Mayor, and *Francis Bacon,* Steward, that they were in Danger,
and afraid of the People. Whereupon the Mayor sent five of the Friends to
Prison by the following *Mittimus,* viz.

" *Norwich* ss.

" WE send you herewith the Bodies of *Thomas Buddery* Woolcomber,
" *John Rust* Sawyer, *Edward Monk* Woolcomber, *William Waymer*
" Boddice-maker, and *Anthony Alexander* Tanner. These are therefore in his
" Majesty's Name, to will and require you to receive and keep them in your
" Custody, till they shall severally find sufficient Sureties for their several
" Appearances at the next General Sessions of the Peace, to be holden for this
" City aforesaid, or be otherwise lawfully discharged. And hereof fail not
" at your Peril. Given under our Hands and Seals the 10th of *July,* in the
" 22d Year of the Reign of our Sovereign Lord King *Charles the Second,*
" *Annoq; Dom.* 1670.

*Mittimus of
5 Persons to
Prison.*

*To the Constables of St. Peter's of
Mancraft, in the City aforesaid, to convey to the Keeper of
the Common Goal, to receive
the said Persons according to
this Warrant.*

" AUGT. BRIGGS, *Mayor,*
" FRA. BACON."

Although this *Mittimus* expressed no such Cause of Commitment, yet a Bill
of Indictment was drawn up against them for a Riot, and presented to the
Grand Jury, but they refused to find it. As for *Anne Whitlock,* at whose
House the Meeting was, they fined her 20 *l.* but her Goods not being worth so
much, Part of that Sum was levied on others, according to the Direction of the
Warrant, which was as follows, viz.

" *Norwich* ss.

" WHEREAS *Anne Whitlock,* of the Parish of St. *Edmund* in this
" City aforesaid, Widow, doth stand duly convicted before us *Augustin*
" *Briggs* and *Francis Bacon,* two of his Majesty's Justices of this City afore-
" said, for wittingly and willingly suffering an unlawful Assembly and Con-
" venticle to be holden in her House upon *Sunday* the 10th of this Instant *July,*
" contrary to the Statute in that Behalf lately made and provided, and there-
" upon stands fined by us the Sum of twenty Pounds for this her first Offence
" against the said Act.

" These are therefore in his Majesty's Name to will and require you, and every
" of you, forthwith to levy the said Sum of twenty Pounds by Distress and Sale
" of the Goods and Chattels of the said *Anne Whitlock,* rendring to her the
" Overplus. And if she shall not have sufficient Goods and Chattels, whereby
" the said twenty Pounds may be levied, then to certify the same unto us, that
" the

*Warrant for
Distress.*

NORFOLK. " the same may be elsewhere levied. And for your so doing this shall be your
1670. " Warrant. Given under our Hands and Seals this 20th of *July* 1670.

To the Constables of Feybridge   " AUGT. BRIGGS, *Mayor*,
Ward, and to either of them.   " FRA. BACON."

Soon after were taken by Distress for Meetings in the said City, as follows, *viz.*

		l.	*s.*	*d.*
Distress for Meetings.	From *John Defrance*, Goods worth	1	6	0
	Anthony Alexander	28	2	0
	William Waymer	0	19	0
	Samuel Duncomb	20	18	6
	Thomas Buddery	1	0	0
	Anne Whitlock	8	0	0
		60	5	6

Samuel Duncomb and *Anthony Alexander* appealed to the Quarter Sessions, but found no Redress, the Mayor and Steward not suffering the Witnesses against them to be produced to their Faces, but the Records of the Court, which had been sworn to in their Absence, were taken for Evidence against them ; nor were they allowed any Copy of those Records before their Trial. They apprehended themselves to be very unjustly used, and represented the Hardship of their Case in the following Letter to the *Mayor, Steward,* and *Court* of *Aldermen,* viz.

" *Friends,*

Letter of S. Duncomb and A. Alexander.

" OUR Oppression is more than we ought always to bear in Silence :
" You cannot be ignorant how some of us have suffered several Ways,
" sometimes in our Assemblies by the rude Multitude, sometimes by Impri-
" sonment, and sometimes by those called *Ecclesiastical Courts.*
" And now we are upon the Brink of Ruin by the Loss of our Goods, &c.
" whereby we are made harbourless in our own Houses, and the Widow and
" the Fatherless have been forced to wander from Place to Place for a Night's
" Lodging, which caused Tears to trickle down the Cheeks of the Fatherless
" Children, which has even melted our Bowels to behold. And what would
" you have us to do ? Do you think we are only wilful, and resolve so to be ?
" Do you think these Things are pleasing to our own Wills (as we are Creatures
" compassed with Flesh and Blood, as you also are) thus to suffer ? The Lord
" be Witness in this Case whether it be so, (as sometimes some of you upbraid
" us) or whether it be not, because that Impulse he has upon our Souls and
" Consciences constrains us to wait upon him, (according to his Light made
" manifest in us) to regulate, reform, and lead into the Life of his Son. And
" for our thus Waiting upon him in the Spirit of our Minds, have we deeply
" suffered.
" And some upon the late Act have made themselves Informers and Wit-
" nesses against us, (Parties and Witnesses both) who would Swear upon
" * Supposition, and falsely for their Advantage : And yet their Oaths were
" allowed in our Absence : And when some of us address'd our selves to the
" Mayor, this was his Answer, *He could not help us,* but advised us to make
" our Appeal ; and when it was answered, *It may be he would take Offence against
" us for it,* he answered, *No, he wish't it might take Effect.* But when it came
" to

---

* The Informers had sworn that *Anthony Alexander* was at a Meeting, though they had not seen him there.

" to Trial, he and the Steward appear'd refolv'd Men that it fhould never go
" on our Sides, and hinder'd the Procedure of our Appeal : And becaufe you
" might fee the Jury could not have brought it in againft us by the Witneffes
" Face to Face, being but *one*, and the Act faid *two*, (and he a Party) you
" made the Records, which were fworn to in our Abfence, to be the Evi-
" dence againft us, and preft it upon the Jury, that if we were there it was
" enough, whether we committed Fact againft the Law or no. Or is that the
" Fact, being at an Houfe above five ? Does the Act forbid that ? O you unjuft
" Judges, would you be thus dealt with your felves ? Think you it not enough
" for us to fuffer the Penalty of the Act when we do an Exercife that it forbids,
" but you will make us fuffer before, fuppofing we intended it ? Do you deal
" thus by Felons ? If they be taken in a Place where they have ftolen, and you
" fuppofe they intended to have done it again, do you punifh them upon Sup-
" pofition of their Intentions ? Surely no. But do you not punifh us becaufe
" you fuppofe we intended to wait upon God (which is not Evil) though we
" did not fpeak one Word ? Is there not a Complaint upon Record againft
" thofe who made Men Offenders for a Word ? And you make us fo for none
" at all. Did you think with your felves, we muft have fuffered from others
" if we had not from you, and that we had as good from you ? If it muft
" have been fo, we had rather it had been fo for your Sakes, for furely the
" Hand of the Lord will be fhortly ftretched forth againft you for thefe unjuft
" Proceedings. The Severity of the Law pretended againft us, you would
" have executed, but you would not let us enjoy the Mercy of it, or what Re-
" lief it affords. Would you be willing to be dealt fo by in the fame Cafe ?
" The Rod that the Lord fuffers to lie upon our Backs now, it will be but juft
" you fhould feel it upon yours. Think upon that : And then who will you
" have to plead for you ? For we have done you no Wrong, nor never in-
" tended it, the Lord knows. So we have not given you juft Caufe thus to
" proceed againft us. And your pretending there is a Law againft us, and you
" were forced to proceed thereby, will not hide your Enmity by which you
" have acted againft us ; for you go contrary thereunto by punifhing us when
" there is no Exercife committed or pretended contrary to the Act. And you
" carried it fo highly againft us, that thofe we employed to plead in the
" Caufe, we perceive, were afraid of your Difpleafure, and fo were fubordinate
" to your Wills, and thereby would not plead it fully according to their Judg-
" ments. And we were ignorant we might fpeak in our Cafe our felves,
" (according to Law) having retained them to plead it for us. So we have fuf-
" fered on every Hand : Well, we do fee there is none to plead our Caufe in
" this Matter but the Lord, who will certainly do it in his own Time : And
" when he utters his Voice by his Judgments upon you, then fhall you know,
" it's a fearful Thing to fall into the Hands of the Living God, with whom it is
" a righteous Thing to recompenfe Tribulation to them that trouble fuch as do
" them no Wrong. And have not you gone about to take the Staff out of the
" Lord's Hand, and prefumed to intrench upon his Prerogative, *viz.* to punifh
" People for the Meditation of their Hearts and Spirits, by Pretence of your
" outward Law, when they do no outward Exercife in Words or Actions ? And
" do you not think the Lord will arife againft you for it, and be terrible to you in
" the End, if you do not repent ? You have been Prefidents in this Cafe, which
" tends to the Ruin of many, and fo you have the more to anfwer ; but we
" wifh you may find Mercy from the great Judge of all the Earth, though
" we did not from you. But you muft alfo expect Judgment, and that with
" Severity, if you do not fpeedily repent, and give Teftimony thereof in
" Words and Deeds. And therefore be not high-minded, but fear ; for the
" Lord can quickly blaft your Honour, and difperfe your Riches. And Woe
" to them that fpoil when they were not fpoiled, (or encourage them that feek
" fo to do) furely the Lord's Hand you will feel heavy for thefe Things. We

" cannot

NORFOLK.
1670.

" cannot fow Pillows under your Arm-holes, but wifh you well as we
" do our felves.

" SAMUEL DUNCOMB,
" ANTHONY ALEXANDER.

" *P. S.* You have always faid to us, (by your Proceedings againſt us) *Bow*
" *down your Souls that we may go over you.* But the Lord will not always
" fuffer you fo to do."

The Mayor fo highly refented this Letter, that he fent them to Prifon for
fcandalous Expreffions, by the following *Mittimus*, viz.

" *Norwich* ſs.

Mittimus of
S. Duncomb
and A. Alex-
ander.

" **THESE** are in his Majefty's Name to will and require you to take
" into your Cuftody *Samuel Duncomb* and *Anthony Alexander*, and them
" fately keep, until they fhall find good Sureties for their Appearance at the
" next Seffions, for fcandalous Expreffions againſt Mr. *Mayor*, and Mr. *Stew-*
" *ard*, and the *Court* of *Aldermen*, and that they in the mean Time be of the
" good Behaviour: And hereof fail not. This 11th of *January* 1670.

*To the Keeper of the Common
Prifon in the faid City.*　　" AUGT. BRIGGS, *Mayor.*"

Samuel Duncomb, being in Prifon, fent a fecond Letter to the Magiftrates,
being as follows, *viz.*

" *Magiftrates !*

Letter of
S. Duncomb
to the Magif-
trates.

" **AS** I know I ought not to feign a Love with Diffimulation to fhun
" Sufferings, fo I know I ought not to let Sufferings extinguifh that
" which is without, as it hath not, though I cannot write to you fo as to pleafe
" you : I confefs, I wifh I could fay *You are far from Oppreffion :* And it
" grieves me that I muſt on the Contrary fay, *You manifeſted your Forwardneſs*
" *to ſtrengthen the Oppreſſors, rather than to relieve the Oppreſſed*, when, (ac-
" cording to legal Proceedings) you could not have done any otherwife, if you
" had given us thofe Advantages the Law doth allow : But you put us by
" having the Evidence *vivâ voce*, according to the ancient Trial of Juries, and
" put us upon difproving that which was fworn in our Abfence, and would not
" grant us a Copy of it before our Trial, that we might know thereby what
" we had to defend, but at our Trial we muſt difprove that we knew not
" what before, or lofe our Goods, fo juſt furprized us : As if you had in-
" tended it on purpofe to be a Snare for us. And for complaining thereof to
" be unjuft, our Liberties are taken from us, our Trades and Credits expofed
" to utter Ruin, whereby you have added Oppreffion to Oppreffion.
" If it be hard to you to bear the laying thefe Things before you, you may
" confider what it is to bear the Suffering of them, *viz. Loſs of Goods*, whereby
" we have been forced to lodge in Straw ; *Loſs of Liberty*, *Spoil of Trade, Spoil*
" *of Credits*, and the *Detriment* that you know accrues to young Tradefmen
" thereby. So that we are unable to maintain our aged Parents, and Relations,
" and Others, as we did help to do when we enjoyed them. Is it not ſtrange
" that the Steward fhould appear fo tender-hearted toward Felons, as to de-
" clare openly, *It is better to err in Mercy than in Judgment* ; and be fo hard
" to us as to err in Judgment thus to the ruinating of us. I remember I have
" read, that King *Charles the Firſt*, in his Sufferings expreſt, that he was fenfible
" *there was nothing worfe than legal Tyranny*, that is, Oppreffion under Pretence
" of the Execution of a Law, for you know Tyranny is not legal. And it
" may be judged how averfe he was to it, by his Judges Proceeding (no doubt

" by

" by his Directions) in the Trial of *John Lilburne* (at *Oxford* I think it was)
" who was active againſt the King in hoſtile Arms : Yet the Judges gave him
" all the Advantages he could take for the Preſervation of his Life, whereby he
" did obtain his Deliverance : By which the King was more honoured, than if his
" Judges had taken away *Lilburne*'s Life, by hindering him of his Advantages.
" And we are not ſeditious Sectaries, or diſloyal Perſons to the King, ñor ever
" were, nor can be ſo proved, whoſe Practices only the late Act takes hold of,
" and not the Practices of any other Perſons, as you may clearly underſtand, if
" you pleaſe to peruſe the Preamble of it. So leaving theſe Things to your
" tender Conſideration, I remain

" *Your Priſoner*

" SAMUEL DUNCOMB.

" *P. S.* I believe ſome of the Juſtices, that ſat in Court at our Trial, were
" not ſatisfied with the Proceedings therein, yet inaſmuch as they were ſilent,
" they cannot be excluded."

ANNO 1672. The following Perſons, being comprehended in the King's
Letters Patent under the great Seal of *England*, were this Year diſcharged out
of Priſon in this County, *viz.* *Edward Sconce, Nicholas Ruſton, Henry Kettle,
Edmund Rack, Thomas Cocherill, Robert Elden, Thomas Munford, Robert Gow-
ſell, Edward Beatley, Joſeph Harriſon, Edmund Patteſon, Mary Cirake, Anne
Holloway, Lewis Gedge, Thomas Watſon,* and *William Hempſtoll.*

ANNO 1674. Remarkable in this Year were the Sufferings of *Joſeph
Harriſon*, a Butcher, dwelling in or near *Fakenham :* This Man, notwithſtanding the Severity of the Law, and its rigorous Execution, ceaſed not to admit
religious Meetings to be held in his Houſe, and endured with Chriſtian Patience
the Penalties of his ſo doing, though often repeated ; for on the 31ſt of the
Month called *Auguſt*, the Parochial Officers, with a Warrant from Sir *Chriſtopher
Calthorpe*, a Juſtice of the Peace, took from him a Bullock, and five Sheep,
worth 5 *l.* and about three Days after, they took from his Stall in the Market,
Beef worth 1 *l.* 12 *s.* On the 16th of *September* they took out of his Orchard
three fat Bullocks worth 9 *l.* And on the 23d, a fat Bullock worth 3 *l.* 10 *s.*
On the 14th of *October*, two Bullocks worth 6 *l.* And on the 28th, a Milch
Cow worth 50 *s.* And ſoon after that, an Horſe and a Mare worth 4 *l.* And in
the Months called *January* and *February* the ſame Year, they ſeized at three
ſeveral Times his Meat in the Market, to the Value of 3 *l.* 7 *s.* 6 *d.*

In this Year alſo, *Edward Pickling*, of *Trunk*, was committed to Priſon for
refuſing to pay Tithes, at the Suit of *Robert Thickſton*, Prieſt of the ſame Pariſh.

ANNO 1675. *Thomas Murford* was preſented at the Quarter Seſſions ; a
Copy of which Preſentment is as follows.

" *City of* Norwich, *and County*
" *of the ſame,* 1675.   ſs.

" BE it remembred, that *Joſeph Teniſon*, Gent. as well for our Lord the
"   King, as for the Poor of the Pariſh of St. *Peter*'s of *Mancraft* in the
" City aforeſaid, as for himſelf in this Behalf, in his proper Perſon cometh
" here in Court of our Lord the King, of the General Seſſions of the Peace
" and *Oyer* and *Terminer*, holden at *Guild-hall*, in the City aforeſaid, on *Mon-
" day* being the 12th Day of *July*, in the 27th Year of our Sovereign Lord
" *Charles the Second*, by the Grace of God, of *England, Scotland, France,* and
" *Ireland*, King, Defender of the Faith, *&c.* before *John Manſer*, Mayor,
" and *Francis Bacon*, Eſq; Steward of the ſame City, and other his Aſſociates,
" aſſigned Juſtices of the Peace of the City aforeſaid, and County of the ſame
" City, to be kept ; and alſo to hear and determine diverſe Felonies and Treſ-
" paſſes, and other evil Deeds perpetrated in the City aforeſaid, and Country
                                                                    " of

NORFOLK.
1675.

" of the fame. And as well for our Lord the King, and the Poor aforefaid,
" as for himfelf, giveth the Court here to underftand, and be informed, that
" *Thomas Murford*, late of the aforefaid Parifh of St. *Peter*, of *Mancraft*,
" in the City aforefaid, and County of the fame City, Yeoman, who for
" one Year laft paft, before the Day of the exhibiting this Information, was
" an Inhabitant within the Paifh aforefaid, and by the whole Time aforefaid
" was of the Age of fixteen Years and above : And that the faid *Thomas*
" *Murford*, from the firft Day of *April*, in the abovefaid 27th Year of the Reign
" of our now faid Lord the King, until the fecond Day of *July* in the Year afore-
" faid, *viz.* by three Months next following after the aforefaid firft Day of
" *April*, did not repair to his Parifh-Church in the Parifh aforefaid, nor to any
" other Church, Chapel, nor ufual Place of Common-prayer, and divine Service,
" on any Lord's Days, or other Days, ordained and ufed to be kept as Holi-
" days, happening between the aforefaid firft Day of *April* and the aforefaid
" fecond Day of *July*, but voluntarily and obftinately hath forborn the fame by
" the Space of three Months, the aforefaid *Thomas Murford* not having a lawful
" or reafonable Excufe or Impediment for his Abfence, contrary to the Form
" of the Statutes in the Parliament at *Weftminfter*, in the County of *Middlefex*,
" holden in the Years of the Reign of our late Sovereign Lady *Elizabeth*, late
" Queen of *England*, &c. the 1ft and 23d in that Cafe made and provided,
" by which the faid *Thomas Murford*, by Virtue of the Statute aforefaid, made
" in the 23d Year of the Reign of the faid Queen, hath forfeited to our now
" faid Lord the King, to the Poor of the Parifh of St. *Peter*, of *Mancraft*
" aforefaid, and to the aforefaid *Jofeph Tenifon*, fixty Pounds of lawful Money
" of *England*, *viz.* twenty Pounds for every Month of the aforefaid three
" Months : Upon which the faid *Jofeph Tenifon* requireth of the faid *Thomas*
" *Murford*, for our faid Lord the King, for the Poor of the Parifh of St *Peter*'s
" of *Mancraft* aforefaid, and for himfelf, the aforefaid fixty Pounds by the
" faid *Thomas Murford* fo as aforefaid forfeited. Whereupon the faid *Jofeph*
" *Tenifon*, who as well prayeth a third Part, according to the Form of the
" Statute made in the faid 23d Year, as well for our faid Lord the King,
" and the Poor aforefaid, as for himfelf, prayeth the Advice of the Court here
" in the Premifes, and due Procefs of Law to be made againft the faid *Thomas*
" *Murford*, &c.

" The faid *Jofeph Tenifon* was fworn here in full Court, according to
" the Statute.

" *Pledges to profecute* $\left\{ \begin{array}{l} \text{John Doe,} \\ \text{Richard Roe."} \end{array} \right.$

Imprifonments and Profecutions for Tithes.

Thus commenced a vexatious Profecution ; of the Iffue of which we have not
a particular Account.

In like Manner alfo *Samuel Duncomb* was profecuted for abfenting himfelf
from the publick Worfhip.

In this Year *John Norris* and *Henry Peede*, of *North-Walfham*, were imprifoned
for Tithes, at the Suit of Efq; *Beecher*. Alfo *John Hart* and *Matthew Bacon*
were committed to Prifon for Demands of fmall Tithes and *Eafter-Offerings*,
at the Suit of *Thomas Clendon*, Prieft of *North-Walfham*, whofe Demand from
one of them amounted to no more than 5 *d.* per Annum. Alfo *Francis Gardener*,
of *Tivetfhall*, was profecuted in the *Exchequer* for Tithes, at the Suit of *Chriftopher Burrill*, Prieft, and committed to *Norwich* Caftle.

More Sufferings of Jofeph Harrifon.

Jofeph Harrifon, who fuffered fo much Spoil of his Goods in the laft Year,
had taken from him alfo in this Year, by eighteen feveral Seizures of Beef in
the Market, to the Value of 18 *l.* 19 *s.* 8 *d.* He alfo fuffered Diftrefs of an
Horfe, Hay, and Houfhold Goods, to the Value of 7 *l.* 5 *s.*

Diftrefs on W. Barber.

In *October* this Year, upon the Information of *John Gibbs*, Prieft of *Geffing*,
William Barber of that Place was convicted for a Meeting at his Houfe, and
fined 20 *l.* for which he had his Goods feized to the Value of 50 *l.* though himfelf was then in Prifon at the fame Prieft's Suit for Tithes.

ANNO

ANNO 1676. About this Time many Warrants, upon Informations given of religious Meetings, were granted by the Justices, *Calthorp, Bedingfield, Crow,* and others, by which were taken, at or near *Fakenham;*

Distresses for Meetings.

	l.	s.	d.
From the Widow *Hemsterly,* thirty five Sheep worth	10	0	0
Francis Hill, seven Cows, a Mare, two Horses, Cloth, and Money, to the Value of	26	16	6
Robert Southgate, of *Twyford,* two Cows, a Mare, and other Goods, worth	9	12	0
Nathanael Uring, of *Walsingham,* two Mares, Yarn, Tobacco, and other Goods, worth	16	12	9
Robert Kirby, of *Holt,* Goods worth	13	5	0
Robert Barwick, William Wood, Anne Bee, Rose Cambridge, John Bee, William Bullard, James Bunting, and *Clemence Simons,* Goods worth	10	18	4
	87	4	7

Some of the Persons last named were poor, and the Distresses made on them, though of no great Value, yet extended to deprive them of their necessary Houshold Utensils, and such other Things as in their low Circumstances, were not easy to be recovered. But peculiarly grievous were the following Cases, viz.

Grievous Case of F. Larder.

The Wife of *Francis Larder,* frequented the Meetings of the People called *Quakers,* though he himself was not of that Persuasion: But for her Offence he was fined, and the Officers took away a Rugg, Blanket, and Bolster, worth 15 s. She still persisting in her religious Course, her Husband was again fined; but when the Officers came the second Time to distrain, they found his Wife sick in Bed, and little Goods in the House; whereupon they reported to the Justice accordingly, and that the Woman was likely to die. But the Justice, whom no Circumstance could move to Compassion, ordered them to go and take the Bed from under her, which Command was prevented from being put in Execution by the poor Woman's Death that Night. She was, with her Husband's Consent, at her Desire, buried in the Burying-Ground of her Friends, the *Quakers:* The Parish-Priest and his Clerk, not being paid their customary Fees, exprest their Indignation by an unusual Piece of Inhumanity; for after the Corps had been interred several Days, one *Thomas Bretland* and his Wife were induced to cause their Servant *Richard Tendrick,* and another Person, whose Name was *Robert Bloom,* to take up the Corps out of the Grave; in doing which they broke the Coffin, which they tied together, and then carried to the Market-place at *Fakenham,* and set it down near *Edmund Peckover's* Door, to the Amazement of the People, who were grieved to see so inhuman an Action: For which no Cause was assigned, but the *Omission* of paying Fees, pretended to be due where nothing had been done.

Inhuman Doings.

Thomas Watson, a very poor Man, who by hard Labour supported his Wife and five small Children, was fined for being at a Meeting. The Officers, pitying his Circumstances, reported to the Justice that the Man had little in the House, except the Bed he and his Family lay on. The hard-hearted Magistrate ordered them to take his Bed, which they did the next Day, and left him and his Family to lodge on Straw. His industrious Wife, after this, endeavouring to help maintain her Children, by baking a little Bread and selling it in the Market, the Officers made a Seizure even of that, at one Time to the Value of 19 d. and at another Time to the Value of 14 d. These Instances shew, that nothing is more destructive of Humanity than a furious and ignorant Zeal: This was farther exemplified in the Case of *Peter Wynna,* a Man so very poor, that the Goods they took from him, worth but 8 s. were the principal Part of the Furniture of his House.

Hard Case of T. Watson and his Wife.

William

NORFOLK.
1676.

An implacable Profecutor.

William Barber, of *Geffing,* was continued in Prifon for Tithes, where he had lain feven Years at the Suit of *John Gibbs* his Parifh-Prieft, a Profecutor fo implacable as to fay, that *he had taken Çare, in Cafe of his own Death, that* Barber *fhould not be releafed.* An Expreffion denoting a *fixed Malice,* as contrary to *Chriftian Charity,* as *Darknefs* to *Light.*

Jonathan Booty, after a Profecution in the County Court for Tithes, at the Suit of *Chriftopher Reeve,* Prieft of *Stratton-Mary,* had taken from him for Tithes four Cows worth 18 *l.*

Death of T. Mathewman in Prifon.

Death of his Wife.

Thomas Mathewman, of *Eaft-Dereham,* was imprifoned for Tithes in *Norwich* Caftle at the Suit of *Richard King,* an Impropriator, in which Imprifonment he died on the 7th of *November* this Year: His Wife, who affectionately attended him in the cold unhealthy Prifon, contracted thereby a Fit of Sicknefs, of which fhe alfo died on the 17th of the next Month.

Vifiting a fick Man deemed a Conventicle.

There dwelt at *Buckenham,* in this County, one *Robert Tillet,* an ancient Man, very weak and confumptive, whom fome of his Friends came to vifit in his Sicknefs: Two Informers, obferving this, crept into their Company; and while they were fitting together, the fick Man fpake a few Words to his Friends concerning his own Experience of the Work of Religion. This the Informers fwore to be a Conventicle, and the fick Man was fined 20 *l.* for which they took away fix of his Cows. About the fame Time they took from *Robert Peartree,* whom they had impoverifhed by former Seizures, the Remainder of his Houfhold Goods, and after that, the very Tools and Utenfils belonging to his Trade.

For Meetings at *Tivetfhall,* were taken

Diftreffes for Meetings.

	l.	*s.*	*d.*
From *John Money,* a Mare, Cow, and Bedding, worth	12	10	0
Thomas Money, fix Cows, a Mare, an Heifer, and Wood, worth	31	0	0
Margaret Money, Widow, her Bedding, and two Cows, worth	10	0	0
John Hunt, two Mares, and a Cart, worth	6	3	6
Mary Satterthwait, Pewter worth	2	0	0
Robert Mills, Yarn, Cloth, Looms, &c. worth	5	5	4
Robert Goodwin, two Cows and a Bull, worth	9	0	0
William Tilney, two Cows worth	8	0	0
And from *William Cattamew,* a poor Man, whom it would have been Charity to have relieved, a Table worth	0	5	6
For a Meeting at *Snare's-Hill,* taken			
From *Edward Rack,* of *Rufhford,* a Cow worth	3	10	0
Richard Hewes, of *Gaythorp,* three Cows worth	10	0	0
	97	14	4

For Meetings at the Houfe of *John Paterfon,* of *Cockly-Clay* near *Swaffham,* were taken

	l.	*s.*	*d.*
From the faid *John Paterfon,* two Hundred Sheep, and other Goods, worth	110	0	0
From *John Hubbard,* Cloth and Bays worth	19	0	0
Zachary Moniman, Goods worth	0	12	0
	129	12	0

Violent Proceedings at Norwich.

Violent in this Year were the Proceedings at *Norwich,* as appears by the following Inftances,

When the Officers came to *Anthony Alexander's* Houfe to make Diftrefs, and took away Goods worth 17 *l.* 19 *s.* One of them, *Erafmus Cooper,* faid to

Alexander's

Alexander's Wife, that *He was come to seize all they had, and would not leave them a Bed to lie on.* They brake the Doors with a Pickax, and behaved so desperately, that some Neighbours wept at the Sight of it. They charged *Alexander*'s Man to help them, and being told how unreasonable it was to require a Servant to take away his Master's Goods ; one of them churlishly answered, *They are our Goods.*

In like Manner, the Officers making Distress on the Goods of *Samuel Duncomb*, brought with them to his House one *Tennison*, an impudent Informer, and the common Hangman. They tarried there several Days and Nights, and kept *Samuel*'s Wife, then big with Child, a Prisoner, suffering her to speak to no Body, and admitting none of the Neighbours to come near her. One of the Informers was so insolent as to say, *I'll make the Mayor wait upon us as often as I please.* The Goods they took at that Time from *Samuel Duncomb* were valued at 42 *l.* 19 *s.*

With like Severity they entred into the House of *Thomas Murford*, in his Absence, and took away four Pieces of Broad-cloth, and twelve Pieces of Linen, worth about 40 *l.* At his coming Home, he appealed to the Quarter Sessions; but the *Recorder*, his Adversary, carried the Cause against him, and also committed him to Prison. When he enquired the Cause of his Commitment, the *Recorder* answered, *You shall know that afterward.* Thus arbitrarily committed, he remained close Prisoner about eighteen Weeks. The said *Thomas Murford* and *Samuel Duncomb*, within the Space of three Months, had Goods taken from them, for their religious Meetings, to the Value of 220 *l.* 19 *s.* About the same Time were taken, for the same Cause, from *Robert Hutchinson, John Sharper, John Fiddeman,* and *John Defrance,* Goods worth 1 *l.* 10 *s.* 2 *d.*

On the 17th of the Month called *July* this Year, *Thomas Atkins* was taken out of a Meeting at *Norwich*, and carried before the Mayor, who tendred him the Oath of Allegiance, and for refusing to Swear, committed him to Prison.

ANNO 1677. *Henry Goddard,* for refusing to pay Tithes, was prosecuted in the County Court by *Christopher Reeve,* Priest of *Stratton-Mary,* and had three Cows taken from him worth 9 *l.* In the same Year *Thomas Tyrrell* was prosecuted to an Outlawry for 6 *l.* demanded for Tithes, at the Suit of *Thomas Crabb,* Priest, and was imprisoned at *Norwich* seventeen Weeks : His Cattle also were distrained to the Value of about 30 *l.* and afterward, on an Execution for the same Tithe, were taken from him eight Cows, four Hogs, two Mares, a Colt, and Linen-Yarn, to the farther Value of 48 *l.* So that for Tithes claimed worth but 6 *l.* he sustained the Loss of his Goods to thirteen Times that Value, and also the Imprisonment of his Person. Hardships insupportable, had they not been alleviated by the Testimony of a good Conscience, supporting the Sufferer under the Weight of such Oppression.

For a Meeting at the House of *Edward Mills,* in *Runhall,* were taken

Prosecutions for Tithes.

Distresses for Meeting.

		l.	*s.*	*d.*
From *John Parker,* a Mare, Colt, Hay, and Wood, worth		7	5	0
John Aggs, two Milch Cows, an Horse, and Mare, worth		12	0	0
Stephen Gooch, two Cows and a Calf, worth		7	0	0
William Stonack, two Cows and a Calf, worth		9	0	0
		35	5	0

ANNO 1678. *Daniel Phillips,* of *Stoak-Ferry,* was committed to Prison for refusing to pay small Tithes, at the Suit of *Jeremiah Cowel* and *Robert Cowel,* Tithe-farmers. And *Nicholas Phillips* was yet continuing in Prison, where he had been above ten Years, at the Suit of *Edward Barnard* of *Dis.* There were also remaining in Prison, for their Testimony against Tithes, *Matthew King, Stephen Wicks, William King,* and *Richard Rouse,* of whom the former two had then been Prisoners about seventeen Years, the Third about fifteen Years, and the Latter almost nine Years. Also *Francis Gardener,* after about three

Long Imprisonments for Tithes.

NORFOLK. three Years Confinement for Tithes, at the Suit of *Christopher Burrel*, Priest
1678. of *Tivetshall*, was taken with a violent Fit of Sickness, and when his Life was
in apparent Danger, Application was made to his Prosecutor to grant him a
Death of little Liberty, but he refused it ; so that he died under close Confinement on
F. Gardener the 7th of *December* this Year.
in Prison.

More Suffer- In this Year also *Joseph Harrison*, several Times before mentioned, suffered,
ings of Joseph for Meetings, nine several Seizures of Beef, and Hides in the Market, to the
Harrison. Value of 7 *l.* 18 *s.* And in the same Year, the Officers also went three several
Times to his House, broke open his Shop-doors, and took thence Beef, Tallow,
and Hides, worth 9 *l.* 10 *s.* The Officers, who made these Seizures, rendered
neither Account nor Overplus to the Sufferer ; they usually sold the Meat
among themselves, and some of them would sit tipling with *Watt* the Informer most Part of the Night. Some of the Justices also would convict upon a
slender Information ; for Instance, Justice *Calthorp* granted a Warrant for Distress, for a Meeting at *Joseph Harrison*'s House, upon the Oaths of *Watt* and his
Wife, who swore that they saw certain Persons come out of the Gate.

Sufferings of It happened in this Year, that *Edmund Peckover*, a Shopkeeper of *Fakenham*,
E. Peckover. an ancient Man, was chosen Overseer of the Poor of that Parish. Now it was
usual with the Justices when they granted Warrants for Distress, to direct them
to the Constables, Overseers, and Churchwardens, of the Place. Accordingly
Edmund was called on to assist in selling some Goods, taken by Distress from a
Neighbour of his own Persuasion, which he refused to do, alledging, *that he
was lame, and not able to sell his own Goods.* This he spoke in the Hearing of
Watt the Informer's Wife, and another Woman who had been twice whipt for
Theft. These Women reported to Justice *Hilliard*, that *Edmund* had said, *He
would not sell stolen Goods :* Upon this the Justice sent his Warrant for him,
and after some Conference told him, *That in regard of his Age he would dismiss
him, if he would promise to execute the next Warrant of that Kind.* To which
he answered, *I may not do my Neighbour such an Injury :* Wherefore the Justice
fined him 5 *l.* and issued a Warrant for Distress, by which his Goods were taken
away to the Value of 24 *l.* 3 *s.* 6 *d.* The Form of which Warrant was as
follows, *viz.*

" *Norfolk* ss.

Warrant for " **WHEREAS** it stands convicted before me, one of his Majesty's
Distress on " Justices of the Peace in this County, by the Oath of two Witnesses,
E. Peckover. " as well as by the Notoriety of the Thing it self, that *Edmund Peckover*, of the
" Parish of *Fakenham* in the County aforesaid, hath wittingly and willingly
" omitted, and peremptorily refused to execute or assist in the Execution of a
" Warrant upon the Goods of *Joseph Harrison*, of the Parish and County
" aforesaid, for that the said *Joseph Harrison* did suffer an unlawful Meeting or
" Conventicle in his Dwelling-house, in *Fakenham* aforesaid, he the said *Ed-*
" *mund* being Overseer for the Poor in the said Parish, and hath for his
" Omission forfeited 5 *l.* according to the Statute, intituled, *An Act for pre-*
" *venting and suppressing of Conventicles.* These are in his Majesty's Name to
" will and require you forthwith to levy upon the Goods and Chattels of the
" said *Edmund Peckover* the Sum of five Pounds by Distress and Sale, ren-
" dring the Overplus to the said *Edmund*, and to return the said five Pounds
" to me, to be disposed of as the Law directs. Given under my Hand and
" Seal at *Carston* this 19th of *February*, in the 30th Year of his Majesty's
" Reign. 1678.

> *To* Francis Page *and* Thomas Jarret,
> *Constables* ; *Mr.* Robert Sheldrake
> *and* Thomas Bretland, *Churchwar-*
> *dens* ; Robert Borlton *and* Henry
> Gogney, *Overseers.*

The

The faid *Edmund Peckover* was a clofe Attender of religious Meetings during the Heat of Perfecution, and had his Goods often diftrained by Warrants grounded on the Act againft Conventicles, by which upon feveral Informations againft himfelf, his Wife, and Son, he had taken from him at feveral Times, in Goods and Money out of his Shop, to the Value of 70*l.* and upwards.

In this Year alfo, for Meetings at *Yarmouth*, were taken from *Thomas Fuller*, his Bed, and Bed-clothes, worth 12*l.* And from *William Waymer*, Goods worth 10*l.* 9*s.*

In the fame Year *John Hubbard*, *Elizabeth* his Wife, and *John Hubbard* their Son, were profecuted in the Ecclefiaftical Court, and excommunicated, for Abfence from the National Worfhip ; as were alfo for the fame Caufe, *Daniel Phillips* and *Elizabeth* his Wife, of *Stoak-ferry* ; *John Paterfon* and *Elizabeth* his Wife, of *Cockly-Clay*; *Bartholomew Hewling* and *Margery* his Wife, of *Shipdam*.

John Laurence and *John High*, of *Wramplingham*, were profecuted on the 23d of Q. *Eliz.* for not going to their Parifh-Church, and fuffered a long Imprifonment for the fame. And for the like Caufe, *John Norris* was imprifoned on a Writ *de Excommunicato capiendo*, and continued Prifoner till he died.

ANNO 1679. *Thomas Fofter* and *John Spoil*, both of *Mulborton*, were imprifoned for Tithes on Writs *de Excommunicato capiendo*, at the Suit of *David Scargill*, Prieft of that Parifh.

Edmund Peckover, profecuted on an old Statute for 12 *d.* each *Sunday*, for Abfence from his Parifh-Church, had taken from him on that Account, Goods worth 6*l.* 5*s.*

ANNO 1680. The aforefaid *Edmund Peckover* was profecuted on the Statute, made againft *Popifh* Recufants, for 20*l.* per Month, for not going to the publick Worfhip, concerning which the following Account was given in a Letter from his Son *Jofeph Peckover*, bearing Date, *October* the 19th, 1680, viz. " Our Adverfaries are wholly bent to ruin us ; they have diftrained for 120*l.* " for the King's Ufe, as they fay, upon the Statute of 20*l.* a Month, and " have taken above forty Pieces of Serges and Stuffs, fome whole, and fome " cut ; alfo feventeen Pieces of Linen Cloth, Calicoes, and *Scotch* Cloth, but " would not let us meafure any, that we know not what they amount to, fo " we have fhut up Shop to fecure our Creditors, and if there be no Likelihood " of a Stop to their Proceedings, we intend to keep open Shop no more, but " to pay where it is owing. One *Samuel Verden*, the Under-Sheriff, with three " of his Bayliffs have done it. They alfo fay, *They will have my Father to* " *Prifon*, though he be very weak."———

About the fame Time, *James Denton*, *John Reeve*, and others, were profecuted on the fame Statute ; and *James Denton's* Malt-houfe was feized on for the Sum of 200*l.* pretended to be due from him to the King.

Toward the Conclufion of the laft Year, viz. on the 21ft of the Month called *March*, *George Whitehead* and *Thomas Burr* were taken at a Meeting in *Norwich* : The Manner of their being apprehended was rude and uncivil ; for one *Chriftopher Nobs*, Clerk of *Gregory's* Parifh, came into the Meeting, pufhing on each Side with his Elbows, and ftruck *Rofe Gedney* fuch a Blow on her Breaft, as made it fore for feveral Days after ; alfo *Charles Alden*, a Vintner, and one of the Singing-Men at the Cathedral, rufhed in, calling out, *Here's*

Sons of Whores : Here's five Hundred Sons and Daughters of Whores : The Church-Doors ftand open, but they will be hanged before they will come there. And whilft *George Whitehead* was fpeaking, he cryed out, *Pull down that Puppy-Dog, why do you fuffer him to ftand there prating ?* Thefe Perfons, and others, made much Difturbance in the Meeting, till at length one of the Sheriffs came, and required *George Whitehead* and *Thomas Burr* to go with him, and he conducted them to the Goal-Door, and there left them : After about two Hours Detention there, they were had before *Francis Bacon*, the Recorder, who

told them, *They muft either pay down a Fine of 20l. each, or go to Prifon.* He alfo afked them, *Whether they would take the Oath of Allegiance ?* They anfwered, *They could not take any Oath for Confcience-fake.* He then told them,

NORFOLK.
1680.

that *He would commit them to Prison till next Seffions, and then the Oath fhould be again tendred them, and they fhould be* Premunired *if they refufed to take it : But if they would pay their Fines, he would not fend them to Prifon.* They perfifting in their Refufal, he told them, *If they would give Security to appear at the next Quarter Seffions, he would not fend them to Goal.* But they not being willing to be bound in fuch a Cafe, he fent them to Prifon by the following *Mittimus,* viz.

" **City and County**
" *of* **Norwich.**

Mittimus.

" **WHEREAS** *George Whitehead,* of the Parifh of St. *Buttolph* in
" *London,* Grocer, and *Thomas Burr,* of *Ware* in the County of *Hart-*
" *ford,* Malfter, have this Day affembled together with feveral other Perfons,
" in Difturbance of the publick Peace, and againft the Laws of this Realm,
" and being required to find Sureties for their refpective Appearance at the next
" general Seffions of the Peace, to be holden for the faid City and County, to
" anfwer the Premifes, which they refufed to do. Thefe are therefore to re-
" quire you to receive and keep the faid *George Whitehead* and *Thomas Burr*
" in the Common Goal for the City and County aforefaid, until they fhall
" be difcharged by due Order of Law, and hereof fail not : Given under my
" Hand and Seal the 21ft Day of *March, Anno Dom.* 1679.

To the Conftables of the Ward of Weft-Wymer,　　　" F. BACON."
and to either of them to convey, and to the
Keeper of the Common Goal aforefaid, to re-
ceive and keep the faid George Whitehead *and*
Thomas Burr, *according to this Warrant.*

Two Days after their Commitment, the Recorder iffued a fecond Warrant, as follows, *viz.*

" **City and County**
" *of* **Norwich.**

A fecond
Warrant.

" **WHEREAS** *George Whitehead* and *Thomas Burr* were lately fent by
" my Warrant, unto the County Goal for the City and County aforefaid,
" for being feditioufly affembled, with fome Hundreds of other difloyal Per-
" fons, againft the publick Peace, and in Contempt of the Laws and Govern-
" ment of this Realm. Now for that the faid *George Whitehead* and *Thomas*
" *Burr* are fufpicious Perfons, and Strangers to this City aforefaid, and being
" unwilling to declare that Duty, which they and every true and well-affected
" Subject ought to bear, by Bond of Allegiance to our gracious King, they
" did feverally refufe to take and pronounce the Oath of Obedience to the
" King's Majefty, duly tendred unto them, and after they were feverally re-
" quired to do the fame by me. Thefe are therefore in his Majefty's Name,
" to will and command you to keep the faid *George Whitehead* and *Thomas*
" *Burr* in the Common Goal for the faid City and County, without Bail or
" Mainprize, until the next General Quarter Seffions of the Peace, to be
" holden for the City and County aforefaid : And hereof fail not. Given under
" my Hand and Seal the 23d Day of *March, Annoq; Dom.* 1679.

To the Keeper of the Common Goal for　　　" F. BACON."
the City and County of Norwich.

At the Quarter Seffions, on the 28th of the Month called *April* 1680, the faid *George Whitehead* and *Thomas Burr* were called to the Bar, and had a long Hearing refpecting the Legality of the *Recorder's* Proceeding, which the major

Part

Part of the Juſtices ſeemed not to approve ; and were inclinable to have ſet them at Liberty. But the *Recorder* inſiſted on the Oath being tendred them in Court, which was done accordingly : And Record of the Proceſs of the Court reſpecting them, was made as follows, *viz.* " *George Whitehead* and *Thomas* " *Burr* are diſcharged of the Matter contained in their two *Mittimus*'s. And " the Oath of Allegiance, and the Teſtament to Swear in open Court, at this " preſent Seſſions, was ſeverally tendred to them : And the ſaid *George White-* " *head* and *Thomas Burr*, having ſeverally refuſed to take the ſaid Oath of " Allegiance, it is therefore ordered, that the ſaid *George Whitehead* and " *Thomas Burr* be committed to the Common Goal of the ſaid City, there to " remain without Bail or Mainprize until the next Quarter Seſſions." And accordingly they were committed again to Priſon.

During their Trial, they offered to ſubſcribe *A Proteſtation* or *Declaration* to diſtinguiſh them from *Popiſh* Recuſants, in the following Words, *viz.*

" I *A. B.* do in the Preſence of Almighty God, ſolemnly profeſs, and in " good Conſcience declare, It is my real Judgment that the Church of *Rome* " is not the real Church of Chriſt ; nor the Pope or Biſhop of *Rome*, Chriſt's " Vicar : And his or their Doctrines of depoſing *Heretical* Princes, and of ab- " ſolving their Subjects of their Obedience : Of Purgatory and Prayers for the " Dead : Of Indulgences, and worſhipping of Images : Of adoring and pray- " ing to the Virgin *Mary*, and other Saints deceaſed : And of *Tranſubſtantia-* " *tion*, or changing the Elements of Bread and Wine into the Body and Blood " of Chriſt, at or after the Conſecration thereof, by any Perſon whatſoever ; " are falſe and erroneous, and contrary to the Truth of God declared in the " Holy Scriptures. And therefore that the Communion of the ſaid Church is " ſuperſtitious and erroneous.

" And I do likewiſe ſincerely teſtify and declare, That I do from the Bottom " of my Heart deteſt and abhor all Plots and Conſpiracies that are or may " be contrived againſt the King or Parliament, or People of this Realm; or " the true *Proteſtant* Religion therein profeſſed. And I do hereby faithfully " promiſe by God's Help to live a peaceable and ſober Life, as becometh " a good *Chriſtian* and *Proteſtant* to do.

" *Witneſs my Hand.*"

The Priſoners alſo would have produced to the Court the following *Certificates*, but the *Recorder* would not ſuffer them to be read, *viz.*

" THESE are to certify all whom it may concern, That *George White-* " head, of the Pariſh of St. *Buttolph Biſhopſgate, London,* hath lived in " the ſame Pariſh for about ten Years laſt paſt, in good Repute, and is " eſteemed a Man of competent Eſtate, and hath fined for all Offices in the " Pariſh, ſave Churchwarden, and hath demeaned himſelf peaceably in his " Converſation, and he hath never been accounted, nor reputed to be *Jeſuit*, " or *Papiſt*, nor any Way *Popiſhly* affected : All Which we certify under our " Hands.

" JOHN FREEMAN ⎱ *Common-Council-Men*,
" THOMAS FYGE ⎰
" JOHN RUSSEN *Deputy*,
" GILBERT EAST ⎱ *Churchwardens*,
" JOHN OSBORNE ⎰

JOHN SUMNER *Conſtable*,
CHARLES BATHURST,
THOMAS DAWSON,
NICHOLAS HARDING.

London, *April* 22d. 1680.

" THESE are to certify any Perſon or Perſons whom it may concern, " that *Thomas Burr*, of *Ware* in the County of *Hartford*, Malſter, hath " lived and been a Trader in Malt for about fourteen Years paſt, and is a
" Man

NORFOLK,
1680.

" Man whom we judge of a good competent Eftate, and of good Credit
" and Reputation among his Neighbours in this Place, and hath never been
" accounted a *Jefuit* or *Papift :* All which we certify under our Hands.

" GILES ROE ⎫ *Churchwardens,*	THOMAS JOHNSON,
" HENRY HART ⎭	RICHARD DICKINSON,
" JOHN LARK ⎫ *Conftables,*	RIVERS DICKINSON,
" WILLIAM MOAKES ⎭	EDMUND FEAST,
" JOHN PERROT,	ISAAC HADSLEY.
" HENRY PEACH,	

Ware *in* Hartfordfhire, *this*
14th *of* April 1680.

The Recorder
difplaced.

About five Days after the End of the aforefaid Seffions, *viz.* on the 3d of
the Month called *May,* Francis Bacon, the *Recorder,* a violent Adverfary of the
People called *Quakers,* was put out of his Office by a Vote of *Common-Council,*
and a Man of more Equity and Moderation was chofen in his Place.

Before the enfuing *Quarter Seffions,* till which they ftood committed, they
found feveral Opportunities to reprefent their Cafe to the *new Recorder,* and
other the Magiftrates ; alfo by Means of fome of their Friends at *London,* a
Letter was obtained from the Earl of *Yarmouth* in their Favour : Their Friend
William Mead alfo ufed his Endeavours for their Relief, and took a Journey to
Norwich on purpofe to affift them to the utmoft of his Power. Thus the Mayor
and Juftices being fully apprized of their Innocence, became willing to difcharge them, and accordingly at the next General Seffions the following Order
of Court was made, *viz.*

" **A**T the General Seffions of the Peace, holden for the City of *Norwich,*
" and County of the fame, before *Robert Freeman* Efq; Mayor of the
" City of *Norwich, John Norris* Efq; Recorder of the faid City, *John Min-*
" *gey* Efq; Steward of the faid City, and other his Majefty's Juftices of
" Peace of the faid City, the 12th of *July,* in the two and thirtieth Year of
" the Reign of our Sovereign Lord King *Charles the Second,* &c. *Annoq;*
" *Dom.* 1680.

Difcharge of
G. White-
head *and*
T. Burr.

" *Proclamation being there publickly made,* That if any Perfon would come
" into the Court, and give any Information or Evidence, or prefer any Bill
" of Indictment againft *George Whitehead* and *Thomas Burr,* Prifoners at the
" Bar, they fhould be heard. And becaufe no Perfon came into the Court to
" prefer any Indictment, or to give any Information againft them, the faid
" *George Whitehead* and *Thomas Burr* are ordered to be *difcharged,* being com-
" mitted by Order of the laft Seffions, to remain in Prifon until this Seffions.

" *Per Curiam.* CARIE."

Thus after about fixteen Weeks Imprifonment they were fet at Liberty.
If the Reader fhall defire to fee the Particulars of their Trial, with the feveral
Points of Law relating to their Commitment, he may find the fame handled at
large in an Account thereof, intituled, *Due Order of Law and Juftice,* inferted
in a Book called *The Chriftian Progrefs of that ancient Servant and Minifter of
Jefus Chrift,* George Whitehead. Printed in the Year 1725.

Death of
M. Mawley
in Prifon.

In a printed Account of the Sufferings of Friends, prefented to the King,
Lords, and Commons, in Parliament affembled, in the Year 1680, we find
an Account of *Mary Mawley,* of *Wortwell,* committed to *Norwich* Caftle, at
the Suit of ——— *Mingley,* Prieft of the Parifh, for the Tithe of a Goofe, and
there kept Prifoner till fhe died.

Imprifon-
ments.

ANNO 1681. *Henry Miller* was committed to *Norwich* Caftle on a Procefs againft him for Abfence from the National Worfhip, as had been fome
Time before, *Francis Balls* and *Jeremy Lucas.*

ANNIS

ANNIS 1682 and 1683. In thefe Years *Anthony Alexander, Mary Booth, John Fiddeman,* and diverfe others of the People called *Quakers,* were kept clofe confined in the City Goal at *Norwich,* lying there in a Dungeon twenty feven Steps under Ground. Great were the Endeavours ufed by their Friends for their Relief, as appears by the following *Letter* and *Narrative,* viz.

NORFOLK.
1682 *and*
1683.

Clofe Confinement under Ground.

A Letter *from* GEORGE WHITEHEAD *and* WILLIAM CROUCH, *to Friends in Prifon at* Norwich; *dated in the Firft Month* 1682-3.

" *Dear Friends,* Anthony Alexander, Mary Booth, John Fiddeman, &c.

" AFTER the tender Salutation of our dear Loves to you all in the
" Lord, thefe are to acquaint you of our Care, and induftrious En-
" deavours, on your Behalf, fince we received your laft Letters; the One
" dated the 19th Inftant, and the Other the 21ft, together with the inclofed
" Letter from the Attorney, and the *Affidavits, Mittimus's,* and the County-
" Goaler's Letter to your Goaler, and alfo Sheriff *Stebbing*'s fevere Order to
" him. In Anfwer to all which, and your Defires fignified, we return you
" this following Account, *viz.*

A Letter *to the Prifoners.*

" 1. We two, whofe Names are hereunto fubfcribed, did Yefterday feek
" for *John Hill,* to whom the faid Attorney directed his Letter, but he was out
" of the City in the Country.

" 2. We fought out Judge *Windham,* and in the Afternoon had Admittance
" to fpeak to him. He was prepoffeft with Sheriff *Stebbing*'s Account againft
" you, and his own Vindication, having rendred you *obftinate, riotous, affront-*
" *ing the Law in your Meetings, and ftanding in the Street contrary to the Pro-*
" *clamation,* &c. But be not difcouraged at fuch injurious Reflections.

" 3. We told him, Sheriff *Stebbing* is your extream Adverfary and Party
" againft you.

" 4. On the Sheriff's Account he alfo reflected on you, as *refufing to give in*
" *Security for your Appearance at the Seffions, and refufing to pay for convenient*
" *Rooms in Prifon,* and faid, that *you chofe a * free Prifon.* This and more
" from Sheriff *Stebbing*'s Account, but ftill we excepted againft him, as not an
" indifferent Perfon.

" 5. We told him, we had Affidavits inclofed in a Letter from Perfons
" indifferent, upon which he called for the Letter to *John Hill,* and opened it,
" and read the *Mittimus* and *Affidavits,* which did caufe fome Calm, &c. having
" before that read the Letter dated the 19th of the Firft Month, which he
" plucked out of G. *Whitehead*'s Hand, wherein you give Account of Sheriff
" *Stebbing*'s being with the Judge, and of his and the Goaler's being more fevere
" to you fince, which Paffages we made Improvement of, to fhew the Sheriff's
" Contradiction to what the King, the Lord-Keeper, and Judge *Windham,*
" had ordered on your Behalf.

" 6. The Judge faid, *he had delivered Sheriff* Stebbing'*s Account to the*
" *Lord-Keeper,* and he gave us back the *Mittimus's,* and *Affidavits,* and faid,
" *we might do what we would with the Affidavits,* &c.

" 7. We gave Account Yefternight to the Meeting of our Friends, of our
" Endeavours with the Judge, and your Letters and the Affidavits were then
" read in the Meeting, who left the Matter to us farther to manage, and
" write to you, which herein we do.

" 8. This Morning we went early to the Lord-Keeper's, obtained Admit-
" tance to him, and fpoke with him in your Cafe and Behalf: He fhewed us
" Sheriff *Stebbing*'s Account againft you. We told him what an extream Ad-
" verfary and Party he is againft you. We delivered him the *Affidavits,* and
" told him they were from indifferent Perfons who had viewed the Goal, and

" we

---

* Such they might chufe, and yet not a deep Dungeon.

NORFOLK.
1682 *and*
1683.

" we defired his tender Notice of them, and to give Report to the King
" accordingly. He received them, and promifed he would deliver them to
" the King.

" 9. *Laftly.* We having thus far endeavoured, and laboured for you, and
" vindicated your Caufe much more than we can here exprefs : To what you
" propofe of drawing up your Cafe to the King, we think it very meet, that
" if you be continued under the fame Hardfhips, you briefly draw up your
" Complaint by Way of *Humble Petition,* or Requeft to the King, fhewing
" your hard Ufage in the moft material Points : For we have lately found
" that fome are apt to reject Complaints at the Council-Board, unlefs the
" Words [*Humble Petition*] be in the Front.

" Thus, *Dear Friends,* having given you thefe brief Notes of our En-
" deavours, being but as a fhort *Index* thereof, we hope that farther En-
" deavours will not be wanting, as the Lord fhall open our Way.

" GEORGE WHITEHEAD,
" WILLIAM CROUCH."

" *A* NARRATIVE *of* GEORGE WHITEHEAD'S *and*
" GILBERT LATEY'S *Application to* King CHARLES *the*
" Second, *on Behalf of their Friends imprifoned at* Norwich.

A Narrative
of an Applica-
tion to King
Charles.

" ON the 23d of the Twelfth Month 1682-3, being the Day the Judges
" appeared at Council, before they went their Circuits, *George White-*
" *head* and *Gilbert Latey* then attending, the Cafe of *Norwich* fuffering Friends
" was delivered at the Council-Board by Sir *Philip Lloyd,* who was pre-engaged
" to prefent it, which accordingly he did, but was obftructed the Reading of
" it, on Pretence that it was not a formal Petition, or not in the ufual
" Form, &c.

" The next Day, being the 24th of the Twelfth Month, *George Whitehead*
" and *Gilbert Latey* went to the Lord Privy-Seal, and fpake to him about the
" faid Cafe of *Norwich* Prifoners being obftructed the Reading at the Council-
" Board, &c. He told them, *that notwithftanding, after that, the King gave a*
" *Moderate Recommendation to the Judges, when they were below, concerning the*
" *Prifoners, to enquire into the State of the Prifoners, and their Ufage,* &c. This
" he told them twice over.

" A little after they the faid *G. W.* and *G. L.* had fpoken to the Lord Privy-
" Seal as before, they went up into the Gallery to fpeak with the King, at his
" coming out of the Park, where after fome Time of waiting, the Duke and
" his Attendants paffed by to meet the King, and after a little Space the King
" and his Attendants came through the Long Gallery towards his Lodgings.
" *G. W.* then ftept up to the King without any Interruption (the whole Com-
" pany being civil) and thus proceeded, *viz.*

" *G. W.* May it pleafe the King to grant us the Favour of a few Words.
" It is in Behalf of many of the King's peaceable Subjects, who are Prifoners
" at *Norwich,* and there like to be buried alive in Holes and Dungeons.

" King. *Can't they fwear themfelves out of Prifon ?*

" *G. W.* Under Favour, fuch are not in Society with us. We intreat
" the King to commiferate the diftreffed Cafe of the Prifoners in *Norwich,* for
" they are burying them alive in Dungeons under Ground.

" King. *Have you a Paper ? If you have a Paper of their Cafe, I'll take it.*
" *G. W.* Yes, here's a Paper. *Which he delivered into the King's Hand,*
" *and he gently took it.*

" *G. W.* They are a poor harmlefs People : Poor Woolcombers, Weavers,
" and Tradefmen, like to be deftroyed in Prifon, in Holes under Ground. We
" intreat the King not to fuffer thefe his peaceable Subjects to be buried alive.

" Gilbert

" *Gilbert Latey* then ftept to the King, *faying*, We are the King's Subjects
" that never did any Thing againft him, having been peaceable, and we can
" truly fay, have ferved him, and we never were againft him, yet our Friends
" are great Sufferers, and they lie in a Dungeon twenty feven Steps deep in
" the Ground at *Norwich*. Wherefore we have moft earneftly fought Relief
" of the King."

George *Whitehead*, in his Account of this Application to the King, obferves,
that his Friend *Gilbert Latey* (as well as himfelf) being tenderly affected with
Friends Sufferings and Hardfhips, fpake to the King in very tender Affection,
under a Senfe of the Lord's Power and holy Fear, which reached the King's
Heart and Confcience (and Others about him) beyond his Utterance, or what
he could in Words demonftrate.

At another Time, *viz.* on the 26th of the Second Month called *April* 1683,
the faid *George Whitehead* and *Gilbert Latey* again attended the King at *Hampton-Court*, of which the faid *G. W.* gives the following Account, *viz.*

" On the 25th of the Second Month 1683, we took Boat for *Kingfton*, in
" the Afternoon, but before we got to *Wandfworth* the Weather began to be fo
" very ftormy and tempeftuous upon the River *Thames*, that we were forced
" to take in at *Wandfworth*, and lodge there that Night at the Widow
" *Springet*'s. Next Morning we arofe by that Time it was well light, and
" walked on Foot to *Kingfton*, it raining almoft all the Way, fo that we were
" much wetted in going thither ; we made fome Stop at *Anne Fielder*'s, at
" *Kingfton*, till we had a little refrefhed our felves, and dried our Clothes at
" the Fire, and then we haftened away to *Hampton-Court*, to meet with the
" King before he went to Council.
" As we went along the Park, toward the Court, we faw at a Diftance
" diverfe Perfons ftanding in the Porch, looking towards us, and one above
" the reft I obferved, believing it was the King by his blue Ribbon, and black
" Cap. I faid to *Gilbert Latey*, *I am perfuaded yonder is the King :* And as we
" drew nearer faw it was the King indeed. And not being willing to go
" abruptly into his Prefence, to open our Cafe to him without his Leave, at
" a little Diftance I called to the King, defiring him to favour us a few
" Words, *&c.* which he prefently granting, one of his Gentlemen that knew
" us, came to us, and gently took off our Hats, and hung them on the Pales
" of a Fence before the Court, and then we went to the King, who was ready
" to hear us.
" Diverfe great Perfons being prefent with the King at the Gate or Porch,
" I proceeded to open our Cafe to him concerning the Continuance of the hard
" Sufferings of our Friends in *Norwich*, in Manner following, *viz.*
" *Firft.* I reminded the King, that our poor Friends in *Norwich* were ftill
" continued under great Durefs and Hardfhips in Goal, in Holes, and a Dun-
" geon under Ground, and defired that the King in his Clemency would
" pleafe to relieve them, further opening their diftreffed Cafe.
" The King anfwered, *It is againft Law they fuffer fo* ; *and I'll take Care
" concerning them.*
" *Note.* I was truly glad when I heard him give this Anfwer, believing
" then, that the Complaints which had been made to him of our Friends Ufage
" and Confinement, and the faid *Affidavits* of Others thereof, had fuch Credit
" and Weight with him, that I hoped he would caufe them to be releafed.
" *Secondly.* The King queftioned us about the Reafon of our not putting
" off our Hats, and ufing the Terms *Thee* and *Thou*, *Yea* and *Nay :* To
" which we gave him Anfwer particularly.
" *Gilbert Latey* faid, if we could put off our Hats to any Mortal, it fhould
" be to the King firft ; but for Confcience-fake we could not to any Mortal,
" but only in our approaching God in Prayer. *To which the King gave no
" particular Reply.*

" *G. W.*

" *G. W. Thou* and *Thee* to one Perfon is Scripture Language, and the true
" Way of Speaking.

" *G. L.* As *Paul* did to King *Agrippa*, Acts xxvi. 2. *viz. I think my felf*
" *happy, O King* Agrippa, *becaufe I fhall anfwer for my felf this Day before*
" *thee, touching all the Things whereof I am accufed of the* Jews, *efpecially be-*
" *caufe I know* thee *to be expert in all Cuftoms and Queftions which are among*
" *the* Jews.

" *G. W. Thirdly.* Concerning *Yea* and *Nay*, we are not ftrictly tied to
" the Expreffions, but fometimes ufe Others of the fame Signification, as *Yes*
" and *No*.

" A great Perfon prefent afked us, *Why do you call him* King ? *Why do you*
" *not call him*, His Majefty ?

" *G. W.* As he is *King*, he has *Majefty* belonging to him : 'Tis included.
" His *Majefty* is his *Greatnefs* and *Power*.

" King. *You fhould not ftand upon thefe Things in Affectation: The Word*
" You *is now become ufual in* Englifh: *And the Word* Yeah *is ufed by Seamen*
" *when they call from the Top of the Maft to be heard upon the Deck.* 'Tis *alfo*
" *a* Dutch *Word, who exprefs it* Yah.

" *G. W.* We affect not Singularity in Words or Behaviour, but defire
" to demean our felves in that Plainnefs and Simplicity, which we are in
" Confcience and Truth perfuaded unto.

" King. *The Words* Thee *and* Thou, *might have been better tranflated out of*
" *the* Greek, *You*.

" *G. W.* If fo, then the Tranflators were as fimple as we the *Quakers*.

" King. *Many of your Friends can Swear, or take an Oath, rather than*
" *lofe their Voices in Elections*.

" *G. W.* Though fome few Perfons have fworn, who have fometimes gone
" under our Profeffion, yet they are not in Society with us, nor we with
" them.

" *G. L.* We are as much diffatisfied with them as the King can be.

" *G. W.* We defire nothing to be done to the Prejudice or Difhonour
" of the King, nor to join with, or promote any Intereft againft the King :
" The Lord knows our Hearts : We have not any Defign or Defire for the
" Subverfion or Change of the Government : Nor can we reafonably be fup-
" pofed to have any fuch Defign, feeing we were deep Sufferers in *Cromwell*'s
" Time, as I my felf was : Therefore there is no Reafon we fhould feek to
" promote any Intereft againft the King, but only defire that God in his
" Wifdom may direct and preferve the King, and that nothing may be done
" or fuffered to the King's Difhonour or Hurt.

" *G. L.* We would not lofe our Point, that we came to the King for,
" that is, the Cafe of our diftreffed Friends in *Norwich*, to whom we defire the
" King to fhew his Princely Clemency for their Relief.

" King. *I will take Notice of their Cafe, and Care about it, that it fhall be*
" *called for in Council*.

" *G. W.* If there be any * Objections againft us (*i. e.* in Council) we pray
" the King to let us know them, and we hope to give fuch Anfwers as fhall
" be fatisfactory.

" King. *You fhall know : I'll take Care about your Bufinefs*.

" *G. W.* We gave *Affidavits* to the Lord-Keeper, which we hope were
" delivered to the King.

" King. *Yes, yes : I'll take Notice of their Cafe, and it fhall be called on in*
" *Council*.

" *G. L.*

---

* *Note.* The Reafon of this Propofal was, that they were informed that Secretary *Jen-*
kins intended to produce a Paper from the Sheriffs of *Norwich*, in Oppofition to the *Affida-*
vits which they had delivered. But it was fuppofed, that the King's favourable Anfwers,
and his confeffing their Suffering was againft Law, and promifing to take Care of their Cafe,
might prevent the Secretary's Intention in that Refpect.

" G. L. We accept it as a great Favour, that we have this Admittance
" to be heard, and pray God to preserve and direct the King.

" G. W. *To the Nobility present,* &c.   And we acknowledge all your Civili-
" ties and Kindness towards us.

" G. W. *To the King as he was with-drawing.* We hope the King will be
" mindful of our suffering Friends in *Norwich.*"

The Issue of their strenuous Applications, and of the King's favourable Reception and Hearing, and his gracious Promises to take Notice of their Case,
was, that at the Summer Assizes 1683, the said Prisoners in the Dungeon at
Norwich, were set at Liberty by the Judge, pursuant, as was believed, to the
Instructions given him by the King.

Imprisonments and Prosecutions for Absence from the National Worship.

In the Year 1682, *Stephen Gooch, Edward Miles* jun. and *Robert Millis*,
were committed to Prison, on Processes against them, for Absence from the
National Worship : And in the Year 1683, *John Aggs, William Barrows,
William Greenwood, Francis Baldwin, Edmund Bedwell, Samuel Pike, Samuel
Claydon, Thomas Fox, Anne Payne, William Moore*, and *Walter Peddiman*,
were also committed to Prison for the same Cause.

Excessive Seizure.

ANNO 1684. *John Roe* and *William Roe*, of *Longham-hall*, Farmers,
having been prosecuted on the Statute for 20*l.* per Month, for twelve Months
Absence from the National Worship, on the 14th of the Month called *April*,
the Sheriff's Officers came to their House to make a Seizure for 240*l.*
and accordingly seized all their Cattle, Corn, and Houshold Goods : On the
next Day they drove away to *East-Dereham* for Sale, twenty eight neat Kine,
worth 40*l.* On the 17th they took an Horse, twenty Milch Cows, and seven
Calves, worth 56*l.* 10*s.* On the 18th they took three Horses, a Mare, a
Cart and Harness, twenty four Stone of Wool, six Comb of Oats, and Sacks,
also six Swine, worth 40*l.* 6*s.* On the 23d they made an Appraisement of
the rest of the Corn and Cattle not yet disposed of : On the 26th they took
away twenty seven Comb of Wheat, five Milch Cows, six Comb of Seed-
Barley, an Horse, a Mare, a Cart and Harness, to the Value of 43*l.* And
on the 28th they took away thirteen Comb of Barley, worth 3*l.* 8*s.* In all
to the Value of 183*l.* 4*s.*

Rude Beha-viour of the Officers.

The Behaviour of the Officers and Assistants, who made this Seizure, was
very rude : They broke open the Doors, Drawers, and Chests, and threatned
the Servants of the House with Sword and Pistol.   To make themselves merry
they roasted a Pigg, and laid so much Wood on the Hearth, that they set the
Chimney on Fire, with which, and their Revelling, Cursing, and Swearing,
they affrighted the Wife of the said *William Roe* to the endangering of her
Life : She being then great with Child, was delivered before her Time, and
the Child died a few Days after. *John Roe* had desired one of his Neighbours
to tarry with him in the House, but they turned him out, telling him, that
the House was none of his, but the King's. Thus the Severity of the Law was
aggravated by the Insolence of those who were employed to execute it.

Abusive Usage of L. Gage.

On the 19th of the Month called *May*, the Officers of *Hempnall* came to
the House of *Lewis Gage*, with a Warrant from *Francis Gardener*, Justice,
fining him 10*l.* 15*s.* upon Information of a Meeting at his House some Months
before, when the Informers pulled him from his Seat, threw him on the Floor,
dragged him, by the Shoulders and Hair of his Head, out of Doors, and laid
him on the Snow, bidding him lie there and rot.   The like Barbarity they also
exercised on several Others at that Meeting.   The Officers took away his
Houshold Goods, worth 20*l.* and four Loads of Hay, breaking open a Door
to come at it : And on the 23d of the same Month they came again, when
no Body was within, and brake open the Door, and carried away most of his
remaining Houshold Goods to a Neighbouring Alehouse, the Keeper of which
had bought three Loads of his Goods before.   The Amount of those Goods,
taken at both Times, was not less than 40*l.*

NORFOLK.
1684.

Seizure of Cattle, &c.

About the same Time, *Jonathan Booty* and *Elizabeth Booty* his Mother, both of *Steaton-Michael*, having been prosecuted on the Statute for 20 *l.* per Month for not coming to Church, had taken from them five Cows, and all their Houshold Goods, not leaving the poor Woman, who was blind and near eighty Years of Age, so much as a Bed or Pillow to lay her Head on. They carried away also his working Tools. The Whole of the Goods, taken from them, amounted to 48 *l.* 3 *s.*

J. Gooding impoverished by many Seizures.

John Gooding, of *Tasburgh*, for a Meeting at his House, on the 30th of the Month called *August* this Year, had Goods taken from him worth 7 *l.* 13 *s.* being the small Remainder of many former Seizures, so that they left him without any Utensils of Houshold, and not satisfied therewith, they took also some of his wearing Apparel. About a Fortnight after they came again, and searched for more Goods, but finding none, abused the Man and his Wife, and threatned to send them to Goal.

Seizing the Effects of R. Southgate.

On the 12th of *September*, the Sheriff's Officers, or Persons who called themselves so, came to the House of *Robert Southgate*, and made a Seizure, leaving a Man in Possession till the 18th, when they drove away five Milch Cows worth 10 *l.* five Swine worth 3 *l.* eleven Sheep worth 3 *l.* and two Horses worth 6 *l.* They also took a Feather-bed, Bedding, and Chairs, worth 7 *l.* A Cart, Harness, Bridle, Saddle, and Pannel, worth 6 *l.* In all 35 *l.*

More Seizures.

On the 26th of the same Month, the Sheriff's Officers entred the House of *Henry Appleyard*, of *Saxlingham-Thorp*, demanding 80 *l.* for the King. They seized all his Goods both within Doors and without, and appraised them at 9 *l.* But when some of the Man's Neighbours, pitying his distressed Case, offered to buy them, they would not part with them again under 13 *l.*

On the 1st of *October*, the Bayliffs of the Hundred came to the House of *Samuel Pike*, of *Hingham*, seized his Goods, and put a Man in Possession till the 7th, when they took away five Milch Cows, and a Feather-bed, worth 15 *l.*

Cruel Usage of H. Ward.

On the 16th of *October*, the Sheriff's Officers came to the House of *Henry Ward*, of *Hellgay*, saying, *They came to seize all he had for* 100 *l. for the King*, which they instantly did, breaking open one Door, and seizing the Keys of the rest, secured them. They kept Possession four Days, swearing and hectoring in a most insolent Manner, to the great Terror of him and his Wife, being both infirm Persons, and near seventy Years of Age.

On the 18th they forcibly entered the Room, where the said *Henry's* Wife, a sickly Woman, lay, and pulled away her Bed out of the Room, scarce giving her Time to put on her Clothes, and leaving her only the Matt and Cords to lie on, while themselves lay on the Bed in another Room.

On the 20th they sold the Goods to several Persons, but refused to give the said *Henry* any Account of them, though often desired. So that the Value of them, which must have been considerable, is to him unknown.

Other grievous Seizures.

On the 14th of *November*, *Robert Allen*, a Bayliff, with two Informers, came and seized Houshold Goods, and Shop Goods, of *Henry Jennipy*, of *Ellingham-magna*, and carried them away to the Value of 18 *l.* not leaving him so much as a Bed to lie on.

On the same Day, the said Bayliff and Informers went to the House of *Winifred Dix*, of the same Town, Widow, (who then was, and had been above five Years a Prisoner for Tithes) and seized all they could find of hers, to the Value of 150 *l.* which they sold for 23 *l.* The Bayliff and his Assistants, with two Waggoners by them employed, consumed in Meat and Drink for themselves and their Horses, to the Value of 5 *l.*

On the same Day also, they went to the House of *John Long*, of *Little-Ellingham*, and took away a Feather-bed, and the Furniture belonging to it, worth 3 *l.*

On the 23d the Sheriff's Officers went to the House of *Robert Jarmin*, of *Shotsham*, demanding 220 *l.* for the King. Having seized what he had, they left a Man in Possession, who with his Horse continued there eight Days. Then they went again to dispose of the Goods, and sold them for 19 *l.* 10 *s.*

On the 29th *Thomas Cockerill*, for a Fine of 10 *l.* 5 *s.* for Meeting, had, by Warrant from Juſtice *Low*, a Seizure made of one Hundred and forty Pair of Shoes, which the Officers left in his Shop till the 1ſt of *December*, and then took away one Hundred Pair of them, worth 10 *l.* 10 *s.* NORFOLK. 1684.

On the 3d of *December*, *Anthony Alexander*, a Tanner in *Norwich*, by Warrant from the ſame Juſtice, had taken from him two Hundred Hides, worth 30 *l.* but valued by the Appraiſers, employed by the Diſtrainers, at 21 *l.* 10 *s.*

On the 26th of the Month called *January*, the ſaid *Anthony Alexander*, for a Fine of 15 *s.* for Meeting had taken from him by Warrant from *Nicholas Helwis*, Mayor, Leather to the Value of 1 *l.* 10 *s.*

In this Year were committed to *Norwich* Caſtle, on Proceſſes for Abſence from the National Worſhip, *Henry Wake*, *John Waſey*, *Matthew Bradbury*, *Katharine Haſlewood*, *Robert Jarmin*, and *John George* ; as was alſo *Nathanael Butler*, upon the Statute for 20 *l.* per Month. *Impriſon- ments.*

ANNO 1685. On the 31ſt Day of the Month called *March*, *Robert Southgate*, for being at a Meeting at *Wells*, had taken from him four Milch Cows, and eighteen Sheep, worth 12 *l.* 10 *s.* And at another Time two Horſes, worth 7 *l.* 10 *s.* *Diſtreſs.*

In the Month called *April*, *Thomas Laws*, *John Wetherby*, *George Bragg*, *Robert Campling*, and *Richard Roberts*, were remaining Priſoners in *Yarmouth* Goal, whither they had been committed in the Year 1682 for refuſing to take the Oath of Allegiance. And at the ſame Time, *John Fiddeman*, *John Cade*, *Thomas Murford*, *John Gurney*, *William Melcham*, *Stephen Amos*, *James Mahew*, *John Elſegood*, *William Kiddle*, *John Fenn*, *Nicholas Comſit*, *Thomas Buddery*, *John Defrance*, *William Waymer*, and *William Clayton*, were continuing Priſoners at *Norwich* Goal, having been for the ſame Cauſe committed thither about the Latter-end of the Year 1683. The Caſe of theſe laſt fifteen, as drawn up by themſelves, is contained n the following *Addreſs*, viz. *Priſoners in* Yarmouth *and* Norwich.

" *An* ADDRESS *of the* PRISONERS *at* Norwich, *to the*
" REPRESENTATIVES *of that City and County, humbly*
" *deſiring them to take our ſuffering Condition into Conſideration.*

" WE, who have been great Sufferers for no other Cauſe but for wor-
" ſhipping God, and becauſe it hath differed in Ceremony from the
" eſtabliſhed Worſhip of the Nation, ſome have termed it Sedition and Re-
" bellion, and have proſecuted us as ſuch, almoſt to the utter ruining of us in
" this World, ſome Times by Laws made againſt ſeditious Sectaries, and other
" Times as *Popiſh* Recuſants, though our Endeavour hath been, and yet is, to
" keep a Conſcience void of Offence toward God and all Men, as our Con-
" ſciences bear us Witneſs, and alſo our Neighbours among whom we have lived,
" who have ſeen our peaceable Behaviour. And farther, our Willingneſs to give
" unto *Cæſar* the Things that are his. And although nothing has been alledged
" againſt us, but the Cauſe of our Worſhip, yet grievous have been our Suf-
" ferings as aforeſaid, witneſs the Priſoners that are at this Day through the
" Nation, as alſo the Havock that has been made upon our Goods for many
" Years paſt by Bayliffs and mercenary Informers, who have not only abuſed
" us, but have domineered over and abuſed the Juſtices and Juſtice it ſelf, for
" baſe and ſiniſter Ends, which has ruined many Families, (of ſuch as were
" always willing to ſubmit to the Sword of Juſtice, that is for the Puniſhment
" of Evil-doers, and the Praiſe of them that do well) as we believe you are
" not unſenſible of. *The Priſoners Addreſs to their Repre- ſentatives.*

" Therefore we do humbly beſeech you, as Opportunity offers it ſelf, that
" you would make Interceſſion on our Behalf, that the heavy Burden may
" be taken off, and the Oppreſſed go free, ſo ſhall we be the more engaged
" to pray for the Proſperity of you and yours.

" Thus

NORFOLK.
1685.

" Thus in Behalf of our felves, and our fuffering Friends, from fifteen of
" us, who have been Prifoners onwards of two Years, becaufe we cannot
" fwear that which we hold and believe our Chriftian Duty, *to wit*, to practife
" true Allegiance to our Prince.

*The 7th of the Month
called* April, 1685.

Oath tendred.

Thefe fifteen, at the Summer Affizes this Year, had the Oath of Allegiance again tendred them in Court, and were recommitted to Prifon. The
Oath was alfo at the fame Time tendred to *J.* Pratt and *William Hemfter-
low*, Prifoners in the Caftle at *Norwich*, and they were returned to Prifon for
refufing to take it.

*Seizure on
J. Booty.*

On the 7th of the Month called *June*, three Informers came to the Houfe of
Jonathan Booty, of *Steaton-Michael*, where they found but three Perfons affembled
befide thofe of the Family, however they determined to make a Conventicle of
it, and lodged their Information with Juftice *Houghton*, who granted his Warrant to levy 20*l.* for the Houfe, and 10*s.* for the faid *Jonathan* and his Wife
being at the Meeting in their own Houfe : And on the 27th of the Fifth
Month following, the faid Informers, with the Conftable and Warden of the
Parifh, came and took away Cattle, Hay, and Houfhold Stuff, to the Value
of 14*l.*

*And on
S. Pike.*

On the 6th of *September* this Year, the Sheriff's Bayliffs, with one *Allen* an
Under-Goaler, and feveral of his Prifoners to affift them, came with a Warrant
from the Sheriff, with an *Eftreat* out of the *Exchequer* for 20*l.* per Month, to
the Houfe of *Samuel Pike* of *Hingham*, demanding 100*l.* for the King, but not
fhewing their Warrant. They feized all his Goods and Chattels, kept Poffeffion of his Houfe fix Weeks, and about a Week after the Seizure fent him
Prifoner to *Norwich* Caftle : They lived upon the Premifes, feeding themfelves
and their Horfes at their own Will and Pleafure ; infolently domineering over
his Wife and Family, and took away two Milch Cows, and three Horfes,
worth 15*l.* A Sow and five Pigs, worth 2*l.* Corn, Hay, and Meflin, worth 49*l.*
Two Carts, a Pair of Harrows, Part of a Plough, with Harnefs, to the Value
of 8*l.* A Bed, Bedding, Brafs, Pewter, and other Houfhold Goods, to the
Value of 7*l.* 3*s.* 4*d.* Two Malt-Quarns, Utenfils, and Tools of Hufbandry,
and other Things, worth 2*l.* 16*s.* Amounting in all, to 83*l.* 19*s.* 4*d.*

*Alfo on
W. Dix.*

The fame Perfons went alfo to the Houfe of *Winifred Dix*, Widow, (from
whom they had laft Year taken Goods worth 150*l.* as before mentioned) and
feized all her Goods and Chattels, both within Doors and without, and drove
and carried away five Cows, two Calves, and a Lamb, worth 17*l.* 15*s.*
Corn, Hay, and Cheefe, to the Value of 32*l.* Four Beds, with the Bedclothes
and Furniture, worth 18*l.* Two Carts and Harnefs, worth 8*l.* Wool, Pewter,
Brafs, and other Houfhold Goods, to the Value of 20*l.* 10*s.* Amounting in
all, to 96*l.* 5*s.*

Hard Cafe.

This poor Widow had at that Time feveral fatherlefs Children, and was
then in Prifon for Tithes, where fhe had been near fix Years. Grievous was her
Cafe, who while under clofe Reftraint and Confinement, fuffered fuch fpoiling
of her Goods for not going to Church, which in her Circumftances was im-
poffible to do.

*More Dif-
treffes.*

The fame Bayliffs took from *Henry Jennipy*, of *Ellingham-magna*, Goods
worth 20*l.* being almoft all he had left of the Spoil they made laft Year.

On the 8th of the fame Month, they took from *Thomas True*, of *Eaft-
Dereham*, the Covering of his Bed, and Yarn, worth 1*l.* 3*s.*

On the 10th they took from *Chriftopher Keddel*, of *Ellingham-magna*, four
Milch Cows worth 10*l.* And two Shotlings, a Silver Spoon, Brafs, Pewter, &c.
worth 12*l.* 19*s.* making together 22*l.* 19*s.*

On the 12th they went with their Affiftants to the Houfe of *Edward Miles*
of *Thaxton*, demanding 120*l.* for the King ; and without producing their
Warrant,

NORFOLK.
1685.

Warrant, took Poſſeſſion of his Effects, *viz.* his Corn, Cattle, Hay, Houſhold Goods, *&c.* which they carried away and conſumed, to the Amount of 116 *l.* 18 *s.*   They kept Poſſeſſion ſeveral Weeks, keeping Horſes and Men there at a great Expence, ſitting up at unſeaſonable Hours in the Night, drinking, ſwearing, and curſing, to the great Terror and Diſturbance of him and his Family.   By the Seizure of his Horſes they prevented the Tilling of his Land in order to ſow his Winter Corn, and by their taking away his Corn and Cheeſe, laid up for his Family's Proviſion, they obliged him to buy Food for his Houſhold, which he had no ſooner done, but thoſe Spoilers, ſometimes ſix or ſeven of them together, preſently devoured what he had bought.   In ſhort, their Proceedings were barbarous and illegal.   The ſaid *Allen*, Under-Goaler, and his Priſoners, made an Inventory and pretended Appraiſement of the Goods, without rendring any Account to the Owners, and carried them off under Colour of having bought them of the Sheriff.   So they never made any Returns of what they had once laid their Hands on.

Barbarous and illegal Proceedings.

On the 22d of the ſame Month, they went to the Houſe of *James Denton* of *Blowfield*, ſaying, *They came to ſeize all he had for the King.*   They got the Keys of his Houſe, and kept Poſſeſſion ; took out of his Cupboard 15 *l.* in Money, and ſo terrified his Wife, who was not of his Perſuaſion, that ſhe borrowed 12 *l.* more for them, to prevent their carrying away her Houſhold Goods : Which Sums of Money, with two Silver Spoons, ſome Books, and other Things they took, amounted to 30 *l.*

Other ſevere Seizures.

On the 24th *Robert Nicholas*, and *George Leveridge*, Bayliffs of the Hundred, made a Seizure of the Goods of *William Stonewich*, of *Cranworth*, and drove away two Cows worth 4 *l.* And on the next Day were carting away his Goods, when ſome of the Neighbours redeemed them by paying the Bayliffs 7 *l.* more.

The ſame Bayliffs took from *Samuel Dover*, of *Attlebury*, three Milch Cows, and two Heifers, worth 9 *l.*

And on the 2d of *October*, they took from *William Freeman*, of *Attlebury*, a Load of Hay worth 2 *l.* and on the 15th, two Load of Hay worth 4 *l.* 10 *s.*

On the 5th of the ſame Month, the ſame Bayliffs went to the Houſe of *John Roe* and *William Roe*, of *Longham* (whom they had grievouſly diſtrained the laſt Year, as before related) and ſeized and drove away twenty two Milch Kine and a Bull, worth 57 *l.* Seven Horſes with Carts, Harneſs, *&c*, worth 46 *l.* And on the 14th they took an Horſe, Saddle, Cloth, and three Cheeſes, worth 2 *l.* 14 *s.* amounting in all, to 105 *l.* 14 *s.*

When theſe Sufferers informed the Sheriff of the Value of theſe Goods, he anſwered, that *He had no Account brought him of any more than 38 l.* but withal threatned the Complainers, that *If they appeared againſt him on this Occaſion, he would ruin them to all Intents and Purpoſes.*

Complainers threatned by by the Sheriff.

From *Henry Skinner*, a poor Journeyman Shoemaker, they took all they could find of his, amounting but to 20 *s.*

From *Simon Brooks*, of *Attlebury*, they took Hay, Corn, and Houſhold Goods, which ſome of his Neighbours, in Compaſſion to him, redeemed for 4 *l.* 10 *s.*

Several Seizures.

They alſo made Diſtreſs on the Goods of *John Enatts*, of *Lumpton*, a Member of the eſtabliſhed Church, for his Wife's frequenting the *Quakers* Meeting, which Goods he redeemed by paying 3 *l.*

In this Year, *Richard Ranſom* was remaining a Priſoner in *Norwich* Caſtle for Tithes ; as was *Daniel Phillips* on a Writ *de Excommunicato capiendo* ; and *Thomas Foſter* on a *Significavit* of Contempt, upon Proceſſes againſt him in the Eccleſiaſtical Court.

In this Year alſo, *Simon Brooks*, of *Attlebury*, was committed to Priſon, and cloſe confined, at the Suit of one *Beetly*, Prieſt of that Town, for Tithes.

Impriſonments for Tithes.

ANNO 1686.   In this and the two preceding Years were taken for Tithe of Corn and Hay, from *William King* and *Martha Hart*, of *North-Walſham*, *Henry Miller*, of *Wickmore*, *John Allen* and *William Booty*, of *Lammis*, *Edward Miles* of *Thaxton*, and *Samuel Pike*, of *Hingham*, ſo much in Quantity as

NORFOLK.
1686.

Tithes.

amounted to the Value of 39 *l.* 12 *s.* And in the fame Years, from *Robert Dey* and *John Goodwin*, of *Tafburgh*, *William Sharming*, of *Branton*, *Nathanael Booty*, of *Coltifhall*, *Elizabeth Ranfom*, of *Gunton*, and *William Beck*, of *Swafield*, Corn and Hay worth 13 *l.* 10 *s.* 6 *d.*

ANNO 1687. Taken this Year from the aforefaid *Robert Dey*, *Henry Miller*, *Nathanael Booty*, *William Booty*, *Elizabeth Ranfom*, *Samuel Pike*, and *Edward Miles*, Corn and Hay to the Value of 18 *l.* 12 *s.*

ANNO 1688. Taken from feveral of the before-named Perfons, and *Thomas Blomfield*, in Corn and Hay, to the Amount of 16 *l.*

ANNO 1689. Taken from the aforefaid *Samuel Pike*, and from *Chriftopher Kiddell*, and *Francis Dix*, of *Ellingham*, Corn and Sheep, worth 5 *l.* 13 *s.* 4 *d.*

ANNO 1690. Taken from diverfe of the Perfons before-named, and from *John Sayer* and *Henry Jenipy*, of *Great-Ellingham*, *Francis Baldwin*, of the fame, *John Prieft*, of *Gunningham*, *William Colby*, of *Coltifhall*, and *Henry Wake*, of *Gaywood*, for Tithes of Corn, Hay, Lambs, and Wool, to the Value of 16 *l.* 7 *s.*

C H A P. XXVII.

NORTH-
AMPTON-
SHIRE.
1654.

NORTHAMPTONSHIRE.

A N N O 1654.

Suffering of W. Dews-berry.

THE firft Suffering of this People in this County was that of *William Dewfberry*, who about the Beginning of *December*, being in the Street at *Wellingborough*, was called to by *Thomas Andrews*, Prieft of that Town, who fpoke to him thus, *Give over deceiving the People, left the Plagues of God fall upon thee.* *William* replied, *Wherein do I deceive them ?* The Prieft anfwered, *In telling them, there is no Original Sin.* *William* afked him again, *Didft thou hear me fay fo ?* To which the Prieft made no Anfwer, but went away. About three Weeks after this, *William* went into the Steeple-houfe, and waited till the Prieft had done, and then fpake to the People, who gave Attention to what he faid. After which he thus fpake to the Prieft, *Thou haft accufed me of deceiving the People ; prove thy Accufation now before the People, or acknowledge the Falfhood of it.* But the Prieft, without giving any Anfwer, departed. Upon this, *William* was haled out of the Houfe into the Yard, where he again preached to the People, who ftood quietly to hear him, till the High-Conftable came, and laying hold of him, led him to the Market-place, faying, *He would bring Evidence againft him for Blafphemy.* After a fhort Time he was let go again, and lodged at a Friend's Houfe that Night. Next Day, being the 28th of *December*, a Conftable came to him with a *Warrant* to apprehend the *Quaker*, but without mentioning his Name : However the Conftable carried him to a Juftice of the Peace, who committed him to *Northampton* Goal by a *Mittimus*, which was faid to contain a Charge of *Blafphemy*, wherefore *Dewfberry* was fomewhat earneft in requefting a Copy of it, but that, though both juft and reafonable, was refufed him. By the fame *Mittimus* the Juftice alfo fent *Jofeph Storr* to Prifon with him, who only came to hear the Iffue of his Friend's Examination, and againft whom no Accufation was laid, but fuch was the Juftice's Prejudice, that he obferved not any Diftinction in their Cafes ; it was enough to him that they were both *Quakers*. In the Prifon they were kept twelve Steps under Ground, among Thieves and Murderers, till the Quarter Seffions on the 10th of the next
Month

Imprifonment of him and J. Storr.

Month, when they were brought before the Bench of Juſtices, where their *Mittimus* was read, but they were again refuſed a Copy of it : Nor did the Juſtices take any farther Cognizance of their Cauſe, but remanded them to Priſon till the next Aſſizes, to be held about two Months after. At this Seſſions *Francis Ellington*, who came thither to hear the Trial of his Friends, was charged by the Juſtices with a Miſdemeanour, reſpecting a Letter he had ſent to one of them ; and under that Pretence they required of him Sureties for the good Behaviour, which he refuſing to give, was alſo committed to Priſon.

Before the next Aſſizes, *Henry Williamſon* having attempted to ſpeak to the People, after the Prieſt had done his Office, was by them ſorely beaten and abuſed, and afterward committed to the ſame Priſon with the Others.

At the Aſſizes, which began on the 10th of the Month called *March* 1654, *William Dewſberry*, *Joſeph Storr*, and *Henry Williamſon*, were brought before the Judges, *Hales* and *Windham*, and were examined in Manner following, *viz.*

*Examination
of* Dewsber-
ry, Storr, *and*
Williamſon,
before Judge
Hales.

Judge *Hales.* *Art thou* Dewſberry *?*

W. Dewſberry. Yea, I am ſo called.

Judge *Hales.* *Where doſt thou live ?*

W. D. I live in the Lord, and I have a Wife and three Children at *Wakefield* in *Yorkſhire.*

Judge. *What cameſt thou into this Country to do, that thou didſt not ſtay in thy own Country with thy Wife and Children ?*

W. D. I ſtaid in that Country with my Wife and Children, until the Father revealed his Son in me, and called me forth from my Wife and Children to declare his Word of Eternal Life, which he hath manifeſted to my Soul in the great Work of Regeneration, in the new Covenant of Life in *Chriſt Jeſus :* The Everlaſting Goſpel I am ſent to preach to thoſe that dwell upon the Earth.

Judge. *I fear it is a Deluſion, and thine own Fancies, and not the Truth.*

W. D. Time will make it manifeſt.

Judge. *Thou draweſt People together, and acteſt againſt Miniſtry and Magiſtracy.*

W. D. As thou ſtandeſt in the Preſence of God, take Heed of hearkning to falſe Accuſations. Miniſtry and Magiſtracy, which is of God, I own : But thoſe that are called Miniſters of Chriſt, and walk contrary to Scripture, I diſown.

Judge. *But who are they that walk contrary to Scripture ?*

W. D. They that abide not in the Doctrine of Chriſt : But have the chief Places in the Aſſemblies ; ſtand praying in the Synagogues, love Greeting in the Markets, are called of Men *Maſters*, which Practice Chriſt cried *Wo* againſt ; and they that walk in it, walk contrary to Scripture.

Judge. *Theſe are ſmall Things to ſpeak of.*

W. D. There is nothing ſmall the Lord commands.

Judge. *Thou ſayſt well.*

Then the Judge enquired of the Court, what they had againſt theſe Men ?

W. D. That is it we would have manifeſt, what Law we have tranſgreſs'd.

Judge. *Produce what you have againſt them, and I ſhall proceed according to Law.*

Clerk of the Peace. *Here are Papers which* Dewſberry *and* Storr *had, which are againſt the Lord-Protector.*

W. D. The Papers they took from me, which they ſay are againſt the Lord-Protector, was the Word of the Lord I was moved to write, which I ſent to him privately with Care, the One in the Fourth Month in the laſt Year, and the Other hath been privately with Care delivered to him ; and privately I kept the Copies of the Papers, until I was apprehended by Virtue of a Warrant granted forth by Juſtice *Pentlow*, and there was not any *Name*, but for One whom he had in Scorn called a *Quaker*, and with that Warrant the Conſtable had me before him, who commanded the Conſtable to ſee if I had any Money ; which was done, and my Money taken from me, and after a little Time he gave it to me again. Then they took thoſe Papers from me, which

which I had privately on me in a Letter Cafe, which here they publifh publickly as an Evidence againft me.

Judge. *Read the Paper.*

When Part of it was read, the Judge bid them *Give over* ; faying, *This Paper is not to be publifhed.*

W. D. It is not my Mind they fhould be publifhed. The Spirit of Truth, that gave them forth, did dircét them privately to the Hands of the *Lord Protector.*

Judge. *How durft thou write to him in fuch an high Language, as from the Spirit of the Lord ?*

W. D. They in whom the Spirit of thè Lord is, write from the Spirit, and he that hath not the Spirit, is none of his.

Judge. *But I fear it is not from the Spirit, for many pretend the Spirit, and the Divine Light, and Revelations : But how fhall we know they are the Truth according to the Scriptures ?*

W. D. The Scripture cannot be known, but by the pure divine Light of Chrift, which enlightens every one that comes into the World ; which pure Light Chrift hath given to every one, a Meafure, to try the Spirits in them, whether they be of God or not : Every Spirit that confeffeth Chrift come in the Flefh, is of God ; but he that denies Chrift come in the Flefh, is the Spirit of Antichrift. And this Light gave the Scriptures forth, which Light leads to Chrift, who reveals the Father to the Soul, which gives up to be guided by him. So comes the Soul to know God by the Revelation of Jefus Chrift, in whom they are known that walk in the Spirit, by their Fruits in all their Words and Works. And the Prophet *Amos,* that had the Spirit of the Lord, and from the Spirit declared the Word of the Lord to the King of *Ifrael,* the People could not bear his Words.

Judge. *Thou fayft well, if thou doft as thou fayft, but this, it may be, will be expected, and I think it will be fair, to give Bail for your Appearance at the the next Affizes.*

W. D. Firft make manifeft what Law we have tranfgreffed, before Bail be required.

After this they were fet afide, and the Judge proceeded to other Bufinefs, till the Court was ready to break up in the Evening, and then the Goaler afked the Judge, *What he fhould do with thofe* Yorkfhire *Men.*

Judge. *Bring them before the Court.* Which was done.

Then fome in the Court faid, *Take off their Hats,* and two of their Hats were taken off, and as they were about to take off *William Dewfberry's* Hat, the Judge faid, *Let it be on,* and bade them put on the Hats of the other two again, which was done at his Command : Then he fpake to *W. Dewfberry,* faying,

Judge. *Now I fee what thou art ; and thy Vizard and Form of fair Words is feen, that thou art not the Man thou pretendeft to be.*

W. D. Vizards and Formality I deny ; but the Power of God I own and witnefs, in which I ftand, and am fubjeét to it, and to the Ordinance of Man for Confcience-fake.

Judge. *Now thou art commanded : Take off thy Hat.*

W. D. Honour is not in pulling off the Hat, but in obeying the juft Commands of God, which is according to the Will of God ; and my Hat offends not any ; but who are offended at it, may take it off : I fhall not refift them. But there is not any Scripture that expreffes any Honour to be in putting off the Hat.

Judge. *What ! muft we do nothing but what is expreft in Scripture, for our Apparel what we fhall put on.*

W. D. Yea, the Scripture faith, *Let your Adorning be with modeft Apparel.*

Judge. *Art thou Judge, that thou ftandeft covered, and wilt not uncover, as other Prifoners do ?*

W. D.

W. D.   What I do, God is my Witnefs, I do it not in Contempt to any, but in Obedience to the Power of God for Confcience-fake.

Judge.   *If you will not ftand as Prifoners, I will not do any Thing concerning you, but here I found you, and here I fhall leave you.*

W. D.   We have been above ten Weeks in the Low Goal, and not the Breach of any Law found againft us : And we do ftand fubjeƈt to the Power of God, what he fuffers thee to do with us.

Then the Judge fpake to *Henry Williamfon.*

Judge.   Henry Williamfon, *where dwelleft thou ?*

H. W.   In *Cumberland* is my outward Being.

Judge.   *What brought thee hither ?*

H. W.   The Lord moved me to come hither.

Judge.   *What to do ?*

H. W.   To declare the Word of the Lord, which he hath manifefted to my Soul through Jefus Chrift.

Judge.   *How doft thou know the Lord moved thee to come hither ?*

H. W.   By the Spirit which he hath given me.

Judge.   *Thou madeft a great Difturbance in the Church : Thou ftoodeft with thy Hat on in the Time of Prayer.*

H. W.   God is my Witnefs : No Difturbance I made, for peaceably I ftood, as the other People did : I fpake no Words : I moved my Hands againft none : And as foon as the Man had done fpeaking, they haled me out, fome by the Hair of my Head, and tearing it, and others dafhing me in the Face with their Books : And whether they broke the Peace or I, judge ye.

Judge.   *It may be Sureties may be required of you for your good Behaviour.*

H. W.   If I have tranfgreffed any Law, I am willing to fuffer by it.

Judge.   *But if you be Men that intend to walk in good Behaviour, as you pretend, it is but a fmall Matter ; and if you will find Sureties to appear at the next Affizes, I will fet you free.*

H. W.   We are of no ill Behaviour, for we are bound to good Behaviour of God, and he that walks in the Truth is of no ill Behaviour.

On the 12th of the fame Month, Judge *Windham* came to the fame Bench where Judge *Hales* was, and being together, they called for the Prifoners, *Dewfberry, Storr,* and *Williamfon,* and again examined them as follows, *viz.*

Judge *Windham.   Take off their Hats.*   Which was done.

Judge *Hales.   Read the Evidence againft them.*

Clerk.   William Dewfberry and *Jofeph Storr* had Papers found on them againft the *Lord Proteƈtor,* and *William Dewfberry* did go into the Congregation at *Wellingborough,* and difturbed the Minifter and the Congregation in ftanding with his Hat on in the Time of the Sermon and Prayer ; and then declared thefe Words, *The Priefts teach for Hire, and the People love to have it fo :* And railed on the Minifter in the Streets, calling him *Hireling ;* and made a great Difturbance in the Market, and then went into *Francis Ellington*'s Houfe, and fpoke forth at a Chamber-Window to the People in the Streets, and fo made a great Difturbance.

Judge *Hales.   What fayft thou ? Didft thou fpeak thefe Words ?*

W. D.   Railing I deny : Neither did I fpeak thefe Words to *Thomas Andrews,* whom they call a Minifter, in the Streets : If you will hear, I fhall declare the Ground of my Going into the Steeple-houfe at *Wellingborough.*   I was going in the Town, near to *Thomas Andrews*'s Houfe, whom they call Minifter, who called to me as I was going in the Streets, *Give over deceiving the People, left the Plagues of God fall upon thee.*   I anfwered him, *Doft thou fay I deceive the People ?* He replied, *I fay thou doft.*   I faid to him, *Make it appear wherein I do deceive them.*   He anfwered, *Thou telleft them there is no Original Sin.*   I then afked him, *Didft thou hear me fay any fuch Words ?*   Then he went away.   Hearing Words he gave forth, which he faid there was fpoken, and was not ; for the Truth's Sake, that not any Lie fhould reft upon it, when the Prieft, *Thomas Andrews,* and the People were met together at the Steeple-houfe,

houfe, I did go in, and fpake not a Word until the People were difmiffed : Then I declared the Word of the Lord to them before they went away. And I fpake to *Thomas Andrews* to prove there before the People, what he had falfely accufed me of, or to own his falfe Accufation, but he did go away, and did not anfwer one Word at all, and all were peaceable, till *Henry Smith*, of *Wellingborough*, haled me by Force out of the Steeple-houfe : And as I was declaring the Truth to the People in the Yard, *William Baw*, called High-Conftable, took me from that Place, and faid, *He would bring Evidence againft me for Blafphemy*, and had me to and fro in the Market, and fo made the Tumult that was made among the People ; but when he could not prove what he faid, he let me go, who went to a Friend's Houfe, and came no more in the Market that Day : So the Peace that was broken, and the Tumult that was made, was by them, and not by me.

Judge *Windham*. Dew/berry, *thou art well known in the North, and in* Yorkfhire ; *there I have heard of thee ; but where waft thou born ?*

W. D. My natural Birth was in *Yorkfhire.*

Judge *Windham*. *Doft thou begin to cant ? Is there any other Birth ?*

W. D. Yea. *Except ye be regenerate and born again, ye cannot fee the Kingdom of God.* Which Birth I witnefs.

Judge *Windham*. *At what Place in* Yorkfhire *waft thou born?*

W. D. My natural Birth was at a Town called *Alliäthorp*, nine Miles from *York*, towards *Hull.*

Judge *Windham*. *Where haft thou been thy Time ?*

W. D. When I was thirteen Years of Age, I was bound Apprentice to a Clothmaker, in the Weft Part of *Yorkfhire*, at a Town called *Holbeck* near *Leeds.*

Judge *Windham*. *Didft Thou ferve thy Time ?*

W. D. I did ftay till the Time was near expired, and then the Wars began in this Nation, and I did go into the Service of the Parliament.

Judge *Windham*. *Doft thou deny all* Popifh *Tenets ?*

W. D. Popifh Tenets I deny ; and all Tenets contrary to the pure Doctrine of Faith in the Lord Jefus Chrift.

Judge *Windham*. *Doft thou own the Scriptures to be a Rule to walk by ?*

W. D. The Scriptures I own, and the pure Light and Power of Chrift Jefus that gave them forth, to guide in an holy Converfation according to the Scripture, and he that walks contrary to it, is condemned by it.

Judge *Windham*. *But if thou and* Fox *had us in your Power, you would foon have your Hands imbrued in Blood.*

W. D. It is not fo : The Spirit of Truth, which we witnefs in us, is peaceable, and doth neither Violence, nor fhed Blood : And all that are guided by the Spirit of Truth, their Hands are bound from offering Violence, or fhedding of Blood.

J. Storr. It is well known in the Nation, their Sufferings and Stonings, and never lift up an Hand againft any.

Judge *Windham*. *It is becaufe you have not Power ; but here is Evidence againft you for breaking the Peace. Will you give Bond for your Appearance at the next Affizes ?*

W. D. It is the Liberty of the Laws of this Nation, that all that profefs the Faith of Chrift Jefus, may walk in Uprightnefs to their Faith in him, without any Breach of the Laws. And I require a Law may be read unto us, that the Evidence brought againft us is a Breach of, that by the Law we may be convinced of the Tranfgreffion of it, before any Bail may be required of us.

Judge *Windham*. *We are Judges, and we conceive and judge what is charged againft you to be a fufficient Ground to require Bail of you, for your Appearance at the Affizes.*

W. D. Though you be Judges, you are Judges of a Law, and are to judge according to the Law, which is your Rule to judge by, and that Law I would have you to read us, and if we have tranfgreffed it, judge us according to it.

Judge

NORTH-
AMPTON-
SHIRE.
1654.

Judge *Windham.* *You are Tranfgreffors of the Law, in that you are not fub-ject to Government and Authority in not pulling off your Hats.*

W. D. We are fubject to the Government and the Power of God, and to the Ordinance of Man for Confcience-fake, but fhew us in Scripture, which is a true Teftimony of the Power of God, in which we ftand, that putting off the Hat is required in Subjection to Authority, and read us a National Law, which is the Ordinance of Man, that requires any fuch Thing.

Judge *Windham.* *It is the Practice and Cuftom of the Nation.*

W. D. The Cuftoms of the *Heathen* are vain.

Judge *Hales.* *From the Evidence which hath been read, we expect Bond for your Appearance, as hath been required, at the next Affizes.*

W. D. Not any Law we have tranfgreffed : If you know the Breach of any Law by us, let it be read, that we may by it know the Ground what Bail is required for, and what we are to anfwer at the next Affizes.

Judge *Hales.* *What fayft thou,* Storr ? *Wilt thou enter into Bond for thy Appearance at the next Seffions ?*

Storr, Where are thofe that have given Evidence againft me, that I may anfwer to the Particulars of thofe Things charged againft me.

Judge *Hales.* *If thou wilt give Bail for thy Appearance at the Affizes, then fhall thofe that have informed againft thee appear Face to Face.*

Storr. We are bound by a ftronger Tie than any outward Bond.

Judge *Hales.* *What fayft thou,* Williamfon ? *Wilt thou enter Bond for thy Appearance at the next Affizes.*

Williamfon. I am not of any ill Behaviour ; but am bound to good Behaviour by the Power of God.

Judge *Hales.* *If you will not find Sureties, you muft lie here till the next Affizes.* Look to them, Goaler.

W. D. Do with us what thou haft Power.

Accordingly they were carried back to Prifon, and there confined, as before, in the nafty Low Goal among Felons, till another Affize. In the mean Time feveral others of their Friends were alfo committed to Prifon, *viz.*

Returned to Prifon.

1. *John Whitehead,* who fome Time before occafionally went into the Steeple-houfe at *Wellingborough,* and tarried quietly till their publick Worfhip was ended, and then afked the Prieft fome Queftions concerning his Doctrine and Practice, to which the Prieft made no Anfwer, but went away, calling him *Madman :* However the People, who generally ftaid, were foon convinced he was not fo ; for his powerful Preaching, and rational Difcourfe, was well accepted by many of the Prieft's Hearers : The Report of which fo nettled him, that he challenged *John Whitehead* to a Difpute at a Time and Place appointed. That Conference made the Prieft yet more uneafy, becaufe he mift his Aim, which was to have fome Matter of Complaint to the Magiftrates. A little Time after, he fends a Meffage to *John* to meet him at Mr. *Pentlow's,* (who was a Juftice of the Peace) that he might hear and determine the Difpute between them. But this Snare was laid too open, and Anfwer was returned, that he muft appoint fome other Place. He then fends for *John* to meet him at a Lecture in the Steeple-houfe, where feveral other Minifters and People were to be : This he accepted, came thither, and quietly waited till their Service was over : Then he propofed a Queftion to the Preachers, which they refufed to anfwer, but *Andrews,* the Prieft, began to accufe *John Whitehead,* who defended himfelf with plain Truth, to the Conviction of many of the People ; fo that the Priefts being drove to their laft Argument, *Byfield,* Parfon of *Torrington,* laid violent Hands on *John,* and dragged him by Force out of the Steeple-houfe. A Warrant was procured to apprehend him as a Vagrant, and he was carried before two Juftices met on purpofe. He told them he was no Vagrant, and that he could prove his Habitation and Manner of Living by one of his Neighbours, a fubftantial Man, if they would admit him to come in. Upon this *Marmaduke Storr* was called, who informed them of the Place of *John's* Refidence, and that he had a Wife and Family whom he reputably maintained. Then

Imprifonment of J. White-head.

NORTH-
AMPTON-
SHIRE.
1654.

M. Storr.

Then they afked *Marmaduke* his Name and Place of Abode, and what was his Bufinefs in thofe Parts. He told them his Name, and that he lived at *Holdernefs* in the Eaftern Parts of *Yorkfhire*, that he was a Grazier, and held Land for that Purpofe, that he came thither to vifit and help his Brother *Jofeph Storr*, a Prifoner at *Northampton*, and was going thence into *Staffordfhire* to renew the Leafe of his Farm then expiring. The Account he gave, both of himfelf and his Neighbour, was fo unexceptionable that the Juftices were at a Stand, and after fome Confultation with the Priefts, dropt the Pretence of Vagrancy, and concluded to enfnare them both another Way. They afked *Marmaduke*, whether he would fwear to the Truth of what he had faid, and finding that he would not, they tendred them both the Oath of Abjuration. They anfwered, that they had fufficiently demonftrated their good Affeétion to the Commonwealth, in affifting it with their Perfons and Eftates in Times of its greateft Straits, and that they were well known to be no *Papifts*, but that they could not Swear for Confcience-fake. They required of them Sureties for their good Behaviour, upon refufing which, they were committed to Prifon on the 17th of the Month called *March* 1654, and at the next Seffions were ordered to be kept till the Affizes. By this Imprifonment *Marmaduke Storr* was prevented from getting his Leafe renewed, fo that his Family were conftrained to remove, and carry off his Stock at a Day's Notice, to his very great Detriment.

E. Ferman.

2. *Edward Ferman*, when the Prieft had ended his Performance in the Steeple-houfe at *Frandon*, and was coming out, went in and fpake to the People. The Prieft, on purpofe to enfnare him, goes back again to his Pulpit, defires the People to tarry, names a Text, and falls to preaching ; but foon left off again, pretending that *Edward* had interrupted him, and under that Pretence charges a Conftable with him, and carries him before a Juftice, who finding no juft Caufe for the Prieft's Complaint, fought another Occafion againft *Edward*, and committed him to Prifon for three Months, under a groundlefs Charge of being a *Vagrant*.

T. Cocket.

3. *Thomas Cocket*, of *Dingley*, hearing of the faid *Ferman*'s Imprifonment, applies to the Juftice who committed him, and acquaints him that *Ferman* was no Vagrant, but an induftrious honeft Man, and of good Repute. The Juftice, inftead of relieving the injured Man, takes Occafion againft the Complainant, who a little before had writ a Letter to one of the Juftices who had fent a Friend of his to Prifon ; which Letter was as follows,

*A Letter
to Juftice
Brown.*

" JOHN BROWN !

" I Went to *William Steel*'s Houfe, where was a Friend Prifoner, and defired
" to fpeak with him, he told me he had an Order from thee that none
" may fpeak with him. Is this to do as thou wouldft be done unto ? Thou
" haft a Light of Chrift in thy Confcience, which bears witnefs with the Law
" of God, and tells thee, thou fhouldft do as thou wouldft be done unto. In
" perfecuting one of Chrift's little Ones, thou haft done it unto him, and Wo
" is thy Portion.

" A Lover of that which is pure in thy Confcience.

The 4th *of the Firft
Month* 1654-5.

" THOMAS COCKETT."

This Letter was called an *abufive One*, and from thence the Juftice took Occafion to require of *Cockett* Sureties for his good Behaviour, and for his refufing to give fuch Security, fent him to Prifon. The Goaler refufed to give him a Copy of his *Mittimus*, but when it was read at the next Seffions, the principal Matter charged againft him, was the writing that Letter, which he therefore defired might be read in Court ; but that was not granted ; and the Juftices ordered his Continuance in Prifon till the next Affizes.

*Imprifonment
of* J. Hutchin
and M. Patte-
fon.

4. *John Hutchin* and *Michael Patteson*, who were fent to Prifon, at the Inftigation of the Prieft of *Wellingborough*, under Pretence of their having
disturbed

NORTH-
AMPTON-
SHIRE.
1655.

Proceedings at
Northamp-
ton *Assizes.*

disturbed him in his Office ; though they had only stood still and silent while he was preaching.

ANNO 1655. At the Assizes at *Northampton,* on the 21st of the Month called *July,* came on the Examination of *William Dewsberry, Joseph Storr, Henry Williamson, John Whitehead, Marmaduke Storr, Thomas Cockett,* and *Francis Ellington,* before *Edward Atkins,* Judge of the Assize ; as follows, *viz.*

Judge. William Dewsberry ! *What art thou here for ?*

W. D. The *Mittimus* will express what I was committed for ; but a Copy of it I am denied by the Keeper of the Goal.

Judge. *What is thy Name ?*

W. D. Unknown to the World.

Judge. *Let us know what Name that is, that the World knows not.*

W. D. It is known in the Light, and not any can know it but him that hath it ; but the Name the World knows me by, is *William Dewsberry.*

Judge. *What Countryman art thou ?*

W. D. Of the Land of *Canaan.*

Judge. *That is afar off.*

W. D. Nay, it is near, for all that dwell in God, are in the holy City, *Jerusalem,* which comes down from Heaven, where the Soul is in Rest, and enjoys the Love of God in *Jesus Christ,* in whom the Union is with the Father of Light.

Judge. *That is true : But are you ashamed of your Country ? Is it a Disparagement for you to be born in* England *?*

W. D. Nay : For the Truth's Sake, I am free to declare, according to the Knowledge of the World : My natural Birth was in *Yorkshire,* nine Miles from *York,* towards *Hull.*

Judge. *You pretend to be extraordinary Men, and to have an extraordinary Knowledge of God.*

W. D. We witness the Work of Regeneration to be an extraordinary Work wrought in us by the Spirit of God.

Judge. *But the Apostles wrought with their Hands in their Callings.*

W. D. They had Callings in the World : Some were Fishermen ; *Paul,* a Tentmaker : But when they were called to the Ministry of Christ, they left their Callings to follow Christ where he led them by his Spirit to preach the Word : And I had a Calling in the World as they had, and in it did abide, until the Father revealed his Son in me, and called me from my Calling I had in the World, to preach the Eternal Word he had made known to me in the great Work of Regeneration.

Judge. *Why didst thou not abide in thy own Country, and teach People in those Parts ?*

W. D. There I did stay, until I was called thence to go where I was led by the Spirit of the Lord ; and as many as are led by the Spirit of God, are the Sons and Daughters of God, and they that have not the Spirit of Christ, are none of his.

Judge. *You say well : For we must in Charity conclude, that every one in this Place hath the Spirit of God in them : But how do you know that you are guided by the Spirit of God ?*

W. D. They that have the Spirit of God are known by their Fruits, and he that believeth in *Jesus Christ,* and is guided by his Spirit, hath the Witness in himself.

Judge. *That is true : Yet notwithstanding I see by your Carriage, that what my Brother* Hales *did at the last Assizes, in requiring Bonds for your good Behaviour, he might justly do it ; for you are against Magistrates and Ministers.*

W. D. Make that manifest wherein we are against them.

Judge. To the Clerk of the Peace. *What have you against these Men ?*

Clerk. Here is an Information given upon Oath by Mr. *Robert Beton,* that *William Dewsberry,* on the 29th of *December* 1654, did go into the Church in *Wellingborough,* and stood with his Hat on in Time of Sermon and Prayer, and after the Minifter had done, he fpake thefe Words, *The Prieſts preach for Hire, and the People love to have it fo : But what will ye do in the End thereof ?* With other railing Words, which made Difturbance among the People.

Judge. *What have you againſt* Storr *and* Williamfon ? But nothing was produced againft them.

Judge. *I ſhall take Courſe, that thoſe that have diſturbed the Miniſters, before I go forth of the Town, ſhall be indiċted.*

W. D. It is the Liberty of the Law of this Nation, that any that are brought Prifoners before thofe that fit to judge their Caufes, may fpeak for themfelves the Truth, to witnefs againft the falfe Information given in againft them, and that Liberty I take to manifeft the Ground of my Going into the Steeple-houfe at *Wellingborough* : As I was going in the Street, *Thomas Andrews* (call'd Minifter of that Town) called to me with thefe Words, *Give over deceiving the People, left the Plagues of God fall on thee.* I replied, *Doſt thou ſay I deceive the People ? Make it manifeſt wherein I deceive them.* He anfwered, *Thou ſayſt there is not any Original Sin.* I then afked him, *Didſt thou hear me ſay ſo ?* To which he would not anfwer, but fled away. I being falfly accufed by *Thomas Andrews,* afterwards when he met with the People at the Steeple-houfe, I went into it for the Truth's Sake, and after he had done, I propounded this Queftion to him, that he would prove there before the People, what he had openly accufed me of, in faying, *there was no Original Sin,* but he would not anfwer, but in Silence fled away : And what I here declare that I did, is not any Breach of the Law of this Nation.

Judge. *But in that you are found wandring in the Country, you break the Law ; for there is an ancient Law, that if any did go from their Dwellings to travel in the Country without a Certificate from ſome Juſtice, they were to be taken as wandring Perſons.*

W. D. If there be any fuch Law, read it to us : And if there be fuch a Law, in thy Confcience thou knoweft it is contrary to Scripture ; for the Apoftles and Minifters of Chrift went to and fro in the Country, preaching the Word of Eternal Life, and there were added to the Church daily fuch as fhould be faved, and the Number of the Saints and Brethren was daily increafed ; and the Law that is in Force in this Nation, doth allow all that profefs Faith in *Jeſus Chriſt,* to have free Liberty to walk in the Faith, which is according to Scripture.

Judge. *Thou haſt an eloquent Tongue, and thou art proud of it.*

W. D. Pride I deny, but the Truth I witnefs, which will judge Pride, and torment all that live in it, until it be deftroyed.

Then the Judge fpake to *Joſeph Storr.*

Judge. *Is thy Name* Jofeph Storr ?

Storr. Yes.

Judge. *What art thou here for ?*

Storr. I have been twenty nine Weeks in Prifon among thofe arraigned for Felony and Murder, and know not for what Caufe I am imprifoned, and never any Accufer appeared to my Face to prove me the Tranfgreffor of any Law, and I defire that my Accufers may appear before my Face, that I may have a Trial according to Law, for Judge *Hales* promifed at the laft Affizes, if I would appear at this Affizes, my Accufers fhould appear to my Face.

The Judge faid no more to him, but afked,

Which is Williamfon ? *What have you againſt him ?*

John Brown, the Juftice that committed him, whifpered to the Judge, who faid no more to *Williamſon,* but called for *Whitehead.*

Judge. *Is thy Name* John Whitehead ?

J. W. Yea, I am fo called.

But he was examined no farther.

J. W. I defire the Liberty which the Law of the Nation allows, that I may be heard fpeak, and have a Trial, having been kept eighteen Weeks in Prifon, and no Accufer hath appeared to prove me the Tranfgreffor of any Law.

Judge.

Judge. *Common Fame is a good Accuſer, though not a good Judge ; yet I am ſatisfied, from what I have heard, to continue you in Priſon, unleſs you will lay in Bond to be of good Behaviour, and appear at the next Aſſizes, for you are by common Fame accuſed to be a dangerous People, and Breakers of the publick Peace.*

J. W. So the People of God (by the common Fame of the World) was in all Ages every where ſpoken againſt, and accuſed to be Diſturbers of the Peace, as *Paul* was accuſed to be a Mover of Sedition, through the whole World.

Then the Judge ſpake to *Marmaduke Storr.*

Judge. *Is your Name* Marmaduke Storr.

M. S. My Name is ſo called : I deſire to have my Trial according to Law, for I was taken in my Journey, and impriſoned from my Management of about ſeven ſcore Pounds *per Annum*, and have never yet forfeited my Liberty, but appeared in ſerving the Common-wealth in its greateſt Straits, for which they are indebted to me about two Hundred Pounds, as my Commiſſion, Debenture, and Claim upon Record, will make appear.

His Cauſe was no farther examined.

Judge. *Which is* Ellington?

T. E. I am ſo called.

Judge. *What are you here for ?*

T. E. I was in Bonds fifteen Weeks for my Appearance at the General Seſſions, and when I appeared there, no Accuſer came to my Face, nor was any Evidence read againſt me, to prove me the Breaker of any Law, and there I was committed, by thoſe called Juſtices, to the Goal, where I have been kept in the Dungeon theſe thirteen Weeks among thoſe arraigned for Felony and Murder, and have been taken from my outward Habitation which was at *Wellingborough*, within ſeven Miles of this Place, and have been deprived from my outward Calling which I lived in, and kept from my Wife and five ſmall Children, and ſo am deprived of the Benefit of the Law of this Nation, which no Felon or Murderer that is here, is deprived of ; for they have Liberty to ſpeak for themſelves, and to have a fair Trial according to Law, which is denied us.

Judge. To the Clerk of the Peace. *Where is your Evidence againſt theſe Men ?*

Clerk. This *Ellington* is a Receiver of theſe Men, and here is a Letter that he writ to a Juſtice of Peace, wherein he doth accuſe the Juſtice of doing Injuſtice, in committing *Dewſberry* and *Storr* to Priſon.

Judge. *Why do you trouble me with that which there is no Matter of Fact in ? I much wonder you ſhould trouble a Judge of the Aſſize with ſuch ſmall Things, and not end them in your own Seſſions, for we come hither to determine greater Matters.* Mr. Ellington ! *I have a great Love to you, bring a Man that lives in this Country : Will you enter into Bond for your good Behaviour, and to appear at the next Aſſizes ?*

F. E. I am of no evil Behaviour, neither to this Day hath any Thing been proved againſt me concerning it, and if it yet can be proved by any one Man here, that I have been of evil Behaviour, or have broken any Law of this Nation, I am preſent to anſwer it, and to give in Bonds for my Liberty.

Judge. *You have tranſgreſſed the Law, in that you come to the Bar with your Heads covered, becauſe it is a Contempt of Authority.*

F. E. There is no Law in this Nation requires any ſuch Thing as putting off the Hat ; if there be any, I deſire it may be read, that ſo before the Country I may be convinced by the Law, before Bonds may be required.

Judge. *I ſhall deal favourably with you, for I ſhall take your own Bond to appear at the next Aſſizes.*

F. E. Firſt prove me a Tranſgreſſor of the Law ; for the righteous Law of God ſaith, *Where there is no Law, there is no Tranſgreſſion* ; and there is no Law in *England* that requires putting off the Hat, therefore it is not a Tranſgreſſion : Therefore I deſire I may have the Benefit of an *Engliſhman*, which is not denied to any Felon here among us ; for I have to this Day ſtood always faithful to the Common wealth, and have not forfeited any Liberty, but have hazarded my Life and Eſtate to procure Freedom, which now I am deprived of.

Judge.

Judge. *If you will not put in Bond for your Behaviour, which I think is very reasonable :* Take him away.

F. E. For my Behaviour, if there be any here that can accuse me, I would have you Countrymen to speak, any of you ; if not, let all the poor People in *Wellingborough,* and the Towns thereabouts, and the Poor in *Northampton,* which I have for these fifteen or sixteen Years employed in carding, spinning, dying, and weaving of Wool, speak what my Behaviour hath been toward them or others : For I have, until they cast me into Prison, employed more poor People at Work about Wool, than any one Man in this Country doth ; yet notwithstanding what I have done, and do, may not I have the Benefit of the Law, as all Malefactors here have.

Judge. *Goaler, take him away.*

Then the Judge spake to *Thomas Cockett.*

Judge. *Is your Name* Cockett.

T. C. Yes : If any have ought to accuse me of, I am ready to answer the Law.

He was not suffered to proceed, but the Judge called to the Goaler to take them away. Howbeit *Marmaduke Storr* spake thus to the People.

M. S. Take Notice, all People, how we are deprived of the Privilege and Liberty that the Law of this Nation allows, in that we may not be heard speak, and have a legal Trial, which is granted to Felons and Murderers.

As they were withdrawing, *William Dewsberry* turned to the Court, and spake thus to the Judge.

W. D. With what Measure thou metest to us, it will be measured to thee again, and the Lord God of Heaven and Earth will judge between thee and us, and will give unto thee, and every one of you, according to the Works you have done, and in that Day you shall know what is now declared is the Truth ; the Lord hath spoken it, in whom we trust, and he will us deliver.

So the Court rose, and the Goaler had them all back to Prison ; where they continued about six Months longer, till the Month called *January* 1655, when they and some others were discharged by an Order from *Oliver Cromwell,* the Protector ; having suffered a grievous Imprisonment without any just or legal Process against them, *viz.*

William Dewsberry and *Joseph Storr,* fifteen Months ; *Henry Williamson, John Whitehead, Marmaduke Storr,* and *Thomas Cockett,* about ten Months ; *Francis Ellington* thirty eight Weeks ; *John Hutchin* and *Michael Patteson,* twenty eight Weeks, and *Edward Ferman* thirteen Weeks.

During their Imprisonment, their Friends were not admitted to visit them, but several who attempted it, were taken up and sent out of the Town with a Pass. *Thomas Goodacre,* desiring to see them, was repuls'd by the Goaler, and going from the Prison met the Mayor and some of the Aldermen in the Street, to whom he spake thus ; *Men ! see what is the Fruit of the Ministry of this Nation, and what it has brought forth, for Wickedness and Persecution abound ; and those that say they are* Christian *Magistrates, and persecute the Innocent, are* Heathens, *and know not God.* Adding, *that they could not bring any Scripture to prove that ever any* Christian *Magistrate did persecute any Man as they had done, who cast his Friends into Prison.* This deserved Reproof so incensed the Magistrates against the Reprover, that they committed him to Prison, where he lay about eleven Weeks. The Mayor of *Northampton,* in this Year, was *Peter Whaley,* a Man of an hasty and Cholerick Disposition : When one *Walter Ferr* came before him with his Hat on, he threw it into the Kennel. At another Time *Michael Gainer* having sent him a Book, he threw it into the Fire. In his Mayoralty *Mary Horne* was committed to *Bridewell,* and *Elizabeth Hunt* to *Northampton* Goal, for certain Expressions of Reproof, which gave much Offence to the Priest of *Wellingborough.*

Thomas Stubbs, exhorting the People of *Daventry* to Repentance, was sent to Prison by a Justice, who, when *Thomas* asked him, *By what Law he proceeded,*

told

told him, *By that Law that says, All* Quakers *must go to Prison* ; though indeed there was no such Law. However he was confined thirteen Weeks, and then released at the Sessions ; but ordered to be sent out of the County : Shortly after he returned, and being at *Isham* Meeting, was taken thence, and by two Justices committed to *Bridewell* as a Vagrant, where he was cruelly whipt, and endured much Hardship, not being suffered to have Necessaries for his Money.

ANNO 1656. On the 26th of the Month called *May*, at a Meeting in a Field belonging to *William Lovel* of *Harding stone*, *Thomas Stubbs* was preaching, when Captain *Pinkerd* came with some Horsmen of the County Troop, saying, *That he had Orders from Major* Butler *to disperse that Meeting* : He asked *William Lovel, whether he owned that Meeting ?* Who answering *Yes*, the Soldiers were ordered to take him Prisoner, which they did, and with him *John Crook, John Samms*, and *Thomas Stubbs*. They were detained in the Field under a Guard some Hours, while the Captain went to the Priest's House to carouse, and consult what to do with his Prisoners. At length the Soldiers were ordered to carry them to *Northampton* Goal. The Goaler opening the Door to receive them, they asked him, *Whether he had any* Mittimus ? He answered, *If you will come in I will receive you.* They replied, *We shall not commit our selves.* Then the Captain ordered his Soldiers to put them in by Force, which was done. The Goaler telling them, *By Captain* Pinkerd's *Order I have received you, and shall detain you.* So he put them into the lower Goal among Thieves and Murderers, and denied even their Wives and Children the Liberty of visiting them. *William Lovel* soon procured an *Habeas Corpus* to remove him to *London*, where he put in Bail to appear at next Term, and returned Home again ; but a few Days after was, by Major *Butler's* Order, taken from his own House, and without any Cause assigned, committed to the Marshal's Custody, where he remained about sixteen Days. He afterwards appeared at the Term, and was discharged : But the others yet continued Prisoners.

Several taken by Soldiers.

In this Year also, *Thomas Goodaire* was taken preaching in a Meeting at *Ould*, and by two Justices sent to *Northampton* Goal, where he lay among Felons, in a Place twelve Steps under Ground, sixteen Weeks. *Henry Hall* and others, going to a Meeting at the House of *John Hart* of *Towcester*, were stopt in the Street, and fined 10 s. each, for travelling on the Sabbath. Several of them had their Horses taken away, and one was set in the Stocks four Hours. *Anne Richardson* was imprisoned eight Weeks at the Instigation of the Priest of *Wellingborough*, to whom a *just Reproof* from her had given *great Offence.*

Diverse other Imprisonments.

ANNO 1657. In this Year *Edward Roberts*, of *Overston*, a Man of exemplary Patience and Innocence, and of a Conversation truly edifying, died a Prisoner, for his Testimony against Tithes, in *Northampton* Goal, at the Suit of *Lionel Godrick*, his Parish Priest, after one and twenty Months Imprisonment. His Prosecutor there before taken from him four Horses worth 28 l. for a Demand of 3 l. 3 s. for Tithes.

Death of E. Roberts in Prison for Tithes.

On the 13th. of *September*, *William Ireland* went into the Steeple-house at *Findon*, and when the Priest had done, and was going out, spake thus to the People ; *Fear God : He is worthy to be feared of all that know him ; and mind the Light of Christ in you, which shews you the Evil of your Ways.* For this Christian Exhortation he was sent to *Bridewell* for six Months, where he was unmercifully whipt, and so cruelly used, that he became exceeding weak, so that he hardly survived the Time of his Imprisonment, but presently after died.

Whipping of W. Ireland.

In like Manner *Anne Corbey*, for exhorting the People at *Burton-Latimer* to fear God, and to mind the *Light of Christ Jesus within them, which was a sure Teacher, and witnessed against the Evil of their Doings*, was imprisoned eleven Weeks in *Northampton* Goal, and together with her, *Anne Peel*, though no Breach of any Law was proved against either of them. For supposed Offences of the like Nature, *Rebecca Peake* and *Mary Bottom* also suffered Imprisonment.

Imprisonments.

In this Year also, the Grand Jury at the Quarter Sessions found two Bills of Indictment against *William Lovel*, one for *Blasphemy*, in saying, *The Scriptures*

W. Lovel indicted.

were not the Word of God; the other for *Slander*, in calling the Ministers, *Ministers of the Devil*: Both grounded on a Misconstru&tion of some Expressions of his : Upon this he was imprisoned about five Months, and was afterwards fined by the Justices 30 *l.*   Next Day after the Sessions, *William's* Wife discoursing with *Francis Harvey*, Chairman of the Sessions, he told her, *That had it not been for him, her Husband had been fined three Times as much* ; *and that it was her Husband's Life* they *thirsted after*, meaning Major *Butler* and *John Brown*, Justices, who were violent Persecutors of the *Quakers* ; as was also *John Mansell*, another Justice in that County.   *William Lovel*, for not paying his Fine, remained in Prison about a Year and an Half, and then was discharged by an Order from *Richard Cromwell* and his Council.

On a like groundless Charge of Blasphemy, *Francis Ellington*, of *Wellingborough*, was indi&ted by the Procurement of one *Lane*, a Priest, and others, who consulted together against him.   *Lane* swore, and his Evidence was accepted, in Contradi&tion to several Ear-Witnesses who were present when the Words charged against him were spoken.   However, the Jury found him *Guilty*, and he was sentenced to the House of Corre&tion for six Months, where he was cruelly whipt, and underwent other barbarous Usage.

Fines.

About this Time *William Vincent, Thomas Ollive,* and *Rebecca Peake,* were fined under the Name of *Sabbath-breakers,* for no other Cause than travelling to their religious Meetings on the First-day of the Week.

Tithes.

William Richardson and *William Page*, both of *Wellingborough*, were imprisoned for frivolous Demands, pretended to be due for Tithe of Calves and Eggs, and for Smoke-Money, and for *Easter-Offerings* ; beside which, the said *William Page* had his Goods taken away on such Pretences, to the Value of 4 *l.*

Distresses.

For Tithes.

In this Year also, for Demands of 10 *s.* 3 *d.* for Tithes, Goods were taken from several Persons, to the Value of 1 *l.* 13 *s.* 8 *d.*

ANNO 1658.   *Thomas Smallbone*, of *Endon*, for 3 *l.* 5 *s.* claimed by the Priest of that Place for Tithes, was imprisoned five Weeks, and had also his Goods taken by Execution, to the Value of 9 *l.*

Hard Sufferings for 4d. claimed for Tithes.

William Vincent, for a Demand of only 4 *d.* for Tithes, was imprisoned in *Northampton* Low-Goal, at the Suit of *Thomas Andrews*, Priest of *Wellingborough*, above a Year among Felons, by whom he was much abused, being a very weakly Man, and having above a dozen Sores about him, by which he was rendered almost unable to help himself, and obliged to go on Crutches. His miserable Case was represented to the Priest, his Prosecutor, who yet shewed no Lenity towards him, but seemed to value the poor Man's Life at less than one Groat.

Several others in this Year, for Claims of Tithes, amounting to 3 *l.* 8 *s.* 4 *d.* had Goods taken from them worth 9 *l.* 10 *s.*

Sufferings for not Swearing.

Grievous were the Proceedings against *Nicholas Day, Peter Mackerness,* and *George Whitlock,* all of *Findon,* who for refusing to take an Oath at a Court-Leet there, were fined 20 *s.* each ; for Non-payment of which, they underwent the Seizure and Loss of their Goods, to the Value of 56 *l.* 2 *s.* 6 *d.*

In this Year also, *Richard Ellard*, having served an Apprenticeship in *Northampton*, was refused his Freedom of the Town, for refusing to take the Oath of Admission, usual on that Occasion.

Grievous Suffering of M. Parker.

ANNO 1659.   *Margaret Parker*, of *Aino* on the Hill, a poor Widow, having three Children, was imprisoned at *Northampton* seven and twenty Months for Tithes of Corn and Hay, less than 13 *s.* 4 *d.* in Value.   This poor Woman's Sufferings were grievous, being close confined among Murderers, Thieves, Whores, and some called Witches, in a close nasty Place, where her Friends were not admitted to see her, otherwise than through the Key-hole of the Door.

We also find imprisoned at *Northampton*, for very small Demands of Tithes, the following Persons, namely,

Prisoners.

Robert Curtis, a poor Shepherd, of *Colebigham* : *Peter Mackerness*, imprisoned above a Year : *John Garret*, forty Weeks : And *John Bett*, of *Aino* on the Hill, seven Weeks.

Elizabeth

Elizabeth Hunt and *Mary Botham* were again imprifoned; the Latter for fpeaking to the People in *Wellingborough* Steeple-houfe, before their Preacher came, thefe Words, *Turn your Minds within to the true Teacher of* Ifrael, *who will never deceive you, for all other Teachers will deceive you.* The Former, applying to the Prieft in the other's Behalf, was alfo fent to Goal with her by the fame *Mittimus*, as a Difturber of the Prieft and People at their Worfhip, though fhe was not there. At the Seffions, on the 13th of the Month called *April*, they were fined 5*l.* each, and continued in Prifon, till releafed by Order of a Committee of Parliament. Some Time before this, *John Green* and *John Rogers* had fuffered Imprifonment for their fpeaking in Oppofition to fome of the publick Preachers of thofe Times.

ANNO 1660. On the 23d of *December*, at a Meeting in the Houfe of *William Atton*, of *Middleton*, where *George Robinfon* was concerned to preach; a Juftice of the Peace being informed of it, fent for *William Atton*; *Robinfon*, to prevent his Friend's fuffering for what himfelf had done, went with him: The Juftice ordered *Robinfon* to be fet in the Stocks, and afterward committed him to Prifon till the next Seffions, when the Juftices tendred the Oath to them both, and alfo to *Daniel Wills*, who came thither to obferve the Proceedings, and upon Refufal committed them all three to *Northampton* Goal, where they lay about three Quarters of a Year. *3 Committed to Prifon.*

On the 27th of the fame Month, *Chriftopher Moore*, of *Richmond* in *York-fhire*, paffing toward *London*, tarried at a Meeting at *Dingly*, where he was taken by a Warrant, and carried before two Juftices, who upon his refufing to take the Oath of Allegiance, fent him to *Northampton* Goal; whither on the 13th of the next Month were alfo committed for the fame Caufe, *Richard Wright* of *Holcott*, *William Darnell* of *Hannington*, *James Pratt* of *Barton*, *Thomas Wright* of *Ould*, and *Samuel Suncock* of *Billing*, who were taken together when met at *Richard Wright*'s Houfe; alfo *John Mafon*, taken by a Conftable in a Friend's Houfe at *Polebrook*. *Many other Imprifon-ments.*

On the 20th of the Month called *January*, *John Parnel*, *Michael Gaines*, *Thomas Hewlett*, *Thomas Hirons*, *Richard Verney*, *William Mather* of *Holmby*, *Oliver Mellows* of *Halfton*, *Thomas Gayling* of *Dufton*, *Daniel Row* and *Henry Row*, of *Dallington*, were taken from a Meeting at the Houfe of *Daniel Wills* in *Northampton*, and fent to Prifon. In the fame Month *John Hart*, of *Towcefter*, *John Butcher*, and *Thomas Hirons*, of *Aftrop*, *John Bett* and *John Borton*, of *Aino*, *Thomas Miller*, *Richard Miller*, *Richard Hewes*, and *William Chandler*, of *Brackley*, were taken out of their own Houfes by Soldiers, and committed to Prifon for refufing the Oaths. And about the fame Time, *Thomas Butcher*, of *Aftrop*, was taken out of his Fields, and fent to Prifon; as was *Samuel Harper*, of *Market-Harborough* in *Leicefterfhire*, who was feized by a Soldier as he was going to a Meeting.

In the fame Month were taken at a Meeting in *Farndon*, *Francis Child*, *Thomas Mackernefs*, and *Thomas Holloway*, all three of *Market-Harborough* aforefaid, *John Goddard*, of *Marfon-Truffel*, *William Rimington*, of *Great-Bowden*, *James Phiggin* and *John Warren*, both of *Oxon* in this County, and committed to Prifon: Alfo from a Meeting at *Attleborough* were taken *William Ward*, of that Place, and *John Gerriott*, of *Findon*, which two only were committed out of twenty feven who were at that Meeting, the Juftice being told that the Goal was fo full it could not hold them. Neverthelefs, on the 24th of the Month called *February* twelve others were thruft in, who had been taken by a Party of Horfe from a Meeting at the Houfe of *William Evans* in *Farthingftone*, namely, *William Evans*, *Francis Evans*, and *George Ayers*, of that Place; *Richard Afhby*, *Thomas Ingram*, and *John Green*, of *Bugbrook*; *John Ayres*, of *Everton*; *Robert Burnall* and *William Robinfon*, of *Eaftcutt*, *Robert Curtis*, of *Colebigham*; *Thomas Poole*, of *Flower*; and *William Afhby*, of *Dalfcutt*. *The Goal filled.*

Singular was the Cafe of *John Lane*, who being come upwards of forty Miles to vifit a Relation in *Yardly-Chafe*, was falfly accufed of being at a *Baptifts* Meeting, and thereupon fent for by a Juftice of the Peace, who committed him *Cafe of J. Lane.*

*Difmal Con-
finement.*

*Difcharge of
Prifoners.*

*Imprifonment
for Tithes.*

*38 Sent from
Meeting to
Prifon.*

*More Impri-
fonments.*

*Sufferings for
Tithes.*

Imprifonments.

to Prifon for refufing to take the Oath of Allegiance. The Number of Prifoners now in *Northampton* Goal was near forty, put into the Low-Goal twelve
Steps under Ground, where they were lockt up every Night among Felons, and
in Winter the Goaler kept the Door faft fixteen Hours together, and they lay
fo clofe one by another, that he who was up laft could hardly fet his Foot between them to go to the Place where he fhould lie. Some of them were fick
for Want of Air, and when their Friends came many Miles to vifit them,
they were not admitted : Their Food and Neceffaries were often kept from
them, fo that their Sufferings were exceeding great.

About the fame Time, *Richard Painter*, *Benoni Bradfhaw*, and *Laurence
Gilgrafs*, were taken out of their own Houfes in *Northampton*, and committed
to the Marfhal's Cuftody for refufing the Oaths. For the fame Caufe, *Thomas
Smith*, *John Chapman*, and *Francis Creake*, were imprifoned among Felons at
Peterborough.

The Generality of the Prifoners before mentioned lay about three or four
Months, and then were difcharged by the King's Proclamation.

ANNO 1661. *Jofeph Gammage*, of *Bugbrook*, was imprifoned in this
County for refufing to pay Tithes.

ANNO 1662. In this Year *Thomas Arnold*, of *Heyford*, and *Thomas Willer*,
of *Brackley*, were committed to Prifon for their Teftimony againft paying
Tithes.

On the 13th of the Month called *July*, thirty eight Perfons were taken at a
Meeting in *Northampton*, of whom twenty five, being Inhabitants there, were
fent to the Town Prifon, viz. *Daniel Wills*, *John Parnell*, *Thomas Hewlett*, *Edward Wallis*, *John Oddell*, *John Lewes*, *Jane Afhby*, *Walter Farr*, *Michael Gaines*
and *Mary* his Wife, *Richard Painter* and *Rebecca* his Wife, *Benoni Bradfhaw*
and *Elizabeth* his Wife, *Laurence Gilgrafs* and *Frances* his Wife, *Thomas Hirons*
and *Alice* his Wife, *Mary* **Cooper**, *Anne Hewlett*, *Anne Cook*, *Anne Tiplady*,
Katharine Bafs, *Sarah Kemp*, and *Elizabeth Hewlett*. The other fifteen were
committed to the County Goal, namely, *William Lovel*, *Richard Green*,
William Green, *Mary Green*, *Philip Haddon* and *Elizabeth* his Wife, all of
Hardingftone ; *Robert Burling*, of *Cotton-End* ; *Thomas Gayling*, of *Dufton* ;
Henry Row and *Mary Dent*, of *Dallington* ; *John Fofter*, *Jane Canfby*, and
Bridget Dilly, of *King's-Thorp* : And on the 28th, *John Hart*, of *Towcefter*.

On the 6th of *November*, *William Mather* and *John Smith*, both of *Welling-
borough*, were taken out of a Meeting at the faid *Mather's* Houfe, and fent to
Northampton Goal, where they lay about three Months. To the fame Prifon
were committed about three Months after, *William Atton* of *Middleton*, *Simon
Mutton* of *Geddington*, *Nathanael Beeby* of *Rowel*, *Thomas Boon* of *Corby*, *George
Almund* of *Medburn*, *Giles Hinfhley* of *Geddington*, *Thomas Cooke* of *Weldon*, and
John Molfoe of *Ochley*, who were taken at a Meeting in the faid *William Atton's*
Houfe.

On the 14th of *December* were taken out of a Meeting at the Houfe of *Mary
Cooper* in *Northampton*, *Edward Wallis* and *Thomas Hirons*, both of that Town,
Thomas Gayling of *Dufton*, *John Forfter* of *King's Thorp*, *Richard Green* and
Matthew Haddon, of *Hardingftone* ; they were committed to Prifon in a nafty
ftinking Place, fcarce good enough for Swine, where five of them remained in
a very cold wet Seafon, till the Seffions on the 16th of the next Month.

ANNO 1663. In this Year *Robert Afhby*, *Arthur Green* the Elder, and
Arthur Green the Younger, all of *Bugbrook*, fuffered Imprifonment for their
confcientious Refufal to pay Tithes. And in this Year alfo, *Peter Mackernef*,
and *Nicholas Day* fuffered Diftrefs of Goods for refufing to pay Steeple-houfe
Rates, or *Eafter-Offerings*.

On the 23d of the Month called *Auguft*, was a large Meeting of two or
three Hundred at the Houfe of *Henry Hopkin* in *Mufkutt*, whither came a Corporal and five Soldiers with a Juftices's Warrant, and entred the Meeting with
their Piftols cockt, yet ftood ftill and heard *John Samm* then preaching. The
Meeting being ended, they took away eight Perfons, namely, *John Samm* of
Haughton-Conqueft,

Haughton-Conqueſt in *Bedfordſhire*, *William Lovel* of *Hardingſton*, *Daniel Wills*, *Benoni Bradſhaw*, and *Laurence Gilgraſs*, of *Northampton*, *George Ayres* of *Farthingſtone*, *Joſeph Gammage* of *Bugbrook*, and *Thomas Dent* of *Kiſlingberry*. The Soldiers took them to an Inn in *Northampton*, whence they were committed to the Common-Goal, and next Day, being the Time of the Affizes there, were brought before the Judge, who tendred them the Oath of Allegiance, and remanded them to Priſon for refuſing it.

On the 6th of *September*, *William Hopkins*, *William Simpſon*, and *Richard Aſhby*, taken at a Meeting in *Bugbrook*, were for the ſame Cauſe committed to Priſon ; as were alſo on the 30th of *December*, *George Warner*, *John Nottingham*, *Thomas Cattle*, and *Thomas Allgood*, who were taken at a Meeting in *Geddington*.

A Fever *in the Priſon, of which ſeven died.*

Toward the End of this Year, twenty two Friends, having been long confined together with ten Felons and Debtors in a cloſe Room, moſt of which was taken up with the Straw on which they lodged, ſo that they had little Space to walk in, a violent *Fever* ſeized firſt ſome of the Felons, to whom as fellow Creatures, and fellow Priſoners, though in a Cauſe vaſtly different, the Friends thought it their Duty to be affiſtant in their extream Weakneſs, and accordingly did what they could for them, till at length the Air being exceedingly corrupted with the Breath of the Diſtempered, a Kind of Contagion ſpread among the Priſoners, and the Friends ſo generally fell ſick, that when called over at the Affizes, only four of them were able to appear before the Judge, who being informed of their ſad Condition, gave a private Order to the Goaler to let them go forth for Air, by which Means ſome recovered, but ſeven of them, being too weak to go out or be removed, died there ; of whom an Account follows in the Beginning of the next Year, viz.

Death of W. Carr.

ANNO 1664. 1. *William Carr*, who was at firſt committed on a malicious Accuſation of ſpreading a treaſonable Paper ; and when at the Seſſions there appeared no Ground for ſuch a Charge, they tendred him the Oath of Allegiance. He lay in Priſon about eleven Weeks, and died on the 25th of the Month called *March* 1664.

R. Aſhby.

2. *Richard Aſhby*, who died on the 26th of the ſame Month.

J. Samm.

3. *John Samm*, a faithful Miniſter of the Goſpel, an inceſſant Labourer in the Work of the Miniſtry, and of an exemplary Life and Converſation. He died on the ſame Day with *Aſhby*.

T. Arnold.

4. *Thomas Arnold*, who departed this Life on the 1ſt Day of the Month called *April*.

W. Ewins.

5. *William Ewins*, who alſo died on the ſame Day.

*J. Gammage.
W. Lovel.*

6. *Joſeph Gammage*, ⎱ who both died on the 11th Day of the ſaid Month
7. *William Lovel*, ⎰ called *April*.

Theſe all finiſhed their Courſe in Peace, and departed in full Affurance of Faith, having their Hope and Confidence firm in the Lord, by whoſe Power they had witneſſed Redemption from a vain Converſation, and who had armed them with the Patience of the Saints to undergo Tribulations and Afflictions for the Teſtimony he had called them to bear, who ſupported them with the Conſolations of his Spirit, and enabled them in the Midſt of their Afflictions to ſing Praiſes unto him, and to bleſs his Name, to the Edification and Comfort one of another, and to the Aſtoniſhment of others who beheld their Piety and Patience.

5 Sentenced to baniſhment.

ANNO 1665. At a Seſſions held at *Northampton* Caſtle on the 4th and 6th Days of the Month called *April*, five of the People called *Quakers* received Sentence of Baniſhment to *Jamaica*, on Conviction for the third Offence in meeting together for religious Worſhip, namely, *William Robinſon*, *Richard Parſons*, *John Coory*, *Elizabeth Harris*, and *Daniel Roe* : And at another Seſſions on the 12th and 13th of the Month called *February*, this Year, four others, viz. *Thomas Allen*, *Francis Child*, *Richard Coe*, and *William Line*, were alſo ſentenced to be tranſported to the ſame Place. In this Year alſo *John Bett*, *John Borton*, *Edward Hardly*, and *John Holcroft*, poor Labourers, had their

4 Others baniſhed.

Other Sufferings.

NORTH-
AMPTON-
SHIRE.
1665.

*Banifhment of
J. Treflove.*

*About forty
taken at a
Meeting and
fent to Prifon.*

*2 Others tranf-
ported.*

*Many others
imprifoned.*

*More Impri-
foned.*

Goods taken by Diftrefs for a Fine of 4*s*. each, impofed for four Weeks Abfence from their Parifh-Church. Likewife *John Garratt*, of *Findon*, for refufing
to take an Oath, when fummoned to ferve on a Jury, fuffered *nine Months* Imprifonment.

ANNO 1666. On the 25th of the Month called *April*, at *Northampton*
Seffions, *John Treflove*, of *Farndon*, was indicted on the Act of Banifhment
for the third Offence. The Foreman of the Jury, impanelled to try him, was
William Smith, of *Farthingftone*, who in *Oliver Cromwell's* Days was a fierce
Stickler againft the Common-Prayer, and then employed to hunt and perfecute
the Innocent : He was now upon the Turn of Times as zealous for what he had
before oppofed, and by his Violence over-awed fome others of the Jury to bring
the Prifoner in *Guilty*, who accordingly was fentenced to be tranfported to *Jamaica* for feven Years.

On the 20th of the Month called *May*, was a Meeting at the Houfe of *John
Mackernefs* in *Findon*, to which a Conftable came with a Rabble of Affiftants,
and told the Friends, that they muft none of them go thence till they had been
before the Juftices, he having a Warrant to fecure them, and as foon as the
Meeting was ended, he, with his Affiftants, dragged about forty of them to
a neighbouring Alehoufe, namely, *Thomas Ollive*, *William Page*, *Robert Cox*,
John Nottingham, *Thomas Page*, *William Mather*, *Elizabeth Ellington*, *Judith
Ollive*, *Alice Ives*, and *Alice Harris*, all of *Wellingborough* ; *John Garratt*, *Jofeph
Garratt*, *Nicholas Day*, *William Miller*, * *Frances Miller*, and *Hannah Day*,
all of *Findon* ; *Richard Pell*, *John Pell*, *Anne Pell*, and *Elizabeth Rofe*, all of
Little-Harradon ; *Elizabeth Bugg*, of the Ifle of *Ely* ; *William Pooley*, *Thomas
Abbott*, and *Chriftopher Davis*, all of *Addington* ; *John Woolfton*, *Laurence Key*,
and *Mary Tarry*, all of *Attleborough* ; *Thomas Auftin*, of *Stanwick* ; and *Anne
Nichols*, of *Rance* ; *Daniel Brown*, *John Bayes*, *William Wooton*, and *Joane
Brown*, all of *Puddington* in *Bedfordfhire* ; *James Pratt*, of *Barton* ; *George
Warner*, *James Warner*, *Thomas Hanfgood*, and *Thomas Cattle*, all of *Kettering*.
They were detained all Night at the Alehoufe, and next Morning put into a
Cart and a Waggon, and fo conveyed to Juftice *Yelverton's* at *Eafon*, who with
another Juftice prefent, fined them 40*s*. each, and for Non-payment fent them
all to the County Goal for fix Weeks.

At the next Quarter Seffions, on the 12th of the Month called *June*, two of
them, *viz*. *Nicholas Day* and *Jofeph Garratt* were indicted for the third Offence.
The Foreman of the Jury was the afore-named *William Smith*, of *Farthingftone*,
againft whom the Prifoners excepted as being prejudiced againft them, but the
Court over-ruled their juft Exception. So they were foon brought in *Guilty*, and
received Sentence of Tranfportation to *Jamaica* for feven Years.

On the 17th of the fame Month, *Thomas Page*, *Thomas Pell*, *Samuel Britton*,
John Biggs, *Anne Mary Page*, *Mary Ives*, *Elizabeth Hackney*, *Anne Cox*,
Ifabel Gibbs, *Mary Bailey*, *Mary Wareing*, *Elizabeth Bull*, *Sarah Bailey*, *Anne
Vice*, and *Mary Houghton*, were taken from a Meeting in *Findon*, kept all
Night in an Alehoufe, and next Day carried in a Waggon to Juftice *Yelverton's*,
who with another Juftice prefent, fevererally fined them, and for refufing to pay
fent them to *Northampton* Goal for fix Weeks, though the Condition of feveral of
them might have moved Compaffion ; one Woman being great with Child,
another having a fucking Child, and feveral poor Widows, having diverfe fmall
Children to provide for.

On the 15th of the Month called *July*, *Richard Pell*, *William Pell*, *Anne
Pell*, *Elizabeth Rofe*, *John Ellington*, *Alice Ives*, *Amy Robinfon*, and *Mary Tarry* ;
fome of whom had been before committed in the Month called *May*, fuffered
fix Weeks Imprifonment, and returning again to the Meeting at *Findon*, were
taken thence, detained one Night in an Alehoufe, and next Day committed to
Prifon.

From

---

* *Frances Miller* had with her a young Child fucking at her Breaft.

From other Meetings, held not long after at the fame Place, were alfo taken and fent to Prifon, *John Haughton, Thomas Preffon, Edmund Macker-nefs, Rebecca Mackernefs, Ellen Garrett, Sarah Bailey, Henry Roe, John Parnel, Michael Gaines, Samuel Gaines, John Gaines, Thomas Hewlett, George Ireland,* and *Alexander Manning.*

On the 19th of the Month called *July, Daniel Wills, Henry Roe, William Griffin, Michael Gaines, John Gaines,* and *John Parnel,* were brought to the Seffions at *Northampton,* to be tried on the Act for Banifhment for the third Offence : One of them, *Henry Roe,* was fentenced to be tranfported to *Jamaica* for feven Years ; but upon fome Doubt arifing, the Trial of the others was poftpon'd, and in Procefs of Time they were releafed. The Trial alfo of *John Lewis,* on the Act for Banifhment, intended to have been that Seffions, was prevented by his Death in the Prifon a fhort Time before.

In the Month called *Auguft, John Pell, John Crick, Robert Wallis,* and *Richard Wright,* were committed to Prifon for being at a Meeting in *Wellingborough :* And in the Month of *September, John Houghton, William Page, John Garrett, John Nottingham, Thomas Page,* and *John Ellington,* taken at a Meeting in *Findon,* were alfo committed to Prifon. Thefe laft fix with others, to the Number of fifteen Men and ten Women, were kept lockt up all Night in an Alehoufe, and next Day the Men were put into a Cart, and the Women into a Waggon, and carried before Juftice *Yelverton,* who figned a *Mittimus* for committing ten of the Men to Prifon ; but another Juftice's Hand being neceffary, he directed his Clerk to carry it to one Juftice *Ward,* not far from *Northampton :* The ten Men were again put into the Cart, and conveyed with the *Mittimus* to the faid Juftice *Ward,* but he refufed to fign it ; upon which the Prifoners were conveyed to *Northampton,* and when there, the two Clerks, viz. *Ward*'s and *Yelverton*'s, bufied themfelves to find out fome other Juftice to fign the *Mittimus,* but could procure none, nor could the Goaler legally receive them without. So the Prifoners, after long waiting, returned every Man to his own Home : But fome Time after, the laft mentioned *fix* were taken by another Warrant and fent to Goal ; *three* of whom, viz. *John Houghton, John Nottingham,* and *Thomas Page,* were afterward fentenced to Tranfportation. The Number of Perfons of this Perfuafion, at one Time under clofe Confinement in the County Goal, was more than fourfcore, of whom many were Farmers and Hufbandmen, lockt up from their Bufinefs both in Hay-time and Harveft, to their very great Lofs and Damage.

ANNO 1667. *Robert Afhby* and *Arthur Green,* before mentioned to have been committed to Prifon in 1663, were yet remaining there at the Suit of one *Whitfield,* Prieft of *Bugbrook,* who during their Confinement made great Spoil on their Effects at Home, taking away fome Times whole Fields of Corn, and fome Times whole Loads of Grain and Hay, far exceeding any legal Claim : At the fame Time preffing the Goaler to keep them clofe confined, which he did, alledging in Excufe of himfelf, that he had afked the Prieft, *Whether he might not let them go out fome Times to fetch in their Provifions and Neceffaries ;* but was anfwered by him, *No ; keep them in, and pine them, and ftarve them.* So that their Imprifonment was very long and grievous. There were alfo yet remaining, clofely confined, thofe fifteen Perfons whom in the two preceding Years we have mentioned to have undergone the hard Sentence of Tranfportation ; under which five of them had now lain two and thirty Months, three others of them twenty eight Months, and none of them lefs than fourteen Months. In this Year alfo we find imprifoned at *Northampton,* under Sentence of *Premunire, Thomas Dent* and *George Ayre,* who had then continued in that State about four Years and three Months. About this Time the Prifoners there thought meet to publifh a Paper declaring their innocent Plainnefs and Integrity, being as follows,

" Some Fruits *reaped already by the* Faithful *that have entred into the*
" Good Land, *of which* Canaan *was a Figure, which we here in the*
" *Fear of the* Lord *declare without boasting, that others may see what*
" *grows in that Land, that are not yet come thither.*

A Paper pub-
lished by some
of the Pri-
soners.

" SINCE the Lord called us, whom the World calls *Quakers*, into that
" Land, where the Light of Christ shineth, we have come to witness the
" Lord's Power fulfilled, that all the Children of the Lord should be taught
" of the Lord, and that the Lord would teach his People himself, and we
" need not that any Hireling Priest teach us ; so we bid Adieu to all Hireling
" Priests and Teachers, and shall not, nor never may, put into their Mouths
" again.

" *Secondly.* Since we came into this good Land, we never have been
" without wise Men among us, that if any Difference hath arisen between a
" Brother and a Brother, we have been made willing to put our Cause to their
" Determination : And so never among the Thousands of those called *Quakers*,
" Brother has never been found to go to Law with a Brother, and that before
" Infidels, such as judge for Gifts and Rewards. So adieu Hireling Priests,
" and deceitful Lawyers : Christ's Government which we live under, will never
" admit of any of you.

" *Thirdly.* And since the Lord hath brought us into this good Land, there
" is not a Beggar found among us, but all are made willing to labour with their
" own Hands, that so they may be serviceable to all in their Generation.

" *Fourthly.* The Civil Magistrates, neither at their Assizes, nor at their
" Sessions, have not at any Time any one of us brought before them for the
" Breach of any just Law of God or Man : Yet we are many of us brought
" before them, as *Daniel* was, and as Christ Jesus said we should, for Things
" concerning our God, and for Righteousness-sake : And for those Things we
" are not ashamed.

" And when Magistrates Eyes come to be opened, and they once come to
" hate the Whore, and to eat her Flesh, and to burn her with Fire, then they
" will see, that the *Quakers* Principles are not destructive to good Government
" nor Governours : But as People come to own their Principles, and to live in
" them, they will ease the Magistrate of a great deal of Labour, and free the
" Nation of a vast Charge, that is now spent needlessly upon Priests and Lawyers,
" and yet for all that no Reformation wrought among the People."

Remarks on the
said Paper.

The foregoing Paper expresses the early Sense of this People respecting mercenary Priests and Lawyers, as having no Place among *perfect Christians* ;
because the true Ministers of Christ are ever ready freely to communicate unto
others their Experience of the Teachings of his Spirit freely given them : And
as to Lawyers, a Government of universal Peace can find them no Employment.

In this and the two preceding Years, *Thomas Cooke* had taken from him, in
Cattle and other Things for Tithes, to the Value of 13*l.* 7 s. And

Tithes.

ANNO 1668. The said *Thomas Cooke* had taken from him for Tithes, two
Acres of his best Corn.

Persecution
revived.

ANNO 1670. In the two last Years we find but few Instances of Persecution in this County ; but upon another Act issued against *Conventicles* in this
Year, the Informers and others again made a Prey on their religious Neighbours, as appears by the following *Extract* of a Letter from *Wellingborough*,
dated the 13th of the Fourth Month 1670.

Extract of a
Letter from
Wellingbo-
rough.

" SOME Days by past, the wicked Ruler's Agents came and streined
" from *Thomas Ollive* sixty Pounds worth of good Cloth at one Time,
" and had Orders to take twenty Pounds from *Francis Ellington*, but forbore in
" Regard of a Deed of Sale for the Security of his Creditors, &c. The
" Friend

" Friend fhewed them what he had referved, but they would not then take it;
" but defired him to go with them to the Juftice, who is a great Perfecutor,
" and when he faw the Deed, he boafted and faid, *It would do the Friend no*
" *Good :* Who anfwered, that *If the late Act had not fruftrated all the Law of*
" *England, his Council informed him, that he might fell his Goods to whom he*
" *pleafed.* So the Juftice bade the Conftable forbear till he had fent to *London :*
" Then he afked the Conftables, *Whether they had taken enough from* Thomas
" Ollive. They faid, *They thought they had.* He replied, *Be fure you take*
" *enough and more, that fo there may be twenty Pounds for the King, twenty*
" *Pounds for the Poor, and twenty Pounds for the Informer, and if you take*
" *Goods enough, then of the Refidue you fhall have one Part, and I will have*
" *the Reft.* They anfwered him, that *They would never receive a Penny on that*
" *Account.* Alfo one *Yelverton,* Knight and Burgefs for *Northampton,* faid the
" fame Words to the Conftables. They alfo took feven Beafts from another
" Friend dwelling near ; and from another Friend one hundred and fixty
" Pafture Fleeces, and moft of his Brafs and Pewter : And from another they
" were ordered to diftrain for feven Pounds fifteen Shillings ; and from another
" as much, who being a Widow's Son, and having nothing in Poffeffion, the
" Warrant was returned to the Juftices, who fent the Conftables back again
" with a Command to take his Clothes : Another Friend was diftrained for
" twenty five Shillings ; another for forty Pounds ; and another for twenty
" Pounds ; befides diverfe for five Shillings and ten Shillings a piece : Alfo
" two or more were diftrained for eight Pounds a piece, and another for
" twelve Pounds.

" The Bifhop of *Peterborough* vifited at *Rowel* laft Week, and there faid
" openly in the Mafs-houfe, after he had given every Officer a Charge to put
" the late Act in Execution ; *That when they met again,* (meaning the Parlia-
" ment) *they would make a ftronger for them, they would get a Law made to*
" *take away their Lands and Goods, and then they fhould be fold for Bond-flaves.*"

This fhews that fome of the leading Ecclefiafticks thought the Laws,
though very fevere, too favourable toward the *Quakers* ; wherefore they not
only urged the Execution of them to the utmoft Extremity ; but would
willingly have extended them to the utter Extirpation of thofe whom in their
miftaken Zeal they deemed to be *Hereticks.*

In this Year, at *Northampton* they met in the Street, being excluded from *Fines for*
their ufual Meeting-place ; for one of thofe Meetings *Edward Cowper* had a *Meeting.*
Fine of 9*l.* impofed on him for himfelf and thirty four others fo affembled, for
which the Officers took away his Goods to the Value of about 16*l.* But when
after a long Time they could find no Body to purchafe them, they were redeemed by fome charitable Neighbours for 3*l.* and returned to the Owner.

Thomas Cooke, for abfenting himfelf from the publick Worfhip, had Goods *T. Cooke.*
taken from him worth 15*s.* He was alfo committed to Prifon, and fuffered
Diftrefs of Goods to the Amount of 7*s.* for the Charges of carrying him
thither.

ANNO 1672. In this Year *Daniel Roe, John Nottingham, Thomas Page,* *14 Difcharged*
John Haughton, Nicholas Day, Jofeph Garrett, William Robinfon, John Cary, *from long Im-*
Thomas Allen, Richard Coe, John Treflove, William Line, Francis Child, and *prifonments.*
Elizabeth Harris, were fet at Liberty from their long and grievous Confinement
in *Northampton* Goal, where fome of them had lain under the difmal Sentence
of Tranfportation between feven and eight Years, and none of them lefs than
fix Years. At the fame Time was alfo difcharged *Thomas Dent,* who had
been confined there under Sentence of *Premunire* upwards of nine Years.

ANNO 1677. *Robert Afhby, John Afhby,* and *Thomas Hafcott,* of *Bugbrook,* *Profecutions*
were imprifoned at *Northampton* for Tithes, and lay there a long Time, at the *for Tithes.*
Suit of *Samuel Clark, Richard Rainsford,* and *William Bugby,* Impropriators or
Tithe-farmers. And not long after, *Peter Mackernefs* was fent to the fame

NORTH-
AMPTON-
SHIRE.
1678.

*Profecutions
for Tithes.*

Prifon for a Demand of fmall Tithes on an *Exchequer* Procefs, at the Suit of the Prieft of *Findon.*

ANNO 1678. *William Tibbs* and *John Green,* of *Bugbrook,* were Prifoners in *Northampton* Goal for Tithes, at the Suit of feveral Impropriators, and alfo of *John Whitfield,* Prieft of that Parifh.

ANNO 1679. The aforefaid *William Tibbs* had taken from him on an Execution for Tithes, by the Sheriff, 40 *l.* for an original Demand of but 6 *l.* and the faid *John Green,* for a Claim of 20 *s.* for Tithes, had an Execution ferved on his Effects for 20 *l.* *John Ayres,* of *Farthingftone,* for a Demand of 20 *s.* for fmall Tithes, had an Execution awarded againft him for 12 *l.* at the Suit of one *Hogg,* Prieft of that Parifh. The fame *John Ayres* and *Henry Hopkins* were alfo imprifoned for refufing to pay Tithes. Likewife *William Miller,* of *Findon,* was committed to Prifon on a Procefs againft him for fmall Tithes in the Ecclefiaftical Court.

William Pooley, of *Addington-Puce,* was profecuted in the *Exchequer,* at the Suit of *Nathanael Hewfon* Prieft, for Tithes of about 6 *l.* Value, for which were taken from him by a Sequeftration, Horfes, Kine, and Hogs, worth 40 *l.* but fome of his Relations afterward redeemed them by the Payment of 20 *l.*

ANNO 1680. *Richard Bradfhaw,* of *Flower* in *Northamptonfhire,* writ a Paper, expreffing the Chriftian Zeal of its Writer againft the Payment of Tithes, and containing a juft Reproof of thofe, who being convinced in their own Judgment that *Tithes are Antichriftian,* do neverthelefs fubmit to pay them for Fear of fuffering, we have thought meet, for the Sake of fuch, to infert the fame, thinking it may be as neceffary now as it was then ; it is as follows,

" *A* Teftimony *to the* T R U T H, *and againft that which makes*
" *a* Profeffion *of* T R U T H, *and yet can pay* Tithes.

" *Friends,*

" YOU that are convinced of God's eternal Truth, but chiefly you that
" have a long Time been convinced of it, and do bear a Teftimony in
" the Affembly of God's People, and alfo againft the falfe Ways and Wor-
" fhips of this World, againft the Hireling and his Wages, in Words ; yet
" notwithftanding thefe Teftimonies, can throw into the Mouth of the *Whore's*
" Merchants : The Lord hath often fhewed me, you are within the Borders of
" *Babylon* ; and thus faith the Lord, *Come out of* Babylon *my People, and touch*
" *no unclean Thing,* for if you partake of her Sins, *you muft partake of her*
" *Plagues,* if you repent not in Time, for the Spirit of the Lord will not
" always ftrive with Man. But this I have farther to fignify unto you, and
" that from the Lord, *There is a Way out of* Babylon, *and out of all her*
" *Borders, and to be feparated from all her Brats :* I do believe I need not fay
" much concerning the Way, for I believe many of you do know the Way,
" and they that do not, let them learn of him who is the Way, the Truth,
" and the Life. *The juft Man's Path is a fhining Light, where the way-faring*
" *Man, though a Fool, cannot err therein.* And it is the Defire of my Soul,
" and the Breathing of my Life unto God, that I with you, and you with
" me, and all that make a Profeffion of the Name of the Lord, may walk
" therein, that we may give no Offence to them that are without, neither to
" the Church of God.

" *Friends,* that which moves in you, and caufes you to pay Tithes, is not
" of the Lord's planting ; therefore *Every Plant which God hath not planted,*
" ought to be plucked up.

" *Friends,* you that pay Tithes, and we that for Confcience-fake cannot pay
" Tithes, yet make a Profeffion of the True God, and all to have the fame
" Teacher : Be cool in your Minds, *Friends* ; and let the true Heart-fearching
" God fearch every Heart with his pure heavenly divine Light and Power, for
" that will do none of us any Harm.

" God

" God is a God of Order and not of Confufion : He doth not lead his
" Children to deftroy the Teftimonies one of another. But you that make a
" Profeffion of the Truth, and yet can pay Tithes, do undervalue the Tefti-
" monies of us who for Confcience-fake cannot pay Tithes, and alfo of many
" of our Brethren who are taken out of the Body, which fealed their Teftimony
" with their Lives, and died Prifoners, being caft into Prifon for their faithful
" Teftimonies againft Tithes : I fay, you that pay Tithes make our Teftimony
" void, as much as in the Strength of the Matter lieth. You that have been
" longer convinced, and fhould be good Examples to the new convinced Ones,
" rather throw Stumbling-blocks in their Way.

" Therefore be not deceived ; he that ferveth to the wicked One, muft receive
" his Wages accordingly ; and he that ferveth to God, fhall receive from God
" his Wages, which will be Peace in his own Confcience. *Friends*, I befeech
" you bear with me, for I do not defire to boaft my felf, but to clear my Con-
" fcience of this Matter, which hath lain as a Weight or Burden upon the
" Seed in me for fome Years. I have confidered, and ferioufly took a View,
" and feen fome lie in Prifon, and fome fuffer deeply the Spoiling of their
" Goods ; and have heard of others in other Countries which have fuffered far
" more deeply than I have feen, for their honeft and faithful Teftimony againft
" Tithes : And alfo feen others make a Profeffion of the fame God, and yet
" pay Tithes ; that troubled me, and often caufed my Soul to be more than
" ufually fad : Then the Lord fhewed me, that we were not all of one Heart
" and of one Mind, and that we did not all obey one Teacher in this Matter.
" God hath raifed up many living Witneffes, that the Subftance is come,
" (bleffed be his holy Name for evermore) which puts an End to all the
" Tithes and Shadows of the Law in the firft Covenant, when the outward
" Temple, and outward Tabernacle; and old Priefthood, were ftanding ; then
" the Priefts offered up for the Sins of the People, and God accepted it : The
" People paid a tenth Part of all which they did poffefs, as an Offering to the
" Prieft, and I do believe that God was pleafed with it in that Day and Time :
" But it is not fo now, for now every Man and Woman muft offer to the
" Eternal High-Prieft, a living and fpiritual Sacrifice of God's preparing.
" Therefore knowing him to be come; *viz.* Chrift, who is the Wifdom and
" Power of God, who put an End to the firft Covenant, to the outward Taber-
" nacle, and outward Temple, and the old Priefthood, and its Tithes, and hath
" ended all the Types and Shadows of the Law, there can be no more pay-
" ing Tithes to the Priefts, nor Impropriators, under the Gofpel Difpenfation,
" and be clear in the Sight of God.

" *Friends*, this Matter of Tithes lieth fuch a Burden upon me, I cannot
" leave it yet ; for that which payeth Tithes, and that which receiveth Tithes,
" are both generated in one Womb : The Wife in Heart know the Mother of
" them both ; for fhe is come in Remembrance before the great God of Heaven,
" and as fhe hath done to others, it fhall be done to her double, for God is
" avenging himfelf of her, for down fhe muft tumble like a great Millftone,
" and muft be confumed, and the Saints rejoice at the Smoke of her Burning,
" though *Babel*'s Builders fee it not.

" Therefore, *Friends*, I befeech you, be you wholly feparated from her before
" it be too late, and you perifh without Remedy. Be warned in Time, *Friends* ;
" let every one turn to the Lord, with our whole Heart, have no Dependence
" upon any Thing but the true and living God, for there is yet a Door of
" Mercy open, and *he that will come, may come, and take of the Water of Life*
" *freely, without Money, and without Price.* Friends, *in the Name of the Lord*
" *there is everlafting Strength :* Therefore, *Friends*, be encouraged in the Name
" of the Lord, you tender-hearted Ones, to whom Tithes is become a Bur-
" den : I dearly intreat you in the Lord's Behalf, Give up and be faithful to
" what you know, and let your whole Dependence be in the Lord alone, and if
" he doth not do that for you, which never Man could do, believe him not ;
" but if he doth that for you, that never Man could do, believe him for the
" Work's

" Work's Sake. *Friends,* the Eyes of all are upon us, fome watching for
" Evil, and fome for Good ; and fome take Notice of our Friends lying in
" Prifon for Non-payment of Tithes, and alfo fee others fuffer deeply the
" Spoiling of their Goods, and alfo fee others pay Tithes, and they know we
" that fuffer Imprifonment, and he that fuffers Spoiling of Goods, and alfo he
" that payeth Tithes, make a Profeffion all of one Religion, and all to be
" guided by the Spirit of God.

" *Friends,* let him be Judge, to whom all Judgment is committed, for
" is this like to reach the Witnefs of God in our Neighbours, and Enemies,
" and them that take Notice of us, and to fignify to that of God in them,
" that we are a People, all of one Heart and of one Mind ? Or will it not
" rather fignify, that we are a double-minded People ? When one ftrives to
" pull down that which another builds, the Building cannot go fo well forwards.

" But notwithftanding all Oppofitions, God will have his Work go forwards,
" and will have a People that fhall bear his Name in Truth and Righteoufnefs :
" Yea, bleffed and magnified be the Name of the Lord, who hath by the
" outftretched Arm of his mighty Power gathered a Remnant into the Cove-
" nant of Light and Life, and to bear his Name and Truth in Righteoufnefs,
" and are made willing through the Love of God (to his Honour be it fpoken)
" to take up the Crofs and defpife the Shame, whom this Teftimony doth not
" concern as to Matter of Charge : Therefore, *Friends,* beware of taking that to
" you which doth not concern you as to Matter of Charge ; but let this Tefti-
" mony go to whom it doth concern, for I know it concerns too many, the
" more's the Pity.

" And, *Friends,* you that are made willing, through the Love of God, to
" bear a Teftimony againft Tithes, I intreat you to be faithful, and let there
" be no private Confenting to Wives, nor Relations, nor Neighbours, paying
" for private Tithes, as Wool, Milk, and Eggs, and fuch Kind of Things,
" and other petty Matters, as the Priefts count their Due, and the great
" Tithes alfo. *Friends,* I fay for the Truth's Sake, and for Confcience-fake,
" let there not be any Thing of that Nature harboured in any of your Breafts,
" and private Confenting to any of thefe Matters, for it is all Abomination in
" the Sight of God : And though you may hide from Man, there is no Hiding
" from God, for the Lord is bringing the hidden Things of *Efau* to Light.
" It is the Defire of my Heart, and the Breathing of my Soul unto God, that
" the Hindermoft of the Flock may come in that Life wherein there is
" Power to refift the Devil in all his fubtil Temptations, and that all that have
" gone aftray, may come to know the true Shepherd's Crook, and fully re-
" turn to him who is the Shepherd and Bifhop of the Souls of the Righteous :
" For the Lord defireth not the Death of Sinners, but rather that they would
" return and live.

" Richard Bradshaw."

This Teftimony carries with it an Evidence of the Sincerity and Uprightnefs
of the Perfon who writ it, and of a true Concern for his Brethren, that they
might be united in the Practice of thofe Chriftian Teftimonies which they made
Profeffion of ; and not draw back for Fear of Sufferings.

ANNO 1682. On the 2d of the Month called *June,* the following Perfons
were in Prifon at *Northampton* for their refufing to pay Tithes, namely, *Nicholas
Day, Edmund Mackernefs,* and *Peter Mackernefs,* on Writs de Excommunicate
capiendo, for Tithes ; the two Former having then lain there about two
Years, and the Latter about five Years : *William Miller,* who had been confined
there about three Years : *Robert Afhby, John Afhby,* and *Thomas Hafcott,* who
had then been Prifoners four Years and an Half : Alfo *John Keming* and
William Barnes, at the Suit of *Harris,* Prieft of *Kiflingbury.*

In this Year *Peter Jahan,* a *Frenchman,* was imprifoned at *Northampton* for
refufing to pay towards the Repairs of the Steeple-houfe ; and for the fame
Caufe *George Mackernefs,* of *Scaldwell,* Hufbandman, was committed to
Prifon

Prison by a Writ *de Excommunicato capiendo*, on the 21st of *December* this Year. NORTH-AMPTON-SHIRE. 1682.

In the same Year, *George Ayres*, of *Farthingstone*, for his Attendance at religious Meetings, had three Warrants granted against him, by *Henry Benson* Justice, for 10 *l.* 5 *s.* each, for which were taken from him, two Horses, six Cows, two Calves, forty one Sheep, a Sow and six Pigs, a Waggon, Corn, Utensils for Husbandry, Wood, Houshold Goods, and other Things, worth 46 *l.* 15 *s.* 11 *d.*

Distress for Meetings.

Besides which, he had taken away for Absence from the National Worship, Pewter worth 15 *s.*

For the same Cause also were taken from *Susanna Bilton* and *William Basely*, Goods worth 4 *l.* 10 *s.*

And from *Benjamin Wright*, of *Blaxley*, for being at a Meeting, were taken Goods worth 6 *s.* 9 *d.*

A violent Promoter of the Distress, made on the aforesaid *George Ayres*, was *John Hutton* the Priest of *Farthingstone*, who presently after his Sermon, or Service, was over, spake to the Parish-Officers about making the Distress, desiring them *to do their Work throughly*. At which Time *Thomas Hogg*, one of the Informers, promised the Parson that he would take Care to see it throughly managed ; and accordingly, the said *Hogg*, with another Informer, a Servant to the Priest, attended the Officers, urging them to take all they could find : But the Officers thinking they had sufficient, did not take away their Bedding, which the Informers would have done, and threatned to come again for the Rest. A short Time after, the said *George Ayres* with his Wife, and *Susanna Bilton* Widow, each of the Women having a sucking Child at her Breast, were sent to Prison for Want of Distress, for Absence from the National Worship, the said Priest *Hutton*, their Prosecutor, having said, as was credibly reported, *that he would rid the Town of them all*. The said *Susanna Bilton*, being in Prison, had taken from her, by Justice *Benson's* Warrant, for being at a Meeting, thirty six Sheep and two Cows, worth 18 *l.* The Sheep and Cows being sold, the Officers brought back 5 *l.* but instead of returning it to the Widow, paid most of it to the Priest for a *Mortuary* claimed by him on the Death of her Husband, and detained another Part for the Steeple-house Rate, till they had but eight Shillings remaining, which the Widow refused to receive, lest she should thereby seem to consent to the unjust Distribution of the Rest.

Prosecution of G. Ayres and others.

Priest Hutton *a fierce Prosecutor.*

John Ayres, of *Litchborow*, for Meetings, suffered Distress of his Goods to the Value of 4 *l.* 14 *s.* 3 *d.* being all the Prosecutors at that Time had Opportunity to come at.

J. Ayres.

On the 28th of the Month called *May* this Year, the aforesaid Priest *Hutton*, attended by his Servant *Matthew Arnold*, and *Thomas Hogg*, Informers, with Constables and others charged to assist them, came to the Meeting at *Farthingstone* with a Justices's Warrant, which they read in the Meeting, and took the Names of some Persons present : After which the Priest, and *Hogg* the Informer, charged the Constables with them, who with their Assistants drew most of them out of the Meeting by Violence, overturning the Forms, and throwing them into the Street. In which Work the Priest's Servant was very active, being commended by his Master for his Industry therein : They nailed up one of the Doors of the Meeting-house, and kept Watch at the other, pretending that they seized the House for the King.

Violent Doings at Farthingstone.

On the 2d of the Month called *June*, *Elizabeth Basely*, *Sarah Daniel*, and *Alice Nicholas*, were Prisoners in *Northampton* for Fines imposed on them for Absence from the National Worship ; and on the 13th of the same, *James Wells* suffered Distress of Goods worth 8 *s.* 8 *d.* for his Wife's being at a Meeting at *Farthingstone*.

Prisoners.

About the 23d of the Month called *July*, *Hutton* the Priest, with *Hogg* the Informer, came to break up the Meeeting at *Farthingstone*, where *Richard Bradshaw* not moving at their Command, they violently haled him out, and caused him to be set in the Stocks, together with *John Gibbins*, and kept them both lockt in near eight Hours. Next Day they procured a Warrant from Juſtice *Needham*, and carried them to him, who tendred them the Oath of Allegiance, and ſent them to Priſon for refuſing it.

On the 17th of the Month called *Auguſt*, *John Hart* and *Nicholas Read*, of *Towceſter*, were committed to Priſon by a Writ *de Excommunicato capiendo*, having been preſented in the Eccleſiaſtical Court, for Abſence from the National Worſhip, by the Wardens of that Pariſh, who had themſelves been firſt preſented there, by the Prieſt of the ſame Pariſh, for Neglect of what he called their Duty.

*More Impri-
ſonments.*

On the 20th of the ſame Month, the following Perſons, having been taken at *Farthingſtone* Meeting, were by the Conſtable and others, at the Inſtigation of Prieſt *Hutton*, put into an empty Houſe, and kept there all Night, and next Day carried before Juſtice *Needham*, a Captain, newly put into Commiſſion of the Peace : Before him the Prieſt alſo appeared, preſſing the Juſtice to tender them the Oaths ; which when they refuſed to take, the Juſtice aſked the Prieſt, *What he ſhould do with them, ſeeing they would not Swear.* The Prieſt readily anſwered, *Make their* Mittimus, *and ſend them to Priſon :* Which accordingly was done. Their Names were *Thomas Smallbone, Richard Ellis, Anne Wells, Hannah Harris, Joane Dillingham, Margaret Simſon, Dorothy Paine, Martha Line, Margaret Adams, Sarah Ingram, Elizabeth Gray, Mary Cumberleigh,* and *Elizabeth Freeman.*

*Employment
in Priſon.*

Some of theſe Women were married, and had Families of Children, others were ſickly, and the reſt Maids. In Priſon they employed themſelves in knitting, ſewing, ſpinning, &c. for their Subſiſtence, having moſt of them little but what they wrought for.

*S. Cox im-
priſoned on
a Writ* de
Excom. Cap.

On the 26th of *October, Samuel Cox*, of *Woodford*, was committed to Priſon by a Writ *de Excommunicato capiendo*, after a Proſecution in the Eccleſiaſtical Court, carried on againſt him by *William Gates*, Prieſt of the Pariſh, for Abſence from the publick Worſhip, and for Marriage Fees claimed by the Prieſt, though he had not been married by him, nor by any of his Function.

Edward Cowper had taken from him for Meetings, Goods to the Value of 9*l.*

*S. Bradſhaw
imprisoned.*

ANNO 1683. On the 23d of the Month called *April*, a Writ *de Excommunicato capiendo* being iſſued againſt *Samuel Bradſhaw*, of *Northampton*, for his not going to Church, he ſurrendred himſelf a Priſoner upon Proclamation.

About the 28th of the Month called *May*, *John Loft*, a Carrier of *Todcaſter* in *Yorkſhire*, was taken from a Meeting at *Whittlebury*, and ſent to Priſon ; of which take the Account given by himſelf in a Letter to *George Fox*, viz.

" *Dear* GEORGE FOX,

*J. Loft's
Letter to
G. Fox.*

" I Was taken Priſoner next Day after I parted with thee at *Whittlebury*
" Meeting, and by one *Longville*, called a Juſtice, ſent to *Northampton*
" Goal, to anſwer at the Seſſions for being at a Conventicle, as he called it,
" and refuſing to give Bond to be conformable to the Church of *England*.
" Since I was brought hither, I have been before them at the Seſſions, and was
" aſked ſome Queſtions, as *Where I lived ?* I ſaid, *I lived in the Fear of the*
" *Lord.* Being aſked the ſame over again, I anſwered, *I live in the Truth.*
" At which they were offended, and ſaid, *They would have no Canting.* After
" I did open my Buſineſs in the Country ſomething to them, and told them
" my Name, and where I lived. Then I was aſked, *If I would take the Oath*
" *of Allegiance ?* I anſwered, that *Chriſt Jeſus, the Everlaſting King, had for-*
" *bidden all Swearing long ago, and therefore I would not Swear.* They ſaid, *I*
" *might have Time to conſider of it, and I might have it read.* I ſaid, *I had con-*
" *ſidered it already :* And willing to ſpeak ſomething more, they hindred me,
" and ſaid, *We will have no Preaching here : Take him away Goaler.* However
" Peace with the Lord is the Portion of all thoſe who ſuffer for Well-doing,
" and through the Lord's Love I have that Peace in my Meaſure with the
" ſuffering Seed. Dear *George*, Friends here in Priſon for the Teſtimony of
" Truth,

" Truth, defire to have their Loves remembred to thee generally, and here
" we have good Meetings, praifed be the Name of the Lord.

Northampton *Goal, the* 11th
of the Fourth Month 1683. JOHN LOFT."

Commitment of T. Poole *and* D. Roe.

On the 15th of the Month called *July, Thomas Poole* and *Daniel Roe* were taken at a Meeting in *Bugbrook*, and carried before the Juftices at *Northampton*, before whom the Prieft of *Bugbrook*, named *Whitfield*, appeared againft them, and would have convicted them on his own fingle Information, telling the Juftices, that *He could not get one Soul elfe in all his Parifh to appear againft them :* But the Juftices would not convict them on his fingle Evidence. Failing in his Purpofe in this Point, he infifted on the Juftices tendring them the Oath of Allegiance, which they did, and upon their refufing to Swear, committed them to Prifon.

Malicious Profecutions.

On the 28th of the fame Month, *William Bafely*, of *Farthingftone*, was taken out of the Field from his Work, and carried before Juftice *Needham*, who, for refufing to Swear, committed him to Prifon, where his Wife was before, as we have already mentioned, and being in Prifon, the Prieft *Hutton* procured a Writ *de Excommunicato capiendo* againft her, and continued her there. Thus, after he had profecuted them for Meetings to the Lofs of all their Subftance, he found Means farther to manifeft the Extent of his Malice, by imprifoning their Perfons without any Profpect of Redemption.

On the 15th of *September, John Bradford*, of *Little-Billing*, and on the 2d of *October, William Tibbs*, of *Bugbrook*, were committed to Prifon by Writs *de Excommunicato capiendo*. About this Time alfo were taken by Profecutions on the Statute for 20*l.* per Month, for Abfence from their Parifh-Church,

Diftreffes for Abfence from the National Worfhip.

		l.	s.	d.
From	*Thomas Cooke*, of *Weldon*, feven Beafts, two Horfes, and Houfhold Goods, to the Value of	27	0	0
	The Widow *Sewel*, five Beafts worth	17	0	0
	Thomas Boone, of *Corby*, thirteen Beafts and five Hogs, worth	20	0	0
	John Bland, of *Brigftock*, one Cow worth	2	0	0
	Roger Booth, Goods worth	3	5	0
	Sarah Palmer	1	7	0
	Samuel Gaines	8	10	0
		79	2	0

Thomas Charles was alfo indicted for the fame Caufe on the fame Statute, and fuffered Diftrefs of his Goods.

Timothy Burberow and *Thomas Mercer*, were committed to Prifon on Writs *de Excommunicato capiendo* ; the Former having been profecuted in the Ecclefiaftical Court for not bringing his Children to be baptized. *Richard Gill* was alfo committed to Prifon on a Seffions Procefs, for Abfence from his *Parifh-Church*.

At the *Lent* Affizes in 1683-4, the Prifoners at *Northampton* delivered the following Petition, viz.

" To the JUDGES of Affize, *and* General-Goal-Delivery *for this County*
" *of* Northampton.

" *The* Humble Requeft *of us whofe Names are here under-written, being*
" Prifoners *in the County Goal belonging to the faid County,*

" SHEWETH,

" THAT we, moft of us living upon our daily Labour, and honeft
" Care to get a Livelihood for our Maintenance in the World, without
" being burdenfome to any, about a Year and an Half fince, being met
" together

Petition to the Judges.

" together for the Worſhip and Service of God at *Farthingſtone* in the ſaid County,
" were ſeized upon by a Conſtable and other Officers at our peaceable and
" quiet Meeting at ſeveral Times, and at *Bugbrook* were brought thence before
" Juſtice *Needham* of this County, who committed us to this Priſon, where we
" remain at this Time : May it pleaſe you therefore, that in Regard of our
" long Confinement, our Condition may be inſpected and examined, as in your
" Wiſdoms ſhall be thought fit, and then to deal with us according to our
" inoffenſive and ſuffering Condition, our Capacities being but mean in Things
" pertaining to this Life, that you would be pleaſed to order our Delivery, of
" which we ſhould willingly accept, and as it is our Duty, ſhall give God
" Thanks, on your and our Behalf, who alone is worthy of Glory and Honour
" over all for ever and evermore. *Amen.* And we, who honour the Lord,
" ſhall by our peaceable Living, ſhew our Love to all in Authority under
" the King, unto whom we are ſubject for Conſcience-ſake.

" RICHARD BRADSHAW,	ELIZABETH FREEMAN,
" JOHN GIBBINS,	MARGARET SIMPSON,
" RICHARD ELLIS,	MARGARET ADAMS,
" JOHN LOFT,	HANNAH HARRIS,
" THOMAS POOLE,	ANNE WELLS,
" DANIEL ROE,	MARTHA LINE,
" JOHN PACKWOOD,	JANE BILLINGHAM,
" JOSIAH PACKWOOD,	SARAH INGRAM,
" WILLIAM BASELY,	DOROTHY PAYNE."
" ELIZABETH GREY,	

This Letter favours of that meek and patient Spirit wherewith this People
endured the Hardſhips inflicted on them, and ſhews with what Humility and
Submiſſion they repreſented their Grievances to thoſe in Authority. Nevertheleſs they were ſtill continued Priſoners.

ANNO 1684. At the Quarter Seſſions in the Month called *April,* the
Priſoners at *Northampton* preſented to the Juſtices a Book intituled *A Treatiſe of
Oaths,* together with the following State of their Caſe, *viz.*

" *A* few Words *to the* M A G I S T R A T E S, *now ſitting in* Seſſions
" *at* Northampton.

The Priſoners
*preſent a State
of their Caſe
to the* Quar-
ter Seſſions.

" U N T O you, we the People called *Quakers* have ſeveral Times wrote
" to conſider, that we, being tender of God's Glory, have from Time
" to Time been willing to perſuade and beſeech you to ſtay your Hand in
" afflicting us upon the Account of Swearing, than which nothing elſe, ever
" ſince we have been a People, could have been more uſed againſt us to cauſe
" our Sufferings, *viz. Oaths :* Although we have cleared our ſelves in that
" Point, anſwering all the Objections that render us Guilty, both in Regard to
" all in Authority, and all others that have ſpoke any Thing againſt our Obe-
" dience to Chriſt Jeſus in that main Point, *Swear not at all* ; not thereby to
" be ſhort to any that hath Authority over us, but if we might, in the Truth
" of our Hearts, ſhould manifeſt our Faithfulneſs both to God and Man. We
" therefore have ſent in our Behalf a Book for you, or as any of you are con-
" cerned, wherein that our Practice of *not Swearing at all* is vindicated and
" juſtified by many learned Men of all Sorts, to read at your Leiſure, that was
" on our Behalf, as a People, preſented to the King and his great Council aſ-
" ſembled in Parliament, as may be ſeen in the Peruſal of the Diſcourſe it ſelf,
" which we hope you will accept of and conſider : In the which we only ſeek,
" that we might but enjoy the Happineſs of living among you in Peace and
" Quietneſs, under the King, in the Land of our Nativity, to be an Help
" according to our Ability for the Proſperity of all that dwell therein.

" And

" And for us who fuffer for Righteoufnefs, this know, it was the Practice of
" all who honoured God in all Ages, to have an high Efteem of Magiftrates,
" being ordained and impowered of God to that high Calling, which if rightly
" difcharged, brings with it the Blefling of God in this World, and they come
" to receive that Wifdom which is from Above, to judge by, betwixt Man and
" Man, to preferve Peace and Unity among the People, which are the World
" of Mankind, which have been led by an evil Spirit from that Obedience that
" of Right is due from all Men to be given to the Lord their God : And
" hence comes Strife, Debate, Murder, and every evil Work, which by the
" Ordinance of the pure God, Magiftrates ought to fupprefs in every Age of
" the World. And all thofe Rulers, Kings and others, that fulfilled their
" Places in giving God the Glory due to his Honour, they purchafed an
" honourable Name in the Truth, and are worthy to have their Names re-
" corded in the Regifter of Life Immortal, and in the Records of Worth
" among Men in this World : So that you may come to have your Names
" among thofe before gone, and amongft the prefent faithful Lovers, and
" Favourers, and Honourers of the Moft High, to whom is Renown for ever
" and evermore.
" And we fend this Book in Love, that you may underftand that our
" Practice in this Point is no Fancy, or from a lewd Spirit, but grounded on
" the Truth of God, and that your Judgment might in the Truth be fwayed
" in this weighty Point."

From Northampton *Goal, the* 9th *Day
of the Second Month* 1684.

The aforefaid Letter and Book were received by Sir *Roger Norris,* who at
that Time appeared favourably inclined toward the Prifoners ; but they did not
obtain any prefent Relief.

At the fame Seffions *Thomas Boughton,* of *King-Cliff,* was profecuted for Abfence from the National Worfhip.

On the 27th of the Month called *May, William Hackney* having been cited
to appear at Seffions for abfenting from the publick Worfhip, furrendred himfelf
there to the Bayliff who cited him, and was by him delivered into the Cuftody
of the Goaler, without any Direction or Order from the Bench.

About this Time *John Loft,* who had been in Prifon above a Year for
refufing to Swear, was fet at Liberty, having fome Time before written a *Letter*
to Sir *Henry Longville,* the Juftice that committed him, a Copy of which here
follows :

" *Friend* HENRY LONGVILLE !

" I N the Fear of the Lord I defire thee to confider how thou haft abufed John Loft*'s
Letter to Sir
Henry Long-
ville.*
" that Power which the Lord hath committed into thy Hand, as thou art
" a profeffed *Chriftian* Magiftrate, in fending any to Prifon, or otherwife
" caufing any to fuffer for their exercifing of Faith in Matters of Spiritual
" Worfhip. Read *John* iv. Verfe 21, 22. there thou mayft fee what Chrift
" Jefus faid to the Woman of *Samaria,* who fpake of God's Worfhip being at
" *Jerufalem,* and that they worfhipped at that Mountain where that Well was
" that *Jacob* bought : But faid Chrift unto her, *Woman, the Hour cometh, and
" now is, that neither at this Mountain, nor at* Jerufalem, *fhall ye worfhip the
" Father : Ye worfhip ye know not what : God is a Spirit, and they that worfhip
" him, muft worfhip him in Spirit and in Truth.* And the Lord knows, I had
" nothing in mine Heart in my going to that Meeting, but in Sincerity to
" perform my Duty to that holy God, who is a Spirit, and muft be wor-
" fhipped in his Spirit's Leadings. And we were not plotting againft the
" King, nor any of his Subjects, but rather praying to God both for him and
" the Nation, that Sin, that provokes the Lord God, might be departed from,
" and that Love to God, and one towards another, might be increafed : And

"so I durst do no other than deny giving Bond to go no more to such Meet-
"ings, whatever my Sufferings had been. Now God being the highest Power,
"who created all Men to serve him, and will call all Men to give an Account
"to him of all our Deeds done in this World, how ought poor Mortals to
"fear before him from the highest to the lowest. So all Magistrates, Kings
"as well as others, ought to honour him, by being a Terror to Evil-doers,
"and Encouragers of all that live a sober and quiet Life in the Fear of the
"Lord; for Christ said to his People that were persecuted for their Love and
"Obedience to him, *Fear not them that can only kill the Body, and afterwards*
"*can do no more, but fear him that is able to cast both Body and Soul into Hell*
"*Fire.* Thou mayst read the xxvth Chapter of *Matthew,* Verse 33, and 34,
"to the End, and there thou mayst see how Christ takes that which is done
"unto his People that suffer for their Love and Obedience to him, as done
"unto himself. And in *Matthew* vth, thou mayst see who are blessed of
"God, the Meek of the Earth, the Merciful, the Poor in Spirit, and they
"that mourn, for they shall be comforted; and, *Blessed are you when Men*
"*shall revile you, and persecute you, and speak Evil of you falsly for my Name's*
"*Sake.* Such as are here mentioned are blessed of the Lord. And in the
"same Chapter thou mayst see, Verse 24 to 37, how Christ Jesus forbids all
"Swearing. So that my Imprisonment, which thou hast caused to come upon
"me, this hard Winter, and last Summer, thou mayst seriously take Notice,
"is the Cause of my writing this; desiring whilst thou hast Time, thou mayst
"prize it, and seek to the Lord to forgive thy Trespass against him by breaking
"his righteous Law writ in thy Heart, and in all Hearts, and in the Scriptures
"of Truth, where Christ saith, *Do unto all Men as ye would they should do*
"*unto you.* Matt. vii. 12. And these weighty Truths being laid to Heart,
"then I know thou will be as ready to set at Liberty, as thou wast rash and
"forward to cast into Prison, him that never did thee any Wrong, nor the
"King, nor never plotted his Harm, nor never will, but wisheth the Ever-
"lasting Good both of him and all People. So having laid my innocent
"Suffering before thee, and as on my Part also forgiven thee, I leave thee to
"the Light of Christ, by which all Men must be judged, saved, or condemned,
"and from him receive the final Sentence of *Come ye Blessed,* or *Go ye Cursed.*
"The Reason is to be seen, *Matt.* xxv. 31. to the End.

Written in Northampton *Goal, the 16th*   " John Loft."
of the last Month 1683-4.

The Manner of the said *John Loft's* Discharge is fully exprest in a Letter
written by himself to *George Fox,* being as follows:

"*Dear* George Fox,

"My sincere and unfeigned Love salutes thee, as one whom the Lord
"hath truly honoured with his Life, and living refreshing Wisdom,
"which is from Above, in which I feel thy Care to preserve what thou canst
"of them the Lord hath gathered from under the Spirit and Power of Error,
"and out of Strife, and whatever would break that Unity that stands in the
"Truth, where is thy Rest, I believe, with the Faithful, that put their Confi-
"dence, not in the Arm of Flesh, but in God alone.

"At the Sessions held at *Northampton* this last Week, I was called before
"him called Sir *Roger Norris,* and several other Justices: One of them was he
"which sent me to Prison, to whom I writ, and as I understood, he shewed it
"them all, not at Sessions, but in the Goaler's Garden, after they were risen
"the first Day; and when they came out of the Garden they sent for me
"before them, and he, call'd Sir *Roger Norris,* called for my *Mittimus,* and read
"it to himself. Then he or some other said, *I was committed for being at a*
"*Conventicle.* I said, *I was at none: I was with a People that met together to*
"*wait upon the Lord, and to worship him, as was the Duty of all Men.* Then
     "they

" they faid, *I was accufed for being a Teacher there:* I faid, *I was no Teacher ;*
" *but we meeting as the primitive* Chriftians *did, and waiting upon God, he taught*
" *us by his Spirit, and this was the Privilege of all the true Church,* or to this
" Purpofe, *and judged I might thus fpeak, when the Lord put Words into my*
" *Mind, and did, and we did pray to God, and exhort one another to that which*
" *is good.* Some then faid, *I was guilty out of my own Mouth.* I faid, *It*
" *was Truth what I had fpoken.* Then fome faid among themfelves, *We may*
" *fine him* 20 *l.* Then he called Sir *Roger Norris,* afked me the *Names of our*
" *Juftices,* and *Where I lived ?* I told them, *I lived about eight Miles off* York,
" *when at Home ;* but faid, *If you intend to have my Goods taken from me, I*
" *am not willing to hurt my felf.* So I told no Names. Then he call'd Sir
" *Roger Norris,* faid, *If I would give Bond, I fhould have Liberty, and appear*
" *if they fent for me.* I faid, *I was not convinced of any Wrong I had done to*
" *any, the King or any of his Subjects ; and fo would give no Bond, but if they*
" *would take my Word, I would promife, if Health and Liberty allowed.* The
" Goaler ftanding by, faid to them, *He will give no Bond, for he told his Brother*
" *he would never own him again ;* [*viz.* if he were bound for me.] But I did
" not fay juft fo to my Brother, though I did hinder him always as much as I
" could, believing the Lord was able, when he pleafed, to work my Deli-
" verance. So at the laft Sir *Roger Norris* faid, *I fhould have my Liberty,*
" *paying the Goaler's Fees.* After the Seffions were over next Day, the Goaler
" when I fpake with him, faid, *He was to tell me from Sir Roger Norris, that*
" *he would remit my Fine, and if I paid my Fees, I might go my Ways.* I faid,
" *I could pay none, being a Sufferer for no Wrong done to any.* After two or
" three Hours he faid, *He would leave it to me, but if I did not anfwer it,*
" *he would truft none more for my Sake.*
" There were no other Friends called, nor fet at Liberty. One that before
" went out upon Bond, writ to them, and laid his Condition before them,
" that he was a poor Man, and had a great Sort of Children, and had little but
" his Hand Labour to maintain them with : However, they did not anfwer his
" Defire. One more was fent to Prifon on a Seffions Procefs. This with my
" dear Love. Going to *Yorkfhire.*

Northampton, *the* 1ft *of*
the Fourth *Month* 1684.   " JOHN LOFT.

" *P. S.* Friends at *Leeds* ftill are fore perfecuted, both by Imprifon-
" ment and Spoil of Goods."

About this Time *John Lane,* taken at a Meeting in *Northampton,* had the
Oath tendred him by the Mayor and Aldermen, and for refufing to take it was
committed to Prifon. Alfo *John King, Richard Baker, Thomas Langford, Jofhua
Hart, John Francis, John Grove,* and *William Afhby,* being taken at a Meeting
at *Whittlebury,* were carried in a Waggon to *Northampton,* and next Day had
the Oath tendred them by the Juftices, and for not taking it were committed to
Prifon.

About the 3d of *September, Nicholas Read,* after above two Years Confinement for his religious Teftimony, died a Prifoner.

On the 31ft of *October, Rebecca Sewel,* of *Brigftock,* for frequenting religious
Meetings, fuffered Diftrefs of fix Cows to the Value of 24 *l.*

On the 23d of *November, Edward Cowper, Thomas Dent, Edward Fofter,
Alexander Manning,* and *John Gill,* were taken from a Meeting in *Northampton,*
and committed to Prifon as Rioters.

On the 8th of the Month called *January, George Warner, James Warner,
Roger Booth,* and *Thomas Gatrell,* taken at a Meeting in the Houfe of *Simon
Mutton,* of *Geddington,* had the Oaths of Allegiance, *&c.* tendred them by
Roger Norris, Juftice, and for refufing to Swear, were committed to Goal.

On the 1ft of the Month called *June* this Year, *Peter Mackernefs* died a Prifoner ; and on the 1ft of *September, Thomas Hafker* departed this Life in the fame
State, having both fuffered Imprifonment for Tithes about feven Years.

ANNO

*Imprisonment
of R. Thorp.*

*Indictments
for Absence
from the Na-
tional Worship.*

ANNO 1685. On the 31st of the Month called *March*, *Richard Thorp* was arrested for 220*l.* for eleven Months Absence from his Parish-Church, and carried to Prison, where he lay five Weeks, and then was removed by an *Habeas Corpus* to the *King's-Bench* at *London*.

At the Quarter Sessions in or about the Month called *April* this Year, *Tobias Brown*, *William Froshly*, *John Knighton*, *Thomas Boon* and *Susanna* his Wife, *Joseph Clark* and his Wife, *Thomas Charles*, *William Line*, *William Chandler*, *Thomas Atkins*, *Anne Winkles*, *Sarah Daniel*, *Alice Nichols*, *Elizabeth Basely*, *Richard Vial*, *John Bland*, *Mary Traslow*, *Thomas Allen*, *Thomas Cooke* and his Wife, *Thomas Cooke* jun. *Simon Mutton*, *Alexander Clark*, *John Thrift*, *Henry Ashby*, *William Griffin*, and *William Chapel*'s Wife, were indicted for Absence from their Parish-Church, and put to considerable Expence and Charge.

In this Year *Thomas Boughton*, one of the Prisoners at *Northampton*, exhibited to the Justices at their Quarter Sessions there, the following *Certificate*.

" *To* His Majesty's Justices *of the* Peace, *of the* Honourable Bench,
" *at the* General Quarter Sessions, *to be holden for the County of*
" Northampton, *and all others whom it may concern.*

*Certificate of
T. Boughton
to the Justices.*

" WE the Inhabitants of *King's-Olliffe*, in the County aforesaid, whose
" Names are hereunto subscribed, do hereby certify, that *Thomas
" Boughton*, of our said Town, being now a Prisoner in the Prison of *North-
" ampton* aforesaid, for not conforming himself to the Church of *England*,
" now established by Law, hath neither himself, nor any of his Predecessors,
" to our best Knowledge, at any Time been taxed or accused for any Dis-
" loyalty: And that his Father, for his Loyalty in the Time of our most
" gracious Sovereign Lord King *Charles the First*, was a great Sufferer, both
" in his Person and Goods, by the rebellious Party: And that the said *Thomas
" Boughton*, now in Prison as aforesaid, hath born all Offices considerable in
" our said Town, and hath discharged his Duty very well in the Execution
" of them, as well in yielding Obedience to the Precepts and Warrants from his
" Majesty's Justices of the Peace, as in doing and performing any other
" Matter, Cause, or Thing, whatsoever, that concerned the same. And far-
" ther that the said *Thomas Boughton*, now in Prison as aforesaid, is a Person of
" an honest and peaceable Conversation, and not at any Time, as we know,
" guilty of any disloyal Practices against the Government as aforesaid; but
" always behaved himself as a peaceable Subject of the same. Witness our
" Hands this eighteenth Day of *December*, in the first Year of the Reign of
" our gracious Sovereign Lord *James the Second*, by the Grace of God of
" *England*, *Scotland*, *France*, and *Ireland*, King, Defender of the Faith, &c.
" *Annoq; Dom.* 1685.

" THOMAS SOUTH, *Rector*, ibm.   RICHARD BUGBY,
" WM. GORHAM,   *The Mark of* ZACHARY LUFF, *sen.*
" RICHARD WILBOROW,   WILLIAM CHRISTOPHER,
" ROBERT HILL,   HENRY ATKINS."

" WE his Majesty's Justices of the Peace for the County of *Northampton*,
" whose Names are here-under written, do certify, that the said *Thomas
" Boughton* is a Person of an honest and peaceable Conversation to the best of
" our Observation, and not at any Time, as we know, guilty of any disloyal
" Practices against the Government, but hath always behaved himself as a
" peaceable Subject of the same. Witness our Hands

" R. NORWICH,
" L. PALMER."

At the fame Seffions were alfo exhibited the following *Certificates*, viz.

" *Northton* fs.

Certificate for
T. Burborow
and others.

" THESE are to certify whom it fhall or may concern, that *Timothy*
" Burborow, *Thomas Fowler*, and *Thomas Mercer*, late Inhabitants of
" the Town of *Aynoe* in the County of *Northampton*, and now Prifoners in
" the faid County Goal, and have been there two of them a Year and three
" Quarters, and the other a Year and a Quarter or thereabouts, upon the Writ
" *de Excommunicato capiendo*, for no other Caufe but Non-conformity, being
" called *Quakers*, are notwithftanding Perfons of a peaceable and honeft Con-
" verfation, and not at any Time, as we know, guilty of any difloyal Prac-
" tices againft the Government, but have always behaved themfelves as peaceable
" Subjects of the fame ; and therefore humbly conceive their faid Offences to
" be pardonable by Virtue of a Warrant dated the 18th of *April* 1685,
" whereby his now Majefty hath been gracioufly pleafed to fignify the fame for
" the Relief of thofe who have teftified their Loyalty and Affection to the
" Government, as in the faid Warrant more largely doth appear. In Teftimony
" whereof we the Inhabitants of *Aynoe* aforefaid, and Neighbours ancient,
" have hereunto fet our Hands this feven and twentieth Day of *December*, in the
" firft Year of the Reign of his Majefty that now is, *Annoq; Dom.* 1685.

" THOMAS NORRIS *Churchwarden*,	EDWARD HOMAN *Churchwarden*,
" WM. BORTON *Overfeer*,	SAMUEL BADING *Overfeer*,
" EDWARD JARVIS *Conftable*,	JO. LAWLEY,
" JO. SPENCER,	HENRY BORTON,
" JOHN BORTON,	WILLIAM HOWES,
" EDWARD GODCHEER,	THO. HANSLAYS,
" GILES SOUTHAM,	EDWARD LETCH,
" LABAN TOMLINS,	JOHN JEFFS,
" WILLIAM JEFFS,	THOMAS TOMKINS,
" JOHN SPENCER,	THOMAS SMITH,
" WM. BORTON *fen.*	MATTHEW BORTON.

" WE whofe Names are under-written, being Juftices of the Peace for
" the County of *Northampton*, do certify, that *Timothy Burborow, Tho-
" mas Fowler*, and *Thomas Mercer*, above-named, are Perfons of a peaceable
" and honeft Converfation, and not at any Time, as we know, guilty of any
" difloyal Practices againft the Government, but always behaving themfelves as
" peaceable Subjects of the fame. Witnefs our Hands the 5th of *January* 1685.

" JO. GARDINER,
" JO. WOODHUTT.

" *Northton* fs.

Certificate for
J. Grove.

" THESE are to certify whom it fhall or may concern, that *John Grove*,
" late of *Whittlebury* in the County of *Northampton*, and now a Prifoner
" in the faid County Goal, and hath been there about a Year and an Half, for
" refufing to take the Oath of Allegiance, (being one called a *Quaker*) is
" notwithftanding a Perfon of a peaceable and honeft Converfation, and not at
" any Time, as we know, guilty of any difloyal Practices againft the Govern-
" ment, but hath always behaved himfelf as a peaceable Subject of the fame,
" and therefore humbly conceive the faid Offence to be pardonable by Virtue
" of a Warrant dated the 18th of *April* 1685, wherein his now Majefty hath
" been gracioufly pleafed to fignify the fame for the Relief of thofe who have
" teftified their Loyalty and Affection to the Government, as in the faid War-
" rant more largely doth appear. In Teftimony whereof, we the Inhabitants

" of *Whittlebury*, and Neighbours adjacent, have hereunto set our Hands this
" seven and twentieth Day of *November*, in the first Year of the Reign of his
" Majesty that now is, *Annoq; Dom.* 1685.

" SIMON WATERMAN ⎱
" ROBERT ASHLEY   ⎰ *Churchwardens*,

" JOSEPH FOSTER *Constable*,
" WILLIAM ROLFE,
" BER. STEPHENS,
" BENJAMIN FOSTER,

JOHN GARDINER,
WOOLSTON BRABROOK,
EDWARD RICHARDS,
SIMON LOVEL,
JOHN HOUGHTON."

"   **W**E whose Names are under-written, being Justices of the Peace for
"   the County of *Northampton*, do certify, that *John Grove* above-
" named, is a Person of a peaceable and honest Conversation, and not at any
" Time, as we know, guilty of any disloyal Practices against the Govern-
" ment, but always behaving himself as a peaceable Subject of the same.
" Witness our Hands this 14th Day of *December* 1685.

" JO. GARDINER,
" JO. WOODHUTT,
" R. NORWICH."

Some Months before these Certificates were signed, the Prisoners had represented their Case to the Members of Parliament for that County, in Manner
following, *viz.*

" *To the* KNIGHTS *and* BURGESSES *for the County of* Northampton,
" *now assembled in* Parliament.

"   **W**E, the poor oppressed and suffering People of God in your
"   County, called *Quakers*, do in the Humility of our Minds, make
" it our Request and Desire, that you would be pleased to take into your
" serious Consideration the great and heavy Sufferings that for many Years
" we have passed through, and still do undergo, only for the Exercise of
" our Consciences toward Almighty God, and to use your friendly and
" *Christian* Endeavours for our Relief ; for several of us have had our Goods
" distrained and taken away by Informers, and our Bodies cast into Prison,
" and one Widow Woman of *Farthingstone*, after her Goods were taken away,
" cast into Prison, having six Children, one then sucking at her Breast, and
" is still a Prisoner. Some fined 12 *d.* a *Sunday*, and for not paying cast into
" Prison. Others, their Cattle seized by Bayliffs for 20 *l.* a Month, and
" drove away and sold, and many suffered Imprisonment at one Time last
" Year, near fourscore of us, and in this last Winter about threescore of us
" crowded together, and four of our Friends died Prisoners the Year past.
" But of late several are now upon Security to appear at the Assizes ; yet
" there still remain in Prison thirty two Men and Women, some upon Bishops
" Writs, and some upon the Oath, most of us having been here above two
" Years, and some three or four Years ; which Sufferings greatly tend to the
" ruining and undoing of many industrious Families that have helped to bear the
" Charge of the Nation, and they who have been in a Capacity to relieve others,
" may by such Means be reduced to stand in Need of Assistance themselves, if
" not timely prevented by your Care and Providence, who are now in a
" Capacity to move in our Behalf, and to use charitable Endeavours for our
" Relief and Liberties. We are not willing to particularize our Sufferings,
" which have been long and many, rather desiring that the Lord may move
" upon your Hearts with Bowels of Pity and Compassion, to the easing of a
"   " poor

" poor afflicted People, who have done neither King nor Nation any Wrong,
" and who are in Sincerity and Truth,

" *Your* Christian *Friends*,

Northampton *Prison,*
the 13*th of the* Fourth
Month 1685.

" JOHN LANE,
" JOHN ASHBY,
" GEO. MACKERNESS,
" THO. BOUGHTON,
" JOSIAH PACKWOOD,

JOHN HART,
RICHARD BAKER,
TIMOTHY BURBOROW,
WILLIAM TIBBS,
JOHN TIBBS.

" Signed on the Behalf of our felves and our Fellow-Prifoners."

About the 7th of the Month called *March* this Year, *John Willoughby* and
William Elfe, Juftices, came to a Meeting at *Northampton*, and took thence
Men, Women, and Children, to the Number of forty five, and fent them to
Prifon. At the next Affizes they were indicted for a Riot, but foon after dif-
charged by a Warrant from the Attorney-General.

*45 Perfons
fent to Prifon.*

Difcharged.

Toward the Clofe of this Year, the feveral Perfons called *Quakers*, then in
Prifon at *Northampton*, either on Writs de *Excommunicato capiendo*, · or for Fines
on *Exchequer* Procefs againft them for Abfence from the Church, or other
Procefles for their religious Affemblies, were generally fet at Liberty by Virtue
of the King's Proclamation. But a fhort Time before, *viz.* on the 9th of the
Month called *March*, *Dorothy Paine* died a Prifoner.

*Death of
D. Paine.*

ANNO 1686. On the 21ft of the Month called *April*, *Thomas Boone*, of
Corby, for being prefent at the Interment of his own Wife, was fined as a
Tranfgreffor of the Law againft Conventicles, and fuffered Diftrefs of his
Goods for that fuppofed Offence, to the Value of 7 *l.* And in the fame Month
Thomas Cooke, of *Weldon*, had taken from him for his attending religious
Meetings, two Horfes, and feveral Houfhold Goods, worth 20 *l.* Alfo *Samuel
Cox*, of *Woodford*, fuffered Diftrefs of his Goods for abfenting himfelf from
the National Worfhip.

*T. Boone
fined for being
at his Wife's
Burial.*

On the 14th of *September*, the faid *Thomas Cooke*, after a Profecution in the
Hundred Court for Tithes, at the Suit of *John Gates*, Prieft, fuftained the Lofs
of Houfhold Goods by Diftrefs, to the Value of 3 *l.*

Tithes.

C H A P. XXVIII.

NOTTINGHAMSHIRE.

A N N O 1649.

THE firft Imprifonment of *George Fox* was this Year at *Nottingham*,
occafioned by his Oppofition to one of the publick Preachers there,
and by his teftifying to the People the Excellency of the Teachings
of the Holy Spirit, and the Neceffity of Obedience thereunto, as
the moft certain and unerring Guide, leading into all Truth, and enabling to
form a juft Judgment of the Doctrines, Sentiments, and Opinions of Men.
His Preaching at that Time was with an holy Zeal and Fervency, effectually
reaching to the Confciences of many that heard him : Neverthelefs, fome took
Offence at his Appearing in their Place of Worfhip, and the Officers of the Parifh
took him away, and put him into a nafty ftinking Prifon : Toward Evening

*Firft Impri-
fonment of
G. Fox.*

they

*The High-
Sheriff con-
vinced.*

*George Fox
grievously
abused.*

*Imprisonments
and Distresses
for Tithes.*

Abuses.

Fine.

Distress.

*Grievous
Abuses.*

they had him before the *Mayor* and *Aldermen,* who after some Examination, recommitted him. Some Time after, the High-Sheriff, whose Name was *John Reckless,* sent for him to his House ; and at his Coming in, the Sheriff's Wife met him in the Hall, and taking him by the Hand, said, *Salvation is come to our House :* For both her Husband and she, were effectually reached and convinced by the Force and Energy of *George Fox's* Testimony, which had wrought such a Change in the High-Sheriff, that he himself, the next Market-day, went into the Streets, and preached Repentance to the People. Some others also in that Town found themselves under the like Concern. This Sheriff lodged *G. Fox* in his own House, entertaining him courteously ; but the Mayor, and some other Magistrates, were the more incensed against him, so that they caused him to be taken from the Sheriff's House, and sent to the Common-Goal, where he remained Prisoner a considerable Time.

After his Release from that Imprisonment, he went into the Place of publick Worship at *Mansfield-Woodhouse,* and there declared the Testimony of Truth to the Priest and People ; but his *Christian* Love met with unkind Reception, for the People fell upon him, and struck him down, almost smothering him, for they beat and bruised him cruelly with their Hands, Sticks, and Bibles ; then they dragged him out, scarce able to stand, and put him in the Stocks, where he sat some Hours ; and they brought Whips, threatning to whip him : After some Time they took him to a Knight's House, where were many Magistrates, who seeing how ill he had been used, after some Threatning, set him at Liberty : But the rude People again assaulted him, and stoned him out of the Town.

ANNO 1658. *John Cowper,* of *Skekbie,* for conscientiously refusing to pay a Demand of 16 *s.* on him for Tithes, had three Cows taken from him worth 10 *l.*

William Claytor, of *Elton,* was *subpœna'd* at the Suit of *Dove Williamson,* a Priest there, into the *Exchequer* at *London,* where he personally appeared, but, not employing an Attorney, was sent to the *Fleet,* as if he had not appeared, and lay there two Years : During which Time, the Priest and his Servants made Spoil of his Goods at Home, carrying off an whole Load of his Corn together. He was afterward sued by the said Priest in the Court of *Common-Pleas,* and a Verdict was obtained against him for 20 *l.* Upon that Verdict, Execution was awarded, and his Goods taken from him to the Value of 42 *l.* He was also detained in Prison three Years and a Quarter.

William Smith, of *Besthorp,* suffered nine Weeks Imprisonment for Tithes. And for the same Cause *Edward Langford,* of *North-Sellingham,* was imprisoned about seven Weeks : And in the next Year he was again cast into Prison, and there remained several Years. *Thomas Elsham,* of *Gerton,* also suffered Imprisonment for refusing to pay Tithes.

About this Time *Mary Leadbeater,* and *Anne Fricknall,* were grievously abused by the People, and set in the Stocks at *Mansfield-Woodhouse,* for some Words they had spoken displeasing to a Priest there.

Robert Wilde, of *Wellerton,* was fined 3 *l.* 6 *s.* 8 *d.* for not putting off his Hat in Court.

ANNO 1659. *George Rogers,* of *Wellam,* for going a few Miles to a Meeting on the First-day of the Week, had his Horse taken, and kept from him two or three Days : After which, they distrained his Goods for a pretended Fine of 10 *s.* for breaking the Sabbath.

On the 7th of *November* this Year, *William Dewsberry,* preaching at a Meeting at *Newark* upon *Trent,* was insulted and much abused by the People : However the Meeting was held, through much Disturbance, and at the Close of it, another Meeting was appointed at the same Place on the 11th of the same Month, being the First-day of the Week, at which, while the Testimony of Truth was declaring, a rude Multitude broke in, thrusting down both Men and Women, buffeting, punching, and stoning them, so that some were knockt down, others had their Teeth beaten out, and their Faces bruised : Women
had

had their Head-clothes pull'd off: After this Manner they continued to abuse about an Hundred Persons who were there religiously assembled; and who bore all patiently, as *Christian* Sufferers. These Things were acted on the Day they call'd their *Sabbath*, by a People who deem'd it a Profanation of that Day to travel five Miles to a Meeting, and whose Consciences could admit them to exercise such Barbarity on the Day in which they would have thought it a Crime to have been employed in any honest Labour.

Pretended Observers of the Sabbath.

ANNO 1660. On the 2d of the Month called *April, Elizabeth Hooton,* passing quietly on the Road, was met by one *Jackson,* Priest of *Selston,* who abused her, beat her with many Blows, knockt her down, and afterward put her into the Water. About the same Time, *William Glasson* was imprisoned fourteen Weeks for saying, that *the Scriptures were a true Declaration of the Word of God, but not the Living Word of God it self.* So gross was the Ignorance and Superstition of those Times.

Abuse.

Imprisonment.

About the Month called *January* this Year, *Thomas Hurst, Thomas Hinley, Thomas Spanald, John Torr, Humphry Need, Mary Gamble, Robert Scrimshaw, Richard Bateman, John Storrs, George Cockran, Thomas Highfield, John Hurst, James Storrs, John Beeby, Richard Brown, Edward Poe, Samuel Hooton, John Leadbeater, Thomas Richardson, Robert Grace, Robert Marriott, Richard Brownly, James Stack, William Glossup, Thomas Crofts, Griffith Lewis, William Smith, Thomas Smith, Robert Carnall, Robert Shaw, Dorothy Kirkman, Anne Flower, Isabel Gregory, Elizabeth Wood, Grace Smith,* and *Anne Webster,* were at one Time Prisoners in the Town and County Goals of *Nottingham,* for refusing to take the Oath of Allegiance; some of them having been taken at their religious Assemblies, others on the Highway, and some as they were going to visit their Brethren in Prison.

Many in Prison for refusing to Swear.

In this Year also, *Roger Storrs, William Thorp* of *Gerton,* and *Robert Morfin* of *Worksop,* were Prisoners for refusing to pay Tithes.

Others for not paying Tithes.

ANNO 1661. *Robert Scrimshaw, Thomas Aukland, Thomas Holywell,* and *John Leadbeater,* were taken from a Meeting at *Sarsfield* by Soldiers, who carried them before their Officers, with whom were two Justices, who tendred them the Oath of Allegiance, and for refusing it, sent them to Prison, where they were lockt up every Night in the Pit among Felons. In the same Year, *John Weaver, Ralph Bateman, Richard Bateman, Thomas Jugall, Edward Aslin,* and *Richard Birkett,* were taken out of a Meeting at *Upton,* and committed to Prison.

4 Lockt up among Felons.

Others imprisoned.

ANNO 1663. In this Year, *Robert Shaw* was imprisoned in the Common-Goal of this County, for his conscientious Refusal to pay Tithes.

Tithes.

ANNO 1666. *John Hart* and *John Reckless* were committed to Prison on the 8th of the Month called *January,* by a Writ *de Excommunicato capiendo,* after a Prosecution in the Ecclesiastical Court, for Absence from the National Worship.

Imprisonment for Absence from the publick Worship.

ANNO 1667. In *September, William Day,* of *Eastwood,* was committed to Prison for refusing to pay Tithes, at the Suit of *Thomas Hewitt,* Priest, and was continued Prisoner about fourteen Months.

Tithes.

ANNO 1669. At a Quarter Sessions, held at *Nottingham* in the Month called *January, Peniston Whaley,* Chairman, in his Charge to the *Grand Jury,* endeavoured to incense them against the *Quakers* by the following Speech, *viz.*

" The Law they are prosecuted by is that in 35 Q. *Elizabeth,* which they
" pretend to be against *Papists.* [*Clerk.* Read the *Preamble to that Act.*
" Which being read, he proceeded] You may see that it was not made
" against them, for the Church of *Rome* is a true Church, as well as any other;
" for a Man, though he be a lame or ill favour'd Man, yet he is a Man, as
" well as a Lord, or an Earl. And though the Church of *Rome* hath some
" Corruptions in it, yet it is a Church as well as any other, and so it could
" not be made against them; therefore it must needs be made against these
" People: You ought therefore to put it in Force, and not pity them. I

Malicious speech of P. Whaley.

" suppofe there was never Rogue hang'd for Robbing, but fome Body pitied
" him. Indeed Sufferings do beget Pity.

" " Thefe *Quakers* are the moft factious People, and hold the moft erroneous
" Doctrine of any People. I'll tell you of their *Principle, Doctrine,* and
" *Manners.* They do deny the holy Trinity, the three Perfons, the Unity in
" the Godhead, Unity in Trinity, and Trinity in Unity : They deny the
" Merits of our Saviour *Chrift,* and fay that he died not for the whole World,
" and that he was no more than an Example of an holy Life, and therefore
" they preach Perfection, which is what none can ever come unto ; for when
" we have done what we can, we are unprofitable Servants. They do deny
" Baptifm and the Lord's Supper : Baptifm you know is the Covenant ; and
" thefe are the two Breafts at which the Church of *England* doth nourifh up her
" Children unto Life eternal : And though the Churches have differed in
" Matters of Exercife, yet they always agreed about the two Sacraments : In
" fundamental Points they did not differ. And undoubtedly, thofe that live
" and die in thefe Opinions, cannot but be damned : And who would beget a
" Child to go to the Devil. Therefore if you would have your Children enjoy
" that you leave them, fupprefs thefe People, and let the full Severity of the
" Law be exercifed on them, and ftricter than the Law, if it can be ; for
" pitying them doth no Good, for they have had nine Years Clemency, and
" they are fo fpread, that if they fpread fo in as long Time more, we muft
" beg : And a great Caufe of this has been, that the Laws have not been
" executed. But if every Conftable would complain if there were any Con-
" venticles in their Town ; and the great Fault doth lie in the Conftables ; and
" it's under this Cover : For many Yeomen are fo proud that they will not ferve
" the Office of a Conftable, but hire fome bafe Fellow, and he is never fworn,
" but hath a Shilling for going to be fworn, but never goes, and that Shilling
" is clear Gain, and fo they will not meddle with their Neighbours, though
" they meet : But we will take fome Courfe to know that you are all fworn
" to do your Office : You fhall either complain of Conventicles, or be forfworn ;
" for they [Meetings] are the only Thing whereby Enterprizes are brought to
" pafs, for if there were a Thoufand People all of a Mind, if they did not
" meet, they could never know one another's Minds by Letters, for that is
" dangerous ; and at Fairs they could not, for thofe happen but feldom : And
" it is at thefe Meetings that they do preach one to another, and contemn the
" Laws, and rail againft Men's Perfons. And if thefe Things be not avenged
" in our Time, they may well be in our Children's Time, and they, an Hun-
" dred Years after may fuffer by our Neglect. But 'tis very like that we in
" feven Years may feel the Effect of it."

This Speech difcovers the Author's *Ignorance* of the *Quakers* Principles to be
equal to his *Virulence* againft them : Yet it feemed to have fome Influence on
the Proceedings of that Court ; at which *John Wood,* for his Non-conformity
to the Church of *England,* was fined two Hundred Marks, and upon his Refufal
to pay that Fine, was committed to Prifon.

About the fame Time *Edward Aflin,* being taken at a Meeting, had the
Oath of Allegiance tendred him, and for not taking it was fent to the Houfe
of Correction.

ANNO 1670. Of the Juftices in this County, the aforefaid *Penifton Whaley*
and *Robert Thoroton* were the moft officious in enforcing the Act againft Conventicles, and by the Warrants of them and others, many Diftreffes were
made on thofe whom no Severities could deter from attending their Affemblies
for religious Worfhip ; for their Conftancy in this Refpect, were taken

		l.	*s.*	*d.*
From *Richard Richardfon,* of *Nottingham,* Goods worth		9	0	0
Charles Moreland		12	0	0
Thomas Heighfield		6	0	0
	Carried over	27	0	0

		l.	*s.*	*d.*
	Brought over	27	0	0
From *John Marſhall*		10	0	0
Edward Poe		1	3	4
William Watſon		0	9	0
Joſhua Oates		1	0	0
		39	12	4

From *Robert Carnell*, of *North-Cullingham*, for a Meeting at his Houſe, the Officers took Goods worth 30 *l.* ſaying, they were ordered by the Juſtice to take three or four Times the Value, that they might afford to ſell good Penny-worths.

From *Robert Shaw* they alſo took away Goods worth 30 *l.* for a Meeting held at his Houſe, though himſelf was at that Time a Priſoner many Miles from Home.

It happened that *William Claytor*, of *Elton*, and *John Barker*, of *Bingham*, were together at a Friends Houſe, where were no others but the Family : One *Chamberlain*, an Informer, came in, and aſked *William* ſome uſual familiar Queſtions, to which he gave him proper Anſwers. The Informer goes to Juſtice *Whaley*, and tells him, *There was a Meeting*, and *that* William Claytor *ſpoke :* Upon which the Juſtice fined him 20 *l.* for Preaching, and cauſed Diſtreſs to be made on his Goods, which amounted but to 15 *l.* ſo they afterward ſeized ſome Sheep of his, to the Value of 4 *l.* more. And from *John Barker* they alſo took Goods worth 12 *l.* *Great Oppreſ-ſion by In-formers and Officers.*

From *Thomas Inghall*, of *Weſthorp*, they took away his Corn, Hay, Carts, and Cattle, to the Value of 97 *l.* The Quantities of his Corn and Hay were ſo great, that ſix or ſeven Perſons were employ'd ſeveral Days together in carrying them away.

Nathanael Price, of *Farnsfield*, a poor fatherleſs Boy, whom his Friends in Charity had put out Apprentice, being taken at a Meeting, and having nothing elſe to diſcharge his Fine, the Officers took away his Coat and Breeches, four Half-pence, his Knife, Sheath, and Sciſſars, ſhewing no Compaſſion to an Orphan under ſuch moving Circumſtances.

At another Meeting *William Claytor*, and ſome others, being aſſembled, and ſitting together in Silence, two Informers came in, and with them ſome of the Town Officers : One of the Informers ſaid, *Take their Names*. W. Claytor aſk'd, *What will you take our Names for ?* The Informer replied, *For a ſilent Meeting*. Nay, ſaid the other Informer, *put him down for a Speaker* ; which they did accordingly, and he was fined by Juſtice *Whaley* for ſpeaking or Preaching, though the Informer had ſpoken as much as he, and on the ſame Subject. So he was fined 40 *l.* as on a ſecond Conviction for Preaching, having been formerly convicted on a like Stratagem as before mentioned. Another Seizure was made of his Goods to the full Amount of that Fine, and when he would have appealed to the Seſſions againſt ſuch illegal Uſage, his Appeal was rejected. A parallel Caſe to this was that of *Joſeph Wallis*, who ſitting ſilent in a Meeting, one *Walker*, an Informer, came in, and aſked him, *When will you give over this ?* Joſeph anſwered, *When wilt thou give over thy Trade ?* Walker return'd, *Not till you give over yours.* Joſeph replied, *Thine will not bring thee Peace in thy latter End.* For this Joſeph Wallis was fined 20 *l.* as a Preacher, and, for that Fine, had a Stack of Hay taken from him by Diſtreſs.

For the ſame Cauſe of religiouſly Aſſembling to worſhip God, were taken

		l.	*s.*	*d.*
From *William Poole*, at *Lodge* in the *Woulds*, Goods worth		3	0	0
Rowland Dawbnell, of *Corpwell*		1	6	0
Henry Doubleday, of *Whatton*		7	0	0
Timothy Garland, of *Mansfield*		5	0	0
	Carried over	16	6	0

Many Diſ-treſſes.

NOTTING-
HAM-
SHIRE.
1670.

	l.	*s.*	*d.*
Brought over	16	6	0
From Robert Moore, of *Mansfield*	4	2	0
Robert Grace, of *Sutton*	6	8	0
Richard Brandrith, of *Sutton* in *Afhfield*	5	15	0
Samuel Hooton, George Cockran, and Mary Lead-beater, of *Skekbie*	8	9	0
Edward Bingham, of *Mansfield-Woodhouse*	25	15	0
John Theaker, of *North-Cullingham*	38	0	0
Thomas Elfon, Thomas Ridge, and William Raworth, of *Gerton*	23	18	0
Jofeph Watts, of *Grefthorp*	24	0	0
George Wheldale, of *Headon*	20	0	0
Mary Snowden, Mary Theaker, Thomas Crane, Faith Sturgis, William Wilfon, and Mary Watfon	10	11	4
William Calvert, of *Carlton*, and John Trufwell, of *Sutton* upon *Trent*	1	17	0
John Smith, Hugh Heale, Matthew Hortley, John Abbot, James Cock, and John Watfon	6	13	6
William Watfon, of *Farnsfield*	19	0	0
Margaret Dring, of *Hollam*	16	18	0
Thomas Sanfom, of *Liverton*	12	0	0
Ralph Bateman	28	0	0
John Englifh, Edward Aflin, John Law, William Wilfon, Alice Smith, Andrew Hodgfon, Laurence Watts, and John Gudderith	12	0	4
William Hudfon, George Rogers, William Rogers, and Lydia Martin	1	16	0
	281	9	2

Diverfe others alfo had their Goods taken by Diftrefs for their religious Meetings, fo that the Sums of the Whole, within this County, amounted in a fhort Time to 598 *l.* 10 *s.* 10 *d.*

Some Refpite.   After this the Storm of Perfecution, in this County, feemeth to have ceafed for a confiderable Time ; fo that we have no farther Accounts of Suffering here, till

ANNO 1676. When it appeared, that the Quietnefs and Eafe, for fome Time enjoyed, was not owing to the favourable Difpofition of the Juftices, but rather to fome Reftraint put on them by thofe in higher Authority, which being again removed, they returned to their accuftomed Severity, and caufed many Diftreffes to be made on the Goods and Chattels of their harmlefs Neighbours for confcientioufly reforting to their religious Affemblies ; for on the 16th of the Month called *April* this Year, upon Information of a Meeting at *Hucknall*, the Parifh-Officers came and took from *John Bullivant*, a Mare and other Goods, worth 3 *l.* He was a poor Nailor, no Houfe-keeper, but dwelt in his Shop : The Juftice, *Thoroton*, judged him to be extremely poor, and therefore ordered the Officers to take all he had, the Coat from his Back, the Hat from his Head, and the Hammer which he work'd with. From *Richard Bateman*, another poor Man, they took moft of the Goods he had, worth about 40 *s.* but fold by them for 3 *s.* 6 *d.* They alfo took the Goods of *William Clay*, of 40 *s.* Value, and fold them for 10 *s.* being urged thereto by the Juftice, who ftrictly charged them to fell the Goods for what they could get, though they fold 10 *l.* worth for 30 *s.* and becaufe they did not fell the Goods within a limited Time, he fined the Conftables 5 *l.* each, and made Diftrefs upon their Goods for the fame. From *Chriftopher Brandreth*, the Officers took a Mare worth 4 *l.* And from *George Cockran*, Goods worth 11 *s.*

Many Dif-trefes for Meetings.

Severity of Juftice Tho-roton.

O

On the 23d of the fame Month, for a Meeting at the Houfe of *Robert Grace,* of *Sutton,* they took from *Thomas Cockran,* two young Beafts worth 3 *l.* And from *William Maulfon,* a Cow and Houfhold Goods, worth 5 *l.* 4 *s.*

On the 28th of the Month called *May,* for a Meeting held in the Street at *Sutton,* was taken from *George Cockran,* a Cow worth 3 *l.* 5 *s.* 4 *d.* From *John Fulwood,* eleven Quarters of Malt worth 10 *l.* 9 *s.* And from *George Hopkin-fon,* Goods worth 12 *s.*

For a Meeting, held about the fame Time, at the Houfe of *Rowland Dabey,* they took from *Edward Richardfon,* of *Kilverton,* a Blackfmith, not only his Hay and Corn, but alfo his Bedding, his Childrens Apparel, and even the working Tools and Utenfils of his Trade, to the Value of 16 *l.* And from *William Maultly, Robert Bullivant,* and *John Smith,* they took Goods to the Amount of 1 *l.* 15 *s.*

For a Meeting at the Houfe of *William Wilfon,* of *Gerton,* were taken from the faid *William Wilfon,* two Cows, the Property of a Neighbour, of whom he had borrowed them : But fuch irregular Seizures were countenanced by the Juftices ; for when the Officers came to diftrain the Goods of *Thomas Fox* for being at the fame Meeting, they found a Quantity of Timber which he had lately fold to one *Thomas Levefly,* and was actually in *Levefly's* Poffeffion ; all which was made appear to the Juftice, and the Bill of Sale produced, neverthe-lefs the Juftice ordered it to be taken away from the prefent Poffeffor, and the Officers acted accordingly : The Value of that Timber was 6 *l.* 6 *s.* 8 *d.* *Stephen Swinfon* had alfo his Goods feized for being at the fame Meeting, to the Value of 2 *l.* 16 *s.* but the Juftices being informed that there was a Cow of his which the Conftable had not taken, they fined the Conftable 5 *l.* for Neglect of Duty, and obliged him to pay 20 *s.* to compound the Affair. From *Thomas Crane,* of *North-Scale,* they took Goods worth 5 *l.*

Illegal Seizures.

For a Meeting at *Fransfield,* they took

	l.	*s.*	*d.*	
From *Ralph Bateman* and *John Bateman,* Sheep worth	33	0	0	*Severe Diftreffes.*
William Watfon, Houfhold Goods, Corn and Cattle, worth	60	0	0	
Andrew Hodfon, Mary Handy, John Wood, and *Stephen Moore,* Goods to the Value of	4	11	4	
	97	11	4	

For a Meeting at the Houfe of *Edward Wood,* of *Ekrin,* Wheelwright, they took

	l.	*s.*	*d.*
From the faid *Edward Wood,* fix Cows, two Heifers, and Timber, worth	25	14	6
John Camm, of *Kirfall,* two Cows, an Horfe, and a Mare, worth	10	5	0
Richard Hind, of *Welley,* two Cows and a Calf, worth	6	10	0
Roger Noble, of *Kirfall,* Pewter and Brafs, worth	0	12	0
Robert Bradfhaw, of *Oxen,* for a Meeting at his Houfe, they took two Mares and four Beafts, worth	20	0	0
	63	1	6

On the 11th of the Month called *June,* for a Meeting held by the Highway-fide, when they were forcibly kept out of their Meeting-houfe at *Knapthorp,* were taken from *Jofeph Humphry,* three Pewter Difhes worth 7 *s.* And from *William Kent, Richard Hind,* and *James Hind,* Goods worth 1 *l.* 2 *s.*

NOTTING-
HAM-
SHIRE.
1676.

*More Dif-
treſſes.*

On the 18th of the same Month, for Meetings at *Kneeſal* on the Common, were taken

		l.	s.	d.
From	*Edward Wood,* of *Ekrin,* Timber and Houshold-Goods, worth	10	10	0
	Thomas Oakland, of *Knapthorp,* almoſt all his Goods, worth	5	0	0
	John Camm, of *Kirſall,* Goods worth	3	0	0
	John Kent, of *North-Layes,* eight young Beaſts, worth	17	0	0
		35	10	0

On the 27th of the Month called *July,* the following Warrant wa
granted, *viz.*

" *To the* Conſtables, Churchwardens, *and* Overſeers, *of the Poor*
" *of* Wellow, *and every or any of them.*

*Warrant for
Diſtreſs.*

" **F**ORASMUCH as *James Hind* and *Richard Hind,* of the said Town,
" are lawfully convicted before me, for having been preſent at a Con-
" venticle or unlawful Aſſembly, on Pretence of Religion, otherwiſe than by
" Law is eſtabliſhed, in *Kneeſal,* on *Sunday* the 25th of *June* laſt paſt. Theſe
" are therefore, in his Majeſty's Name, to require you to levy of each of the
" Offenders ten Shillings a piece, being formerly convicted, by Diſtreſs and
" Sale of Goods, which Sums you are to deliver to me to be diſtributed
" according to Law. Hereof fail not, as you will anſwer the Contrary at your
" Perils.
Given under my Hand and Seal, the 27th Day of *July,* 28° *Car.* 2
Annoq; Dom. 1676.
" Robert Thoroton."

By this Warrant *James Hind* had his Bedclothes taken from him, worth
but 13 *s.* And from *Richard Hind* they took away an Hog, worth about 10 *s.*
We ſhall next ſubjoin a Copy of a Warrant of Diſtreſs for a Meeting at
Mansfield.

" Nots. *ſs.*

" *To the* Conſtables, Churchwardens, *and* Overſeers *for the*
" *Poor, and* Thirdboroughs *of* Sutton *in* Aſhfield *and*
" Hucknall, *and every or any of them.*

*Another
Warrant.*

" **F**ORASMUCH as *Robert Grace* and his Wife, *Elizabeth Brand-*
" *rith, John Blackburne, Samuel Whitworth, Elizabeth Whitworth, Eliza-*
" *beth Fello,* and *Sarah Clay, Richard Bateman, Joseph Roberts, Francis Clay,*
" and *Margaret Whitworth,* of your ſaid Towns, are lawfully convicted before
" me, for having been preſent at a Conventicle or unlawful Aſſembly, on
" Pretence of Religion, otherwiſe than by Law is eſtabliſhed, in *Mansfield,*
" on *Sunday* the 9th of this Inſtant *July.* Theſe are therefore, in his Majeſty's
" Name, to require you to levy of the ſaid *Robert Grace,* for his own Offence
" and his ſaid Wife's Offence, the Sum of one Pound, being formerly con-
" victed; and the ſaid *John Blackburn, Samuel Whitworth, Elizabeth Whitworth,*
" and *Elizabeth Fello,* of every or each of them, the Sum of five Shilling
" a piece; and of the ſaid *Margaret Whitworth,* the Sum of five Shillings for
" her own Offence, and the Sum of two Pounds by Reaſon of the Poverty of
" *Richard Bateman, Joseph Roberts, Sarah Clay,* and *Francis Clay,* formerly
" convicted, by Diſtreſs and Sale of Goods, which ſaid Sums you are to
" deliver

" deliver to me to be diftributed according to Law. Hereof fail not as you
" will anfwer the Contrary at your Peril.
    " Given under my Hand and Seal the 25th Day of *July*, 28° *Car.* 2.
    " *Anno Dom.* 1676.

" ROBERT THOROTON."

Purfuant to the foregoing Warrant, Diftreffes were made on the Goods of feveral of the Perfons therein mentioned.

Alfo for a Meeting at *Sutton* in *Afhfield*, were taken about the fame Time,

		l.	*s.*	*d.*	
From	*William Day*, a Mare, an Heifer, Pewter, Brafs, and Bedding, worth	14	10	4	*Diftreffes.*
	Thomas Farnfworth, of *Scaftworth*, five Cows, worth	14	0	0	
	Robert Spavold, five Cows worth	13	0	0	
	Robert Nicholfon, an Heifer worth	1	3	4	
	Zachary Bower, a Cow worth	2	10	0	
	George Greaves, four Cows worth	13	0	0	
	John Wilfon, a Mare worth	4	10	0	
	Gervafe Creafe, Pewter worth	0	14	0	
	John Torr, of *Scrooby*, four Oxen and an Heifer, worth	17	0	0	
	William Kirkby, of *Geatforth*, feven Beafts worth	12	10	0	
		92	17	8	

For Meetings at the Houfe of *John Seaton*, of *Blythe*, were taken

		l.	*s.*	*d.*
From	the faid *John Seaton*, all his Houfhold Goods, Cattle, Horfes, Swine, Carts, and other Utenfils of Hufbandry, with Wood, Stone, and Brick, worth	100	0	0
	George Greaves, of *Blythe*, Hay, Corn, Beafts, Swine, Houfhold Goods, and other Things, worth	36	0	0
*	*Henry Upton*, of *Harwooth*, two Oxen and three Cows, worth	14	0	0
	William Kirkby, fix Beafts, five Horfes, and Houfhold Goods, worth	25	0	0
	Jofeph Hudfon, of *Matterfea*, five Cows, ten Swine, Corn, Hay, and Houfhold Goods, to the Value of	12	10	0
	John Birks, of *Scaftfworth*, Horfes and Cows, worth	18	0	0
	Zachariah Bowers, Cows, Calves, Horfes, Corn, Hay, Carts, Ploughs, and other Utenfils, Bedding, Pewter, Brafs, and other Goods, worth	51	8	10
	Thomas Denton, two Calves and other Goods, worth	2	17	0
	Thomas Farnfworth, of *Scaftfworth*, Cattle, Horfes, Corn, Hay, Carts, Ploughs, Harnefs, &c. four Beds, and other Houfhold Goods, worth	40	11	0
	Edward Hickfon, of *Tickhill*, an Heifer worth	3	5	0
	Carried over	303	11	10

* They took at another Time from *Henry Upton*, all the Refidue of his Goods.

	l.	*s.*	*d.*
Brought over	303	11	10
From *John Lambert*, of *Tickhill*, an Heifer worth	3	10	0
Gervase Lambert, Houshold Goods, Leather, working Tools, and Hay, to the Value of	8	0	0
John Cornsall, Corn, Beds, Bedding, &c. worth	10	0	0
George Hopkins, Goods worth	0	15	0
William Emly, of *Mansfield*, Goods worth	23	0	0
	348	16	10

Amount of Distresses.

The Distresses made this Year, for the Cause of their religious Assemblies only, amounted to 712 *l.* 8 *s.* 4 *d.* many of which were exorbitant, and the Fines frequently laid and levied, upon flight, and sometimes false Informations : The Law did indeed admit the Sufferers to appeal to the Quarter Sessions, but the Justices, more tender of one another's Honour than of the *Quakers* Grievances, seldom gave them any Relief.

Partiality of Justices on Appeals.

One *John Sayton* was informed against, and fined 20 *l.* by Justice *Thoroton*, for being at a Meeting in the Parish of *Blythe*, at a Time when he was at the Distance of more than sixty Miles from thence : He appealed to the Quarter Sessions, and with much Difficulty obtained an Hearing of his Case : The Jury finding the Matter clear, brought in a Verdict for the Appellant ; whereupon *Peniston Whaley*, one of the Justices, ordered them to go out again, but one of them answered, *We are agreed, and have well considered the Matter* : Whereupon the Justice in a Rage flung off the Bench, and said, *You deserve all to be hang'd* ; adding, that *they were as bad as Highwaymen* ; and said, *he hoped the King would take away Juries, for this*, said he, *will not do.* Thus *Sayton* was acquitted, and the Jury dismist, to make Room for another more agreeable to the Purposes of the Court. Next Morning another Jury was impanelled, and another Appeal of the like Nature came on. The Case was that of *William Hudson*, whom the Evidence could not prove to have been at the Meeting he was charged with, and though eight of the Jury were pickt Men, known to be against the Appellant, yet the other four stood out, and no Verdict was agreed on till about eight at Night, when one of those four being taken ill, and needing Refreshment, Justice *Whaley* told them, *If they did not agree, they should be kept there till they died, and as one of them died, the Court would chuse another, till they were all dead* : They were over-awed into a Compliance, and after the Court was adjourn'd, privately gave in a Verdict against the Appellant. When one of the Jury said, *He would gladly do Equity* ; Justice *Thoroton* replied, *You have nothing to do with Equity.*

Villany of Informers detected.

By such partial Proceedings of the Justices, Informers were encouraged, and took little Regard to their Assertions, seeing their most groundless Testimonies were accepted for incontestable Truth, and all Proceedings against them were so manifestly discountenanced. However, in one notorious Piece of Deceit they were detected : The Case was this : On the 26th of *November* 1676, certain Informers came to a Meeting at *Blythe*, and finding no Preacher there, resolved to make one. So they came out again, and consulted with their Associates ; one of whom, *Edward Butterworth*, goes into the Meeting, and demurely seats himself there, till the Informers came again : Then *Butterworth* stood up, and said, *Blessed are the Peacemakers*, with some other Words ; upon which *Thomas Sharp*, one of the Informers, lays hold on him, pulled him out of the Meeting, and delivered him to the Constable, who carried this pretended Preacher before Justice *Sands*, where *Sharp* appeared to make Information against him. But the Justice, observing the Fellow's Behaviour, suspected him and examined him, *Where he lived* ? He answered, *At* Broughton, *eight Mile from* Lincoln. The Justice ordered him to be brought again next Day, when Sir *Ralph Knight* being also present, they again examined him, and he still asserted that he lived at *Broughton* : *Sharp*, the Informer, being also examined

upon

upon Oath, affirmed, *that he never faw the Man before in all his Life.* But between thefe two Examinations, the following Certificate had been procured, and was produced before the Juftices, *viz.*

" THIS may certify whom it may concern, that we whofe Names are under-written do teftify, that *Edward Butterworth* and *Thomas Sharp*, of " our Town of *Newark*, are very well acquainted and near Neighbours, living " together in our Town, and both in a Street ; moft of our Town well know it.

> " JOHN MILNER,
> " THOMAS MERRYWEATHER."

Upon this the Juftices ordered *Butterworth* to find Sureties for his Appearance at Seffions, or elfe to be fent to *Nottingham* Goal, but as the Conftable was conveying him thither, he made his Efcape. About three Days after, he came to the Juftices, and two of the Informers with him, who were bound for his Appearance at Seffions. But we do not find any farther Proceeding in this Affair ; for though the Deception was clearly difcovered, and the Perjury of *Sharp* the Informer, made manifeft, yet the Juftices let the Affair drop ; for they were too favourable to fuch grofs Offenders ; as on the Contrary, when fome Parifh-Officers, either out of Compaffion to the Poor, or Unwillingnefs to prejudice their Neighbours, were remifs in executing Warrants, the Juftices were very fevere, as in the Cafe of one *Creffie*, a Conftable of *Blythe*, whom they fined 5 *l* for omitting to execute a Warrant of Diftrefs ; and for that Fine he had taken from him, two Cows and other Goods, worth 9 *l*. 4 *s*. 1 *d*.

Thomas Farnfworth, John Birks, and *Zachariah Bowers*, for refufing to Swear, when fummoned to ferve on a Jury at a Court-Leet, were fined, and had their Goods taken away by Diftrefs for the faid Fines.

We find not many Inftances of Perfecution in this County after the Year 1676, except that many Land-Owners, and Occupiers, had their Corn taken out of the Fields for Tithes ; of which the Priefts, and others, took large Quantities : The Value of the Tithes, fo taken, with the Perfons Names from whom they were taken, between 1686 and 1690, of which we have an Account, were as follows, *viz.*

	l.	*s.*	*d.*
At BLYTHE, from *John Seaton, George Greaves, John Wilfon, Thomas Buck, Charles Hopkinfon, Jofeph Shipporah*, and *John Bullivant*	28	14	5
At EVERTON, from *John Camfall* and *Gervafe Lambert*	2	19	4
At CLARBROUGH, from *John Richardfon, John Gunthorp, Jofeph Turnhill*, and *William Hudfon*	15	0	6
At SCAFTFORTH, from *Robert Spavold* and *John Jephfon*	9	19	0
At WILLOUGHBY, from *James Camm* and *George Camm*	8	0	8
At LANHAM, from *Gervafe Harrifon*	17	10	11
At SOUTH-LEVERTON, from *Thomas Sampfon*	17	3	10
At KNEESAL, from *John Machon*	7	7	6
At MAPLEBECK, from *John Camm*	9	7	0
At KIRSALL, from *Solomon Johnfon* and *Roger Noble*	3	4	3
At SUTTON, from *John Trafwell, Hugh Heald*, and *Richard Tacy*	24	19	0
At GRASSTHORP, from *Jane Smith*	4	11	0
At SCROOBY, from *John Torr* and *Robert Jephfon*	12	8	0
At TICKHILL, from *Anne Lambert*	4	7	6
At HARWORTH, from *George Greaves*	5	10	0
At NORTH-CULLINGHAM, from *Robert Carnell*	1	6	8
At HUCKNALL, from *John Longford*	0	10	0

Car. over 172 19 7

NOTTING-
HAM-
SHIRE.
1686 *to*
1690.

	l.	*s.*	*d.*
Brought over	172	19	7
At SUTTON in ASHFIELD, from *Nathanael Clay*	1	6	8
At SKEKBIE, from *William Mason*	1	16	8
At OXTON, from *Francis Scothorn*	0	8	6
At FARNSFIELD, from *Anthony Smith*	0	10	0
At EPERSTON, from *Richard Roe*	2	12	10
	179	14	3

Distress and Imprisonment of G. Harrison.

In the Year 1689, *Gervase Harrison*, of *Lanham*, was prosecuted in the Ecclesiastical Court for small Tithes and *Easter-Offerings*, at the Suit of *Richard Bradley*, Vicar of that Parish : The Parson's pretended Claim was only for Trifles, *viz.* For three Communicants 6 *d.* for six Calves 2 *s.* 2 *d.* for twenty five Lambs 6 *s.* 3 *d.* for Wool of thirty six Sheep 6 *s.* for one Chicken 2 *d.* for Eggs at *Easter* 4 *d.* for Hemp and Growth 3 *d.* For not appearing to answer to these Demands, which were rather fictitious than real, the poor Man was denounced *Contumacious* ; and upon Certificate thereof to two Justices they granted a Warrant, by which he was committed to *Nottingham* Goal, where he lay nine Weeks, two of which he was kept in the Dungeon.

C H A P. XXXII.

S U F F O L K.

Anno 1655.

T HE firſt Inſtance of Perſecution in this County was that of *John Porter*, a Man licenſed to ſell Wares up and down the Country. He being, on a Firſt-day of the Week, at the Houſe of *Richard White* in *Wickhamſtyth*, as he ſat reading in a Book publiſhed by one of his Friends, *Edward Harvey*, a Juſtice of the Peace, came in with a Conſtable, and ſnatcht the Book out of his Hand, ſaying, *You Rogue, what will you not pull off your Hat to the Protector? You are a ſeducing Fellow, and read ſeducing Books: You ſhall be bound to appear at the Seſſions, or go to Priſon.* Accordingly he gave Bond, and did appear at the Seſſions, where the Majority of the Juſtices, at the Perſuaſion of the ſaid Juſtice *Harvey*, ſeemed determined againſt him: *Harvey*, an embitter'd Man, on this Occaſion turned Informer, and took his Oath, that *the ſaid* John Porter *did carry a Pack at his Back, and ſold* Quakers *Books.* *Porter* produced his Licenſe for travelling in the Way of his Trade, ſigned by five or ſix Juſtices and Officers, but the Court would take no Notice of it: They ſentenced him to be whipt; which Sentence was

Cruel Uſage and barbarous whipping of J. Porter.

Juſtice turns Informer.

SUFFOLK.   moſt barbarouſly executed on the Market-day at *Mendleſham*, where the poor
1655.   Man, tied by his Hands, was hung up on a Butcher's Spirket, till the cruel
            Executioner gave him above twenty Stripes with a three-corded Whip, ſo that
            the Fleſh and Skin hung in Flakes torn in pieces on his Back, a miſerable
            Sight, exciting Compaſſion even in the Hard-hearted among the Spectators.

            On the 30th of the Month called *July* 1655, *George Whitehead*, *John Har-
            wood*, and *Richard Clayton*, paſſing through *Buers*, a Town in *Suffolk*, the ſaid
            Richard Clayton did fix a Paper on the Door of the Steeple-houſe there, being
            as follows, *viz.*

Copy of a   " IF you do ſet up ſuch Miniſters as ſeek for their Gain from their Quarter,
Paper fixed   "   you ſet up ſuch as the Prophet *Iſaiah* diſapproves of, *Iſai.* lvi. 11. And
on the Steeple-   " you that do ſet up ſuch as bear Rule by their Means, you ſet up ſuch as the
houſe Door at   " Prophet *Jeremiah* and the Lord diſapprove, *Jere.* iv. And you that ſet
Buers.   " up ſuch that ſeek for the Wool, and make a Prey upon the People, you
                     " ſet up ſuch as the Prophet *Ezekiel* diſapproves of, *Ezek.* xxxiv. And you
                     " that ſet up Hirelings, you ſet up ſuch as *Micah* diſapproves of, *Micah* iii.
                     " And you that ſet up ſuch as are called of Men *Maſter*, ſtand praying in the
                     " Synagogues, have the chiefeſt Places in the Aſſemblies, you ſet up ſuch
                     " as Chriſt diſapproves, 2 *Pet.* ii. 14. And if you ſet up ſuch as perſecute,
                     " and cauſe People to be ſent to Priſon for ſpeaking the Truth in the Syna-
                     " gogues, you ſet up ſuch as go in *Cain*'s Way to Envy, *Jude* Ver. 11. And
                     " you that ſet up ſuch as receive Gifts and Rewards, the Wages of Unrigh-
                     " teouſneſs, you ſet up ſuch as mind earthly Things, whoſe God is their
                     " Belly, which the Apoſtle diſapproves, *Phil.* iii. 9. And you that ſet up
                     " ſuch Teachers, ſtrive to keep God's Labourers out of his Vineyard, which
                     " Chriſt and his Apoſtles diſapprove. And you that ſet up ſuch as will not
                     " ſuffer another to ſpeak that ſtands by, when any Thing is revealed, but ſend
                     " him to Priſon if he do, you ſet up a perſecuting Spirit full of Diſorder,
                     " and are judged by the Apoſtle's Life and Doctrine, who was a Miniſter of
                     " *Jeſus Chriſt*, both you that ſet up, and them you do ſet up, who ſaid, *All
                     " may propheſy one by one*, 1 *Cor.* xiv. 3. And ſo you all by this Spirit are
                     " judged to be in the Spirit of Error, and to be ſuch as would quench the
                     " Holy Spirit of God, and deſpiſe Prophecy, and dare not try all Things,
                     " manifeſting your ſelves to be Haters of the Light, and diſapproved of the
                     " Prophets and Apoſtles, and their Practice and Life. And you that ſet up
                     " ſuch as give *David*'s Quakings, Tremblings, Cryings, Roarings, Propheſy-
                     " ings, and Praiſes and Prayers in the Metre mixt together, you ſet up ſuch
                     " as have not the Spirit of Underſtanding, which Spirit brings to know the
                     " Time of praying, and praiſing, and groaning, and crying, and trembling
                     " and quaking, and propheſying : He that hath the Underſtanding witneſſeth
                     " theſe Things in their Places ; but you that give Scorners, and Drunkards
                     " and Swearers, and Perſecutors, *David*'s Conditions, for he was ſcofft at when
                     " he was in ſuch Conditions, and theſe do ſo now at thoſe that are in ſuch
                     " Conditions. And if you ſet up ſuch as take Tithes, you ſet up ſuch as the
                     " Apoſtle denies, for the Apoſtle ſaith, *That the Prieſthood was changed, and
                     " the Law changed alſo*, *Heb.* vii. And if you ſet up ſuch as before men-
                     " tioned, you ſet up ſuch as are contrary to the Scriptures, and plant no
                     " Vineyard for God, nor labour in his Vineyard, for firſt they muſt plant a
                     " Vineyard, before they eat of its Fruit, 1 *Cor.* ix. 7."

            This Paper being ſtuck up, ſome People came together to read it, to whom
George Whitehead and *John Harwood* gave a Chriſtian Exhortation to live in the
Fear of the Lord, and to turn from the Evil of their Ways, &c. While they
were ſpeaking, a Conſtable came, and carried them before *Herbert Pelham*,
an *Eſſex* Juſtice, then at *Buers*, who examined them, though officiouſly, being
out of his Precinct, and then ſent them, together with *Clayton*, to *Thomas
Waldegrave*, a Juſtice at *Smallbridge*, not far from thence, who having aſk
                                                                              them

them a few Queſtions, left them in the Conſtable's Cuſtody, till *Pelham* and he
had laid their Heads together. The Iſſue of their Conſultation was, that
Richard Clayton was, by *Waldegrave's* Order, publickly whipt as a Vagrant,
and ſent out of the Town the ſame Day with a Paſs : A Proceeding not
juſtifiable by Law, *Clayton* being a Man of Reputation, and known to have
an Eſtate of 20*l.* per *Annum* at *Gleaſton* in *Lancaſhire*. *John Harwood* was the
next Day ſent to *Edmundſbury* Goal, and *George Whitehead* the Day following ;
a Copy of whoſe *Mittimus*, with his own Remarks thereon, we here inſert, *viz.*

Whipping of
R. *Clayton.*

Impriſonment
of J. *Har-
wood and*
G. *White-
head.*

" *To the Conſtable of* Buers, *and to the Keeper of the Goal at* Bury.

" Suffolk *ſs.*

" **I** Send you herewithal the Body of *George Whitehead*, of *Orton* in the
" County of *Weſtmorland*, *(a)* an idle wandring Fellow, and *(b)* a common
" Diſturber of the Peace of this Nation, requiring you, in the Name of his
" Highneſs the *Lord Protector*, &c. to receive him into your Goal, and him
" there ſafely to keep, that he may be forth-coming before the Juſtices at the
" next Seſſions for the Peace, to be holden for this County at *Bury*, then and
" there to be proceeded with according to the Law : And hereof I require
" you not to fail. This 1ſt Day of *Auguſt* 1655.

Mittimus of
G. *White-
head.*

" THO. WALDEGRAVE."

George Whitehead's own Remarks on this *Mittimus* were as follows,
" *Obſerv.* *(a) An idle wandring Fellow.* This is falſe in Fact, as well as
" ſcurrilous and diſdainful, for
" 1. I am well known to be no ſuch Perſon, for after my Parents took
" me away from that noted School at *Blencoe* in *Cumberland*, at the Requeſt
" of ſome Friends, I taught a private, then a publick School.
" 2. After that, I was at my Father's Houſe Part of a Summer, and then
" was not idle, but induſtrious in what was proper for me, not being educated
" either in *Idleneſs*, nor willing to eat the *Bread of Idleneſs*, that I might
" prevent all Reflection and Reproach againſt me on that Account.
" 3. And when it pleaſed God to call me by his Word from my Father's
" Houſe, and out of my native Country, to preach the Everlaſting Goſpel,
" therein I laboured faithfully, and travelled in the Service thereof, accord-
" ing to the Grace and Ability given me of God, in his dear Son Chriſt Jeſus.
" *(b)* *A common Diſturber of the publick Peace of this Nation*, is alſo un-
" juſtly charged againſt me, for I was, and am, of a peaceable Converſation,
" being alſo a Miniſter of the Goſpel of Peace.
" How came I to be termed *an idle wandring Fellow* in the *Warrant* of
" Commitment, ſeeing that in the *Indictment* at Quarter Seſſions, I was called
" *Labourer ?* Thus Self-contradictory was this our Proſecutor. Where Envy
" is, there is Confuſion. Could he reaſonably think himſelf more diſhonoured
" by my giving him his own Name of *Thomas Waldegrave*, than he was by
" his own injurious and illegal Proceedings againſt us ?"

*Remarks on
the ſaid Mit-
timus.*

A few Weeks after the Commitment of *George Whitehead* and *John Harwood*,
George Rofe was ſent to the ſame Priſon by Juſtice *Gurdon*, his *Mittimus* being
as follows, *viz.*

Suffolk *ſs.*

" *To the Keeper of the Common Goal at* Bury St. Edmund's,
" *and his Deputy or Deputies there.*

" **F** ORASMUCH as upon Examination of *George Rofe*, late of
" *Halſted* in the County of *Eſſex*, Glazier, and upon Examination taken
" upon Oath before us againſt the ſaid *Rofe*, ſufficient Cauſe appears to us,
" whereby

Mittimus of
G. *Rofe.*

SUFFOLK.
1655.

" whereby we enforce *Rofe* to find two able and fufficient Sureties for his per-
" fonal Appearance at the next Seffions of the Peace, to be holden for the
" Franchife of *Bury* St. *Edmund*'s, and thence not to depart without Licenfe
" of the Court : And forafmuch as the faid *George Rofe* refufeth to find
" Sureties, we therefore herewithal fend you the Body of the faid *George Rofe*,
" requiring you, in the Name of his Highnefs the *Lord Protector* of the
" Commonwealth of *England*, to receive him into the faid Goal, and him
" there fafely to keep until the next Seffions, if in the mean Time he the faid
" *George* (being by his own Confeffion one now ufually called a *Quaker*) fhall
" not find fuch able and fufficient Sureties for his Appearance as aforefaid.
" Dated at *Affington* the 3d Day of *September* 1655.

" JOHN GURDON."

The Juftice avenges the Prieft's Quarrel.

Thus was *George Rofe* imprifoned by a *Mittimus* affigning no Breach of Law, nor any Matter of Fact, as a Caufe for requiring Sureties, nor indeed had he given any juft Occafion of Offence, except his afking a Queftion of the Prieft of *Stoke*, after his Sermon there, at which the Prieft was difpleafed, and the Juftice, to avenge the Parfon's Quarrel, took this extrajudicial Courfe to fend the poor Man to Prifon. The *Mittimus* indeed fays, that he confeffed himfelf one called a *Quaker*, but that Confeffion could be neither a legal, nor reafonable Caufe for his Commitment.

Indictment of Whitehead, Harwood, *and* Clayton,

Fined and recommitted.

Imprifonment of G. Fox *the Younger.*

At the next Quarter Seffions, held at *Edmundfbury* the 9th of *October*, *Whitehead*, *Harwood*, and *Clayton*, were indicted as *Common Difturbers of the* * *Magiftrates and Minifters*. The Juftices who committed them were their fole Accufers, and incenfed the others againft them ; and an ignorant Jury being impanelled, by Direction of the Court, prefently found them *Guilty* of the Indictment : Whereupon they were fined twenty Nobles each, and recommitted to Prifon till Payment. *George Fox*, of *Chafefield*, commonly called *George Fox the Younger*, to diftinguifh him from the other of that Name, was prefent at their Trial, and obferving the hard Treatment of the Prifoners, and efpecially the Prejudice expreffed by Juftice *Gurdon* againft them, and being troubled thereat, fpake thus to the faid Juftice as he was coming out of the Seffions-houfe, viz. *Repent of thy unjuft Actions this Day, for otherwife thou canft not efcape the juft Judgments of God.* Upon this *Gurdon* laid hold on him, and had him before the Bench, who demanded Sureties till the next Seffions, which he not complying with, they fent him to Prifon with the others.

Imprifonment J. Laurence.

On the 14th of the Month called *Auguft*, *Jofeph Laurence* was committed to the County Goal at *Ipfwich*, being charged with *Railing againft the Minifters of God's Word, and calling the Worfhip of God*, Babylonifh. A Charge founded only on fome cafual Words of his, who, when two Perfons came to him and demanded Tithe for the Prieft, had faid, *That he fhould not pay Tithes for the upholding of* Baal's *Prieft, or any* Babylonifh *Worfhip*.

H. Marfhal *imprifoned, indicted, and fined.*

On the 22d of *November*, *Henry Marfhall*, of *Cambridgfhire*, for fpeaking a few Words to the Prieft of *Boxford*, after his Sermon and Prayer were ended, was, by Order of Juftice *Gurdon*, firft fet in the Stocks about an Hour, and then fent to *Edmundfbury* Goal. At the next Quarter Seffions he was indicted as a *Peace-breaker*, and fined twenty Marks ; for Non-payment of which he was fent back to Prifon : Thus he fuffered a three-fold Punifhment for one pretended Offence, viz. the *Stocks*, *Imprifonment*, and *Fine*. At the fame Seffions *George Fox* was called, but no Indictment was laid againft him, nor did any Accufer appear ; yet the Court fent him back to Prifon till another Seffions, at which he was not called : Whereupon he afked his Liberty of the Goaler, but he would not grant it, neither would he fhew him any Order or Warrant for his longer Detention.

The

---

* Though neither of them had fpoken a Word to any Magiftrate, or Minifter, before they were taken into Cuftody.

The Ufage of thefe five Prifoners at *Edmundfbury* was very hard ; for they were lodged in the common Ward among Felons, in a low Dungeon-like Place under the Market-houfe, with a damp Earthen Floor, where they lay upon Rye-ftraw. The Goaler was alfo very angry with them, becaufe they contributed not to his Avarice, nor would buy any of his Strong-liquors, as fome of the other Prifoners did ; but thefe Perfons were temperate, and drank only Water, by which he could gain nothing. Befides, they frequently teftified againft the Drunkennefs, Swearing, and other Diforders in his Houfe, and reproved him for his Hypocrify, who, while he fuffered fuch Things, made great and high Pretences to Religion, he being a Member of a *Prefbyterian* Church, and would on the Day called *Sunday,* call his Prifoners together, pretend to give them Inftructions, and exercife a Kind of formal Devotion among them. When G. *Whitehead* told him of his Hypocrify therein, his Fruits being fo contrary, his Daughter faid, *What ! do you call my Father an Hypocrite, who has been a Saint thefe forty Years ?* For thefe Caufes he was exceedingly embitter'd againft them, fo that he did often ftrike them on the Face, and grievoufly abufe them both by Words and Actions : And the Tapfter, Turnkey, and other of his Servants, and fome of the drunken Prifoners, encouraged by his Example, did frequently abufe them with Blows, and fometimes took away their Food and other Neceffaries, faying, *The Goaler gave them Leave fo to do :* And one of the Prifoners faid, *If he killed them, he fhould not be hang'd for it.*

It would be too tedious to relate one Half of the Sufferings they underwent, which the Goaler and his Servants were fo confcious of, that they ufed their Endeavours to prevent its being known, by taking away from the Prifoners their Pen and Ink, and often prohibiting their Friends from coming to vifit them, pretending an Order from the Juftices that none of them fhould be admitted. Under this miferable State of Captivity and tyrannical Ufage they continued many Months : The Manner of their Deliverance thence will be related in our Account of the next Year.

In this Year alfo *William Seaman,* of *Mendlefham,* and *Elizabeth Lockwood,* were committed to *Ipfwich* Goal, for fpeaking to a Prieft, after he had ended his Sermon in the Place of publick Worfhip at *Mendlefham.* At an enfuing Seffions *Seaman* was fined twenty Marks, and fent again to Prifon, where he was cruelly ufed by *John Story,* Goaler. In the fame Year *Henry Baker,* of *Thrandleftone,* going on the Firft-day of the Week to a Meeting at *Mendlefham,* had his Horfe taken from him, but redeemed next Day by his Mother's paying 10 s. And fhortly after, in his Return from a Meeting at the fame Place, his Horfe, Bridle, and Saddle, were taken away, worth 5 l. *John Eweings* and *Jane Hawes,* for riding to a Meeting, were fet in the Stocks fix Hours, by the Direction of Juftice *Harvey,* who, becaufe the Conftable in their Favour removed the Stocks to a warmer Place than they were ufed to ftand in, for that Act of Humanity fent him to Prifon.

ANNO 1656. It happened on the 10th of the Month called *June,* that *George Harrifon* and *Stephen Hubberfty,* two Preachers, came to the Houfe of *Anthony Appleby* at *Haverill* ; they had not been long there before a Multitude of People befet the Houfe, curfing, fwearing, threatning, and throwing Stones at the Door till about Midnight. Next Morning they renew'd their Rage, fwearing they would have thefe Men, or pull the Houfe down, not unlike the wicked *Sodomites* at the Door of *Lot :* At length with one Accord, they made an Onfet and broke the Gate to pieces, and entring the Houfe, haled out the harmlefs Strangers, and defperately beat and kickt them, driving them along the Street with halloeing and fhouting, and ftoned them beyond the Town's End. When *Anthony Appleby* complained to a Juftice of the Peace of this Riot, and grievous Abufe of his Friends, the Juftice would not hear him, becaufe he had his Hat on, but ordered the Conftables, that *If any of that Perfuafion came to Town, they fhould bring them to him to be punifhed.* About this Time alfo, *John Greenwood* was fent to *Edmundfbury* Goal, and detained there feveral Weeks, for no Offence, except that of prefenting a Book to

SUFFOLK.
1656.

Two Women imprisoned.

Prosecutions

Distress for Meeting.

Application to Cromwell.

A Letter to Judge Atkins.

Justice *Gurdon*, of *Assington*, intituled, *The Wise taken in his own Craftiness.* Some displeasing Truths that Book contained so irritated the Justice, that he by an Act of arbitrary Power imprisoned the Giver of it, who had broke no Law. As if the Office of a Magistrate were an Exemption from just Reproof. Equally impatient of Contradiction were the Priests, who procured the Imprisonment of *Margaret Gray* and *Anne Blakeling*, who had presumed to call in question either the Truth of their Doctrine, or the Validity of their Call.

George Sherwin, being prosecuted in the *Exchequer* for Tithes, at the Suit of Dame *Vere Gaudy*, of *Debingham*, for refusing to Swear to his Answer exhibited in that Court, was committed to *Melton* Goal on the 2d of the Month called *January*; as was on the same Day *John Simpson*, of *Kenton*, for the same Cause, at the Prosecution of *Charles Gaudy*, for Tithes. About the same Time *William Warn*, of *Wellingworth*, was also imprisoned in the same Goal for a Demand of but 9 *s.* for Tithe. Also *Joseph Laurence*, for 2 *l.* 14 *s.* demanded for Tithes, had Goods taken from him to the Value of 10 *l.* Likewise *Richard White*, of *Wickhamskith*, was prosecuted in the County Court, at the Suit of *Austin Gibbett* Priest, for a pretended Debt of 16 *l.* 15 *s.* borrowed, and 3 *l.* 5 *s.* for Tithes. The Debt, a meer Pretence, was dropt, at the Trial, but the Tithe was granted by the Jury, and he had three Cows taken for it worth 12 *l.*

Anthony Kettle, of *Edwardstone*, for going to a Meeting on the First-day of the Week, had his Goods taken by Distress, to the Value of 12 *s.*

In this Year the Prisoners at *Edmundsbury* and *Ipswich* found Means of representing their barbarous Usage to some of their Friends at *London*, who applied to *Oliver Cromwell*, and his Deputy *Fleetwood*, on their Behalf, who issued Orders to the Justices to enquire into their Case; upon which Enquiry the cruel and illegal Treatment of the Prisoners from the Goaler, his Servants, and others, was so fully made appear, that they reproved him for it, and charged him to suffer no such Abuses for the future. This awed them into a Degree of better Behaviour, and the Condition of the Prisoners became more tolerable. An Application was also made to Judge *Atkins*, at *Bury* Assizes, on the Behalf of *George Whitehead*, in an unusual Manner, as appears by the following Letter, *viz.*

　　" *Judge* ATKINS!

" WHEREAS I have offered myself unto thee for my Friend *George*
"　　*Whitehead*, to lie in Bonds, or what else might be inflicted on him,
" so he may go forth free, or to lay down my Life for him, I was and am
" willing; but I have not yet received any plain Answer, whether thou wilt
" grant my Desire, *yea* or *nay*; so that since I have spoken of it twice to
" thee, I have been at the House where thou lodgest, to know thy Mind in
" the Thing, and I could not get so much Liberty as to speak to thee:
" Therefore this is to desire thee to send me a few Words, whether my Body
" will be taken a Pledge for his, or else to give Order that I may come to
" thee. So I desire thee, in the Name of the Lord, not to slight this, but
" consider and resolve of it in the Sight of God, for the Thing is to be
" valued; and herein I do own the Scriptures, and witness them, and the
" fulfilling of them in me by *Christ Jesus*, who suffered and laid down his
" Life for his Flock, and *Greater Love hath no Man than this, to lay down his*
" *Life for his Friend*, which I witness, wherein I am subject to the Commands
" of Christ, and see them fulfilled in me.

Bury, *the* 20*th of the*
Sixth Month 1656.

　　" MARGARET SUTTON."

Christian Love demonstrated.

　　This Letter, though it shews the poor Woman's Ignorance in point of Law, and the Extent of the Judge's Power, yet it aptly sets forth the Perfection of *Christian* Charity, and the exceeding Love and Bowels of Compassion in
Christ

Chrift Jefus, which faithful Sufferers for his Sake have one towards another ; for the fame Woman had been alfo for fome Time imprifoned at *Bury,* by the Procurement of a Prieft there, whom fhe had been concerned to reprove. The Fervency of her Concern for *G. Whitehead* had induced her to travel from her Habitation in *Weftmorland,* the Place of his Birth, to follicit for his Liberty. Whether the Judge, at his Return to Court, made any Report of this Affair, does not appear ; however, at length, after frequent Application to *Oliver Cromwell* and his *Council,* wherein *Mary Saunders,* a waiting Gentlewoman in the Protector's Family, was very ferviceable, the following Order was iffued, *viz.*

" Thurfday, *the* 16*th of* October, *at the Council at* Whitehall.

" **O**RDERED by his Highnefs the Lord Protector and his Council,
" that the *Quakers* imprifoned in *Colchefter* in the County of *Effex,* and
" *Edmundfbury* and *Ipfwich* in the County of *Suffolk,* be forthwith releafed and
" fet at Liberty. And it is referred to Sir *Francis Ruffel,* to take Care that
" the fame be done accordingly ; as alfo to confider how the Fines fet upon
" them, or any of them, may with moft Conveniency be taken off and dif-
" charged : And likewife to take Order, that upon their being fet at Liberty
" as aforefaid, they be forthwith fent to their refpective Homes.

Order of Council.

" W. JESSOP,

" *Clerk of the Council.*"

This Order was carefully executed by Sir *Francis Ruffel,* a confcientious and compaffionate Man, and averfe to Perfecution, who fent his Clerk to the Prifon at *Bury,* to fee them fet at Liberty, which was done accordingly ; though he did not order them to be fent Home, but, in Kindnefs, gave them an Order or Warrant, to produce in their Defence, if Need fhould be, that fo they might travel without Moleftation.

Sir Francis Ruffel's *charitable Difpofition.*

In the Time of their Imprifonment, *George Fox the Younger* and *George Rofe,* received a Gift and Part of the Miniftry of the Gofpel, and became ferviceable Preachers ; and the latter of them travelled afterward through diverfe Parts of *Europe* and *America.*

Minifterial Gift of G. Fox and G. Rofe.

ANNO 1657. On the 1ft of the Month called *April,* was a Meeting in the Yard or Orchard of *Jofeph Deinfey,* of *Nayland,* where *George Whitehead* preaching, was apprehended by a pretended Gentleman, who rufhed in with Soldiers and others, and pulled him down with Violence, and had him away to Juftice *Gurdon,* who gave him much threatning Language, and when *George* defired him to hear with Moderation, he anfwered, *You are a moderate Rogue :* And when *George* calmly reproved him for his hard Speeches, he deridingly bad him, *Go* Quake. *George* afking him again, *Whether he defpifed Quaking?* he anfwered, *Yes, I do defpife Quaking.* After fome Examination, which the Clerk took in Writing, and which the Juftice required *George* to fign, but he refufed, as being partially taken ; the Juftice told him, *He fhould be whipt, and if he came again into that Country, fhould be branded on the Shoulder ; and if he came a third Time fhould be hanged.* To which *George* mildly replied, *I am no fuch Perfon as thou haft mentioned : Thou art an old Man, and going to thy Grave, thou doft not know how foon the Lord may put an End to thy Days, and difappoint thee of thy evil Defigns againft me : However, I fear not thy Threats, if the Lord, whom I ferve, require my Return into thefe Parts, I muft obey him.* The Juftice faid, *I know I am an old Man.* *George* added, *Thou art old in Iniquity, it is high Time for thee to repent.*
The Juftice then iffued the following Warrant, *viz.*

G. White-head *taken preaching at* Nayland.

Violence of Juftice Gur-don *reproved by G.* White-head.

" *To*

SUFFOLK.
1657.

Warrant for whipping G. Whitehead.

" To the Conflables, and all other Officers whom it may concern, and
" to every of them.

" **B**E it remembred, that one *George Whitehead*, a young Man, about twenty
" Years of Age, who confeffeth himfelf to have been born at *Orton* in
" *Weftmorland*, being this prefent Day found vagrant and wandering at *Nayland*
" in this County, contrary to the Laws of this Nation, and being thereupon
" brought before us, two Juftices of the Peace for this County, is by us
" ordered to be openly whipp'd at *Nayland* aforefaid, till his Body be bloody, as
" the Law in fuch Cafe enjoineth. And he is to pafs thence from Parifh to
" Parifh by the Officers thereof, the next Way to *Orton* aforefaid, before the
" firft Day of *June* now next enfuing.
" Dated at *Affington* in this County of *Suffolk*, the firft Day of *April* 1657."

Signed by JOHN GURDON, *and another Juftice.*

*Cruelly exe-
cuted.*

This Warrant was the next Day executed by a foolifh Fellow, whom the
Conftable had hired, who with a long fharp Whip laid on unmercifully, having
neither Fear nor Wit to reftrain him, till the People cried out to ftop him,
fo that *George's* Back and Breaft were cut and wounded with many long bloody
Stripes, the Marks whereof were feen a great While after. He was enabled
to bear this rigorous Punifhment with a Patience and Courage becoming his
Chriftian Caufe, and his Spirit was fo raifed in the Inftant of his Sufferings,
that he fang Praifes aloud to the Lord, who had counted him worthy to fuffer
for his Name's Sake. After this cruel Execution, he was conducted the fame
Day on his own Horfe, by the Conftable and others, to *Sudbury*, and from
thence to *Clare* and *Haverill*, the Officers, to whom the Warrant was directed,
admiring to fee a young Man fo well habited, and on fo good an Horfe, pafs'd
as a Vagrant. On the Edge of *Cambridgfhire*, his innocent Appearance fo
wrought on the Conftable, that he gave him up the Warrant, and bade him go
his Way. So he returned to *Halfted*, *Coggefhall*, *Colchefter*, *Sudbury*, and other
Places in thofe Parts, where the Report of his Suffering raifed in the People a
great Curiofity and Defire to hear him, the Meetings were much frequented,
and the Teftimony of Truth greatly fpread and prevailed.

*Profecution of
G. Rofe, and
36 others, at
Hadleigh.*

In the Month of *November*, on a Firft-day of the Week, was a Meeting at
Hadleigh, to which the Mayor came, and afked, *Who was their Chief ?* It was
anfwered, *The Lord is Chief among us.* Whereupon he ordered his Affiftants to
pull down *George Rofe*, who was preaching, and to take him away with thirty
fix others, who were put into a Dungeon fome Hours ; after which, he demanded 10 s. of each of them, which they refufing to pay, eighteen of them
were kept all Night in Prifon, and on the Morrow, being Market-day, they
were all fet in the Stocks. *Roger Hawkins* alfo fuffered the like Punifhment fix
Hours, for going to a Meeting but half a Mile from his own Houfe : Alfo
Anthony Kettle, of *Edwardftone*, for the fame Caufe, was punifhed in the fame
Manner.

*Sufferings for
refufing to
Swear*

William Seaman, of *Bromfwell*, for refufing to Swear at a *Court-Leet*, was
fined 20 s. and had his Mare worth 6 l. taken away for that Fine. Some
Time before this, *John Wateridge*, being chofen Conftable, and refufing to
take the ufual Oath of Admiffion into that Office, was fent to Prifon ; and
upon his Difcharge thence, the Goaler kept back a Cloak of his worth 40 s.
for 4 s. 4 d. demanded for Fees.

*and for not
attending the
publick Wor-
fhip.*

Richard Cooke and *Thomas Wood* were committed to Prifon, from the Seffions
at *Edmundfbury*, on a Prefentment for not reforting to their Parifh-Church at
Afhfield : And for the like Caufe, *Richard Chandler* of *Nayland*, and *Henry
Clark* of *Affington*, were fined 2 s. 6 d. each.

*Imprifonment
of W. Alex-
ander.*

In this Year *William Alexander*, of *Needham*, for fpeaking to the Prieft of
that Town, after his Sermon, was imprifoned at *Ipfwich* till Seffions, then
fined 5 l. and recommitted for refufing to pay it.

John

John Dunks, of *Colchester,* for speaking to the People in *Nayland* Steeple-house, after the Priest had done, was taken up as a Vagrant, though but a few Miles from his own Habitation, publickly whipt, and sent away with a Pass.

The Prejudice and Spleen which *Robert Gurdon* and *John Fordingell,* Justices, entertained against this People, is apparent by the following Warrant, *viz.*

" FORASMUCH as it appears unto us upon Oath duly taken
" before us, that the Parties whose Names are under-written, being
" of the Age of sixteen Years at the least, are suspected or reputed to be
" *Papists* or *popishly* affected, these are therefore, by Virtue of a late *Act of*
" *Parliament for discovering, convicting, and repressing of* Popish Recusants, to
" will and require you forthwith to summon all and every such Person or
" Persons aforesaid, either by Delivery unto every one of them a Note in
" Writing, or leaving the same at their Dwellings or usual Places of Abode,
" to appear personally at the next Quarter Sessions, which are to be holden for
" the Franchise of *Bury* St. *Edmunds,* to do and receive that which by the
" Court shall be enjoyned them, and thence not to depart without Licence of
" the Court. Dated at *Sudbury* this 12th Day of *December* 1657.

" ROBERT GURDON,
" JOHN FORDINGELL.

" N A M E S,
" *Anthony Kettle* Yeoman, and *Sarah* his Wife : *Ambrose Kettle* the Younger,
" and *Sarah* his Sister : *Ambrose Hale,* and *Anne Edwards* Widow."

They appeared accordingly, but those Justices, who shewed such a Willingness to proceed against them, failed of their Purpose, and no farther Process appears upon Record.

Rebecca Lucas, Widow, about eighty Years of Age, and her Daughters *Rebecca* and *Mary,* were summoned to appear before the Mayor of *Hadleigh,* who charged the old Woman to suffer no more Meetings at her House, nor to lodge any *Quakers,* threatning to quarter Soldiers on her, if she did ; he also told her Daughters, that he had nothing against them, but their being *Quakers.* A few Days after, the two Daughters were taken from their aged Mother, and sent to *Bridewell,* under Pretence *that they ought to put themselves to Service* ; but in Truth, as the Constable plainly told them, because *they were not of the Mayor's Religion.*

About this Time *John Sewel,* having offended one of the Priests, was put into the Stocks at *Haverill,* and as he was sitting there, his Brother *Ambrose Sewel* and one *John Hill* came to him and talked with him ; for which Act of Friendship they were committed to *Edmundsbury* Goal. An arbitrary Proceeding, without any Rule either of Law or Equity. The same *John Sewel* was afterwards sent to the House of Correction.

It happened, near the same Time, that *William Gardener,* of *Petestry,* casually falling into Discourse with one *Adkinson,* Priest of *Livington,* in the Presence of a Justice of the Peace, the Priest charged him with *Denying the Scriptures to be the Word of God* : *William* desired the Priest to *Prove by the Scriptures that they call themselves so.* The Priest quoted *Luke* viii. 11. *The Seed is the Word of God,* and insisted, that *the Scriptures were that Seed.* After which, repeating his Charge with some Aggravation, *William* answered, that *He lied in so charging him, for that he did own the Scriptures.* Whereupon the Priest struck *William* with his Bible, and bruised his Face, and in all Probability would have proceeded to farther Violence, had not the Justice, ashamed of his Actions, pulled him away, and restrained him.

ANNO 1658. On the 12th of the Month called *July, George Whitehead* riding through *Hoxon,* and meeting *Edward Willan,* Priest of that Place, exhorted him *to fear God, and cease from Iniquity* ; after which they had some

SUFFOLK.
1658.

G. White-
head *hurried
to Prison by
Night.*

E. Crofs
*abufed by a
drunkenPrieft.*

*Profecutions
for Tithes, and
grievous Im-
prifonments.*

Death of
J. Caufton.

*Imprifonment
of* A. Kettle.

Conference about the Church, till the Prieft, impatient of Contradiction, grew angry, and taking *George's* Horfe by the Bridle, forcibly ftopt him, till others came, who carried him before *Anthony Barry,* a Juftice of the Peace, to whom the Prieft complained that *George* had called him *Perfecutor,* though that was after he had affaulted him in the Street, and threatned to pull him off his Horfe : However, the Juftice, willing to gratify the Parfon, fent *George* to *Ipfwich* Goal, under Pretence of his having broke a late *Act of Parliament,* made againft *Vagrants, idle, loofe, diffolute Perfons, Fiddlers,* &c. which the Juftice faid, was made only for *Quakers.* They hurried him away to *Ipfwich* on Horfeback by Night, being about twenty Miles. In the Prifon there, he found the aforefaid *William Alexander,* and two others of his Friends, whofe Company was a great Solace in that Confinement, which was in the Common Ward, and their Lodging upon Straw. At the next Quarter Seffions he was fined 20 s. and continued in Prifon about fixteen Weeks, till the Death of *Oliver Cromwell,* upon which he was difcharged.

In *September* this Year, *Edmund Crofs,* a Grocer of *Woodbridge,* was grievoufly abufed and beaten in his own Shop, and had an Earthen-pan broken about his Head, and his Face much cut therewith, by a Prieft, whom he had reproved for his Drunkennefs and Debauchery, of which he had been notorioufly guilty. The Prieft added to his Blows many opprobrious Words, calling *Edmund, Rogue, Witch, Devil, Papift,* and whatever elfe his drunken Rage did fuggeft.

In this or the preceding Year, *John Fryer* and *James Norton,* both of *Felixton,* were imprifoned at the Suit of *Miles Gowty,* Impropriator, for Tithes, and after thirteen Weeks Imprifonment, the *former* had taken from him for the fame Tithes, two Cows and two Calves worth 9 *l.* and while in Prifon, for another Demand of 18 s. for Tithe, fuffered Diftrefs of Goods, to the Value of 4 *l.* The *latter,* for Tithes of 25 s. Value, had Goods taken away worth 3 *l.* 15 s. Not long after thefe Diftreffes, other Seizures, yet more exorbitant, were made on the fame Perfons for Tithes, the faid *John Fryer,* for a Demand of 1 *l.* 5 s. having Goods taken from him worth 14 *l.* and the faid *James Norton,* for a Claim of 3 *l.* 10 s. made for only one Year's Tithe of Land, rented but at 12 *l.* 13 s. *per Annum,* fuffered the Lofs of his Goods, to the Value of 16 *l.* About this Time alfo, *Arthur Goddard* was arrefted for Tithes, at the Suit of *Richard Rogers,* * Prieft of *Clopton,* and after he had been fix Months in Cuftody, his Profecutor obtained a Warrant from two Juftices to make Diftrefs for the fame Tithe, and took away about four Times its Value. Hard was the Cafe of *John Caufton,* imprifoned in *Ipfwich* Goal, in the coldeft Time of the Winter, three Months in an open Room, under a cruel Keeper, where, through the extreme Hardfhip he endured, he contracted a Sicknefs of which he there died. *Arnold Nunn* was alfo fent to Prifon, for Tithes, about the fame Time with *Caufton,* and detained there nine Months : And for the fame Caufe *William Tummiet* was confined in the fame Prifon, by an Attachment out of the *Exchequer.* As was *Richard White,* of *Mendlefham,* for refufing to Swear to his Anfwer to a Bill exhibited againft him, for Tithes, in that Court. There was likewife at the fame Time *John Eaftling,* a Prifoner there for Tithes.

Anthony Kettle, being cited before two Juftices, on a Complaint of *Gregory Pretty* a Prieft, for Subtraction of Tithe, the faid Juftices iffued their Warrant for Diftrefs ; and becaufe, in fome Difcourfe there, *Anthony* contradicted the Prieft, and bluntly, though truly, had told him, that *He lied,* the Juftices de-manded Sureties of him for his good Behaviour, and for refufing to give them, fent him to *Ipfwich* Goal. The Juftices expreft themfelves with much Warmth, and particularly one of them faying, *He hoped to have a new Law, whereby they fhoul curb the* Quakers ; and the other telling the faid *Anthony,* that *He fhould have Punifhment by the Bufhel.*

Thoma

---

* This Prieft came with the Officer, called *Arthur* Jefuit, and other reproachful Names feized him with his own Hands by the Collar, and had probably done him much Harm, had he not been prevented by a feafonable Reproof from one of his own Hearers.

Thomas Bircham, of *Feverton*, was imprifoned at *Blyborough* for 12 s. claimed SUFFOLK. by *John Carry*, Prieft there, for two Year's Tithe ; and *Thomas Judye*, of 1658. *Afhfield*, was kept clofe Prifoner at *Edmundfbury*, for refufing to pay Tithes.

Thomas Bond had taken from him, for Tithes, 3 *l.* 10 *s.* a Sum equal to the Yearly Rent of the Land from which it was demanded. *John Coleman* alfo was a Sufferer by Diftrefs for Tithes : And the Widow *Posford*, of *Clopton*, was fued for Tithes in the County Court of *Ipfwich*, and caft there on the Statute for treble Damages.

Imprifonments, Diftreffes, and Profecution, for Tithes.

ANNO 1659. In this Year were taken for Tithes,

		l.	*s.*	*d.*	
From *William Driver*, of *Tremlie*, for 1 *l.* 14 *s.* demanded, Goods worth	}	12	0	0	Diftreffes for Tithes.
Thomas Pinfon, of the fame, for 14 *l.* 1 *s.* demanded, Goods worth	}	57	0	0	
William Burroughs, of *Great-Finborough*, for 30 *l.* 8 *s.* 6 *d.* demanded, Goods worth	}	40	0	0	
Arthur Goddard, of *Clopton*, for 3 *l.* 10 *s.* demanded, Goods worth	}	14	0	0	
Richard White, of *Mendlefham*, for 4 *l.* demanded, Goods worth	}	15	0	0	
Anne Shipman, of *Crettingham*, for 1 *l.* 10 *s.* demanded, Goods worth	}	6	0	0	
For 55 *l.* 3 *s.* 6 *d.*	Taken	144	0	0	

Lucie Oxe Widow, her Son-in-Law *Chriftopher Sharp*, and *Lucie* his Wife, were caft into *Melton* Goal, at the Suit of *Francis Davis*, Prieft of *Clifford* ; though the Son and Daughter had no Property in the Land, out of which the Tithe was claimed, being only Servants to their Mother.

Hard Cafe.

On the 17th of the Month called *April* this Year, a remarkable Occurrence happened in the Place of publick Worfhip at *Felixftone*. One *Jofeph Scott*, a Quaker, went in before the Prieft had entred on his Office, and ftood ftill ; on Sight of him the Prieft was fmitten with fudden Fear and Faintnefs, and faid to the People, *I had thought to have done fomething at this Time, but here is one come in with a Spirit of Contradiction, fo that I find much Weaknefs upon me, and cannot :* Having fpoken this, he took his Hat, and went out. As he was going, *Jofeph Scott*, who till then had faid nothing, fpake thus, *When the Blind leads the Blind, needs muft they fall :* At which the Prieft feemed much difturbed, and told him, *His Mouth fhould be ftopt.* At the next Quarter Seffions the Prieft got him prefented, and committed to *Ipfwich* Goal, where he lay a confiderable Time.

A remarkable Occurrence.

Thomas Pinfon went into the Steeple-houfe at *Aldborough*, where he ftood ftill and faid nothing, but was forthwith pulled out by the Hair of his Head, kept Prifoner one Night, and then fent out of Town by the Magiftrates, who ordered the Ferryman to carry him over the Water.

T. Pinfon.

Robert Davis, a Conftable, having fome Prefentments to make at a Seffions in *Woodbridge*, becaufe he could not for Confcience-fake Swear to the fame, was committed to *Melton* Goal, and his Prefentments were rejected.

A Conftable imprifoned.

Obfervable was the Chriftian Courage and Intrepidity of *George Fox* the *Younger*, who, when he was preaching in a Meeting at *Dunftall*, was violently oppofed by one *John Tokely*, who in a furious Manner came toward him with a drawn Sword, but when he faw that *George* faced him without Fear, he retired, and fetcht a Gun charged, which he fired at him, and the Shot went over his Head, but *George* continued preaching undifturbed, which his Oppofer obferving, from the Force of a fudden Conviction, cried out, *Your Faith is ftrong,* and fo went away.

Chriftian Courage of G. Fox the Younger.

At another Time, the fame *George Fox* preaching in the Market-place at *Aldborough*, was put out of Town by the Bayliff, but foon returned, and had a Meeting there at a Widow's Houfe the fame Evening, whence he was taken and

His Sufferings.

SUFFOLK.
1659.

and fent to Prifon, where he was not long detained, for, four Days after we find him again preaching to the People in the Steeple-houfe at *Sowold*, after the Prieft had done : But his *Chriftian* Concern for them was ill requited by the ruder Sort, who beat him, threw him violently upon the Stones, and haled him through the Streets to the Bayliff's Houfe, who committed him to Prifon, and ordered him to be put into the inner Ward; to prevent his fpeaking to the People.

We fhall next lay before our Readers the Copy of a Prefentment exhibited at the Quarter Seffions for this County, *viz.*

" *Ipfwich, Suffolk.*

Prefentment of Timothy Grimble.

" THE Jury for his Highnefs *Richard*, Lord-Protector of the Common-
" wealth of *England*, *Scotland*, and *Ireland*, and the Dominions and
" Territories thereunto belonging, upon their Oaths do prefent, that *Timothy*
" *Grimble*, late of *Ipfwich* in the County aforefaid, Mariner, at *Ipfwich* afore-
" faid, on the 7th Day of *January* 1658, and continually after, until the Day
" of the taking this Inquifition, hath received into his Houfe, countenanced,
" harboured, and fupported diverfe *diffolute, idle, loofe, and fufpected Perfons,*
" *Difturbers of the publick Peace*, to the Jurors unknown, commonly called
" *Quakers*, of evil Converfation, doth alfo keep *Diforder, evil Rule and Govern-*
" *ment in his Houfe*, to the great Nufance of his Neighbours, and other People
" of this Commonwealth, and againft the Peace.

" John Mall,	John Douty,
" Charles Wright,	Samuel Humphry,
" Joseph Haymor,	Robert Groves,
" Richard Thurston,	John Hamont,
" Robert Stebbing,	John Gray,
" Edward Keene,	Richard Clopton,
" Edmund Darby,	William Goodale,
" Thos. Wright *jun.*	Thomas Grigg,
" John Jolley,	Richard Humphry,
" Peter Cole,	Thomas Brook."

To this Prefentment an *Anfwer* was written by fome of the *Friends* concerned, and figned by *Robert Duncon, George Whitehead*, and *Robert Graffingham :* The Subftance of which *Anfwer* is contained in the following *Abftract, viz.*

Anfwer to the the faid Pre-fentment.

" LET all fober People obferve how envious thefe Jurymen and Inquifitors
" have appeared againft *Timothy Grimble* and his Friends, *&c.*

" For, *firft*, their Prefentment being grounded and made up of falfe Accu-
" fations, grofs Lies and Slanders, the Meeting that we had at *Timothy's* Houfe
" (which was the 6th Day of the Eleventh Month 1658) was a peaceable
" Meeting for the Service of God and his Worfhip, and the Holy Truth therein
" held forth, and no Caufe thereby given for thefe Jurors, or any others, to be
" offended at fuch a Meeting, which was both according to the Law of God,
" and alfo tolerated by the Government. What Enmity and Malignity there-
" fore appears in fuch a fcandalous Prefentment, thus to defame an honeft Man
" for fuffering a peaceable Meeting, and entertaining quiet innocent People
" at his Houfe, who ought by Law to be protected, and not punifhed for the
" Exercife of their Religion, or Confcience toward God.

" 2. As for thofe called *Quakers*, whom *Timothy Grimble* received and har-
" boured in his Houfe, who, they fay, are unknown to the Jurors, fome of
" their Names are *Robert Duncon, Robert Graffingham, Jofeph Scott*, and *George*
" *Whitehead :* They are well known to be fober honeft Perfons, and alfo
" refponfible where they live.

" *Note.* What a large Confcience did appear in thefe Jurors, who could
" fwear againft Men *unknown to them*, and upon Oath prefent them fo highly
" criminal, as being no other than *diffolute, loofe, idle, lewd*, and *fufpected*

" *Perfons*

" *Perfons,* while unknown to thefe their Accufers, and Swearers againft SUFFOLK.
" them.

1659.

" 3. We afk you Jurors, wherein did we called *Quakers,* whom you have
" fworn againft, *difturb the publick Peace?* And what *evil Converfation* can
" you charge or prove againft us? If you cannot prove Matter of Fact
" charged, and by you fworn againft us, be afhamed thereof. Surely thofe
" Magiftrates, or that Court that have fuch a Prefentment as yours, ought
" not to truft your Oath to the fame, but to examine you of the particular
" Crimes or Accufations charged, you having grofly, and very unjuftly, de-
" famed *Timothy Grimble,* and his Friends called *Quakers,* for which you are
" accountable. Let the Magiftrates inquire of you, what *fufpected Perfons he*
" *hath harboured continually,* and try you from what Ground you have caft
" fuch Afperfions upon fober honeft Men? And what *Diforder, evil Rule* and
" *Government,* doth *Timothy Grimble* keep in his Houfe? What fober honeft
" Neighbour will fay, that they are annoyed or difturbed by *Diforder, evil*
" *Rule* or *Government,* kept at *Timothy Grimble's*? Produce your Proofs for
" thefe your Accufations, or elfe, like forfworn Perfons, for-ever ftop your
" Mouths, and let Shame cover your Lips, for have you herein acted either
" like *rational Men,* or *Chriftians?* Or done as you would be done by? Would
" you take it well to be prefented or indicted for entertaining your Friends, as
" you have prefented, and grofly mifreprefented *Timothy Grimble* for harbouring
" his Friends?

" 4. Many can witnefs, that the Meetings we had at *Timothy Grimble's*
" Houfe in *Ipfwich,* were peaceable and lawful: And thofe Priefts and Pro-
" feffors, who were offended at them, had done more honeftly and difcreetly,
" if they had come to our Faces in our Meetings, to have manifefted openly,
" what *Lewdnefs* or *Errors* were practifed or held forth by any of us, if they
" could, rather than go behind our Backs, to inftigate the Magiftrates againft
" us, without any juft Caufe. But thofe who have thus acted in the Dark
" againft the Innocent, their Deceit is made manifeft to their Shame; and the
" more, by grofly abufing innocent People, as the faid Jurors and their
" Abettors have done.

" 5. *To Swear at all* is a Tranfgreffion againft Chrift's Doctrine: But to
" prefent Lies and Slanders upon Oath, to caufe the Innocent to fuffer, is a
" much greater Offence, which thefe Jurors have done againft *Timothy Grimble,*
" and his Friends called *Quakers,* who are Witneffes againft all *Idlenefs, Diforder,*
" *Loofenefs, Lewdnefs,* and *evil Government,* whatfoever; though thus the
" Wicked have made Lies their Refuge, and like Men mad with Envy, have
" forged fuch Slanders againft honeft Men, as are contained in the faid Pre-
" fentment. So that we may even fay with the Prophet, *They that were mad*
" *againft us, were fworn againft us,* Pfalm cii. 8."

To the foregoing *Obfervations* we think it not improper to annex *George*
Whitehead's Letter

" *To the* Inhabitants *of* Ipfwich, *both* Teachers *and* People, *viz.*

" OH! the Pride, Highmindednefs, and Self-conceitednefs, which abounds
" in the Town of *Ipfwich*; and Oh! what a Feignednefs, Hypocrify, and
" Will-worfhip is among the Profeffors, who ignorantly worfhip an unknown
" God according to their own Wills, who have gotten Words of the Saints,
" and of the Scriptures of Truth, but the Light which led the Saints they are
" out of, and have grieved and quenched the Spirit of it, when it hath ap-
" peared in their own Confcience, to convince them of Sin and Evil; fo that
" their Sin remains in them, and the Curfe of God hath Power over them
" that live in Pride, Deceit, Superftition, and ungodly Converfation.

" There hath been a Zeal ftirring for the Lord in feveral of them formerly,
" according to what they knew, but now much Deadnefs, Coldnefs, Emptinefs,

G. White-
head's *Letter*
to the People
at Ipfwich.

" and

" and Barrennefs is over their Spirits, and Unrighteoufnefs hath the Pre-
" eminence among them. The Teachers have gotten the Saints Words to
" fpeak of, and are painted over with an empty Profeffion, and a feigned
" Humility, but inwardly they are proud, covetous, and rebellious, refifting
" the Truth, and make a Trade upon the Scriptures, *Teaching for Hire, and*
" *Divining for Money* : Such the true Prophets of God cried againft, for they
" are as *Women that few Pillows under Peoples Arm-holes, fpeaking Peace to the*
" *Wicked, where there is no Peace.* And they are *as Foxes in the Deferts, that*
" *are greedy, waiting for their Prey.* And much Wilfulnefs and Slavery is in
" the proud and covetous Priefts, and in many of the Profeffors, *who will*
" *not bring their Deeds to the Light,* neither dare they *try all Things,* as the
" Apoftle commanded, but cry out againft us called *Quakers,* behind our
" Backs, but would not be tried Face to Face, nor fuffer others to come and
" try us Face to Face, though for the Truth's Sake, feveral of us have fuffered
" among them *in Prifon.* So that many of the Teachers *incenfe the People*
" againft us, and that which we profefs, which is the TRUTH : So are they
" kept in Slavery and Ignorance. And fo you Profeffors in *Ipfwich,* Chrift
" may juftly fay to you, *I was a Stranger, and ye took me not in. I was in*
" *Prifon among you, and you vifited me not : Inafmuch as ye did it not to thefe*
" *little Ones that believe in me, who have fuffered among you, ye did it not to*
" *me.* Yet this from the Lord I declare unto you, that the Day of Vifitation,
" and the Kingdom of God, is come nigh unto you, and Wo unto them that
" ftill walk in Filthinefs, refifting and *hating the Light,* which is God's Witnefs
" in their own Confciences, which doth convince them of Sin and Evil, and
" reproves them when they commit it. Take heed how you always refift the
" Truth, fince the Lord hath warned you, left you perifh in your Iniquities,
" and your Blood lie upon your own Heads, and upon your Teachers, who
" retain the Wages of Unrighteoufnefs, and exercife Lordfhip over you,
" to keep you in Ignorance from the *true Light in your felves,* which Chrift
" hath *enlightned* you withal, which all muft come to and follow, who ever
" come to be faved from the *Wrath of God,* and from the Curfe which abideth
" upon the Children of Difobedience. Away with all your empty Profeffions,
" and let fuch as *name the Name of Chrift depart from Iniquity.* Away with
" all your proud and covetous Teachers, who preach for Hire, who make a
" Trade upon the Saints Words, which were fpoken forth freely from *the Spirit*
" *of Truth.* Away with all your Pride, gaudy Attire, and Superfluity of
" Naughtinefs ; the Lord is grieved with you becaufe of thefe Things, you
" are not come to the *modeft Apparel* outwardly, nor to the *true Adorning* in-
" wardly, which is not coftly nor gaudy Attire, but it is that of a meek and
" quiet Spirit, which is of great Price with the Lord. *How long fhall the*
" *Lord wait to be gracious to you,* and yet ye refift his Grace, which hath ap-
" peared unto you, *to teach you to deny Ungodlinefs and Worldly Lufts, and to*
" *live foberly and godly in this evil World.*

" How long fhall the Lord warn you, and yet you repent not ? How oft
" fhall he call you, *by his Light in you,* out of your Filthinefs, and yet you
" anfwer him not, nor hearken to his Voice ? How often fhall the Lord
" knock at the Door of your Hearts, and yet ye open not ? Yet know that
" his Spirit will not always ftrive with Man : But it cometh to pafs, that they
" that *will be filthy, muft be filthy ftill.* Therefore, as you love your Souls,
" take *Warning.*

" From a Friend to all that defire to know the Lord, and one who, for
" the Gofpel's Sake, hath lately fuffered fifteen Weeks, or above, in
" *Ipfwich* Prifon.

Suffolk, *the* 1ft *Day of the*
Ninth Month, 1658.

" GEORGE WHITEHEAD."

Thus

Thus inceffantly, either by Preaching or Writing, was this Servant of Chrift employed in the Exercife of the Talent he had received, for the Benefit and Inftruction even of thofe who perfecuted him, and often returned Scorning and Abufes for the *Chriftian* Labour of Love beftowed upon them.

Sufferings for Meeting.

We return to the Sufferings of fome others about the fame Time, *viz.* *Robert Duncon, Robert Mann, Bartholomew Bridges, Robert Davies,* and *William Gardener,* who going to a Meeting at *Aldborough,* on the Firft-day of the Week, had their Horfes taken from them, which for a pretended Forfeiture of 10 s. each, were fold for 20 l. and no Part of the Price returned to the Owners. Others, going to the fame Meeting on Foot, were put into the Stock-houfe or Cage. Alfo *Henry Mather* and *John Burch,* riding to the fame Meeting, had an Horfe taken from them worth 6 l. and a great Coat valued at 20 s. for a Fine of 10 s. each, for a pretended Breach of the Sabbath.

In this and the preceding Years, we find taken by Diftrefs, toward repairing the Houfes for the then National Worfhip,

		l.	s.	d.	
From	*Anthony Kettle,* of *Edwardftone,* for 1 l. 1 s. 6 d. demanded, Goods worth	7	9	0	*Diftreffes.*
	Anthony Appleby, of *Haverill,* for 1 s. 8 d. demanded, Goods worth	0	12	0	
	George Evan, of the fame, for 6 d. demanded, Goods worth	0	14	0	
	William Driver and *Thomas Pinfon,* for 1 l. 12 s. demanded, Goods worth	2	6	0	
	For 2 l. 15 s. 8 d. Taken	11	1	0	

ANNO 1660. On the 25th of the Month called *May, Thomas Cofley,* of *Badfey,* was caft into Prifon at *Melton,* for refufing to pay Tithes. In this Year alfo were taken for Tithes,

Imprifonment and Diftreffes for Tithes.

		l.	s.	d.
From	*James Norton,* for 12 l. 12 s. 6 d. demanded, Goods worth	18	0	0
	Arthur Goddard, for 6 l. 19 s. 8 d. demanded, feven Cows worth	28	0	0
	William Tudderman, for 4 l. 10 s. demanded, five Cows worth	22	0	0
	For 24 l. 2 s. 2 d. Taken	68	0	0

On the 3d of the Month called *June,* a Meeting was held in the Houfe of *William Gardener,* of *Pettiftry,* to which came a Company of armed Horfe-men, who pulled down *Jofeph Fuce* then preaching, and carried him with *William Gardener* to Juftice *Rivet,* but he, after fome Examination, inclined to difcharge them : Whereupon they, who took them, applied to another Juftice, who releafed *Fuce,* but committed *Gardener* to Prifon.

Imprifonment of William Gardener.

Toward the Conclufion of this Year we find the following Perfons in the feveral Goals of this County, who had been generally committed for refufing to take the Oath of Allegiance, being moft of them taken out of their religious Meetings, and fome from their own Houfes and lawful Employments, *viz.*

In EDMUNDSBURY Goal, thirty three, *viz.*

A Lift of Pri-foners in the feveral Goals of this County.

William Burrough a Man of eighty Years of Age, *James King, Edward Dikes, John Peach, Robert Serjeant, Robert Prick, Robert Debedge, Henry Hubbert, John King, John Middifh, Jeffery Bullock, John Grafper, Richard Waite, John Crifmas, Thomas Smith, John Partridge, Thomas Manning, Thomas Sickleprice, Edward Hindes, Samuel Dearfley, James Nunn, Roger Hawkins, William Hayle, Jofeph Riddlefden, Samuel Afton, Caleb Lambert, Robert Clark, John*

SUFFOLK.
1660.

John Woodgate, William Woodgate, Charles Woodgate, George Lamb, Joseph Atkin, and *Joseph Burrough :* Moſt of theſe dwelt at *Sudbury, Lavenham,* and Parts adjacent.

In BLYBOROUGH Goal, nine, *viz.*

Richard Townſend, Thomas Burcham, John Coleman ſen. *John Coleman* jun. *James Fulcher, Roger Cole, William Bennett, William Thurton,* and *John George :* Two of theſe, *Richard Townſend* and *John George,* were taken from their Labour, *Thomas Burcham* out of his Bed, and the other ſix from a Meeting at *Leoſtaff.*

In MELTON Goal, thirteen, *viz.*

John Birch, John Camplin, Stephen Brightwell, Godfrey Brightwell, John Fryer, Thomas Bond, John Bennett, Nicholas Bennett, John Bennett jun. *William Gardener, James Norton, Charles Bond,* and *Arthur Goddard :* All theſe were ſummoned to the Quarter Seſſions at *Woodbridge,* held the 16th and 17th of the Month called *January,* and being there, had the Oath of Allegiance tendred them : They continued in Priſon about four Months.

In ALDBURGH Goal, four, *viz.*

John Manning, Arthur Cowel, Robert Davis, and *Samuel Bridges :* Of whom the firſt three lay there about eighteen Weeks, and the other about eleven Weeks.

In IPSWICH Goal, twenty three, *viz.*

Thomas Simonds and *Henry Hall,* taken from a Meeting at *Hoxon. Robert Duncon,* apprehended as he was viſiting his Friends in *Ipſwich. William Wall, Anthony Garball,* and *Robert Pearce,* taken out of a Meeting at *Wallingſworth William Seaman, William Fiddeman, Henry Mather, John Lamb,* and *Henry Grimble,* taken from a Meeting at the ſaid *Grimble's* Houſe in *Ipſwich. John Smys, William Alexander, James Harling,* and *Thomas Gardener,* apprehended in a Meeting at *Needham. Samuel Moulſon, Timothy Cleeveland, James Tompſon, John Spicer, Mary Grimble, John Rackham,* and *Roſe Parker,* taken at a Meeting in *Ipſwich. Alice Bream* was ſent to Priſon for admitting Meetings at her Houſe.

Beſide thoſe before mentioned, *Frances Smith, Roſe Palmer,* and *Margaret Catmore,* for frequenting Meetings at *Ipſwich,* were committed cloſe Priſoners to the *Bottom* in *Aldburgh.*

More Impriſonments.

ANNO 1661. At a Seſſions at *Ipſwich,* on the 17th of the Fifth Month *George Painter* eighty ſix Years of Age, *Henry Driver, Thomas Cooke, Benjamin Reeve, Richard Sparhawke, Diana Fryer, Thomas Pinſon, John Pinſon,* and *Joſeph Scott,* were indicted for being at Meetings, and committed to *Melton* Goal ; and about the ſame Time, *William Seaman, Abraham Cole,* and *John Birch,* were ſent to Priſon for refuſing to give Sureties for their Appearance a Seſſions.

On the 29th of the Month called *Auguſt, Robert Laſt* was committed to *Ipſwich* Goal, and kept there twenty Weeks, becauſe he had ſuffered ſome Neighbours to meet at his Houſe, where a Friend, who came to viſit him, gave ſome religious Exhortation.

Commitments from the Quarter Seſſions.

At a Quarter Seſſions, held at *Beccles,* on the 13th of the Month called *January, William Bennett, William Thurton, Matthew Elmy, Elizabeth Barker Richard Townſend, John Coleman,* and *Roger Cole,* were committed to *Blyborough* Goal. And two Days after, at *Woodbridge* Seſſions, *Joſeph Scott, Thomas Cooke, Benjamin Reeve, Richard Sparhawke, Diana Fryer,* and *Henry Driver* were ordered to continue in Priſon, whither they had been committed near ſix Months before. In the ſame Month *John Wateridge, Nathanael Shriefe,* and *Edward Vineyard,* were taken out of a Meeting at *Rickengill,* and committed to *Ipſwich* Goal, where they found *Joſeph Fuce,* ſent thither ſome Time before for refuſing to take the Oath of Allegiance.

Priſoners for Tithes.

In the Month called *February* this Year, were Priſoners for refuſing to pay Tithe ; in IPSWICH Goal, *Richard White :* In BLYBOROUGH Goal, *Ralph Randall*

Randall, near eighty Years of Age : And in MELTON Goal, *Robert Man* of SUFFOLK.
Dallingoe, Abraham Cole of *Bromfwell,* and *Robert Davis.* In this Year alfo was
taken from *Robert Laft,* for Tithe of about three Acres of Meadow-Ground,
an Horfe and an Hide worth 2 *l.* 18 *s.*

ANNO 1663. *Thomas Peck* and *Thomas Dockin* were committed to *Ed-* Prifoners for
mundfbury Goal, on the 12th of the Month called *July,* for refufing to take the not Swearing,
Oath of Allegiance.

We fhall next infert the Cafe of *John Shipman* and *Thomas Virtue,* as delivered
to the King on the 5th of *November* this Year, viz.

" *For the* KING *and* Council.

" *A* fhort Relation *of the fad and cruel Ufage of two of the King's*
" *peaceable Subjects,* JOHN SHIPMAN *of* Cretingham *in the County*
" *of* Suffolk, *and* THOMAS VIRTUE *of* Clopton *in the fame County,*
" *both of them of that People who are in Scorn called* Quakers.

" T HE faid Perfons being informed againft by the Sheriff's Bayliffs, Cafe of John
" and by the Bayliffs of the Liberty, where the faid Perfons dwelt, Shipman *and*
" upon a Statute made againft *Popifh* Recufants, and for their not being at the Thomas Vir-
" publick Worfhip for eleven Months paft, at a Quarter Seffions holden at tue.
" *Woodbridge* in the faid County, *John Sicklemore* being Judge there, Judg-
" ment was paft againft them by the Juftices there, for each of them to pay
" 20 *l.* a Month for eleven Months, eleven fcore Pounds a-piece, and fince,
" the Bayliffs aforefaid have taken away Goods worth 68 *l.* 15 *s.* from *John*
" *Shipman,* and 35 *l.* worth from *Thomas Virtue,* and do threaten to take more
" from them, until they be fatisfied for the Fines of twice eleven fcore Pounds,
" although the whole Eftate of *Thomas Virtue* is not judged to be worth half
" fo much ; fo that if the King fhew not fome Kindnefs to thefe poor Men,
" the faid *Thomas Virtue,* his Wife, and fix Children, are like to be left
" deftitute : And farther, the faid Perfons were for the fame Caufe, both kept
" in Prifon ; the one of them a Year and an Half, the other a Year and a
" Quarter, before their Goods and Cattle were taken away.

" And the faid Bayliffs do threaten, that they will inform againft feveral
' others of the People aforefaid upon the fame Account.

" Therefore our Requeft to the King is, that he would take Care that the
" faid Sufferers may be relieved, and that they may not thus deeply fuffer
" for Confcience-fake, who wifh well to the King and Government."

By thus reprefenting their Cafe to the King and Council, it is probable that Effect of their
he farther Seizure of their Eftates for thofe Fines was prevented ; and the In- Application.
tention of their Profecutors totally to ruin thefe honeft Men, was difappointed. Other Impri-
In the fame Year *John Wateridge,* of *Hepworth,* was committed to Prifon fonments.
by a Writ de Excommunicato capiendo, the Effect of a Profecution in the Ecclefiaftical Court for Non-conformity to the Church. In this Year alfo at *Bury*
Affizes, *Edward Manning* was fined 40 *s.* for not putting off his Hat in Court,
and refufing to pay it, was committed to Prifon, where he lay about eight
Years.

ANNO 1664. In this Year *Henry Gofling* and *Robert Linge* were impri-
foned at *Ipfwich* for Tithes : Alfo *Robert Duncon, John Edwards,* of *Felfham,*
Blackfmith, *Jofeph Riddlefden,* of *Boxford,* Hufbandman, *Robert Rodwell,* of
Wiverftone, Carpenter, *Thomas Woods,* of *Badwell-Afh,* Linen-weaver, and *Henry*
Spark, were committed to the fame Goal by Writs de Excommunicato capiendo.

ANNO 1665. *James Palmer,* for abfenting himfelf from the National
Worfhip, was committed to Prifon ; as were alfo *James King* of *Edmundfbury,*
and *Thomas Ledeman,* by Writs de Excommunicato capiendo.

SUFFOLK.
1666.

Death of
J. Tompfon.

Prifoners for
Tithes.

A great Suf-
fering for
Tithes.

Diftrefs.

Imprifonment.

Diftreffes, &c.
for Tithes.

Fines and
Diftreffes for
Meeting.

ANNO 1666. *Edward Hall*, and *Anne* his Sifter, for not conforming to the publick Worfhip, were fent to *Edmundfbury* Goal, and continued Prifoners there upwards of twenty Months.

James Tompfon, Timothy Cleveland, and *John Tompfon*, coming to vifit their Friends in Prifon at *Ipfwich*, were taken and confined there eight Weeks, by which Confinement the faid *James Tompfon* contracted a Sicknefs, of which he died foon after his Difcharge thence.

ANNO 1667. In *November* this Year *William Beets*, for his Teftimony againft paying Tithes, was committed to *Edmundfbury* Goal, where was Prifoner alfo at the fame Time, *William Bennet.*

ANNO 1668. *John Fryer*, and *Anne* his Wife, were imprifoned at *Edmundfbury*, at the Suit of *William Coppinger* Prieft, for Tithes : This Imprifonment was to them a very great Suffering, they being taken away from feven fmall Children, dependent on their Care and Induftry.

In this Year were taken out of the Meeting-houfe at *Ipfwich*, by Diftrefs, a Table and Forms to the Value of 5 *l.* 12 *s.*

Jonathan Haddock, for being at a religious Meeting in *Chelmondifton*, was imprifoned fome Days, and had his Goods taken away by Diftrefs, to the Value of 5 *l.* 12 *s.*

ANNO 1669. *John Hill*, of *Ipfwich*, for a Demand of 3 *l.* 12 *s.* for Tithe, had his Goods taken away to the Value of 6 *l.* His Wife, affrighted and abufed by thofe who made the Diftrefs, fuddenly fell in Labour, and was delivered of a dead Child. In this Year alfo, *Edward Melfop*, taken at a Meeting in *Chelmondifton*, was not only imprifoned, but alfo had his Goods taken away to the Value of 7 *l.* 7 *s.* thus fuffering a twofold Punifhment for one pretended Offence.

ANNO 1670. In the Month called *April, John Bennet* the Elder, *John Haddock, Daniel Camplin, R. Bridges, R. David*, and *John Laurence*, taken at a Meeting at the Houfe of *John Fiddeman*, were committed to *Melton* Goal, till the Seffions at *Woodbridge* a few Days after, where they were fined 50 *s.* each. About the fame Time *Jonathan Haddock*, for being at a Meeting in *Dallinghoe*, was imprifoned four Days, and had his Goods taken away by Diftrefs to the Value of 3 *l.* 12 *s.* And for being at another Meeting a few Days after, his Horfe, worth 5 *l.* was taken from him, at a Time when he and his Wife were going a Journey.

Upon the Publication of the *Conventicle-Act* this Year, the Meetings in this County were frequently informed againft : Of the Profecutions which followed, we have fome particular Accounts, *viz.*

I. For Meetings at HAVERILL.

Profecutions
for Meetings
at Haverill.

Rigorous
Execution of
Warrants.

No fooner came the Act in Force, than *Robert Dawkins*, a Parifh-Officer of *Haverill*, and *Elias Dowty*, an Informer, appeared very active in coming to the Meetings there, which were conftantly held both on the Firft and Fourth Day of the Week, and taking the Names of the Perfons prefent, gave Information to *Gervas Elways*, a Juftice of the Peace, and he iffued his Warrants for Diftrefs fo often, that the whole Eftates of the *Quakers* there were thought too little to fatisfy them. Thofe Warrants were executed with the utmoft Rigour, the aforefaid *Dawkins* encouraging the other Informers and Officers, faying, *Come Sirs, let's do what we do quickly, for this Trade will not laft long.* When they had carried away all the Goods out of one Friend's Houfe, they alfo took the Wood out of his Yard, and when a Neighbour defired them to leave a few old Hop-poles to boil fome Milk for the Children, they refufed it. From another, for a Fine of 10 *s.* they took Cotton-Yarn worth 18 *l.* From a third the Team of Horfes out of his Plough. And when they had made Spoil of a poor Weaver's Goods, they brake his Loom in pieces with the Work in it, the only Means he had to get Bread for himfelf, his fick Wife, and a young Child. The Diftreffes, taken in a few Months Time, were of the following Values, *viz.*

From

	l.	s.	d.	
From *Robert Sharply, Anthony Appleby,* and *Daniel Gridley*	138	0	0	SUFFOLK. 1670.
John Salmon, Giles Barnadiston, and *William Reynolds*	32	5	0	
Thomas Hall, John Edwards, and *John Bird*	2	9	0	
Thomas Evans, George Evans, and *Richard Power*	89	5	0	
	261	19	0	*Amount of Diftreffes.*

After all this Spoil, they were kept out of their Meeting-houfe fix Months *Farther* together in Winter, when they met in the open Street, as conftantly as before, *Abufes.* and underwent many and grievous Abufes. At firft a Juftice of the Peace came perfonally, and commanded them to be difperfed : Afterward the Officers came from Time to Time, and endeavoured to drive them afunder by Violence, till at length, partly weary, and partly afhamed of their Actions, they employed two Watchmen with Halberts, who pufhed the Friends up and down the Streets, frequently ftriking, and fometimes threatning to kill them, adding, that the Juftices had told them, *The Law could not punifh them if they did :* But one of thefe Watchmen, being hurt by a Fall, fell fick, and feveral of the Perfons, whom he had abufed, relieved him in his Diftrefs, which *Chriftian* Charity being taken Notice of by his Fellow, he, though naturally of a rugged Temper, was fo affected therewith, that he refufed to officiate in that Poft any more, and meeting one of them whom he had evil entreated, faid to him, *I defire you to forgive me ;* adding, *The Bleffing of God is among you.* After this the Officers employed another Watchman, who was as rough as the former for fome Time, till by Degrees, the Patience and Meeknefs of the *Effects of* Sufferers over-ruled his Fiercenefs, fo that he would come and fit on the *Chriftian* Threfhold as quiet as a Lamb, all the Time of the Meeting. Thus weather'd *Patience.* they the Storm, and by a paffive Fortitude furmounted the Trials and Troubles they met with.

II. For Meetings at H O X O N. *2. For Meet-*
Taken by Diftrefs *ings at Hoxon.*

	Goods worth			
	l.	s.	d.	
From *John Amefon,* for Meetings at his Houfe	25	0	0	
John Sweat, John Gofling, John Dickinfon, and *Peter Martin*	3	2	0	
John Edwards and *Robert Bound*	22	2	6	
	50	4	6	

So officious was Juftice *Dade,* as to impofe a Fine on *John Edwards* upon a *An Officious* bare Suppofition of a Preacher's being prefent at *Hoxon,* when the Meeting was *Juftice.* wholly held in Silence : A Copy of the Warrant he iffued on that Occafion, is as follows, *viz.*

" *Suffolk* fs.

" WHEREAS *John Edwards* and his Wife, of our Town, have *Warrant* " been duly convicted before me, for unlawfully affembling at the *granted on* " Houfe of *John Amefon,* of *Hoxon* within this County, upon the 22d Day of *Suppofition of* " *May* laft, under Colour or Pretence of exercifing Religion in other Manner *a Preacher.* " than according to the Liturgy of the Church of *England,* for which a Fine " of 5 s. is impofed upon each of them, it being their firft Offence within " the late Statute *for preventing and fuppreffing feditious Conventicles.* And " forafmuch as the Preacher of the faid unlawful Affembly, his Name and " Habitation is not known unto me, I do impofe upon the faid *John Edwards* " eight Pounds in Part of the faid Preacher's Fine, which he fhould have paid, " if his Name and Habitation had been known, and he thought able to have " paid the fame ; which Sums of eight Pounds and ten Shillings, you and " every

SUFFOKL. " every of you are, in his Majefty's Name, charged and commanded to
1670.   " demand of him the faid *John Edwards*, and upon his Refufal to pay the
        " fame, to levy it by Diftrefs and Sale of his Goods and Chattels, rendring
        " to him the Overplus, and the Money fo levied, forthwith to deliver to me,
        " to be diftributed according to the Ufes in the faid late Act fet forth and
        " declared : And hereof fail you not at your Perils.   Given under my Hand
        " and Seal at *Tanington*, the 14th Day of *June* 1670.

  To the Conftables, Churchwardens, and   " DADE."
  Overfeers of the Poor of Wingfield.

3. For Meetings at Elmfutt.

III.   For Meetings at E L M S U T T.

	Goods worth		
	l.	*s.*	*d.*
Taken from *Jofeph Burroughs*, for a Meeting at his Houfe	26	0	0
Philip Smith, *Deborah Wood*, and *Margaret Baker*, for being at the fame Meeting }	1	1	0
	27	1	0

4. For Meetings at Edmundsbury.

IV.   For Meetings at E D M U N D S B U R Y.

On the 3d of the Month called *July*, *Matthew Warren*, Alderman, with
James Cobb and *Robert Sheape*, Juftices, and fome Conftables, came to an
Affembly fitting in Silence, took feveral of their Names, and turned them all
out : On the 10th of the fame Month they came again, and did the like : On
the 17th they fet a Ward at the Door of the Meeting-houfe, and kept the
Friends out, who neverthelefs met, ftanding together near the Door, whereupon
the Alderman and Juftice committed *James King*, *Edward Dikes*, *Henry
Hubbard*, *George Gibfon*, *Robert Serjeant*, and *Thomas King*, to Prifon ; he
alfo iffued Warrants of Diftrefs for the two former Meetings, by which were
taken

	Goods worth		
	l.	*s.*	*d.*
From *Thomas Tillet*, the Owner of the Houfe where they met, though he was not a *Quaker* }	44	0	0
Henry Hubbard and *James King*	13	3	8
Edward Dikes, *John Peachy*, and *Robert Serjeant* }	19	1	6
Thomas Simons, *Sufanna Butcher*, and *George Gibfon* }	3	1	0
	79	6	2

They who made the Diftrefs on *Edward Dikes*, entered his Corn-chamber,
threfht out what they thought fit, and would not let him fee it meafur'd.

Robert Yardly, for a Meeting at his Houfe in *Buxhall*, had his Goods taken
away, to the Value of 13 *l.* 10 *s.*

5. For Meetings at Herringfleet *and* Beccles.

V.   For Meetings at HERRINGFLEET and BECCLES.

	Goods worth		
	l.	*s.*	*d.*
Taken from *Martha Crofswell*, for Meetings at her Houfe	27	0	0
Margaret Shorton, of *Pakefield*	6	10	0
Matthew Thirton, of *Kirtly*	8	11	0
	42	1	0

VI. Fo

VI.   For Meetings at I P S W I C H.

	Goods worth			SUFFOLK.
	l.	*s.*	*d.*	1670.
Taken from *Jonathan Haddock*	18	2	0	
Robert Simons, Joseph Tomson, and *Thomas Melsup*	3	12	0	6. For Meetings at Ipswich.
John Lamly jun. *Timothy Cleveland,* and *Robert Rushforth*	11	10	0	
Samuel Swann, Edward Melsup, and *Robert Mann*	3	15	0	
	36	19	0	

Edward Melsup had also his Goods, worth 1 *l.* 10 *s.* taken away for refusing to bear Arms in the *Militia.*

On the 4th of *September, Robert Brightwell,* of *Ufford,* was arrested for Tithes, at the Suit of *Richard Lufkin,* Priest of that Place : He was afterward sued to an Execution, and lay in *Melton* Goal nine Years, notwithstanding the Priest, his Prosecutor, had without Law taken a Mare out of his Stable, worth 8 *l.* and had also sent his Servants, who carried away whole Loads of Corn at a Time. *Long Imprisonment for Tithes.*

Robert Huntington was also imprisoned this Year, for Tithes, in *Ipswich* Goal.

ANNO 1671. On the 23d of the Month called *June, Edward Plumsted,* of *Old-Newton,* was committed to *Ipswich* Goal by an *Exchequer* Process, for Tithes, and was detained there several Years.

ANNO 1672. In this Year *Edward Hall, Anne Hall, Edward Manring, John Bragg, John Sparke, James Lilly* and *Thomas King,* were discharged out of Prison, in this County, by the King's Letters Patent for releasing such of this People as were then confined at the King's Suit. *Release of Prisoners.*

ANNO 1673. *Thomas Ellis,* of *Glensford,* for suffering a religious Assembly at his House, had his Goods taken away, which, though really worth 16 *l.* 5 *s.* were sold for no more than 40 *s.* *Distress for Meeting.*

John Hill, of *Ipswich,* was committed to the County Goal, by a *Significavit* from the Ecclesiastical Court, on a Prosecution for Tithes, at the Suit of one *Kaebeck,* a Priest in *Margaret's* Parish in *Ipswich.* Also *Samuel Freeman* was imprisoned by a Writ *de Excommunicato capiendo,* at the Suit of *William Maxey,* Priest. In this Year also, *Edward Melsup* was committed to the County Goal at *Ipswich,* for refusing to pay toward the Repairs of the Steeple-house there. *Imprisonments for Tithes.*

	l.	*s.*	*d.*	
ANNO 1674. *Leonard Pearson,* of *Heavingham,* for permitting a Meeting at his House, suffered Distress of five Cows worth	22	0	0	*Distresses.*
Also *John Harvey* and *Tobias Abbey,* for being at the same Meeting, had Goods taken away, to the Value of	0	17	0	
	22	17	0	

John Downham, of *Assington,* was imprisoned in *Bury* Goal by a Writ *de Excommunicato capiendo,* at the Prosecution of one *Garraway,* Priest of *Westerton,* for Tithes. *Imprisonment on a Writ de Excom. Cap.*

	l.	*s.*	*d.*	
ANNO 1675. Taken by Distress for religious Meetings, From *Robert Sharp,* of *Haverill,* Grocery Wares worth	15	0	0	*Distresses for Meetings.*
George Evans, working Tools, and other Goods, worth	4	0	0	
Daniel Catlin, Wood, Weavers Tools, and Utensils, worth	2	0	0	
	Car over	21	0	0

		l.	s.	d.
	Brought over	21	0	0
From *Ferdinando Salmon*, Brafs and Pewter worth		8	12	0
Mary Fifh Widow, a Barrel with Beer, and other Things, worth	}	0	6	0
Daniel Gridley, Fuftians worth		27	0	0
		56	18	0

SUFFOLK.
1675.

Excommunication.

On the 17th of the Month called *June*, *George Glanfield* was arrefted upon a *Significavit* of Excommunication for not paying Tithes, and committed to Prifon. Being there, he was ferved with a Seffions Procefs for not going to the publick Worfhip.

Grievous Profecutions for Tithes.

Thomas Kendall was fued in an Action of 67 *l.* for two Years Tithe of Land not half that Yearly Rent, at the Suit of *William Batty*, Prieft of *Hitcham*, and committed to Prifon, where he lay fixteen Months, and then being in a weak State of Health, was hurried in one Day above fixty Miles to *London*: He was, by reafon of his Weaknefs, carried to *Weftminfter-hall* in a Chair, and from thence committed to the *Fleet*. His Profecutor was heard to fay, that *All the Stock on this poor Man's Ground, and all the Goods in his Houfe, were no more than fufficient to fatisfy him.* He at the fame Time profecuted the poor Man's Wife and Daughter at the Quarter Seffions, for abfenting themfelves from the National Worfhip, employing Bayliffs to take them up, and threatning their Ruin.

Profecutions for Steeple-houfe Rates.

We find in this Year *Edward Hindes*, of *Sudbury*, committed to Prifon for refufing to pay 2 *s.* 6 *d.* toward the Steeple-houfe Rate: And for the like Caufe, *George Evans*, *Robert Sharp*, *Daniel Catlin*, and *Daniel Gridley*, all of *Haverill*, were committed to *Bury* Goal. One of the Profecutors of thefe laft four, was *Robert Darkin*, a Woolendraper, who, when *Daniel Gridley*'s Wife reproved him for his Cruelty in promoting Informations againft her Hufband, and fending him to Prifon, telling him, that *Such Actions might provoke God againft him*, he called her *Bitch*, and *Whore*, and profanely faid, *What do you tell me of God?* He alfo beat her twice down to the Ground, caufing her Leg and Arm to bleed, and faid, *He would leave the* Quakers *there not worth a Groat.*

Cruel Ufage of Prifoners.

On the 29th of the Month called *January* this Year, *William Falkner* and *John Manning* were committed to Prifon on Writs *de Excommunicato capiendo*, for Abfence from their Parifh-Church: The Keeper of the Goal, *Thomas Watfon*, was very cruel to them, and kept them twenty three Weeks together in a Place called the *Bottom*, among Felons, without fuffering them to have either Chair or Stool, or fo much as a Stone, to fit on.

Death of G. Grainger.

In the fame Year *George Deane*, of *Amerton*, was taken from his Work by an Apparitor and a Baylift, on a *Significavit* of Excommunication for not going to the publick Worfhip, and by them carried to *Ipfwich* Goal. As they were going thither they met *Giles Grainger*, againft whom they had alfo a like *Significavit* for the fame Caufe, and took him alfo to the fame Prifon. Being there, they were alfo ferved with a Seffions Procefs. The Goaler lodged them on a Bed where a Perfon had lately lain fick of the *Small-Pox*, by Means whereof *Giles Grainger* took that Diftemper, and died of it: His Wife coming to vifit him in his Sicknefs, was detained by a Seffions Procefs for the fame Caufe as her Hufband. *Giles* was a poor Man, who rented a fmall Farm of about 16 *l.* per *Annum*, himfelf and Wife being all his Family, except a Child of three Years old, which fhe had left at Home. The forrowful Circumftances of this poor Woman were fo far from being commiferated by the Prieft of the Parifh where fhe had lived, that his Agents foon after took from her Corn to the Value of 4 *l.* 10 *s.* being twice as much as the real Value of the Tithe could amount to. In this Year alfo, *Samuel Freeman* the Elder, of *Shotley*, and *Elizabeth Stotte*, were imprifoned on Proceffes at Seffions, for Abfence from the National Worfhip.

Oppreffion of a poor Widow.

William

William Scarce, of *Wortham,* was prosecuted in the Ecclesiastical Court on a SUFFOLK. bare Presumption of his not being legally married. He was excommunicated 1675. and committed to Prison, although indeed he had beeen married, before he was called a *Quaker,* after the accustomed Rites of the Church of *England.*

ANNO 1676. *William Greenwood,* of *Brisit,* had taken from him for Tithes, by a Warrant from the Manour Court, three Cows and an Heifer worth 10 *l.* 10 *s.*

ANNO 1677. On the 16th of *October, John Shipman,* of *Crettingham,* was imprisoned for Tithes of Herbage, at the Suit of *Stephen Trappit,* Priest : And in this Year also, *Edmund Hankins,* of *Boxford,* was sent to Prison for Tithes, by a Writ *de Excommunicato capiendo,* at the Suit of one *Bromhall,* Priest of *Polsted.*

Taken at several Times this Year for Meetings, by Warrants from *Jeffery Burwell* and *Thomas Bright,* Justices,

		l.	*s.*	*d.*
From *John Hayward,* of *Bayton,* Goods worth		25	0	0
Thomas Lucas, of *Packenham,* Goods worth		0	15	0
Thomas Balbrook, of *Woolpit,* two Cows worth		7	0	0
Thomas Judy, of *Wethersden,* whose Dwelling-house the Spoilers broke open, two Cows, a Bed, *&c.* worth		13	0	0
Thomas Woods, of the same, two Cows worth		6	0	0
		51	15	0

From *Edmund Bally* they took a Mare, two Swine, and other Things, worth 9 *l.* 10 *s.* which Mare was the Property of another Person, and the Owner of her was advised by Council, to take Witness with him and demand his Mare, and if they refused to deliver her, he might take her where he could find her. He did so, and finding her in a Pasture where the Constable and Informer had put her, took her Home. Whereupon Justice *Burwell* issued his Warrant to apprehend the Owner of the Mare, and threatned to send him to Goal for Felony in taking his own, and so terrified the poor Man, that he got from him 20 *s.* in Hand, and obliged him to find a Bondsman for Payment of 5 *l.* more ; for which the Justice arrested the Surety, and made it cost them ?9 *l.*

The Constables also broke open the House of *Alexander Cooke,* cutting his Door in pieces. This was done by the Constables, at the Instigation of one *Thomas Bally,* an Informer, who, though as to his Person he was a very Cripple, took very much upon him, and acted with great Insolence ; for coming one Day to a Meeting, he ordered a Guard to be set at the Door, and directed his Associates to bring the Stocks thither, and caused *Anthony Hayward* to be set into them : Being asked, *By what Authority he did so ?* He answered, *I am Warrant, I am Constable, I am Justice myself.*

ANNO 1678. In this Year was a violent Prosecution of this People for their Meetings held at *Woodbridge,* on such of them as dwelt there and at other adjacent Places, a special Warrant being granted by the Justices to the Constables for that Purpose, of which the following is a Copy, *viz.*

" *Suffolk* ss.

" WHEREAS Complaint has been made unto his Majesty's Justices
" of the Peace for the said County, by the Inhabitants of your Town,
" against certain seditious Persons, who in Defiance and Opposition to his
" Majesty's Laws made for the Peace and Welfare of the Nation, and against
" special Warning given them to the Contrary (in regard of this more than
" ordinary suspicious Time of Danger from such *Jesuitical* Male-contents, as
" may hereby take Advantage to creep and farther seduce them) do notwith-
" standing

SUFFOLK.
1678.

" ftanding, under Colour or Pretence of the Exercife of Religion, in other
" Manner than according to the Liturgy and Practice of the Church of *Eng-*
" *land*, contrary to the late Act in this Cafe provided, and againft the Peace
" of our Soveraign Lord the King of *England*, meet, and of late in great
" Numbers, from feveral Parts of the Kingdom, to the greater Sufpicion
" and Terror of his Majefty's liege People, at a fpacious Meeting-houfe nigh
" the Church in your Town, lately built and erected by them for that Purpofe,
" where they may, at fuch Meetings or Conventicles and unlawful Affemblies,
" contrive Infurrections, or other evil and dangerous Practices againft the
" Church and State, as late Experience hath fhewed. Thefe are therefore,
" in his Majefty's Name, ftrictly to charge and command you, and every of
" you, that you repair to the faid new Meeting-houfe, or other Houfe or Place
" in your faid Town where they fhall at any Time hereafter, during your
" Office, fo affemble or attempt to meet, five Perfons or more, of the Age
" of fixteen Years or upwards, Subjects of this Realm, over and befides
" thofe of the fame Houfhold, where there is a Family inhabiting at fuch
" Times of their Meeting, as you fhall by diligent Enquiry find out, for
" the preventing, fuppreffing, and difperfing fuch feditious Conventicles, by
" charging and commanding them, in the King's Majefty's Name, peaceably
" to difperfe and depart forthwith to their feveral Homes and Abode, and
" not break his Majefty's Peace by meeting in fuch an unlawful Manner ;
" and if any of them, after fuch lawful Charge and Warning given, fhall
" refufe or neglect to obey the fame, and not immediately difperfe and
" depart from thence, you are hereby required to take what particular and
" fpecial Notice you can of all fuch Perfons, their Names and Sir-names,
" and Places of refpective Abodes, and what they do at fuch Meetings contrary
" to his Majefty's Laws, and to give Account thereof to one of his Majefty's
" next Juftices of the Peace for the County aforefaid, before whom you are
" alfo to bring as many of them as you can take, for the more effectual pro-
" ceeding againft them according to Law : And in cafe Entrance be denied
" you, or any Oppofition offered, that then you break open and enter the
" faid Houfe to the Purpofe aforefaid, and call in fuch farther Aid and
" Affiftance as you fhall find neceffary for the fuppreffing and difperfing of
" them, and better Prefervation of his Majefty's Peace herein : And hereof
" fail not. Given under our Hands and Seals this 18th Day of *December* 1678.

To the Conftables of Woodbridge,
and to every of them, for the
Execution hereof.

" J. BARKER,
" R. BROOK,
" NICH^s. BACON,
" THO. BACON,
" JOHN BRAME."

Profecutions
in Confequence
of that War-
rant.

In Confequence of this Warrant the Conftables foon began to act, for on
the 22d of the fame Month, they kept the Friends by Force out of their
Meeting-houfe, and being met in the Street, Juftice *Bacon* came and committed
John Bennett, Richard Woods, John Laurence, Edward Rigges, Benjamin Free-
man, Thomas Fox, Matthew Skinner, Jofeph Fuller, Thomas Virtue, William Page,
and *Robert Tompfon*, to *Melton* Goal, where the faid *Robert Tompfon* died a
Prifoner foon after. For other fucceeding Meetings, Warrants for Diftreffes
were iffued, by which many deeply fuffered. *John Bennett*, of *Woodbridge*,
being fined 9*l.* 15 *s.* had his Goods feized worth 10 *l.* 12 *s.* which being under-
fold, fell fhort of the Fine, wherefore Juftice *Batty* fined the Conftables for
Neglect of Duty, becaufe they did not break open the Man's Dwelling-houfe
and take more. At another Time the Juftices, *Batty* and *Bacon*, came in
Perfon, and ordered the fame Man's Doors to be broke open, and his Goods
taken away worth 40 *l.* and at a third Time, Juftice *Bacon* himfelf got in at a
Window,

Window, and ordered the Inside Lock of the Door to be taken off, and Goods to be seized worth 16*l.*

		l.	*s.*	*d.*
From	*Joseph Fuller*, of *Dillings*, they took an Hayſtack and an Horſe worth	12	0	0
	John Smith, of *Haſketon*, a Feather-bed, two Bolſters, and a Cover, worth	3	10	0
	Robert Collington, of *Caſegrove*, a Mare worth	5	0	0
	Thomas Mann, of *Grandeſburgh*, Hay and Wood worth	11	0	0
	John Laurence, of *Boulge*, Hay, Plough, Harrows, &c. worth	5	10	0
	Peter Croſs, of *Woodbridge*, ſeventy eight Ells of Linen, &c. worth	9	14	0
	Richard Wood, of the ſame, Lead and other Things worth	3	0	0
	William Bedford, of *Woodbridge*, ſeventy five Yards of Linen worth	2	9	0
	Jonathan Seaman, ſix Quarters of Wheat, and Bedding, worth	17	0	0
	Clement Carter, Goods worth	2	10	0
	Thomas Lind, of *Melton*, Hay and Steel worth	3	10	0
	William Skinner, of *Dallingo*, Hay worth	2	10	0
	William Pearts, of *Woodbridge*, Deals and Forms worth	5	0	0
	Edward Rigges, of the ſame, ſix Quarters of Wheat worth	13	0	0
	Nathanael Keeble, of *Tunſtall*, two Horſes, two Mares, and a Cart, worth	19	0	0
	Robert Davie, of the ſame, two Coats worth	1	10	0
	Thomas King, of *Ufford*, Goods worth	1	7	0
		117	10	0

In this Year *Robert Prick*, of *Bury*, was a Priſoner for refuſing to pay toward repairing the Steeple-houſe, and for *Eaſter*-Offerings, having been then confined fourteen Months: And for the like Cauſes *Benjamin Reeve*, of *Debenham*, was kept cloſe Priſoner in *Ipſwich* Goal: Alſo *George Lea*, of *How*, was committed to Priſon for Tithes, at the Suit of *Robert Manton*, of *Letheringham*, Impropriator: Likewiſe *George Driver*, of *Clopton*, was caſt into Priſon by a *Significavit* out of the Eccleſiaſtical Court, at the Suit of the Wardens, for not going to the National Worſhip: As was alſo *James Fiddeman*, of *Ipſwich*: And in the ſame Year *Martha Glanfield*, of *Hackſtead*, Widow, on a Writ *de Excommunicato capiendo*.

Imprisonments for several Causes.

Theſe were alſo proſecuted, and Seizure was made on their Effects, by the Statutes againſt *Popiſh* Recuſants, *viz.*

Prosecutions as Popiſh Recusants.

	l.	*s.*	*d.*
Stephen Boldo and *John Page*, to the Value of	3	10	0
Thomas Judy, of *Aſhfield*	12	0	0
Thomas Woods, of *Wetherden*	5	0	0
	20	10	0

ANNO 1679. For their Conſtancy in publickly aſſembling to worſhip God, Goods were taken by Diſtreſs of the following Values, *viz.*

	l.	*s.*	*d.*
From *Robert Johnſon* of *Ufford*, and *William Page* of *Debbidge*	2	2	0
Godfrey Brightwell of *Bredfield*, and *Samuel Tonel* of the ſame	1	4	0
Car. over	3	6	0

Diſtreſſes for Meetings.

		l.	*s.*	*d.*
Brought over		3	6	0
From *Susanna Partridge*, Harrows and other Utensils of Husbandry		0	15	0
Francis Knock of *Shotsham*, and *George Stuard* of *Sutton*		1	0	0
John Shotter, *Thomas Brown*, and *William Sadsby*, all of *Wickham Market*		1	14	6
Daniel Churchman of *Petistry*, *Thomas Virtue* of *Debbidge*, and *John Bally* of *Bayton*		4	16	0
Thomas Lucas, *John Ransom*, and the Widow *Adkins*		5	15	0
George Gibson of *Bury*		4	10	0
The said *John Bally* and *Thomas Lucas*, for visiting a poor Widow in her Sickness, were informed against as holding a Conventicle, fined, and had their Goods taken away, worth		8	10	0
		30	6	6

Imprisonment of W. Bennett.

ANNO 1683. On the 12th of the Month called *August*, the Parochial Officers of *Woodbridge*, excited thereto by *Edward Brume*, Priest of that Place, came to the Meeting there, and two of them, *John Firman*, Churchwarden, and *Robert Chapman*, Constable, violently seized *William Bennett*, being on his Knees at Prayer, and haled him and several others before *Edmund Jenny*, Justice, who committed them to *Melton* Goal, where *William Bennett* was close confined till Sessions, when he was indicted for being at a Riotous Assembly : He used many Arguments to shew that the religious Meetings he frequented were peaceable, and purely to worship God, and pleaded *Not Guilty* to the Indictment : He was then required to give Bail for his *Appearance at another Sessions, and to be of the good Behaviour* ; which refusing to do, he was recommitted till another Sessions, and brought with others upon his Trial before

His Trial.

Christopher Melton, Chairman : He pleaded his Cause with so much Force of

The Jury's Verdict rejected and alter'd.

Reason, that the Jury brought in their Verdict *Not Guilty*. At which the Chairman being displeased, persuaded them to return and alter their Verdict : upon which they brought them in *Guilty of an unlawful Assembly* : The Chairman thereupon ordered *William*, who was a sickly Man, to be carried to *Ipswich* the

Hardships occasioning his Death.

same Day in order to be fined, it being in the sharpest Time of that Winter, so remarkable for Extremity of Cold : In going thither he was very wet, it snowing hard all the Way ; and being come thither late, and many other Prisoners with him, for want of Beds, he was obliged to sit up all Night in that wet cold Condition, which so much weakned him, that he never got over it. He was called at the Sessions there, fined 20*l.* and sent back to Prison ; where he remained close confined till another Sessions at *Ipswich*, when he was called into Court, and nothing said of the Fine ; but the Clerk of the Court told him, *they had a particular Order from the King to deal with him*, and so tendred him the Oath of Allegiance, and for refusing it remanded him to Prison, where he grew weaker and weaker, till he died on the 23d of the Month

His Death and Character.

called *June* in the next Year. He laid down his Life about the fiftieth Year of his Age, being *an innocent and faithful Man, of good Report among his Neighbours, and left a sweet Savour behind him.*

Imprisonments for Meeting.

On the 18th of *September*, *Jonathan Haddock*, *John Spurling*, *Joseph Clarke*, *Thomas Simons*, *William Rowland*, and *Thomas Melsup*, having been taken at a religious Meeting, were, by Order of Sessions, committed to *Ipswich* Goal : As were for the same Cause, on the 6th of the Month called *January*, *Esther Rowland*, *Mary Rose*, *Mary Grimble*, and *Sarah Clark* : And on the 28th of the same Month, *Edward Melsup*, *Alice Melsup*, *Sarah Church*, *Mary Cock*, *Samuel Swann*, and *Anne Goddard*.

About

SUFFOLK.
1683.

About the fame Time *Thomas Fowler, George Cole,* and *William Pitchers,* were imprisoned in the County Goal for Absence from the National Worship. For Fines for being at *Woodbridge* Meeting, was taken

		l.	*s.*	*d.*
From	*Peter Smith,* of *Melton,* an Horse worth	1	15	0
	Nathanael Keeble, a Cow worth	1	15	0
	Matthew Skinner, Goods worth	2	18	0
		6	8	0

ANNO 1684. In the Month called *April, William Swaites* and *Joshua Bangs* were Prisoners in this County for Tithes: In the next Month *Francis Lemon* was a Prisoner at *Ipswich* for Tithe, having continued in that State above four Years: Also *Samuel Freeman, William Fiddeman,* and *George Deane,* who had been there confined, on Writs *de Excommunicato capiendo,* about six Years.

Prisoners for Tithes.

At the Sessions, held at *Edmundsbury* on the 14th of the Month called *April, Samuel Cooper, James Greenwood, William Greenwood, Henry Parker, Sarah,* Wife of *John Bennett, Jane Woods, Hannah Woods, John Boreham, Anne Sewel, Henry Collins, Daniel Groom, Benjamin Dowman,* and *Edward Hawkins,* Prisoners, who had been committed without Bail or Mainprize for refusing the Oath of Allegiance, were brought into Court, and most of them refusing to plead to an Indictment drawn up against them, one of the Justices, named *Hull,* urged the Bench to pass Sentence of *Premunire* upon them, but the other Justices, being more moderate, gave them farther Time till the next Sessions, yet continued them in Prison, where the Goaler kept them close confined, having been threatned by Justice *Hull* for letting some of them have a little Liberty: Whereupon they drew up the following Petition

Proceedings at Sessions.

" *To the* K I N G,

" *The* Humble Petition *of eighteen Persons, commonly called* QUAKERS, " *Prisoners in* Bury *Goal in* Suffolk,

" S H E W E T H,

" T H A T we the aforesaid Prisoners were first committed to this Prison " by Justice *Hull,* near eight Months ago, for peaceably meeting to- " gether to worship God according to our Persuasions; and at Quarter " Sessions following he caused all to be Indicted upon the Act of 13 and 14 " *Car.* 2. and moreover at the same Sessions, caused the Oath of Allegiance to " be tendred to thirteen of us, and at Sessions following preferred Indictments " thereupon with a second Tender of the Oath, pursuing hard to have the " Sentence of *Premunire* past upon us, only because for Conscience-fake we " cannot Swear, and not for any Disaffection to the King and Government, " and caused other five of the said eighteen of us to be indicted for two " Months Absence from the Church, and detained Prisoners thereupon, tending " to the Ruin of us, our Wives, and Families; which we believe is not the " Desire of the King, of whose Favour and Clemency we have had better Expe- " rience, nor of our Neighbouring Magistrates in this County, who have seen our " peaceable Lives and Conversations among them, but of the aforesaid *Joseph* " *Hull,* who hath caused Men and their Wives to be shut up together in Pri- " son, Parents and Masters from their Children and Servants, Husbands from " their Wives, tender Children and Families, most of us poor and in a mean " Capacity, some who might of their honest Labour have provided for them- " selves and Families, are already reduced to Want by Imprisonment.

Petition to the King.

" We therefore the said Petitioners do humbly intreat, that the King will " be pleased to grant us our Liberty to take Care to follow our honest " Vocations, before we and our Families are utterly ruined.

" *And we the Petitioners, as in Duty bound,* &c."

On

On the 19th of the Month called *May*, *William Stiles*, *Richard Ellgood*, *John Brooks*, *Edward Lea*, *Thomas Bayley*, *John Edwards*, *Henry Clow*, and *Elizabeth* his Wife, *John Elsdean*, and *John Browes*, were Prisoners in the County Goal at *Ipswich*, upon Processes for not going to Church : Also *Peter Cross*, *Thomas Mann*, *Samuel Leggett*, *William Peart*, *Thomas King*, *Richard Burton*, *William Page*, *Clement Carter*, *Robert Johnson*, *Samuel Kimble*, and *John Laurence*, were confined in the same Prison for going to Meetings, and refusing to Swear.

On the 25th of the same Month, *Edmund Jenny*, a Justice of the Peace, attended with the Constables of *Woodbridge*, came to the Meeting there, and took from thence *Robert Brightwell*, *John Shooter*, and *Nathanael Keeble*, and committed them to *Melton* Goal.

At the forementioned Sessions, held at *Edmundsbury* on the 10th of the Month called *April*, *Joseph Riddlesdale*, *Joseph Chisnall*, *John Bennett*, and *Ambrose Sewel*, Prisoners for Absence from the National Worship, were indicted, and refusing to plead, were continued in Prison. And at the same Sessions *Samuel Folks* was fined 40*l.* for two Months Absence from Church, and ordered to remain in Prison till Payment. He was shortly after returned into the *Exchequer* for this and other Fines on the like Account, amounting in all to 680*l.* and Process was issued out of that Court for the Sheriff to levy the same: For the same Causes also, *Henry Parker*, and his Wife, *John Folkes*, *Elizabeth Hives*, and *Anne Laws*, were continued under Confinement.

At the Affizes, which began at *Edmundsbury* on the 10th of the Month called *July*, the same eighteen Prisoners who had petitioned the King, as above related, presented their Case to the Judge, *viz.*

'' *The* C A S E *of diverse Persons called* QUAKERS, *Prisoners in* Bury
'' *Goal*, *humbly presented to the* Christian *Consideration of Judge*
'' MONTAGUE, *the 12th of the Fifth Month* 1684.

'' HERE is now in this Prison eighteen of us, who were committed
'' near ten Months ago, for being peaceably met together to worship
'' God according to our Persuasions, and indicted for the same upon the Statute
'' of 13 and 14 of this King, and since that, the Oath of Allegiance was
'' tendred to thirteen of us, twelve whereof were indicted upon *Premunire*, and
'' the rest of us indicted for two Months Absence, *&c.* one whereof fined 40*l.*
'' and to lie in Prison till Payment ; the others continued upon the said In-
'' dictments, which we need not enlarge upon, it plainly appearing by the
'' Calendar, being also not unknown to the Magistrates in this Part of the
'' County, whose Moderation we do acknowledge, since we have appeared
'' before them, to be such, as that, we believe, they did not desire our utter
'' Ruin. And we desire of God, who is Love, and from whom all Good
'' comes, still to incline the Hearts, and augment the Pity and Compassion of
'' those in Authority towards us ; for indeed our Condition is very sad and
'' lamentable, Man and Wife shut up together in Prison, all taken from Oc-
'' casions and Employments ; Parents and Masters from their Wives, Children,
'' and Families, some whereof have been great Sufferers formerly.

'' And this we can say, and that truly, that several aged People among us
'' are already exposed to Ruin, as to the Things of this World, by this their
'' long and close Imprisonment, who before of themselves did, with God's
'' Blessing, and their honest Endeavours, get a comfortable Livelihood in their
'' several Employments, and might have done so still : Others there are, if
'' still continued, like to be dispossest of House and Home, and what they
'' have seized upon by the Land-Owners, the Farms going to Ruin, Loss and
'' Spoil, for want of the Farmers ; several Instances we could give, which
'' would be too tedious now to mention.

'' Before last Sessions some few of our Friends, upon urgent Occasions,
'' obtained a little Liberty to go to their own Homes, as in particular one who

'' was

" was Overfeer of the Parifh where he lived : Another, whofe Wife died, &c.
" However, Juftice *Hull*, as is fuppofed, receiving Intelligence that fome
" Liberty was given, which indeed was but to a few, took Occafion fo to
" threaten the Goaler, that fince the laft Seffions not one Perfon of us,
" how urgent foever Occafions were, could get Leave to go to our own
" Homes ; yet Word was brought to one Man, that his Wife lay weak, like
" to die, and defired to fee him, which could not be obtained, fo clofe hath
" our Confinement been fince laft Seffions.

" What Caufe have we ever given to be thus hardly dealt withal ? God (we
" befeech him) clear our Innocency in this Matter ! Hath not our Converfation
" been peaceable towards the Government and our Neighbours ? And God,
" who knows the Secrets of all Hearts, knows that we have no other
" Intent than to live peaceably under the Government, and that we do not
" refufe to take the faid Oath out of Wilfulnefs, Stubbornnefs, and Contempt,
" but only for Confcience-fake, in Obedience to the Command of Chrift.

" Having thus ftated our Cafe truly as it is, we intreat thee to yield us
" fome Relief from thefe our hard Bonds and Imprifonments, that we
" and our Families may not be wholly expofed to Ruin."

A few Days before the faid Affizes, *Thomas Kemp*, *Jonathan Crifmas*, and
Thomas Clark, all of *Sudbury*, were fetcht out of their own Houfes by the
Conftables of the Town, by Warrant from *Jofeph Hull*, *Thomas Waldegrave*,
and *John Cordwell*, Juftices, then fitting at the Sign of the *Crown* in *Sudbury*,
who tendred them the Oath of Allegiance, and for refufing to Swear, committed them to Prifon ; where *Thomas Kemp* died on the 26th of the Month
called *March* following.

The following Account is extracted from a Letter writ by *Jofhua Bangs*,
a Prifoner at *Edmundfbury* for Tithes, *viz.*

" A Few Days before the Affizes at *Edmundfbury*, which began the 10th
" of the Fifth Month 1684, *Roger Thompfon*, employed by *James
" Englifh*, Bayliff of *Lackford* Hundred, and another Perfon with him, took
" two who were called *Quakers*, at *Mildenhall*, upon an Affize Procefs. One
" of the two they took with his Horfe and Cart, near a Mile from his then
" Refidence, who was without his Hat, being alfo then in Apparel about his
" Occafions ; yet the faid *Roger Thompfon* would not permit him to go Home,
" and get his Hat and Clothes, before he went to Prifon, nor give him fo
" much Time as to unyoke his Horfes, but forced him away, leaving the faid
" Horfes in a Cart in the Yard, where they, after the Prifoner was gone,
" forced into a Garden-place, and deftroyed Beans, and what grew there, be-
" fides what they could eat, to the Damage of the Owner. The other they
" took away from his Grafs-mowing, not fo much as fuffering him to call at
" his own Houfe, notwithftanding it fell in Courfe for him to go not far from
" thence in his Way toward Prifon. *Note* alfo, that thofe two Perfons who
" were thus pofted from their Employments, took Occafion to alight off their
" Horfes at a certain Place where the Bayliffs call'd to take another upon
" Affize Procefs, but becaufe the faid two Prifoners made not fo much Hafte
" on Horfeback again as the Bayliffs would have them, they got a Line about
" one, and dragg'd him upon the Ground feveral Rods : Nor did the other
" Perfon efcape the Rage and Cruelty of *Roger Thompfon*, who ftruck him,
" and farther faid, *If he kill'd him, he fhould not be hang'd for him, becaufe he
" was an excommunicated Perfon.* So they were had to Prifon that Night,
" about eleven Miles from the Place where they were taken to *Bury* Prifon,
" to which they were committed.

" But when thefe two Perfons from *Mildenhall* aforefaid, with two others
" which were brought upon Affize Procefs from *Ipfwich* County Goal, namely,
" *John Brews* and *William Greenwood*, came before *William Montague*, who

SUFFOLK.
1684.

" that Affize fat Judge at the Crown Bar ; he difcharged them all of their
" Imprifonment, faying, *Their Goods fhould be diftrained for their Fines,* which
" were 3 s. each Perfon for three Weeks Abfence, &c."

Death of J. Chifnall.

On the 24th of the Month called *July, Jofeph Chifnall,* Prifoner as aforefaid,
for Abfence from the National Worfhip, died in *Bury* Goal, where he laid
down his Head in Peace, calling upon the Lord a little before his Departure.

Profecution of the Aged and of the Blind.

About this Time *Mary Cleveland, Anne Goddard, Jane Newham, Mary Cocke,*
and *Mary Grimble,* were taken at a Meeting in *Ipfwich* by Conftables and an
Informer, who carried them before *John Burrough,* Bayliff of the Town, and
he committed them all to Prifon, though the very Sight of them might have
been a reafonable Motive to Compaffion, for the faid *Mary Grimble* and *Anne
Goddard* were either of them near eighty Years of Age, and the faid *Mary
Cleveland* was of like Age, and quite blind, fo that fhe was led between two
Men to the Bayliff's Houfe. Certainly this Magiftrate was over officious in
this Cafe, for he could not juftly apprehend any real Danger to the Government from an Affembly of fuch Perfons.

Proceedings at Edmunds-bury Seffions.

At *Edmundfbury* Seffions in this Month, Juftice *Hull* again urged the Court
to pafs Sentence of *Premunire* upon the *Quakers* who had appeared at the
former Seffions, but the other Juftices refufed, and ordered the Clerk to draw
up their Cafe in order to be laid before the King and Council, and fo protracted
the paffing Sentence till another Seffions.

Commitment on Sufpicion.

On the 5th of *September, Edmund Jenney,* Juftice, came again to the Meeting-houfe at *Woodbridge,* after the Meeting was concluded : But the Juftice
obferving *Jonathan Seaman* walking in the Lane from the Meeting-houfe, fent
him to *Melton* Goal, on a Prefumption of his having been at the faid Meeting.

Sentence of Premunire.

At the Quarter Seffions on the 13th of *October,* the aforefaid Juftice *Hull,*
being Chairman, paffed Sentence of *Premunire* upon *Samuel Cooper, James
Greenwood, Henry Packer, Jane Wood, Hannah Wood, Anne Sewel, Henry
Collins, Daniel Groom,* and *Benjamin Dowman :* Under which hard Sentence
they were remanded to Prifon.

On the 19th of *November,* the following Petition was prefented to the King
at *Newmarket* by *Anne Groom,* viz.

" *To the* KING,

" *The* Humble Petition *of* SUSANNA COOPER *and* ANNE GROOM,
" *of* Suffolk.

" SHEWETH,

Sufan Coo-per's & Anne Groom's Pe-tition to the King.

" THAT we have lately prefented a *Petition* to the King at *Newmarket,*
" in Behalf of our Hufbands *Samuel Cooper* and *Daniel Groom,* with
" eight innocent Perfons more, who after long Imprifonment for their tender
" Confciences, are fentenced to a *Premunire* ; the one whereof employing at
" leaft two Hundred poor People in the Woolen Manufactory, when at
" Liberty : And it being only in the King's Power to relieve them, and fet
" them at Liberty.

" We therefore the Petitioners humbly pray, and wait to know the
" King's Pleafure concerning our faid Hufbands, &c. We being
" come on purpofe out of *Suffolk* to feek Relief.

" *And we the Petitioners do, as in Duty bound, pray,* &c."

Commitments on the Statute of 20 l. per Month, &c.

Ifrael Roberts, Edward Hart, Stephen Carter, Stephen Levitt, and *John Rivett,*
taken on Seffions Procefs, were indicted for three Months Abfence from the
Church, on the Statute for 20 l. per Month, and had alfo the Oath of Allegiance tendred them at Seffions, and for refufing to Swear, were committed to
" clofe

clofe Prifon : Alfo *Thomas Humphrey*, of *Clare*, was taken by Conftables out his Shop, and carried to the Seffions, where the Oath of Allegiance was tendred him, and he, for refufing to take it, was fent to Prifon.

Imprifonments for Meetings at Ipfwich.

On the 22d of the Month called *February*, *Margaret Greenwood*, *Elizabeth Gofling*, *Mary Vincent*, *Elizabeth Story*, *Hannah Pinborrow*, and *Ruth Gofling*, taken at a Meeting in *Ipfwich* by Conftables and an Informer, were committed to Prifon by *William Neave*, Bayliff of that Town. And a few Days after, the fame Informer came with a Warrant, and apprehended *Sarah Clark*, of *Ipfwich*, for being at the fame Meeting, and carried her before a Juftice of the Peace, who fent her to Prifon.

ANNO 1685. This Year commences with the Commitment of *Mary Port* and *Jane Laurence* to *Ipfwich* Goal, and of *Katharine Brightwell*, *Martha Bourne*, *Elizabeth Posford*, *John Brightwell*, and *Andrew Freeman*, to *Melton* Goal, by *Edward Jenney*, Juftice, who attended by *Jofeph Cooper*, Conftable of *Woodbridge*, had taken them at a Meeting there.

Fines and Recommitments.

On the 19th of the Month called *April*, at *Woodbridge* Quarter Seffions, thofe imprifoned at *Melton*, were fined, and recommitted to Prifon.

On the 2d of the Month called *May*, at the County Seffions in *Ipfwich*, thofe in the County Goal were called, and refufing to give Sureties for the good Behaviour, generally remanded to Prifon.

Proceedings at Ipfwich Seffions.

On the 5th and 6th of the fame Month, at the Seffions for the Town of *Ipfwich*, the Friends in the Town-Prifon were brought forth, and fome who lay for fmall Fines were fet at Liberty, their Neighbours paying for them ; but *Edward Melfup*, *John Spurling*, *Thomas Melfup*, *Anne Goddard*, *Sarah Clarke*, *Mary Rofe*, *Mary Cox*, *Alice Melfup*, *Elizabeth Gofling*, *Margaret Greenwood*, *Elizabeth Story*, *Mary Vincent*, * *Ruth Gofling*, and *Hannah Pinborrow*, were required to find Sureties for the Good Behaviour, and for not doing it, were returned to Prifon, the Juftices giving the Goaler a ftrict Charge to keep them very clofe.

Imprifonments for Meetings.

On the 10th of the fame Month, *Edward Jenney*, Juftice, with the Conftables of *Woodbridge*, came again to the Meeting there, and the Juftice caufed a *Mittimus* to be made for the Commitment of *Sarah Bennett*, *Elizabeth Piggott*, *Deborah Shutter*, *Sufan Partridge*, and *William Bedford*, to *Melton* Goal.

The Number of Prifoners remaining in the feveral Prifons in this County, on the 29th of the Month called *May* 1685, were

Number of Prifoners.

In EDMUNDSBURY Goal. Under Sentence of *Premunire*, for refufing to Swear, thirteen : And on an Indictment for Abfence from the publick Worfhip, four.

In IPSWICH County Goal. For not paying Tithes, four : And by Procefs at Seffions and Affizes, for Abfence from the National Worfhip, twenty feven.

In IPSWICH Town Goal. For meeting together to worfhip God, thirteen.

In MELTON Prifon. For meeting together to worfhip God, nine.

In SUDBURY Goal. For Abfence from the National Worfhip, and for refufing to Swear, eight.

In all feventy eight.

After which Time we have no Account concerning them. It is probable they were generally fet at Liberty at the Summer Affizes that Year, according to the Proclamation of King *James the Second*, bearing Date the 8th Day of *April* 1685.

Fines remitted.

There were in the Month called *May* this Year, Procefies out of the *Exchequer* againft the People called *Quakers* in this County, for Monthly Abfence from their Parifh-Churches, fo called, to the Amount of 33300 *l*. The making Diftreffes for which, and the Ruin of many Families thereby, was alfo prevented by Means of the aforefaid Proclamation.

C H A P.

---

* *Note.* The faid *Ruth Gofling* being very fick in Prifon, the Magiftrates, on Application to them, ordered her Difcharge.

Index of People

(Page references as in Besse)

Cambridgeshire 84-99   Essex 190-208   Huntingdonshire 261-268
Leicestershire with Rutland 330-346   Lincolnshire 346-361
Norfolk 486-518   Northamptonshire 518-551   Nottinghamshire 551-562
Suffolk 657-687

Index of Places